THE POLITICS OF
FORMOSAN NATIONALISM

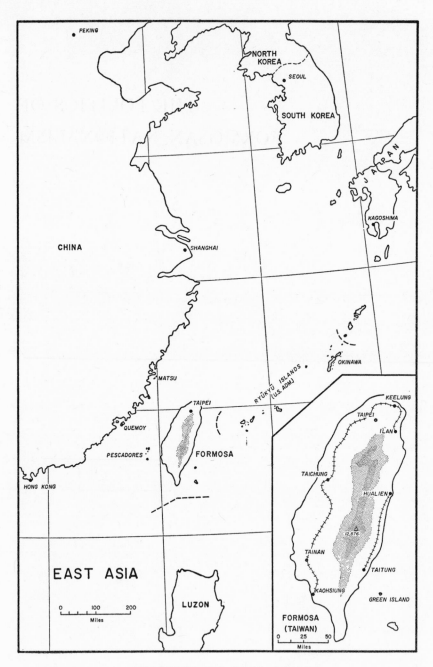

FORMOSA IN EAST ASIA

THE POLITICS OF FORMOSAN NATIONALISM

Douglas Mendel

UNIVERSITY OF CALIFORNIA PRESS
BERKELEY AND LOS ANGELES 1970

University of California Press
Berkeley and Los Angeles, California
University of California Press, Ltd.
London, England
Copyright © 1970, by
The Regents of the University of California
SBN: 520-01557-6
Library of Congress Catalog Card Number: 78-94982
Printed in the United States of America

TO THE PEOPLE OF FORMOSA

"To dream the impossible dream,
To fight the unbeatable foe,
To bear with unbearable sorrow
To run where the brave dare not go . . .
To reach the unreachable star
Though you know it's impossibly high,
To live with your heart striving upward,
To a far, unattainable sky."

CONTENTS

TABLES

INTRODUCTION

The purpose of this book is to describe and explain native-born Formosans' views of their past, present, and future. Both the Communist and the Nationalist Chinese regimes insist that Formosans are no different from Chinese on the mainland, and that the island of Formosa—or Taiwan, as both Chinas call it—is as much an integral part of historic China as Tibet or Outer Mongolia. That concept was recognized by the Cairo Declaration of 1943 in which President Franklin Roosevelt and Prime Minister Winston Churchill pledged to restore the island to the Republic of China after the defeat of Japan. The same idea, that Formosa is part of China, has been the basis of the Nationalists' possession of the island, their international status in the United Nations, and their goal of "mainland recovery." On the other side, the idea has also been used by Peking to justify its announced intention of "liberating" what it calls "China's territory of Taiwan" from Chiang Kai-shek and his Kuomintang (KMT) party, and thus prevents any reconciliation between Peking and Washington. Both regimes, each purporting to be the real Chinese government, oppose any future status for Formosa as a separate "Formosan nation," regardless of world opinion or the wishes of the Formosans, who are the silent majority on the island.

Nationalist China regards any separatist Formosan movement as treasonous, punishable as such, because its international status as the Republic of China (ROC) would vanish in the transition to a "Republic of Formosa." Only one-fifth of the inhabitants of Formosa today are post-1945 Nationalist refugees from the mainland, but their elite dominate the government in Taipei, now the Nationalist capital, and they would lose thousands of jobs if the island's present two-level (Chinese national and Formosan provincial) government were consolidated under native Formosan control. If Formosa were a separate entity, without claim or allegiance to the nation of China, it would not need the large civil and military bureaucracies which consume 50 per cent of the islanders' taxes and curtail civil liberties in the name of martial law. It is possible, however, that although the dual myths of "mainland recovery" and "Formosa as a part of China" sustain the morale of the two million mainlanders on Formosa—the majority of whom are poor or lower middle class—perhaps two-thirds of them could be reconciled to accept political rule by the eleven million Formosans.[1]

Communist China contends that the status of Formosa is an "internal problem" to be settled either by negotiation with its Nationalist enemies or by armed "liberation." It scorns any attempt by the United Nations or by individual states to mediate the issue or impose a plebiscite, and has tried to undermine Nationalist confidence in the United States by suggesting that Washington prefers a "one China, one Formosa" solution, anathema to both parties in the Chinese civil war.

The opposing attitudes of Peking and Taipei have posed special problems for the U.S. and the Soviet Union. In 1954 and 1958, Communist shelling of Quemoy threatened to provoke a Sino-American conflict, but the offshore islands remain a base of Nationalist operations against the mainland. "Both sides seem to fire over each other's heads just to keep the war going," said an American airman in 1962 after years of duty in the area. The two Chinas have expected their allies to support their respective civil war objectives, as shown by Peking's resentment of Russian disinterest in its 1958 attack on Quemoy. But Moscow evidently did not want to be drawn into a Sino-American war over the offshore islands, and we can assume that Washington is equally opposed to a Nationalist invasion of the mainland. Neither superpower seems likely to lend material help to either China if it would mean a direct confrontation or thermonuclear war.

Other nations, whether recognizing Peking or Taipei, find it embarrassing to espouse the cause of Formosan native separatism. Japan, for example, the colonial ruler of Formosa from 1895 to 1945, recognizes only Nationalist China but is a principal trading partner of both Chinas and vulnerable to their conflicting pressures. Many non-aligned or geographically distant members of the United Nations have found their hope of a "one China, one Formosa" compromise blocked by the refusal of either Chinese regime to tolerate a separate status for Formosa.

Our concern in this book is more with the political attitudes of native Formosans than with those of Nationalist mainlanders or with foreign attitudes toward either Nationalists or Formosans. International implications are vital to any overall consideration of the Formosa problem, however, and we shall return to them later.

A study of Formosan nationalism reveals an excellent example of comparative colonialism and suppressed nationalism, both of which are topics of interest to students of Afro-Asian countries. The people of Formosa were ruled briefly by the Spanish, the Portuguese and the Dutch, then for more than 250 years by Manchu China until Japan acquired the island in 1895, and they were not permitted self-determination in 1945. "In the years after world War II almost all the former colonies of Britain, France, Belgium, Holland, and other nations achieved independence, but Formosa merely changed from Japanese to Chinese control," noted Matsumura Kenzo, a Japanese elder statesman, in 1961.[2] Whether or not one believes that the Formosan majority is under Chinese colonial domination today, the reaction of native Formosans to their past Japanese and present Chinese overlords is relevant to any study of Asian colonialism.

"Formosans couldn't govern themselves because they have no managerial elite, no experience in self-government, and no deep commitment against communism," said a notably pro-KMT professor at Columbia University. The late Dr. Chiang Mon-lin, postwar chairman of the Sino-American Joint Commission on Rural Reconstruction in Formosa (JCRR), considered Formosans "just another variety of Chinese similar to the provincial mainlanders who used to complain when the central government sent officers from the capital to govern them."[3] But nationalism is a sense of identity, usually aroused by common experiences in a struggle against overlords from another locality. It needs no unique religion, language, or other objective basis, nor can it be denied on the ground of previous inexperience in self-rule. National identity is essentially emotional.

The principal focus of this book is on native Formosan attitudes, since these constitute the real test of nationalism, but evidence is also drawn from reports of foreign observers between 1945 and 1967. After some background chapters on the growth of Formosan identity, the book deals with contemporary native Formosan reaction to Nationalist Chinese efforts to mold the island into a "model province" socially, economically, and politically, and to make eleven million Formosans docile, if not loyal, Chinese citizens.

The account of Formosan reactions to Chinese cultural, economic, and political policies concludes with a discussion of the role of Formosans in the Nationalist armed forces. The bulk of the 600,000 troops are native conscripts: would they favor an invasion of the mainland or even retention of the offshore islands? Does military service make young Formosans loyal Chinese Nationalists, as the schools and adult propaganda are also designed to do, or are such programs counterproductive? A major source of data for the book was provided by a sampling of several hundred Formosan ex-soldiers who are now students, businessmen, or political refugees in Japan and the United States.

The final chapters deal with the policies and attitudes of the United States and Japan toward Formosan nationalism, with Formosa's future prospects. Will the Nationalist regime evolve peacefully into a "Sino-Formosan" or purely Formosan state, be incorporated by force or diplomacy into mainland China, or collapse in the face of an aroused native majority? Can Formosans expect assistance from the United States and Japan, the two nations most intimately involved in their island's defense and other scholars.

Any work on such a controversial topic as Formosan nationalism must rely on many native and foreign sources who cannot be identified for security reasons. Therefore, the reader is entitled to know as much as possible about the writer's qualifications, research methods, and approach. To remain objective, I have tried to maintain a certain detachment so that personal preferences would not distort my view of the data or cause me to mistake ideals for probabilities. "Don't write a book," advised one of my best informants in southern Formosa. "Only your government leaders can promote real freedom for this island; try to educate them and not the American public." The duty of a political scientist, however, is to make his research available to the public as well as to governments and other scholars.

One of many tactics shared by both Nationalist and Communist Chinese leaders is to impugn the motives and integrity of their critics, subjecting them to vitriolic abuse. "You're just a propagandist . . . a paid agent of a few misguided Formosan students abroad!" claimed some Nationalist spokesmen in 1966. The Peking Foreign Language Press accused me of being a "mouthpiece for American imperialism conniving to thwart the liberation of Formosa."

My own commitment to freedom for all peoples, including those living under rightist dictatorships, was demonstrated by my personal support of the defense of Western Europe and South Korea against the Communist threat after 1945; and like many other Americans, my ancestors fought to free the United States from British rule. In writing this book, however, I have tried to let the data speak for themselves, with personal comments explicitly labelled.

My interest in Formosan affairs was first stimulated by the comments of Japanese I interviewed in 1957 for a book on Japanese foreign policy.[4] "The natives of Taiwan do not hold Chiang Kai-shek in high esteem, so it is wrong to make Taiwan a province of China when the islanders are different from Chinese," was a comment typical of several prewar Japanese residents of Formosa. An official of the Japanese Embassy in Taipei later in 1957 corroborated the existence of this psychological gap between native-born Formosans and mainlander Chinese on the island, as did U.S. State Department members in conversations before my departure for a year in Formosa in mid-1961.

During the academic year 1961–1962 I held a Fulbright senior lectureship at Tunghai University near Taichung city in central Taiwan—having applied for the position because of the opportunity it would provide to test conflicting hypotheses about Formosan political attitudes after almost a generation of Nationalist rule. On my arrival in September 1961 a Chinese member of the U.S. Educational Foundation (the local Fulbright office) confirmed by assumption that Tunghai, as an American Protestant mission-supported school, would probably be less subject to governmental interference than universities in Taipei. The location of the university, midway between Taipei in the north and Kaohsiung in the south, facilitated travel along the entire west coast of the island, and teaching duties occupied only three mornings a week.

For the first few months, however, I made only exploratory visits to test the responsiveness of shopkeepers, farmers, and other persons in Taipei, Taichung, Tainan, and Kaohsiung. "The Nationalist regime is very sensitive about certain issues," the Chinese-American cultural officer at the U.S. Embassy in Taipei had warned, "and if you publish anything critical of your host government we may ask you to return home at your own expense." Formosan newsmen to whom I had been introduced added specific warnings against asking questions on such forbidden topics as mainland recovery, the legitimacy of the KMT regime, and Formosan separatism. Therefore, these rules were followed: (a) avoid all sensitive political topics in lectures or talks with students and faculty on the residential Tunghai campus; (b) meet Formosans in city shops and rural villages where a foreign professor can go without arousing police suspicion; (c) lead into political questions only when the contact has been willing to discuss the island's economic, social, or physical management;

and (d) seek introductions from American diplomatic sources or Formosans willing to guide me to men they consider the best informed in their area.

"Don't try to do any political interviewing inside Formosa," advised an American colleague with a deep interest in Chinese politics. "It would be too dangerous for your respondents." Others who had studied in Formosa believed it would be safe to talk in native homes or isolated places. "Obviously you cannot use the scientific mass public opinion surveys you employ in studying Japanese attitudes," said Dr. Edwin Reischauer, then U.S. Ambassador to Tokyo. Reischauer had visited Formosa in late 1960 to ask both mainlanders and Formosans their choice for American president. "All the mainlanders preferred Nixon and all the Taiwanese wanted Kennedy, an obvious reflection of their differing views on the first [1960] TV debate, when Kennedy opposed United States defense of the offshore islands and Nixon supported it. You should ask similar indirect questions to gauge the opinions of the native majority," he advised.

The interviews on which so much of this book is based were conducted with more than 1,000 Formosans, inside the island, in 1957, 1961–1962, 1963, and 1964; and with Formosan students and businessmen resident in Japan and the United States between 1963 and 1968. Some informants were among the Formosan political elite in appointive and elective positions; others were former officials or underground spokesmen well known to the American Embassy. Few of these can be safely identified unless they have since died, and less prominent Formosans (shopkeepers, students, laborers, and farmers) would be unknown to the reader even if identified.[5]

"You will find your Japanese very useful here," said a Chinese professor who briefed our Fulbright group and who knew I spoke no dialect of Chinese although my Japanese was fluent. Several academic colleagues in the United States had found Formosans extremely hospitable when they spoke in Japanese, and Japanese correspondents related similar experiences.

A special effort was made to talk with Formosans who had not risen high during the Japanese period, and to seek the opinions of Formosans under 25 (few of whom could speak Japanese in 1962) through the reports of Mandarin-speaking colleagues and personal interviews in Japanese or English with Formosan graduate students in Japan and the United States. Some may object that I could not use scientific survey methods or talk with Formosans in either the Taiwanese or the Mandarin dialect. Nonetheless, by making full use of the writings and direct impressions of other American scholars who had full Chinese language competence during their years of research in Formosa, it was possible to surmount that barrier of language—and, to some extent, of age and class. Moreover, a great many Formosan students interviewed in Japan and the United States came from middle-class families, not only from the Formosan elite who are sometimes thought to be the only pro-independence advocates.

The Nationalist regime on Formosa does permit public criticism of graft, social crimes, and administrative malpractices, so it was safe to discuss inflation, taxes, unemployment, and living conditions, which could often lead to more directly political subjects. For example, a special defense surtax, announced and imposed overnight in 1962, afforded an ideal opportunity to question people on their opinions of the high defense tax burden and the system, amounting to taxation without representation, which allows only a handful of Formosans in the national legislature.

Informal contacts were as useful as indirect types of questioning, since it was not possible to seek introductions from the top down, as I had done in Japan. Occasionally, one could locate a useful contact by repeating anti-Nationalist slogans in Japanese while walking along city streets at night: "Taiwan under the pigs is hell," or "Taiwan is a police state but Japan is a democracy." Chinese within earshot could not understand, but a sympathetic Formosan passerby might follow the speaker and offer to tell him inside stories or introduce him to other people.

Since leaving the Fulbright lectureship in mid-1962, I have talked at length with overseas Formosan businessmen, students, and expatriates around the world. There have also been discussions of the Formosan problem with Japanese and American diplomats, scholars, newsmen, and others experienced in the affairs of the island.

Because of the limited nature of the study, only enough background on Nationalist Chinese policies is given, in appropriate chapters, to place Formosan reactions in proper context. There is no dearth of reports, yearbooks, articles, and other works giving the Nationalist Chinese interpretation of the postwar history of Formosa, and many of these are cited in the text and footnotes.

I should like to express my thanks to those who provided funds for the study: the U.S. Educational Foundation in China, the Contemporary China Committee of the Social Science Research Council, the American Philosophical Society, and the Faculty Research Committee of the University of Wisconsin. None of these bears any responsibility for the views expressed herein. Three Formosan graduate students in the United States served as research assistants on the project between 1964 and 1968, and their usefulness in translating Chinese materials was exceeded only by the value of their personal accounts of life in Formosa. American and Japanese academic colleagues in the field of Chinese studies have given expert advice and counsel, while many members of the Japanese and United States governments have discussed Formosan opinion with me during the past seven years. The principal help, however, came from the people of Formosa—particularly those at home and abroad who risked their personal safety to provide necessary data—to whom the book is dedicated.

The name "Formosa" is generally used in the book instead of the "Taiwan" employed in Chinese and Japanese, not only because it is more common in the Western world but also because émigré Formosans prefer the old Portuguese name to indicate their rejection of both prewar Japanese and postwar Chinese domination.

The decision to place the notes at the back of the book has been the author's, not the publisher's.

1

THE GROWTH OF
FORMOSAN NATIONALISM

The physical aspect of Formosa is one of the few points on which Peking, Taipei, and native-born Formosan inhabitants all agree. Shaped like a tobacco leaf, the subtropical island is about 240 miles long and 85 miles across at its widest point, with an area of 14,000 square miles— about the size of Massachusetts, Connecticut, and Rhode Island combined. It lies 120 miles east of the Chinese coast, some 400 miles southwest of Okinawa, and north of the Philippines. The Pescadores (Penghu) group of islands off the southeast Formosan coast, together with some smaller ones, is considered part of Formosa itself, unlike the Quemoy and Matsu island groups a few miles off the mainland.

Collectively, all these islands have been governed since 1945 by the Republic of China and since 1949 as the one Chinese area free of Communist control. Of the 13.5 million inhabitants recorded by a 1968 newspaper census, over 11 million are native to Formosa, and 2 million are post-1945 Nationalist settlers from the Chinese mainland. There are also approximately 170,000 aboriginal tribesmen and a few thousand Chinese in the offshore islands.[1]

Few Americans are as concerned or informed about Formosa as they are about Communist-ruled mainland China—which, with over 700 million people, is the most populous nation in the world and a hostile power officially committed to an anti-American policy. The growing nuclear capacity of Communist China, its support for "wars of national liberation" (as in Vietnam), and its domestic turbulence during the Proletarian Cultural Revolution have received much publicity and provoked widespread discussion in the United States. Yet, when the University of

Michigan tested popular awareness of Communist China in mid-1964 (see Table 8–1), three in ten Americans did not know mainland China had a Communist government.[2] Only 60 per cent of those who did know that most of China was under Communist rule knew anything about "another Chinese government . . . Nationalists, Republic of China, Chiang Kai-shek, Formosa, or Taiwan." The degree of ignorance about Formosa, an island protected by an American defense treaty and recipient of over $5 billion economic and military aid since 1950, is probably no less today.

Therefore it is doubtful that many Americans know much about the natives of Formosa who constitute four-fifths of its population. The outside world is likely to have a stereotyped view of Formosa, commonly described as "Chiang Kai-shek's island fortress," "the Nationalist stronghold," or "Free China's base to recapture the mainland." "Do you realize there are two million natives among the eight million Nationalists here?" asked an American businessman on a Taipei-bound plane in 1963. He had no idea his statistics were in reverse.

Chinese tradition considers anyone of Chinese ancestry, however removed from China geographically or historically, to be a member of the Chinese family. It is on this basis, as well as de jure sovereignty from 1683 to 1895 and Allied agreements during World War II, that both Peking and Taipei consider Formosa an integral part of China. China had never felt at home in the Western system of national states, and even revolutionary leaders of modern China retain a patronizing sense of suzerainty toward outlying areas—in contrast to the familiar Western definition of nationalism as "a body of people who feel they are a nation." Many Formosans might agree with Rupert Emerson, who wrote that nationalism is "the sense of a singularly important national 'we' which is distinguished from all others who make up an alien 'they.'"[3]

"If speech, similar customs, and race determine nationality," asked one native Formosan, "why did your American ancestors fight for independence from England? They were far more British than we are Chinese." In addition to a sense of common identity, Formosans today share other attributes of the "ideal" nation. From the time they were colonized by the Dutch in 1624, they have known and hated a succession of foreign overlords. They have lived on a compact and isolated territory and—in the words of one scholar who refers to the Formosan dialect and Japanese as "native languages learned and spoken in the homes of most Formosans"—have shared "the common historical experience

which (for the better part of a century) was and is different from that
of mainland China." [4]

The growth of Formosan nationalism concerns us more than the study
of how other colonial peoples developed their sense of identity, but comparative comments will be included occasionally when relevant.[5] The
problem of all incipient or submerged nationalisms is how to achieve actual political control. As *Time* magazine wrote of Israel: "A nation becomes a state when it has the power to occupy and hold a given amount
of space and when other nations recognize this fact. It may smack too
much of raw force. . . . Yet these basic conditions—identity, tradition,
ability to stake out a territory, govern it and win recognition—are the
only real criteria for sovereignty." [6]

"The internal imponderable in Taiwan," says A. T. Steele, "is not
whether the native-born Taiwanese would like self-government—they
would hardly be human if they did not—but rather the intensity of their
feeling on the matter." [7]

Early Settlement and European Colonial Rule

Formosa's earliest inhabitants came from the Malay-Indonesian-Philip-
pine area in prehistoric times. Their descendants are today's 170,000
tribal aborigines, most of whom inhabit the central mountains, although
some have been assimilated into coastal villages and a few live near
Taipei or Sun-Moon Lake, where their settlements are a tourist attrac-
tion. Nationalist officials consider the aborigines the only "Formosan natives."

Chinese and Japanese pirates and sailors presumably stopped off at
Formosa earlier, but the first known permanent Chinese settlement was
in the sixteenth century, near the site of Tainan. About the same time
Portuguese sailors, from whose exclamations of "Ilha Formosa" ("island
beautiful") it got its name, were probably the first Western visitors to
the island, which Portugal soon annexed.

In that age of European exploration and colonization the Spanish and
the Dutch were also attracted by Formosa's strategic location in the sea
lanes between Southeast Asia, China, and Japan. The Dutch were persuaded by the declining Ming Dynasty to transfer their trading station
from the Pescadores to Formosa. "There was no official with whom [the
Dutch captain] could confer," according to one historian, "nothing to
suggest Chinese authority on the island . . ." [8]

For about forty years thereafter, the Dutch East India Company exploited the island's southern coast near their base at Tainan, holding tenuous authority over 25,000 farmers who had migrated in the previous century from the Fukien and Canton coast of China and perhaps 75,000 tribesmen.[9] Deerskin, sugar, dried meats, and other native products were exported by the Dutch to China and Japan. Relics of Dutch domination remain at Tainan and its shallow port of Anping, and at Tamsui, where the British consulate occupies the original Dutch fort.

The Ming dynasty collapsed in 1644 as the alien Manchu (Ch'ing) invaders swept over the mainland. Eighteen years later, in 1662, the son of a famous Ming pirate led his refugee band across the Formosa Straits, expelled the Dutch, and made Formosa his personal kingdom. This son of a Chinese pirate and a Japanese mother is known to history as Koxinga (Cheng Cheng-kung) and is revered for different reasons by Communists, Nationalists, and Formosan natives. To Communist Chinese, Koxinga is the hero who expelled "the red-haired barbarians" (i.e., the Dutch) from Formosa. The Nationalists think of him as a loyal Ming warrior who provided a refuge on his island fortress for thousands of Chinese opposed to the alien Manchu dynasty, and who plotted unsuccessfully to overthrow the Manchus in a "glorious counterattack." The Communists remember that Koxinga's grandson, in 1683, surrendered Formosa to the Manchus' mainland regime, which then incorporated it into Fukien province across the straits.

Every modern nationalist movement as a matter of course tries to strike its roots as deeply as possible into the past by reviving national legends and heroes, so it is not surprising that many Formosans consider Koxinga the creator of the first independent state on Formosa and the symbol of its dual heritage from China and Japan. Some refer to his regime as "the first and only time the island was independent of foreign control and ruled by a majority of its inhabitants using the Fukien dialect." [10]

Actually, Koxinga's brief twenty-year dynasty was most notable for bringing into Formosa mainland refugees, who by 1690 probably outnumbered the aborigines. Land taken from the latter was put into rice, sugar, and vegetables by the new Chinese settlers. But, considering their division into Canton and Fukien peasants, Hakka outcasts, and political refugees, there is probably more romance than reality in attempts to trace the beginnings of Formosan national identity to the seventeenth century.

The First Period of Chinese Rule

From 1683 until the Sino-Japanese War of 1894–1895, Formosa was under the careless and weak control of the Manchu dynasty, whose capital was in far-off Peking. "Officials from the mainland lived mostly in the few towns and squeezed the island farmers by means known only to Chinese bureaucrats," according to a Formosan elder statesman. "Until just before the end of their rule in the late nineteenth century, they gave us nothing and took everything." Between 1683 and 1843 there were fifteen major rebellions.[11]

The two centuries of Manchu administration saw the gradual spread of settlers from the southwest to the northern end of Formosa as immigration from the mainland increased. No reliable census was taken before the first Japanese attempt in 1905, but the Manchu regime had estimated that 150,000 persons were in settled areas in 1683. This number grew to about 1,300,000 at the end of the eighteenth century, 2,546,000 at the time of Governor Liu Ming-ch'uan's 1893 census, and almost 3 million in 1905. Assuming the usual high death rate in a primitive society with subtropical diseases, the population increase in the eighteenth and nineteenth centuries must have been mainly due to immigration. Thereafter, however, Japanese policy discouraged mainland immigrants, so that most native Formosans today are descendants of settlers who came from Fukien and Canton in the two centuries of Manchu rule.[12]

Since two-thirds of Formosa is mountainous land unsuited for agriculture, the farmers among the settlers from the mainland at first remained close to the western coast. The Hakkas, discriminated against by the Fukienese majority, tended to settle in the upland foothills where they fought both the aborigines (who retreated to the east) and other ex-mainland groups on the coastal plain. The American Consul James Davidson tells of several major revolts, some by settlers against Manchu officials, others by the pathetic tribal natives against the more "advanced" immigrants, who defeated them with arms and alcohol. "Quite naturally . . . this entailed the undying hatred of the entire savage population . . . a condition which has continued to the present day." [13]

Western observers on Formosa before 1895 reported that laws and security measures were neither enforced by the Manchus nor accepted by the settlers. One such observer, quoted by Davidson, wrote: "Though industrious, the emigrants have deservedly a reputation for insubordination and lawlessness. They associate much in clans, and clannish attachments and feuds are cherished among them." [14] The Chinese officials of that period were generally rapacious in the face of Peking's indifference to the distant island, and the heavy taxes, demand for graft money ("squeeze"), and other similarly onerous practices of the officials earned them little respect from the Formosans. Chinese administrators found it dangerous to venture beyond the island's few garrison towns. In 1871 and 1873, when the Japanese government demanded the punishment of east coast tribesmen who had killed some shipwrecked Okinawan fishermen, the Chinese government repudiated all responsibility for the central mountains or the narrow east coast of Formosa. Nor did Peking's emissaries give much better protection to west coast farmers, who resented the poll tax, camphor tax, salt fees, and land rents they extracted.

A British consul reported: "Great fear was always entertained of the rebelling of the Formosans, and to provide against this soldiers required for service in Formosa were not enlisted from the island but brought over from the mainland. . . . The military affairs were in a great state of corruption, too many officers leaving their posts defenseless and putting in their pockets the money intended for their men." [15] Some of the lawlessness was the work of brigands, but many revolts sprang from genuine grievances of Formosan farmers against the mandarins and troops in their midst.

According to George Mackay, a Canadian missionary who wrote in 1896 of conditions before the Japanese takeover, "From the highest to the lowest, every Chinese official in Formosa has an 'itching palm,' and the exercise of official functions is always corrupted by money bribes. The mandarin supplements his income by 'squeezing' his attendants and every man who comes within his grasp. His attendants have the privilege of recouping themselves by 'squeezing' all who through them seek favors from the mandarin. In the matter of bribing and boodling the Chinese official in Formosa could give points to the most accomplished office-seekers and money-grabbers in Washington or Ottawa." [16] The Reverend Mr. Mackay had spent twenty-three years in Formosa, including the allegedly "good period" under Governor Liu Ming-ch'uan, and knew both the Sino-Formosans and the aborigines better than any other Westerner of his time.

Whether the many revolts of Formosans against mainlander rule in the eighteenth and nineteenth centuries signified a growing native identity is doubtful. Most writers seem to think they were a negative resistance to external rule rather than a sign of positive nationalism. Maurice Meisner thinks it "highly questionable that the Formosans felt any special sense of nationhood during the more than two centuries of Ch'ing rule. It is true that popular opposition to the Manchus was particularly intense in Formosa and the frequency of peasant rebellions became proverbial . . . Yet there is no evidence to suggest that these . . . revolts were significantly different in character or motivation from the local peasant rebellions . . . that were chronic throughout most of Chinese history." [17] Professor Ong Jok-tik, one of the more articulate Formosan refugee scholars in Japan, agrees that even the large-scale rebellions in 1721, 1787, and 1870 were "peasant uprisings; they cannot be considered independence movements in the strict sense of that term." [18]

Before 1895, no true island-wide government existed on Formosa. The vast majority of the settlers were not only illiterate but unable to travel far beyond their villages or to understand those who had come from a different mainland area. Without means of communication or transportation, living a precarious existence and lacking either an intellectual middle class or knowledge of modern nationalism, the people on Formosa whom the Manchu court ceded to Japan in 1895 were in no position to mount an effective protest against external rule.

Some American specialists on Formosa agree with the Australian Sinophile, W. G. Goddard, that Chinese provincial governor of Formosa (Liu Ming-ch'uan) deserves more credit than he has received for his achievements between 1887 and 1891.[19] Liu had hoped to modernize the island's defenses, communications, and tax base. He moved the capital from Tainan to the relatively new city of Taipei, probably because of its proximity to the ports of Tamsui and Keelung, and tried to conduct a land survey to clarify the confused system of squatters' rights. He also planned a system of roads, and paid Western engineers to construct a rail line from Hsinchu, south of Taipei, to Keelung, north of the capital. "Although no railway had yet been constructed by officials in the whole Empire of China, Governor Liu decided that Formosa should have one . . . If the reader is acquainted with affairs in China and has noted the extremely conservative tendencies of the mandarins . . . he will no doubt observe with some surprise the progressive spirit exhibited by Liu Ming-chuan," [20] says Davidson. Development of the port of Keelung, electricity in Taipei, and other plans came to an end, however, because of a combination of indifference in Peking and combat with aboriginal tribes.

The consensus of native opinion today agrees with Davidson that Liu's reforms were either ineffectual or too late. Construction of the railway, for example, was so poor that the Japanese rebuilt it soon after their occupation of the island. (The fate of that railway is reminiscent of the highly vaunted Cross-Island Highway, completed by the Nationalists in 1960 to connect Taichung with Hualien across the central mountains, but closed by rock slides and washouts during much of the year.) There was in any case a limit to what could be accomplished by one man operating within the moribund system of Confucian China, a system wedded to the past and contemptuous of Western learning.[21]

Formosa Under Japanese Rule

The Sino-Japanese war of 1894–1895 was fought for control of Korea and southern Manchuria rather than Formosa, where (prior to the peace treaty) no battles were fought. China was more concerned with her continental tributaries than with three million unruly islanders across the Taiwan Strait, and when the Treaty of Shimonoseki was negotiated, Chinese Imperial Viceroy Li Hung-chang ceded Formosa and the Pescadores to Japan.

The short-lived "Republic of Formosa" that followed is still the subject of much controversy. Formosans today would probably agree with Consul Davidson's view that the Chinese Governor in Taipei issued his 1895 declaration of independence only at the instigation of mainlander officials and without popular support inside Formosa.[22] Pro-Chinese sources, however, insist the "independence" attempt was a genuine resistance movement loyal to China, and consider it a precursor of the 1911 Republic on the mainland. One doubts that many Formosans—except the wealthy, who were divided on the issue—either regretted the departure of Chinese mainland officials or welcomed the invading Japanese troops; they were too uninformed and apathetic.

Japanese forces met with little resistance in northern Formosa after landing on May 26, 1895, but ran into heavier obstacles in the south from disease and native rebels. Japan considered her occupation of all major towns complete by the end of October 1895 at a cost of 200 combat deaths and several thousand victims of disease. Davidson, who accompanied the Japanese troops, reported that some Formosans volunteered to join the Japanese while mountain tribesmen wanted to add more mainland Chinese heads to their collection. The Japanese, of course, were superior in weapons, strategy, and discipline during the "pac-ification" decade that followed.

Contemporary observers described Formosa as less than beautiful when viewed on the spot rather than from offshore: "Dirty water was rushing around the houses . . . and some people lived together with dogs and pigs. Though there were public toilets (in Taipei), excrement was found everywhere . . . the inhabitants seemed to possess no knowl-edge of sanitation. A large number of prostitutes with advanced syphilis appeared around the city." [23] An Englishman in Tainan, the oldest cul-tural capital, noted: "Education lagged far behind. . . . Pressed so hard to earn a living, they [Formosans] had no time for learning. Farmers and coolies did not receive even elementary education; merchants could read and write, but their knowledge was limited to bookkeeping and business correspondence. . . . Ninety per cent of males were completely illiter-ate, and female literacy was naturally lower." [24]

Opium addiction and epidemic diseases, compounded by unsanitary conditions in the towns, endangered the health of colonial personnel, and lack of educational facilities hampered efficient administration. The 62-mile narrow-gauge railway from Hsinchu to Keelung was inoperable, and few roads had been improved (postal delivery between Taipei and the south took over one week), so the new rulers had to improve the transport system and other facilities needed for minimal administrative efficiency. Japan herself was then in the midst of the rapid technological development that occurred in the Meiji era (1868–1912) and could apply this expertise to her first colony.[25]

In addition to maintaining order, the Japanese—through their colonial police—kept a close and paternalistic watch on urban social conditions and rural development. Their record in Formosa might be summarized as successful in every material way, but not in winning Formosan loyalty. Formosans today sometimes refer to the Japanese period as "the era of the dogs," although "It is not an altogether unflattering term," they ex-plain. "We had never enjoyed such security before and, even though the Japanese police were strict, they were fair and honest—no squeeze."

Formosa's first reliable census was made within the first dozen years of Japanese rule. A Chinese scholar has stated it was "the most complete and accurate in the Far East and surpassed even the data collected in most European countries." [26] A land survey was also conducted with the dual purpose of regularizing the vague traditional tenure system and al-lowing for collection of more land taxes. Currency, weights, and meas-ures were standardized: essentials for economic growth and a market economy. Goto Shimpei, deputy to General Kodama Gentaro, the fourth Japanese governor of Formosa, is credited with many of these stabilizing reforms of 1898–1906, including the beginnings of government-sponsored research on Formosan and aboriginal customs.[27]

Transport and communications improved quickly as the Japanese built a series of modern railways, the biggest of which was the 200-mile Keelung-to-Kaohsiung main trunk line down the west coast connecting principal cities. By 1940, Formosa had almost 1,000 miles of government rail lines and 1,800 miles of narrow-gauge mountain and sugar plantation private lines. The mountain railroad on Ali Shan (Mt. Ali) has been called "a brilliant Japanese engineering feat which took 12 years to accomplish . . . to tap the timber resources [which] had not been developed by the Chinese." [28] Japan also extended a railway from Keelung in the north down to Suao, a small port on the east coast, and another from Hualien to Taitung on the southeastern coast. Engineering studies, confirmed by postwar Chinese experts, showed that the two missing links (Suao-Hualien and Taitung-Pintung) needed to complete a round-the-island railway were impractical to construct and maintain. Instead, the Japanese carved a spectacular 72-mile road out of the steep east coast cliffs from Suao to Hualien, one of the most scenic roads in the world.

A Chinese scholar recently praised "the *daisha*, or push-car, which was brought to the island by the Japanese and helped to develop the mountain land. . . . In 1938 the aggregate mileage of the push-car line was 586 miles carrying 3 million passengers and 553 million tons of freight for the year." [29]

The Japanese expanded Keelung and Kaohsiung harbors, and began relocating Hualien to higher ground north of the old port—a project which the Nationalists have continued in their effort to make Hualien a "free port" in eastern Formosa. It is doubtful, however, that officials of Kaohsiung, now Formosa's second largest city and an expanding industrial port, would agree with the claim that "during World War II, Kaohsiung developed into an important naval base, ranking with such important ports in Japan proper as Osaka, Kobe, and Nagasaki." [30]

During the 1920's, Japan strove to build hydro-electric plants in the Formosan mountains and an irrigation system for the southeastern plains. Their most notable successes were the power station at Sun-Moon Lake in the central foothills, and the Chianan irrigation system. Sun-Moon Lake is a small artificial lake about 2,200 feet in elevation, not far from Taichung, and has become a noted tourist resort enjoyed by visitors oblivious of the fact that the adjacent power plant has been described as "the greatest achievement of the Japanese period in Taiwan, [and] is now considered the TVA of the Far East, [making it] possible for the island to support aluminum, chemical, and steel alloy plants." [31] The Chianan irrigation system between the city of Chiayi south of the Choshui River and the mouth of the Tsungwen River at Tainan (hence the name Chianan) was also completed in the 1920's to irrigate about 457,000 acres of land through 10,900 miles of small canals. "After the system went into operation the land used for growing rice increased by more than 74 percent and the sugar-cane land by 30 percent . . . production of rice per unit area nearly doubled and the total rice production increased nearly eight times," [32] according to the Chinese author Hsieh Chiao-min.

If a Chinese scholar can praise these Japanese engineering feats so highly, we can understand why Formosans credit such inheritances from the Japanese occupation with much of their island's subsequent prosperity. The same Chinese writer declares: "Taiwan's industries reflect credit on the former Japanese rule of the island, and its present industrial structure has been built on the good foundation left by the Japanese." [33] In the same vein, Neil Jacoby has written that Japan's record on Formosa "is worthy of observation by contemporary development administrators. While the motive was self-interest, Japan's policies were enlightened. Japan sought to demonstrate that it was a civilizing force in Asia." [34]

A more dubious economic improvement of the Japanese period was the introduction of a new strain of rice (called Ponlai or, in Japanese, *horai*) which was 20 per cent more productive than the native Formosan variety and preferred by the Japanese for its flavor. The new type required more fertilizer, however, and was not a net boon to native farmers forced to plant it for the Japanese market.[35]

Commercial sugar, banana, and pineapple production on Formosa originated with Japanese, who valued these crops for their own market. Sugar production rose 1,300 per cent between 1905 and 1935; by 1940 Japan—thanks to its island colony—ranked seventh in world sugar production. Poultry and hog production increased tenfold during the Japanese period. Japanese consumers were at least as important then as today to the Formosan farmer. Furthermore, before 1945 Formosa was within the yen bloc and exempt from Japanese tariffs.

Probably the Formosans were happy to share in the expanding industrialization of the Japanese economy. Bicycles, radios, textiles, watches and clocks, and other consumer goods flooded into Taiwan in payment for its rice, sugar, and primary crops. Formosan economists have calcu-

lated that national income rose from US $209 million in the years be-
tween 1911 and 1915 to $772 million between 1936 and 1940 (or from
$61 to $136 per capita).[36] One of the island's most eminent elder states-
men maintained that these figures proved the 1930's were Formosa's
most prosperous period, unmatched by the Nationalist regime until
1963. The meaning of economic statistics often varies with each interpreter; but as the American scholar Meisner so aptly wrote, "Whether
the Formosans were actually better off under the Japanese than they are
now is less important than that most articulate Formosans think this to
be true." [37]

Both Nationalist and Communist Chinese insist that the Japanese occupation of Formosa drained the island's resources, resulting in low
wages for native-born workers, and benefit only to the imperialist rulers.
"Why, no Taiwan-born Chinese was able to rise higher than station-mas-
ter on the Taiwan railway!" exclaimed Shen Chang-huan, later Foreign
Minister of Nationalist China, during our first encounter in 1957.[38] The
next evening, however, I attended a government dinner in a pavilion recently donated to Taipei's central park by a Formosan businessman
whose wealth had been accumulated prior to 1945. Later, between 1961
and 1967, I met dozens of other Formosans who had either profited financially or risen to high government positions under the Japanese.

The life of the ordinary rural Formosan did not change as much under
Japanese rule as the life of the expanding middle class in the cities. Urbanization is not an unmixed blessing, but for good or ill the impact of
modernization strikes the cities first. "Taihoku [Japanese for Taipei] is
now a thoroughly Japanese city in every respect . . . With fine macad-
amed streets, imposing buildings, and well-stocked shops, it excels perhaps any city of its size in the whole empire of Japan. The streets are
also generally cleaner and better cared for than under the Chinese regime," wrote Davidson in 1903.[39]

By 1940, the last year unaffected by World War II shortages, the
number of hospitals and of modern medical personnel had risen from a
handful in 1897 to 386 and 2,500 respectively. Medicine was one field in
which Formosans could rise without political discrimination, and many
promising sons of Formosan families chose that career as a way to higher
education in Japan, leading sometimes to a quasi-political career later at
home. Opium addiction was reduced from 130,500 cases in 1905 to 14,-
600 in 1935 while the death rate from all causes fell from 32 per 1,000
(1906–1910) to 20 per 1,000 (1936–1940). Malaria and cholera virtually disappeared as the Japanese extended health and police sanitation

units throughout the island and established a standard in general public health administration that was high for the Far East. No wonder that despite curtailment of mainland immigration the Formosan population doubled during the fifty years of Japanese rule.

Education for the Formosans was a lesser and later goal of the Japanese colonial administration. Elementary schools had been established in all towns and cities by 1920, but as late as 1932 only one-half of qualified Formosan boys (and one-fifth of the girls) were attending grade school. Ten years later, however, over 90 per cent of Formosan and 75 per cent of aboriginal children were enrolled in the six-year free and compulsory primary schools.

Japanese middle and higher schools on the island, including after 1928 the Imperial University at Taipei, were filled with Japanese students but very few Formosans. The Presbyterian Seminary in Tainan, a major private college, was a great influence on the island's intellectual growth. Many sons of wealthy Formosans entered universities in Japan proper, since the sea journey to Japan was cheap and popular. And as the Japanese regime switched to a more liberal assimilation policy between 1920 and 1937, Formosan children were admitted more readily to the secondary schools originally built for Japanese children only.

All schools of Formosa and most publications officially used Japanese; by 1944, about 70 per cent of the Formosans were literate in that language. Yet, as in Korea, Formosans managed to retain their own language and many customs in the face of Japanese pressure for assimilation, which was especially strong after World War I. After 1918 Formosan college students in Japan began publishing a journal called *Taiwan Chinglian* [The Young Formosan], which urged the Japanese government to conform to the Wilsonian spirit of that era by granting Formosa greater democratic representation. Formosan political activity at that time seemed freer in Tokyo than inside Taiwan itself; nevertheless a growing number of educated youths from upper-class families spearheaded the self-government movement on the island.

Politically, the early period of military rule in Formosa gave almost plenary power to the colony's Governor-General whose edicts, under Law 63 of 1896, had force in the territory equal to the laws registered by the Imperial Diet. Japan itself had a highly centralized administrative state with commensurate police power, a weak representative system, limited civil rights, and various "thought control" laws. The Japanese had gone to Formosa believing its inhabitants to be even less capable of self-government than their own citizens, and their pre-1919 policy al-

lowed little political freedom to Formosans. Eventually elective municipal councils were permitted, and Law 63 was rescinded in 1929, but during Japanese rule no Formosan mayors or higher officials were popularly
chosen.

World War I saw parliamentary rule and a measure of democracy
come to Japan, and some liberalizing of Japan's colonial administration
in Formosa as a consequence. Itagaki Taisuke, one of the more democratic leaders of Japanese politics, visited Taipei in 1914 to organize a
Taiwan Assimilation Society (*Taiwan Dōkakai*) and urge equal rights
and treatment for the colonials in practice as well as in existing but dor-
mant policy. Such Formosans as Lin Hsien-t'ang (Rin Ken-do in Japanese) tried their best to use assimilation to raise the political standards
of their own people. "Self-government" became a more radical slogan
later in the 1920's as Lin and others began publishing journals and staffing schools.

The first high school for Formosans opened at Taichung in 1915,
eight years after Lin Hsien-t'ang had been advised by the famous
Chinese scholar, Liang Ch'i-ch'ao, "to imitate the ways of the Irish in
dealing with Britain, namely to work with prominent Japanese politicians to check the power of the government-general and reduce its
oppression of the Formosans." [40] "An ironic method of throwing off the
yoke of colonialism is for young students in the imperial country to be
the vanguard of the liberation movement. Formosa was no exception in
this respect," [41] wrote Dr. Ong. Lin later played a dual role of organizing the *jichi* (self-government) movement inside Formosa and financing
many Formosan students' education in Japan. He became so well known
and popular that many Formosan informants felt he would have been
elected president in any free Formosan state after 1945.

The story of Formosan political activity before 1945 is too involved for
more than a brief summary here.[42] There were 18 incidents of armed resistance to Japanese rule between 1895 and 1915, after which tactics
shifted to political means. An historian sympathetic to the Nationalists
reports over 8,500 annual political arrests from 1895 to 1919, 6,500 annually in the 1920's, and 3,400 annually in the 1930's, but few of the rebels were executed or given long prison terms.[43] By and large, Formosans
eschewed violence, relied on the conscience of Japanese liberals and
worked for gradualist reform rather than extremist goals.

The violence of the March 1st 1919 Movement in Korea and the May
4th Movement in China, both directed against Japanese colonialism, had
shocked and puzzled the Japanese. Nevertheless Tokyo, in the flush of

the Allied victory of World War I, decided to appoint a civilian governor in Formosa and make a few concessions to Formosans. In turn the
Formosans increased their demands, petitioning in 1921 for election of
an assembly to screen the budget and restrict the law-making power of
the Japanese governor. Similar petitions were sent to every session of the
Japanese Diet until 1934, with the signatures of hundreds of influential
Formosans, headed by Lin Hsien-t'ang who in 1921 had organized a Taiwan Cultural Association (*Taiwan Bunkakyokai*).[44]

The government-general in Taipei began to crack down on the Taiwan Cultural Association in 1923 after its members had sponsored lectures, meetings, and seminars throughout the island, but most of those
arrested were soon freed to continue their activities. Organization of the
Taiwan Sugar Farmers Union in 1925 was typical of the more effective
techniques by which native Formosans persuaded their Japanese overlords to implement requests that were ostensibly innocuous. The Japanese regime had started farmers' organizations as early as 1907, with the
usual objective of raising production and controlling the villages where
most Formosans lived, and Formosan intellectuals later tried to work
through these mass organizations to arouse the peasantry. But these Cultural Movement leaders split in 1927 over whether the organization
should be cultural or action-oriented, with the latter, supported by the
few Marxists in the group, winning out. Thereafter, personal and ideological divisions split the Formosan movement.

Despite the confusion of the many Formosan political movements
between 1921 and 1938, it is still possible to distinguish some of the ideological differences among the factions. Probably the largest group of
Formosans believed with Lin Hsien-t'ang that gradualism and modera-
tion would win increasing concessions from Japan, and that Formosans
should not ally themselves with either the mainland KMT or Chinese
Communist Party (CCP) because to do so would only antagonize
Japan. Another group, of which some members were to hold high positions in the Nationalist government after 1949, believed the ascendancy
of Chiang and the KMT in 1928 would indirectly benefit them.

A third group saw the guerilla campaigns of the Chinese Communists
as the best model for their own liberation from Japan. Whether this latter group, sometimes called the Taiwan Communist Party, wanted alliance with the CCP as a tactic to gain Soviet and Chinese Communist
aid for Formosan independence, or favored the merger of Formosa into
a future People's Republic of China is debatable.

A fascinating lady Marxist, Hsieh Hsueh-hung, born to a poor Formosan family in 1900, grew up to lead a checkered career. It began before 1920 with three years in Japan; she then worked in the Taiwan Cultural Association until 1925, when she moved to Shanghai. She was encouraged by the Chinese Communist Youth Corps to study in Moscow, where she met Tokuda Kyuichi, the Japanese Communist leader. Later she worked in Tokyo and Shanghai before smuggling herself back for underground work in Formosa. There, with 107 fellow-subversives, she was arrested in 1931.[45] (The Communist Party was illegal at that time in Japan, Formosa, and Korea.) Miss Hsieh surfaced after World War II and joined the 1947 Formosan revolt. She then fled to Communist China, where she was at first honored, but later rejected when the Chinese Communists accused their few Formosan comrades of "bourgeois nationalism" after the wilting of the "Hundred Flowers" campaign in 1958.

Naturally, the Japanese regime did its best to suppress, subvert, or disrupt extremist Formosan political movements. It encouraged the moderates and bought the loyalty of the more susceptible; spread rumors designed to sow discord among the leadership of Formosan factions; and imprisoned only the most radical extremists. "The Japanese police did not interfere in our city elections, and there was no dominant party like the KMT today," commented a southern Formosan who had been active politically under both regimes. "We Formosan candidates were treated more fairly by the prewar Japanese parties than the mainlander Chinese KMT leaders treat us now."

Ideological disputes were greater in the Formosan underground prior to World War II than in the recent anti-Nationalist movement. The true natures of the KMT and the CCP were, after all, less familiar to the Formosans between 1921 and 1938 than later, and many Formosan activists in those years could argue with sincerity for collaboration with a mainland party.

One of the most noted Japanese scholars sympathetic to prewar Formosan grievances was Professor Yanaibara Tadao, later president of Tokyo University, whose book *Teikokushugika no Taiwan* [*Taiwan under Imperialism*], published in 1929, is still an inspiration to many Formosans in demonstrating that some eminent Japanese favored their independence. "The middle class may become united with the propertied class and lead a united people's movement for political freedom . . . This has been seen in the history of Ireland and appears to be a law of political development in colonial territories," wrote Yanaibara.[46]

To sum up: political freedom under Japanese rule did not keep pace with economic, public health, and educational developments, although comparison of the Japanese record in Formosa with their rule in Korea, American rule in the Philippines, and probably with most colonial regimes before 1945, might rank Formosa above other prewar colonies.

Nonetheless, Japanese discrimination against the Formosans, socially and economically as well as politically, even in the relatively liberal and prosperous later years of occupation, is undeniable. "But remember the alien Japanese among us never constituted more than 6 per cent of the population, whereas the mainlanders today make up almost 20 per cent and include far more pensioners and lazy bureaucrats," said an eastern Formosa official in 1962.

By the 1960's, Formosan memories of Japanese colonialism had become intertwined with the more recent experience of Chinese Nationalist administration. Some observers think that only the more literate of the Formosans retain a favorable image of Japan, and that the vast majority of farmers and youth have been influenced to a much greater degree by postwar Nationalist indoctrination. The Formosans I met, however, regardless of age, social class, or other differences, all cited the comparative virtues of Japanese rule—not because they were pro-Japanese, but to emphasize their dislike for the Nationalists. Among those interviewed, in addition to intellectuals, were farmers, waterfront laborers, pedicab drivers, and many too young to have personal memories of Japan's occupation.

In retrospect, Formosans appear to have realized that the half-century of Japanese rule had prepared the ground for a genuine sense of national unity. It had provided the first effective island-wide administration, substituted comparatively modern education for old superstitions, cut off most ties with mainland China, raised living standards far above those on the turbulent Asian continent, and encouraged a cash crop economy, with per capita foreign trade 39 times greater than China's and higher than that in Japan itself.[47] The growth of urbanization, along with the rise of an articulate middle class, helped to weld the Formosan population together at the same time that the irritant of the Japanese presence further united it.

2

REVULSION AGAINST
EARLY NATIONALIST RULE

When Japan attacked Pearl Harbor and other United States bases in the
Pacific, her leaders must have known that war with the United States
could end with the loss of all colonial territories, including Korea and
Formosa. At the Cairo conference in November 1943, Churchill and
Roosevelt promised President Chiang Kai-shek that "all the territories
Japan has stolen from the Chinese, such as Manchuria, Formosa, and
the Pescadores, shall be restored to the Republic of China." [1] George
Kennan wrote later that the Cairo declaration was apparently drafted by
Harry Hopkins after consultation with the President and the Chinese:
"Of all the acts of American statesmanship in this unhappy chapter [on
wartime diplomacy in Asia], the issuance of this declaration, which is so
rarely criticized, seems to me to have been the most unfortunate in its
consequences . . . This thoughtless tossing to China of a heavily inhabited and strategically important island which had not belonged to it in
recent decades, and particularly the taking of this step before we had any
idea of what the future China was going to be like, and without any consultation of the wishes of the inhabitants of the island, produced a situation which today represents a major embarrassment to United States policy, and constitutes one of the great danger spots of the postwar
world." [2]

Washington discarded plans to invade Formosa during the Pacific war
for strategic reasons (Okinawa was a better base for the planned invasion
of Japan) [3] and decided not to occupy the island after V-J Day. Furthermore, Nationalist China was not only an ally of the United States
against Japan, but the only Allied claimant to Formosa. American policy

was not conspicuously far-sighted in 1945, nor did the native Formosans evince much anti-Nationalist sentiment at that time.

"If we had been given a vote in 1945, we probably would have approved Chinese rule," said Dr. Thomas Liao in 1963. Other Formosans, too, admit to their "glorified image of the fatherland caused by our ignorance of China and the Chinese." [4] It was only after the Nationalists proved themselves objectionable on Formosa that the native islanders rose in revolt.

George Kerr, a veteran of prewar Taiwan, predicted in 1945: "The Chinese will inherit exceptional political advantages [with Formosa] . . . no warlordism, no developed political parties, and no highly organized secret service or anti-Chinese subversive activity. For the Far East, living conditions are high . . . the grinding poverty encountered on the China coast is not to be seen . . . the most serious causes for civil unrest are absent." [5] (The islanders also had a ten-year experience with the mechanics of local elections, but the Nationalists were to prove more interested in a docile population whose natural wealth could be enlisted in the mainland civil war.) Cut off from its Japanese source of fertilizer and commercial goods, no longer able to sell Japan its agricultural surplus, and deteriorating from wartime neglect, Formosa needed only minimal rehabilitation and some international aid until Japan could be restored as its natural trading partner.

According to the U.S. State Department, "China found Formosa in favorable circumstances since Japan had made constructive use of the great natural resources of the island and the living standards were higher than anywhere on the Chinese mainland. It possessed a good industrial complex and was more than self-sufficient in foodstuffs." [6] A professor who had been among the few hundred Japanese allowed to remain on the island after the Chinese takeover recalled in 1963 that "we all went down to greet the Chinese troops carrying Nationalist flags, and the Formosans really were sincere in welcoming the new government. But the mainland troops were so poor and shabby that the Formosans were disillusioned even before experiencing the graft and corruption that led to the 1947 revolt. They'd been used to smartly-dressed and disciplined Japanese soldiers who were clean, neat, and well-behaved. Now these KMT troops were filthy, illiterate, and treated the Formosans as an occupied people." [7]

At first, only a few thousand Nationalist troops were sent to govern Formosa under General Chen Yi, who had been named administrator-general of Formosa pending establishment of a civilian regime. But

Chen, the former governor of Fukien province, soon surrounded himself with other mainland officers who acted as commissioners to control the island economy. The mainlanders of that first "wave"—as Kerr describes them—then sent for their friends and relatives to share the booty of the prosperous island. "The second wave," says Kerr, "was followed by a third composed of coolies [brought] from the diseased and illiterate masses of Shanghai slums . . . bubonic plague and cholera appeared on Formosa in 1946 for the first time in thirty years." [8]

It is important to remember that the occupying mainlanders governed Formosa as an occupied territory, not as a liberated Chinese province. They resented the local population, partly because it had prospered under Japanese rule, and tended to regard the Formosans—who had adopted the food, dress, customs, and culture of Japan—more as enemies than as brothers. General Chen Yi and his colleagues distrusted those who had achieved higher education or risen to high position under Japanese rule as "collaborators" to be purged of their tainted culture and re-educated as Chinese. Few Formosans were appointed to policy positions by Chen; many were dismissed from their jobs to make way for mainlanders.

The economic collapse of Formosa was the most serious consequence of the first eighteen months of Chinese rule. Nationalist officials were accustomed to padding their low pay with assorted squeeze: every merchant and citizen had to pay for government permits, and the consequent red tape provided increasing opportunities for bureaucratic corruption. The arrogance of the mainlander soldiers, and the payoffs expected by all KMT officials, antagonized large numbers of Formosans, especially in the cities where mainlanders were concentrated. Formosans had received discriminatory treatment from their Japanese overlords; they did not expect those they had regarded as fellow-Chinese to treat them so shabbily. Widespread corruption had been unfamiliar; now it ranged from outright thievery from stores and private homes to looting of factories and warehouses and massive diversion of Formosan goods and leftover Japanese supplies to the mainland black market. According to Kerr again: "Conscript peasants from China stole or commandeered bicycles but, unable to ride, carried them on their backs . . . by January 1946, members of the American Army's Formosa Advisory Group were predicting serious uprisings against Chen Yi." [9]

The Mainlander government placed all Japanese property under state control, and within a short time, says a U.S. Foreign Service witness, "at least 90 per cent of all the industry and agriculture of the island was controlled by some branch of the Government . . . Private and free enterprise in the island, restricted by the Japanese, was fast disappearing under the Chinese." [10] A commissioner of Chen Yi's regime was assigned to organize all tea production under one government bureau; another brought all sugar under his control; a third supervised all foreign trade (with excellent opportunities for personal profit); while the Monopoly Bureau controlled the sale of matches, alcohol, camphor, and tobacco.

Formosan fishing boats were diverted by Chinese officials to carry stolen goods to the mainland; banks began making heavy loans for commercial rather than industrial purposes; the value of the currency dropped steadily, and unemployment mounted after factories shut down for lack of raw materials. During 1946, it was estimated that 80 per cent of the native-born Formosan industrial workers lost their jobs, and between November 1945 and January 1947 commodity price indices rose 700 per cent for food, 1,400 per cent for fuel and building materials, and 25,000 per cent for fertilizer—largely the result, in Kerr's words, of "the drain of Taiwan wealth from the island, with little or no return to it . . . There is substantial evidence . . . that large quantities of grain were smuggled out or went into private control of officials." [11]

Mainlander graft included not only a multiplicity of fees for every commercial permit (to move, store, sell, or buy goods on credit) but also, even when no legal fee was required, "unfortunate administrative delays" unless the person paid a suitable amount to the appropriate official. "I've wanted to revisit my aging parents in Tokyo," said a Japanese woman who had married a Formosan during World War II and had not seen her family in twenty years, "but I cannot afford the payoff to get my passport." That was in 1962. Such petty corruption was commonplace, to my own knowledge, as late as 1969, and it appears to have been far worse between 1945 and 1947.

Not only capital goods and rice vanished into the mainland black market. So did everything from 500,000 tons of sugar to doorknobs, watermeters, and even sewer pipes, stolen from residential areas at night. UNRRA relief supplies shrank by an estimated 50 per cent as they passed through the hands of Chen Yi's lieutenants. Within a year, middle-class Formosans had reached the edge of bankruptcy.[12]

Formosans learned not to trust the courts for any redress of grievances against mainlander officials because, even though many lawyers and judges were Formosan, the police and secret police were controlled by Chen Yi. Many mainlander-run economic syndicates had their own independent armed police to enforce blackmail, bribery, and squeeze. When one native Formosan dared to bring charges in a county court against a mainlander policeman who had beaten him, the Formosan judge, as well as court aides sent to arrest the accused policeman, were themselves removed from office, beaten, and presumably killed. Even so, at the risk of retaliation, the native press often publicized the regime's misdeeds. "To neutral observers," says Kerr, "it was apparent that the men from the mainland were amazed and baffled to find these despised 'colonials' insistent on their rights before the law. These were not the docile, illiterate peasants and coolies they had been accustomed to exploiting on the mainland." [13]

Educational standards deteriorated as friction between Formosans and mainlanders disrupted the schools, especially the high schools and colleges whose Formosan students and teachers frequently clashed with mainland administrators and police. But for the first year and a half of postwar Chinese rule, most respected Formosan elders cautioned the more impatient youth against reckless opposition, admonishing them to "wait until President Chiang hears our complaints and the new Chinese constitution is extended to us; that will correct these temporary problems."

As the American Ambassador to Nanking, Dr. John Leighton Stuart, later reported to President Chiang Kai-shek, three acts of the KMT government in early 1947 "crystallized Formosan resentment toward economic policies and toward individuals in the Government." [14] These were (1) postponement by Chen Yi to December 1949 of the application of the new Constitution to Formosa; (2) the announcement that formerly Japanese-owned real estate might be sold at auction to favored mainlanders, who would then be allowed to evict or raise the rent of Formosans who had been living on it; and (3) the February 14, 1947 decision to place absolute control of all external trade and most domestic production and commerce in the hands of a few mainlander officials.

The first of these acts disillusioned hitherto moderate Formosan leaders who had told their compatriots that as soon as the new Chinese constitution took effect on the island, locally elected officials would give them better control over police and public services. Instead, it now appeared that Chinese military occupation would continue for nearly three more years and that Formosans would have neither security of person nor equality of property rights.

Rents had been an exception to the general inflation after the war; thus the second Chen Yi announcement was resented by Formosans living in ex-Japanese houses who felt they (and not mainlander realtors) deserved compensation for fifty years of Japanese colonialism. The third action confirmed Formosan fears that "carpetbagger" mainlanders would use their political power to acquire a total monopoly of the island's economic wealth.

It is therefore understandable that Formosans were ready to revolt against their Nationalist overlords by February of 1947. Some conceded that Nationalist officials were faced with a few problems beyond control, such as the wartime neglect of the island's civilian economy by Japan; the repatriation of 300,000 Japanese including many skilled technicians; and American bombing damage to parts of the island. But "there really wasn't much bomb damage in Taipei," said the chairman of the Taiwan Cement Company in 1961.[15] "Here in Kaohsiung," recalled a high official in 1962, "the worst-hit area was the Japanese residential area, rather than docks or factories." The Nationalists continue to claim even today that wartime damage was extensive; other sources, however, minimize the extent of damage and its effect on the economic problems of postwar Formosa.[16]

The loss of Japan as a trading partner was more disruptive to the economy than the evacuation from Formosa of Japanese technicians, most of whom might have remained if requested. In any event, the island economy was mainly agricultural and could have sustained itself even with reduced industrial production. One is forced to conclude that the major causes of Formosa's disintegration were within the power of the Nationalist regime to solve, and that for eighteen months most Formosans gave that regime the benefit of every doubt.

The "2-28" Revolution

On the evening of February 27, 1947, Chinese agents of the Tobacco and Wine Monopoly Bureau, accompanied by four policemen, walked through a crowded Taipei park to check for unlicensed vendors of cigarettes. They caught a widow in her forties and confiscated her cigarettes and cash, knocking her down when she protested. When those nearby tried to defend the woman, the police fired several shots into the crowd and killed at least one person. This was the spark that ignited groups of Taipei citizens—already angered by an earlier incident on Keelung—who marched on the police headquarters to demand arrest of the policemen responsible for the shooting. Later that night, the local police claimed to have turned the murderers over to the military police, which the latter denied. Another crowd, who urged a newspaper editor to print the tobacco woman's story, was told the government would forbid publication.

The following morning, a larger crowd decided to march to Chen Yi's headquarters and on the offices of Tobacco and Wine Monopoly demanding immediate punishment of the policemen, compensation to the bereaved families, relaxation of the tobacco monopoly, and apologies. About 1:00 p.m., as the crowd approached, Chen Yi's guards fired machine guns into it and killed several persons. This marked the beginning of a general uprising against Chinese officials, which spread to every city on the island as rebels who had seized the Taiwan Broadcasting Station notified the populace, and Chinese police began hiding from enraged civilians. Chen Yi declared martial law later on the 28th, moving army units into the cities to quell the rioters, who by then were burning offices of reputedly corrupt officials, but had avoided indiscriminate attacks or looting.

The events of the next two weeks, the most dramatic in the island's history, cannot be given here in detail; but the main features are vital to an understanding of postwar Formosan nationalism and the continuing gap between the native majority and their mainlander overlords.[17]

"For about the first week in March, we saw no armed Chinese on the streets of Taipei, and the Formosans seemed to control every city because Chen Yi had too few troops to suppress the massive demonstrations," Ralph Blake, then the American consul in Taiwan, said later.[18] "The mainlanders seemed to stay off the streets or seek shelter in foreigners' houses," recalls a Japanese professor who witnessed the events in Taipei: "Young Formosan students patrolled the streets and tried to keep any ruffians in order. They would speak to people in Japanese, because that was the best way of telling if a person was local or mainlander, and if you could reply in Japanese you were safe." Native islanders roamed the streets looking for symbols of the hated mainlanders and beating up police. All mainlander Chinese, regardless of rank or occupation, became targets of the Formosan mobs. Some Chinese were stoned, and cars were burned, but the few looters were severely punished by Formosan crowds.

Meanwhile General Chen Yi agreed to negotiate with an ad hoc Committee of Settlement composed of conservative members of the appointive municipal and provincial councils. He also agreed to receive reform suggestions from the Committee by March 10; promised not to bring more troops into the city from outlying areas; allowed a voluntary Youth

Corps to maintain order in Taipei under supervision of the mayor and police chief; and restored communications. Clashes between armed patrols and civilians continued, however, and a group of mainlander railway officials sought temporary asylum in the American consulate across the street when a crowd protested the railway police shooting of passersby.[19]

Taipei newspapers, pleading for public order to permit peaceful negotiations with the Nationalist general, strongly backed the Settlement Committee (branches of which were springing up throughout the island) and faithfully reported developments. On March 2, they claimed that the Governor had been unable to bring troops up from the south because citizens of Hsinchu (a city between Taipei and Taichung) had removed rails from the tracks. Moderate Formosan leaders had difficulty in persuading their more cynical colleagues of the Governor's sincerity and both tactical and personal divisions among the native leaders prevented genuine unity.

In some cities, such as Hualien, mainlander officials put up little resistance as native committees took control between March 1 and 3. In Kaohsiung, however, the army commander (later Defense Minister), General Peng Ming-chi killed several rebel leaders on March 6 before capitulating to the aroused populace.

Informants who now live abroad have told me of many specific occurrences during that week of native Formosan rule. They say that sometimes aborigines came down from the hills to join the rebels; that mainlander civilians in charge of the power system and other services frequently proved to be politically neutral; and that even some military police and army units handed over their arms to the rebels. Says Kerr: "Events of the week also demonstrated that Formosans could operate the technical economy of the island by themselves, thus destroying Chen Yi's argument that they were a 'backward people' requiring constant guidance." [20]

By March 6, the Settlement Committee had drafted its reform proposals which it submitted to the General the next day. The 32 points called for immediate local elections, abolition of irresponsible police units, appointment of more Formosans to higher positions of policy, and a breakup of the economic monopolies. All the points were reformist: none asked for separation from China, although some looked toward local control of the island's armed forces. It must nonetheless be noted that posters appeared about this time urging either extreme autonomy or expulsion of the KMT, and some groups around the island surely shared that desire. The rebels' principal spokesmen, however, were moderate, peaceful, and rather naïve.[21]

The General's agent, Major General Chang Wu-tao, assured the Settlement Committee on March 8 that "the demands for political reforms in this province are very proper. The Central Government will not dispatch troops to Taiwan . . . I can risk my life to guarantee that the Central Government will not take any military actions against Taiwan . . ." [22] Chen Yi himself made contradictory statements, however, and some "half-mountain" Formosans (i.e., those who had migrated to the mainland and returned with the Kuomintang) questioned even the moderate-type of proposals suggested.

Several thousand mainlander troop reinforcements of the 21st Division, Shanghai, landed at Keelung north of Taipei on the night of March 8 after their machine-gun fire had cleared the dock area. They carried American and Japanese equipment as they marched toward the capital to begin a month of retaliatory massacre.

Chen Yi's men had succeeded in infiltrating and deceiving the Settlement Committee, like the Russians in Budapest ten years later. It became evident that the KMT command had never intended to make any concessions to the Formosans, but had used the first week in March to identify the Formosan activists both individually and as types (college students, teachers, and doctors, among others).[23]

As the reinforcements began their slaughter in Taipei March 9, Chen Yi dissolved the Settlement Committee, allegedly for having "exceeded its authority," and ordered the arrest of almost everyone connected with the previous ten days' movement. Few of the designated Formosans in the northern cities had time to escape, unlike their colleagues in the south who were able to flee the advancing Nationalist troops. "The troops came to our door and asked my father to go with them for questioning. Despite pleas by my mother, we never saw or heard from him again," one of my students told me in 1962. His father was a university dean, one of the more eminent of the marked men. Some of these were beaten and killed on the spot, but large numbers of doctors, lawyers, editors, and businessmen were simply taken away. High school and university enrollment lists were used to round up dissident students and, if they were not found, some family member was taken as hostage. Ong Jok-tik, who escaped the dragnet, has told me of the murder of his elder brother. "All Taiwanese dissidents became known during the time of the revolt, and many were put in sugar bags, bayonetted, and thrown into the river off the big Taipei bridge," recalled a Japanese professor who was one of the few foreign witnesses to the massacre.[24]

Some American and European residents also witnessed the month-long reign of terror. A Canadian nurse remembers running out seven times during that period to treat wounded persons or carry them to her mission hospital. Kerr tells of another foreigner who "saw a youth forced to dismount from his cycle before a military policeman, who thereupon lacerated the man's hands so badly with his bayonet that the man could not pick up his machine." [25] The area near the American consulate was sacked on March 10 as the troops killed many shopkeepers and looted at will. The number of persons killed in the Taipei area alone has been estimated at over 2,000 with 1,000 more in Keelung, but no reliable figures were ever published because the regime responsible for the slaughter remained in power. During the massacre only a few government newspapers were published, others having been banned. By March 17, the troops advanced down the main road toward the center and south of the island.

In my travels through Formosa during 1961 and 1962, I asked people in all walks of life from peddlers to county magistrates for their memories of the 1947 massacre. In Hualien on the east coast, the sister of a shopkeeper broke down in tears as she recalled men, women, and children of that port city forced to kneel on the bank of a stream before the troops mowed them down with machine-gun fire. "The pigs never asked whether we were involved in the revolt or had committed any political act at all; they just assembled people at random, especially those who seemed prosperous." Well-to-do Formosans were probably singled out as targets less because they had waxed fat under Japanese rule than because they constituted an incipient political elite among the conquered islanders.

Another Hualien shopkeeper, after the store had closed and he could speak privately, told of troops who had commandeered a regular passenger bus in Taipei as it was ready to make the 8-hour trip to Hualien. "The Chinese officer threw out all the passengers and ordered his troops into the bus. The driver, knowing the troops were on their way to terrorize the Hualien area, told the girl conductor not to board the bus but rather to take a hastily scribbled note to his wife. Then he drove the busload of troops along the narrow road carved out of the steep cliffs overhanging the Pacific Ocean. As he approached the steepest point, where the road was hundreds of feet above the surf, he veered sharply to the left and drove over the cliff to certain death below." (Years later, the bus driver was rumored to have jumped to safety and lived in hiding ever since.)

The tale of the bus driver is still known throughout the island, even by those too young to have experienced the events of March 1947. Whether apocryphal or not, it is passed by word of mouth as a symbol of that unforgettable month and my knowledge of it helped convince Formosans in other areas of my sincere interest in the true history of their island.

In Taitung, on the southeast coast, a Formosan official told of mainlander troops' attacks on aboriginal villages when they learned that the tribes had helped the anti-Nationalist Formosans. The more militant tribes had indeed harbored old grudges against the Manchu mainlanders, but most victims were as innocent as their Formosan neighbors.

A foreign missionary attached to the Presbyterian Seminary at Tainan in 1962 said that almost every student's family included some relative who was killed in 1947. "Christian Formosans were one of the groups resented by the Nationalists," he explained, "because of their contact with foreigners, and their known devotion to the Formosan language and welfare."

Some of the Kaohsiung veterans of 1947 now living abroad have confirmed reports of 2,700 slaughtered in that great southern port city. "Peng Ming-chi was called the 'butcher of Kaohsiung' for very good reasons," a Kaohsiung worker told me in 1963. "One of the lawyers you interviewed yesterday narrowly escaped death because the mainlander who was police chief in 1947 accused him of not providing him refuge in the days of native rule. The complaint failed only because the accused man had important friends among the Formosans who served the KMT." Many wealthy businessmen either voluntarily or through blackmail served as apologists for the Chen Yi regime to the enraged masses. After the slaughter ended in late March 1947, these men managed to save their families, wealth, and hopes for future service within the regime. Some were genuine puppets of the Nationalists, but most appear to have had more complex motivations.

The few leftists among the 1947 leadership accused men like Lin Hsien-t'ang (the prewar autonomy activist) of "posing as an elder statesman during the Settlement Committee talks when the uprising began . . . He protected the mayor of Taichung, informed on the revolutionaries, and hindered the struggle of the masses in secret. After the arrival of Defense Minister Pai, Lin denounced the revolution as instigated by 'traitor-bandits' and was handsomely rewarded." [26] But, in fact, Lin had soon escaped to Japan where he died shortly after. Mutual recriminations for the failure of the movement have continued among the survivors abroad ever since.

Some Formosans, like one university-educated family in southern Formosa, resolved to have nothing further to do with the regime and to live in seclusion. "How could we ever trust those pigs again when they broke all their promises to us and lured so many to their slaughter? Even some who played their game were killed or ruined financially," they told me in 1962.

"We lost a whole generation of leaders in that terrible month of 1947," remarked a Kaohsiung city official as we looked down on the city from a mountain which was once the site of a Shinto shrine but had become largely a Nationalist military zone. "Those who escaped either went abroad or into hiding on the island; others learned their lesson—not to challenge the regime. Some of us work to improve the lot of our fellows, even through the government, but the courageous ones who could have been great politicians are gone. See those cement pillboxes on the streetcorners down there? They are not really designed to defend us against a Communist invasion, but to remind us never to try another 1947."

Estimates of the total number of Formosans killed in 1947 range from 10,000 to 20,000 if one counts prisoners presumed dead and those who disappeared.[27] Several hundred, perhaps up to 3,000, managed to flee the island and became political exiles in Hong Kong and later Japan. Shopkeepers in Taichung told of a few refugees still living in the mountains, where many fled from central Formosa after they beat off two attacks near Sun Moon Lake. "A few mourners may go to Buddhist temples every year secretly about 5 a.m. on February 28," said Thomas Liao in 1962, "but the Nationalists have never permitted any open commemoration of that date."

The Aftermath. After the islanders had been terrorized into submission by the massacres of March, the central government at Nanking replaced Chen Yi with Wei Tao-ming, former Ambassador to the United States, and changed the status of the island from a militarily administered territory to one of the thirty-five provinces of China, as it had been before 1895. Censorship and martial law were relaxed, government enterprises converted partially to private ownership, and many mainlander officials replaced by pliable Formosans who had remained loyal to the government in the 1947 crisis. Most of the administrative reforms were more formal than real, as the security police continued to ferret out any remaining sources of native dissidence. The armed fist was concealed by a velvet glove, however, partly because of official American and liberal Chinese criticism aroused by the March massacres.

Russell Fifield, then an American diplomat in China and later a University of Michigan professor, noted that "most foreigners on the island are inclined to believe that considerable time must elapse before the new regime can be fairly evaluated . . . Past experience of Chinese rule, which lasted from 1683 until 1895, does not suggest that its return would be in the best interests of the island or of its inhabitants . . . If the Formosans were in a position today to decide their own fate what would they do? Many of the foreign residents who have been there a long time and can speak fluently the principal language [the Taiwan dialect] of the people are convinced that they would seek a trusteeship under the United Nations, with the United States as the principal trustee. After the termination of the trusteeship, these foreigners believe, the Formosans would welcome an affiliation with China provided the Chinese had meanwhile put their own house in order. In the event that a stable China did not emerge, they would prefer to be independent." [28]

How did the Nationalists explain the "2-28" incident? Rather than blaming wartime damage, disruption caused by the transfer from Japan, and Chen Yi's personal errors, the Nanking Defense Minister sent to investigate the uprising declared that "the revolt was due to the instigation of Communists, the training of the Japanese, and the ambitions of Formosan politicians." These three charges were repeated in later works of the Nationalist regime and its foreign advocates. Geraldine Fitch, for example, wrote in 1953: "To what extent Communists, planted on the island to make trouble, had fomented the uprising which Chen Yi quelled with such ruthlessness, I do not know. Oddly enough, the Chinese characters for '2-28' can be written so as to mean 'Communist.' Perhaps the day was chosen for the incident." [29]

W. G. Goddard, writing in 1966, began by blaming the Japanese and the Formosan politicians:

> The moment [the Japanese] knew that defeat was inevitable, they set in motion their plan to make the return of Chinese control as difficult as possible. A similar plan operated in Indonesia to hamper the return of the Dutch. Local independence movements were organized and selected men, trained by the Japanese, were entrusted with the campaign . . . When defeat did come, and the Japanese left Formosa, these Formo-

sans, with arms supplied by the Japanese, roamed the island, fanning the flames of revolt against the return to China and claiming independence for Formosa. They were few in number, and when they failed to gain support they left for Japan, where they carried out their campaign, which still continues but with diminished virulence. Their brief activity in Formosa was assisted by a small number of disaffected Formosans who, having fled the ruthless oppression of Japanese colonialism to China in past years, now returned in the hope of receiving posts of authority in the island. Disgruntled and disappointed in not realizing their ambitions, they joined up with the Japanese-inspired independence movement, and they, too, eventually found their way to Japan. At times an echo of their bitterness can be heard from the pages of certain periodicals in America and elsewhere . . . Chen Yi, from the beginning, never tried to win the good will of the people, and his misrule, together with his arrogant personality, brought about public indignation and the subsequent uprising. His dismissal won popular support for the Chinese government and from that time the independence movement began to peter out. At no time had it been popular. The disturbance of February 1947 had been directed not against the Chinese Government, but against the despotic rule of Chen Yi.[30]

Ambassador Stuart insisted that Communism "in any form was of the most negligible importance on Taiwan" in March 1947, and Russell Fifield among other local observers agreed that "actually there are very few Communists in Formosa [and] it is probably incorrect to blame the Communists for the revolt." [31] According to a Formosan graduate student who came to the United States about 1963, "Schools on the island still teach that a Communist girl named Hsieh was in charge of the riots, but we students didn't believe it and neither did our teachers." [32] Communism had been effectively suppressed by the prewar Japanese administration, and no CCP mainlanders are known to have come to the island during the first years of Nationalist rule. None of my Formosan or foreign informants between 1961 and 1968 thought the 2-28 incident had been sparked, organized, or led by Communists, Formosan or mainlander. Miss Hsieh and her few leftist colleagues were on the fringe of the spontaneous island-wide revolt.

Japanese influence, if meant to imply efforts to promote anti-Nationalist movements inside the island, is an equally specious explanation for the revolt. If however "influence" is defined as Japanese education of the

Formosans in efficient government, honest police, and orderly economic development, the charge is valid. Educated Formosans who compared the rule of the prewar Japanese "dogs" with the postwar Chinese "pigs" found the latter definitely inferior. Fifty years of Japanese influence in Formosa did not make the natives pro-Japanese, but they did provide a standard to which the postwar Chinese Nationalists failed to measure up.

To blame Chen Yi personally for the uprising is rather like blaming General Tojo for the Pacific War. Personalism is a traditional Chinese theory of politics, but even Chen Yi could not have engineered such a massive despoliation of Formosa or the betrayal of its people in 1947 without considerable help from other Nationalist officials both on the island and in Nanking. After Chen was relieved of his Taiwan post in mid-1947, he was appointed a field commander in the mainland civil war; only after he had attempted to sell out to the Communists did President Chiang order his arrest, in March 1949, and return him to be executed in Taipei, the scene of his earlier crimes, on June 16, 1950. "What poetic justice to execute him on the same spot where Formosans had been killed!" said a leading Formosan refugee in 1961. "But would they have done that if he hadn't betrayed Chiang?" [33]

Five months after the suppression of the Formosan incident, General Albert Wedemeyer led a mission to China and reported to the Secretary of State as follows:

> Our experience in Formosa is most enlightening. The administration of the former Governor Chen Yi has alienated the people from the Central Government. Many were forced to feel that conditions under autocratic rule [of Japan] were preferable. The Central Government lost a fine opportunity to indicate to the Chinese people and to the world at large its capacity to provide honest and efficient administration. *They cannot attribute their failure to the activities of Communists or of dissident elements.* The people anticipated sincerely and enthusiastically deliverance from the Japanese yoke. However, Chen Yi and his henchmen ruthlessly, corruptly, and avariciously imposed their regime upon a happy and amenable population. *The Army conducted themselves as conquerors.* Secret police operated freely to intimidate and to facilitate exploitation by Central Government officials . . .
>
> The island is extremely productive in coal, rice, sugar, cement, fruit, and tea. Both hydro and thermal power are abundant. The Japanese had efficiently electrified even remote areas and

also established excellent railroad lines and highways. Eighty per cent of the people can read and write, the exact antithesis of conditions prevailing on the mainland of China. There were indications that Formosans would be receptive toward United States guardianship and United Nations trusteeship. *They fear that the Central Government contemplates bleeding their island to support the tottering and corrupt Nanking machine and I think their fears well founded.*[34] (Emphasis added.)

For two years after the March massacre Formosa received little attention from the Nationalist regime on the mainland, or from the United States. Police brutality and economic oppression were somewhat moderated under Governor Wei Tao-ming, who made a sincere though largely ineffective effort to ameliorate conditions. But when the Chinese Communist armies crossed the Yangtse River in January 1949 and began their final southern campaign, Chiang Kai-shek replaced the civilian Wei with his old friend, General Chen Cheng, who restored military rule on the island to prepare for the worst, which soon occurred: the influx of one million Nationalist refugees, about half of them troops, across the strait to Formosa. American observers reported the newcomers "brought with them the mainland inflation . . . The island is badly and inefficiently run at a time when the best possible efforts are needed unless developments on the mainland are simply to be transferred to Formosa." [35]

The 1949 State Department "White Paper" (Department of State: U.S. Relations with China, 1949) claimed that Formosan hatred of the mainland Chinese increased after 1947. It was thus startling, at the time of my first visit to Taipei in December 1957, to hear the counsellor of the American embassy assure me that "we no longer make any distinction between Formosans and mainlanders—the gap has narrowed with education and prosperity and will disappear very soon." Explanation of the discrepancy came in June 1961, when a China specialist in the State Department briefed me before my Fulbright year on Formosa by contradicting the Taipei officer's 1957 statement: "That's one reason why that officer is no longer in the [Foreign] service: we all say things like that in public, but most of us know better privately." [36]

George Kerr wrote in 1965: "So long as Chiang Kai-shek, his family, or his Party and Army govern Formosa, this [1947] betrayal will not be forgotten or forgiven." [37] The attitudes of the vast majority of Formosans interviewed between 1961 and 1968 bore out Kerr's prophecy.

3

FORMOSAN RESPONSE TO
CULTURAL INTEGRATION

"The most depressing thing about this island is the mutual disadmiration society in which both mainlanders and Formosans look down on each other." This comment of a young American diplomat assigned to the Formosan affairs desk of the Taipei embassy in 1962 describes the continuing gap between the two groups despite Nationalist disclaimers of any cultural gap.

This chapter deals with what Mark Mancall has termed "a deep-seated self-consciousness of Taiwanese as Taiwanese" that is not limited to the older generation educated before 1945.[1] "The mainlanders look on us as outsiders because we do not speak Mandarin well," said a Christian Formosan leader in 1962, "but our youngsters know perfect Mandarin and yet can see for themselves the discrimination against Formosans in employment and politics." [2] Among themselves, Formosans of all ages tend to use the Formosa dialect.

Formosans who were over the age of thirty in the early 1960's, and had therefore received a Japanese education, are often, and rightly, assumed by the mainlander elite to retain idealized memories of the Japanese period and a bitter recollection of the 1947 massacre; and in consequence they are sometimes suspected of divided loyalties. The Nationalist regime knows they understand the Japanese language and admire Japanese customs more than their children who grew up after 1950. After all, about three-fourths of the Formosans at the end of World War II were competent, if not fluent, in Japanese. The Nationalists therefore pin their hopes on indoctrinating the Formosan younger generation.

Because attitudes of younger Formosans are especially important in terms of the future, it is significant that an unexpected result of the post-war upsurge of higher education has been the creation of a large number of educated young Formosans repelled by the hypocrisy of Nationalist ideology, and by the unfulfilled promise of Sun Yat-sen's "Three Principles"—"nationalism, democracy, and people's livelihood."

In this chapter we shall see how the continued use of non-mainlander language and customs has reinforced the Formosans' own cultural self-consciousness, and then discuss educational developments, especially their impact on Formosan identity both in formal schooling of the young and in adult indoctrination. The chapter closes with Formosans' objections to what they consider retrogressive Chinese culture patterns imported by the mainlander regime or revived from the pre-Japanese Formosan past.

Persistence of the Japanese Heritage

Even a defender of the theory that Formosans are essentially a Chinese subculture has written: "How could Taiwanese fail to be different from residents of Fukien when they had a distinctive historical experience prior to 1895, were isolated from the mainland for half a century, and for the same half century were ruled by Japanese, not by Chinese—by a modern industrial power, not by an underdeveloped half-nation?" [3] The impact of Japanese rule on Formosa has been discussed earlier, but the persistence of the Japanese cultural heritage over two decades after 1945 requires special explanation.

The prevalence of the Japanese language in Formosa today is noted by visitors who find their ability to speak it an open sesame to native hospitality. An American officer, for example, was reportedly given a free taxi ride through Taipei when the driver heard him speak Japanese. Several American newspaper correspondents and research scholars have employed Japanese-speaking interpreters for better rapport with Formosans over forty.[4] A Formosan official who guided me around Taitung spoke almost entirely in Japanese both with his friends and in a village of tribesmen we visited.[5]

"We understand some Japanese from the radio and movies and from our parents' talk, even when we don't speak it well, so please use it rather than English, which is harder for us," requested a group of Taipei university seniors in 1962 as we began to discuss their political ambitions.

When Formosa was ceded to Japan in 1895, the majority of the natives spoke Taiwanese, some spoke Hakka, a very few Mandarin, and the mountain tribes a variety of dialects. Japan set up the first public schools on the island and Japanese became a unifying tongue for all the inhabitants. As a matter of pure convenience, therefore, Japanese bridged the communication gap among the several linguistic groups in Formosa. Furthermore—an increasingly important consideration—Western words and scientific terms can be spoken and written more easily in Japanese than Chinese, while Japanese trade, investment, and tourism inspire many Formosans to retain or learn the language.

An indication of the islanders' competence in Japanese is that Radio Peking broadcast a Japanese-language program of news and music to the island every night at the hour when local Formosan stations all carried the Nationalist government's daily propaganda news. "They [the mainland Communists] must know that many of us turn the dial to avoid that, and try to appeal to our Japanese nostalgia," explained a shopkeeper. (The Nationalist government did not jam Radio Peking but forbade listening to any mainland broadcasts.)

No primary or secondary school run by the government teaches either Japanese or the Taiwan dialect, but the eldest son of a Taipei druggist whom I frequently visited was enrolled in a Japanese-language course at Taiwan National University, the largest on the island. "The class has over 200 students," he said, "and is too crowded for good teaching methods, but I can't afford to go to one of the private language schools." When Taiwan opened its first television station, the regime—disregarding the fact of technical and financial assistance for the station from Japan—required all Japanese commercials and programs to be dubbed in Chinese.[6] "Our record of not suppressing the several tongues found on Taiwan is commendable, although we probably are too touchy about Japanese," admitted the Taipei China News in 1967.[7]

A Japanese periodical reported a few years ago: "Taiwanese are most enthusiastic in listening to the NHK [Japanese government radio corporation] broadcasts in Japanese and send 200–300 letters a month responding to the NHK programs. To show its appreciation, NHK created a special program, 'Thank You for Your Tidings', from April 1962 and it was reported there were 200 letters from Taiwan listeners to this program in April." [8] The Tokyo broadcasts include American-style popular music which many Formosans prefer to the Chinese-type music on their local stations. Here again there is no overt political significance to the use of Japanese, any more than when the tourist expresses play "Sayonara" as they roll into Taipei station.

The widespread sale of Japanese popular magazines, especially those with women's fashions and romantic or sensational fiction, is a matter of cultural preference as well as of anti-Nationalist feelings. Whenever I went to a Taichung barber shop, the radio was tuned to Japanese music and the tables were full of Japanese periodicals. "I wish we were allowed more of these," the owner complained. "Many come from our friends who carry them back in their luggage from Tokyo, and each copy gets plenty of use for years."

"None of the really good Japanese journals is allowed, because they occasionally carry stories from Red China," explained a Taipei bookseller. "The government also frowns on our pirating any Japanese book and is extremely strict in censoring such works brought in by travellers." Japanese is permitted, however, in newspaper ads for Japanese products and in commercial advertising generally. There seems also to be a brisk black market trade in Japanese records and magazines outside the narrow confines of the few newspapers and magazines approved for import.

Formosans have also retained a few other vestiges of the 50 years of Japanese rule. Every large town and city on the island has its *sushi, tempura,* and other varieties of Japanese restaurants, catering to Formosan clients. The most luxurious of these blend Chinese and Western cuisine with their Japanese food, and tend to be cleaner and quieter than their strictly Chinese counterparts. "No mainlanders come here," said the owner of such a restaurant in Taipei, "but neither do many Japanese tourists, who prefer to stay out of town at the Peitou hot-springs resort." Although all the hot springs on the island were originally developed to cater to the Japanese taste, Peitou is "the only place where the service is still *reigisaho* [polite]," according to a young Taichung businessman.

Some Formosans cite every difference between their inherited Japanese culture and that of the mainlanders on the island as proof of Formosan cultural separatism. "Those mainland pigs don't even know the best rooms in a hot-spring hotel," said the wife of a Formosan businessman. "Every time we go to one, we see the *gaishojin* [literally, 'people from outside the province'] in the less desirable rooms and refusing to remove their shoes!" It is the general Formosan desire to retain Japanese cultural forms and language, as proof of the non-Chinese nature of their island's tradition, that makes these practices significant.

Looking to contemporary Japan as a model of economic growth and material development is a popular Formosan habit. Mayor Kao of Taipei returned from a foreign tour in 1967 to say: "We have done a lot to develop Taipei, but compared with Tokyo and Seoul, we are not doing enough and not progressing fast enough." [9] The same month, a Chinese travel expert advised his government to imitate Japanese practices: "The success of tourism in Japan should be a lesson to us." [10] Materially, the Nationalists see no danger in accepting such advice, but the indirect impact on Formosan consciousness may be to reinforce the image of Japan as the most democratic model in Asia.

Persistence of the Formosan Dialect

Japan had enforced the study and use of its own language; punished harshly the speaking of Formosan (i.e., the Taiwanese dialect derived from the Fukien coast) and pushed the diffusion rate of Japanese from an estimated 3 per cent in 1920 to 71 per cent in 1944.[11] The Nationalists, on the other hand, though formally discouraging Taiwanese in favor of Mandarin, wink at the continued use of the Taiwan dialect in the armed forces where Mandarin is legally required, and elsewhere too. According to a local newspaper, "A member of the Taipei City Council complained he did not understand what was going on at the municipal government or the city legislature because most of his colleagues and the city officials spoke in the local dialect . . . In a written statement to Mayor Henry Kao, [he] demanded an explanation of why his men do not speak Mandarin in conducting official business." [12]

Further indication of the regime's tolerance of the Formosan dialect is the 1966 report that 126 of the 158 motion pictures made in Taiwan during the previous year were in Taiwanese.[13] When I was there, the new TV channel showed a Taiwan-dialect play every evening in prime time, and radio stations often played native folk songs. Yet several Formosan Presbyterians who wrote a native dialect textbook using romanized characters in 1949 were advised against reprinting it in 1964 by a fellow-Presbyterian (Chua Pue-he), then serving as a minister without portfolio in the central government, who argued: "The regime is opposed to the diffusion of the Taiwanese language through romanization, which it could and would interpret as similar to Peking's recent use of a romanized script."

The United States Information Agency reported in its *Communication Fact Book: Taiwan* (Washington, D.C.: February 1962) that "although all but one of the commercial radio stations are owned and operated by mainlander Chinese, their programs are predominately in Taiwanese . . . More and more advertisers in buying airtime asked for Taiwanese operas, dramas, popular songs, or storytelling. The average adult Taiwanese cannot speak Mandarin with any degree of fluency . . . Public information personnel operate in a social and economic environment sharply bifurcated by the contrasting habits, language and backgrounds of the indigenous Taiwanese and mainlander refugee groups." Fulbright grantees were even warned in the official State Department guide books not to mix mainlander and local servants in the same household because their language and customs were so different.

Announcements on railway trains and long-distance buses, and in many other public places, are made first in Mandarin and then in Taiwanese. "After a few more years, when the older people are even more outnumbered by the Mandarin-educated generation, we can stop the Taiwanese," predicted a railway official. It seems probable, however, if Taiwanese continues to be perpetuated in the home and communal associations, as in recent years when all overseas students of my acquaintance have spoken Taiwanese exclusively among themselves, that use of the dialect may continue for generations.

Education and Indoctrination

The Nationalist regime appears to have learned in 1947 that peaceful efforts to win Formosan loyalty would be far more effective than openly harsh suppression of native discontent. Increasingly dependent upon United States aid, the regime could not afford to antagonize American observers again, particularly since it wanted help from Washington to build a viable Formosa. The Nationalists had great hope of molding the postwar generation of Formosan children into "pure" Chinese who spoke Mandarin, knew the writings of Sun Yat-sen, and would follow Chiang Kai-shek in the reconquest of the mainland. The refugee regime realized that it must rely on Formosan youths to replace aging mainlander soldiers for both defense of the island and eventual counterattack, and that the loyalty of those troops would be vital. American advisors stressed also the importance of training civilian Formosans to be more productive workers in the fields and factories. Therefore, education at every level, from formal schooling to the mass media, assumed both political and economic importance.

We have seen that Japan gave prewar Formosans a good primary education and vocational training, but relatively little higher education. Literacy was probably over 70 per cent in 1945, and higher in the urban areas of Formosa, where thousands were admitted to secondary schools in the 1930's. Primary school enrollments rose from 26,000 in 1904 to 244,000 in 1924, and 933,000 in 1944; [14] between 1944 and 1964 they more than doubled (but so did the population).

There were almost 500 junior high schools at the end of the Japanese occupation, nearly half of whose 16,000 students were Formosan, and about 30 higher commercial and normal schools. The six-year primary schools were free and compulsory in the latter period of Japanese rule, while 10,000 aborigine children attended special schools in the mountains. The one university, Taihoku Imperial, enrolled fewer than 500 students (mostly Japanese), but many of the present 70 universities in Taiwan have been raised from technical and normal schools as in postwar Japan and the United States.

The present regime extended free public schooling to nine years in 1968, which will require 5,000 additional classrooms and a proportionate increase in the number of teachers.[15] Until 1968, about half the elementary school graduates could pass the entrance examinations for junior high school, and two-thirds of those who completed that level went on to senior high school. The cramming required to pass entrance exams to junior high schools before 1969, and higher level schools today, evidently takes a heavy toll on the health of students, according to surveys of student weight and eyesight.[16]

About 14,000 of the 50,000 annual applicants for admission to universities can be accommodated in the institutions of higher learning, few of which are really of university calibre.[17] "So many primary students still attend two-shift schools or are crowded 95 to a room that it will take at least until 1970 before all can be admitted to junior high, and the teacher-student ratio must be improved," noted a Formosan graduate student in 1966. "Japan required many years to finance its postwar 9-year system, and her people enjoy triple our per capita income."

The competition of education, industrial investment, and defense for a greater share of the national income promises to remain very keen. In 1963, only 13 per cent of Taiwan's total government revenues went for formal education, compared with about 50 per cent for defense, and the American Agency for International Development estimated illiteracy among Formosans over age 12 at 28 per cent.[18] The Ministry of Education claimed in 1962 that the average annual expenditure per student ranged from $21 in primary school to $178 in universities. By 1967, the Taiwan Provincial Department of Social Affairs reported one-fifth of the labor force to be illiterate and predicted that the total labor force would grow by 22 per cent before 1971.[19]

Most teachers in elementary schools are native Formosans but mainlander teachers predominate in secondary and higher education. Mandarin is the language of instruction, and texts are rigorously screened to give students a neo-Confucian and pro-Nationalist orientation. Every Monday morning, according to student reports, Sun Yat-sen's Three Principles of the People are reviewed, and continued as a required subject through the university level. The teaching methods in Formosa are heavily formalistic with rote memory, standardized lectures, and regurgitational examinations. Dr. George Mackay's description of the old Chinese school system in 1872–1894 applies all too often in the crowded schoolrooms of modern Formosa: "Unconsciously the style and sentiments of the books are absorbed, but originality in either thought or expression is not only undesirable but utterly impossible." [20]

Formosans who observed the entire period of postwar education, from the early neglect and mismanagement of 1945–1949 to the outward progress of recent years, are aware of several shortcomings. They note that whereas Article 164 of the Republic of China Constitution provides that "expenditures for educational programs, scientific studies, and cultural services shall not be less than 15 per cent of the total national budget, 25 per cent of the total provincial budget, and 35 per cent of the total municipal or county budget," [21] the national government actually spends less than 4 per cent of its budget for education in Formosa. The bulk is diverted to the Nationalist's expensive military program.

Another educational shortcoming, admitted by members of the Control Yuan (Nationalist China's equivalent of the old censorate), is the overcrowding of schools.[22] Some first-grade classes are said to contain as many as 96 pupils, while classes at the Taiwan Normal University, theoretically limited to 50, usually have over 70 students. Low teacher salaries are a perennial complaint, and one reason why fewer than 10 per cent of Formosan scholars return to the island after completing their studies abroad. Grade school teachers in Taipei received about $25 monthly in 1962 and university professors from $45 to $100 per month. A Stanford Research Institute study for the Chinese Ministry of Education in late 1962 confirmed the lack of wage incentives to attract men into the teaching profession and predicted a shortage of 1,200 secondary school teachers, 1,400 mechanical engineers, and 1,200 accountants by 1967.[23]

Teachers sometimes earn extra cash by conducting extra-curricular cram sessions for primary and high school students who are taking entrance exams for the next level.

Bernard Gallin, who studied one rural Formosan area intensively, blames both the economic problems of village life and the impractical content of textbooks: "No attempt is made to give the children a written vocabulary which would equip them to read simple agricultural magazines . . . several years after graduation, many of these young people are again functionally illiterate." [24] Farmers Associations begun under Japanese rule, continue to provide extension-type programs theoretically of great value, but too often marred by the employment of urban teachers ignorant of farm problems.

Higher education is more relevant to our concern with Formosan nationalism because it is usually the university graduates who provide political leadership in any culture. The rote memory process, low teaching salaries, and difficult admission requirements which prevail in lower schools also obtain at the university level, where the 80,000 full-time day students are likely to double in the 1970's. Financial and curricular weaknesses are more serious for college students and faculties, however, and —in addition to the authoritarian political atmosphere which alienates those in the humanities and social sciences—help explain the movement of these groups to more hospitable environments.

Professors receive a modest rice and research stipend in addition to their low salary (usually under $100 U.S. monthly), and are often provided with housing on the campus or nearby; but the shortage of research funds and equipment affects all disciplines. Many college and university teachers have migrated to the United States and Europe for economic reasons.

Late in 1966 an American journalist who had spent two years teaching at Tunghai University reported in the *Wall Street Journal*: " 'The political situation at home often figures in the foreign students' desire to stay in the United States,' says James M. Davis, Institute for International Education vice president. He says many natives of Taiwan still strongly resent the Nationalist Government which took over the island in 1949. Many of the 2,000 Taiwanese currently studying here don't intend to go home until major changes have been made in the Nationalist regime, according to a Taiwanese student organization." [25]

University people are more likely than other groups to object to the gap between traditional Chinese respect for scholarship and the power of the military and party ideologies in both Nationalist and Communist

China. They find it safer, however, to couch their criticisms in terms of poor student facilities, low faculty salaries that inhibit research, and the tendency for old professors to monopolize desirable faculty positions.[26]

On the small residential campus where I lived and taught, over two-thirds of the students were Formosan. Twenty of the 100 faculty were American or British; only one economist and a physical education instructor were Formosan. The Chinese and most of the American professors could see little friction between the Formosan and mainlander students, nor did I detect any political discontent during my residence. "Teach them democracy as you know it," advised a staff member of the Chinese Fulbright Foundation on my arrival in 1961. "You were assigned to Tunghai University because it is private, away from Taipei, and has less government supervision than the universities here in Taipei."

But later we discovered that the Tunghai dean had quizzed students applying for a summer program in Japan about their political attitudes, and that another administrator was in charge of KMT loyalty checks on the campus. "You didn't realize it when you were lecturing to us," said one of the students who later came to the United States, "but Mr. X in the class was the KMT spy." Formosan students claimed they showed no hostility toward their mainlander fellow-students in the dormitories, where all lived unsegregated, but maintained separate friendships and activities off-campus. "We would go to the movies twice or three times a week, and the mainlanders would go in their own group. Naturally, we were afraid to tell you these things because we knew you were being watched and we did not want to hurt our chances of getting passports to study abroad. I am sure that other students were also afraid of talking politics with you, because to have too close relationships with foreign professors is to be suspected."

The anonymity of a large Taipei commuter university proved more conducive to communication between professors and students, despite the tighter on-campus controls, than the "one big family" atmosphere of rural Tunghai. Once, after a guest lecture at a university in Taipei, one of the seniors invited me to talk with his fellow-students at a private home. "We never associate with the mainlanders in our class once we are off-campus," he explained, "and we want to tell you our political ideas in privacy." [27]

A university graduate who is well qualified to compare Japanese and Nationalist educational policies, made the following criticisms of postwar educational practice on Formosa: "Most Nationalist policies are carried out under such beautiful words and slogans as 'fellow-country-men' and 'restoration of Taiwan to the fatherland,' but Taiwanese students are treated as second-class citizens because the heads of public schools, colleges, and universities and the Minister of Education are always mainlanders. During Japanese rule, we were also misruled, but openly as a colony, not under the disguise of so many slogans; education under Nationalist rule is nothing but a tool of the KMT party whose leaders make policies seldom in consultation with the real educational experts on the island."

On the other hand, I noticed that all students and faculty appreciated the Nationalist regime's tolerance of pirated textbooks, which made American texts quickly available at about one-seventh the original price. "Sure, we have excessive freedom for economic piracy," commented one cynical student at the Kaohsiung Medical College, "but the Chinese believe only in piracy and prostitution, not political freedom." After seeing the shortage of Western texts in South Korean universities during 1962, I could not criticize the pirate publishing in Formosa, but it did make the Formosan intellectuals keenly aware of the Nationalist Chinese concept of liberty as permissible only in non-political areas.

The Press and Mass Organizations

The press in Formosa is allegedly free of censorship, but every editor and writer consulted during my stay admitted he would be severely punished if he printed any criticism of the President or foreign policies, although the Republic of China Constitution (Article 11) guarantees the freedoms of speech, teaching, writing and publication. An editor of the Central News Agency, Nationalist China's news outlet, defended the right of the regime to ban newspapers and magazines considered offensive to public security by saying: "We are still at war, you know, and civil liberties must be controlled." [28]

Nationalist China also has a military information news service, under the political section of the Ministry of National Defense; the *Central Daily News*, a KMT party organ, the *Taiwan Hsin Sheng Pao*, official organ of the Taiwan Provincial Government; a newspaper of the provincial KMT party; and the *Young Warriors' News*, designed for troops by an agency of the Defense Ministry. Government-owned newspapers and magazines naturally carry official news and the party line while privately owned journals are careful to criticize only approved targets (graft and corruption by Taiwanese politicians; inefficiency generally; and administrative details).

The editor of one newspaper in central Taiwan made it clear to me in 1962 that the name of his paper, *The People's Voice of Taichung*, did not mean I could use its resources to study political opinion without the cooperation of the local police chief, a mainland general, the mayor's office, and other officials. "You'll find no real criticism of the Nationalist regime's political system in any publication," said the mayor of one city on the island, "so look behind the scenes." When asked about censorship, reporters for the *Central Daily News* in Taipei spoke politely of the weather and excused themselves from further conversation. The more famous censorship cases will be covered in Chapter 5, but we should note here that restrictions on newsprint, assertedly justifying limitations on the number and size of newspapers, and other administrative techniques, are used to control the press.

We have already seen that radio and television are similarly controlled, and the government-owned network dominates through the Broadcasting Corporation of China (BCC): "Broadcasting stations cooperate with the Government Information Office in disseminating . . . information." [29]

The government also controls the Central Film Studio (which owns large theatres in Taipei): the Taiwan Provincial Government Studio; and a studio operated by the Political Department of the Defense Ministry. The latter ministry is the core of all propaganda and loyalty enforcement work in the island.

In addition to forbidding establishment of new journals, banning some existing journals (such as the *Free China Fortnightly*), restricting the size of newspapers, and charging some editors with irrelevant crimes in order to frighten others, the regime exercises drastic censorship of incoming and outgoing mails. No Japanese paper or journal with political content is allowed into the island, and nothing from or about mainland China. "I have to fly to Tokyo to buy data on the Communists' agricultural programs, then hand-carry them back in my briefcase," Dr. Chiang Mon-lin told me at our first meeting in 1957. I quickly looked at the door to see if anyone was listening to such heresy, although the 71-year-old former president of Peking University seemed unconcerned.[30] Many American scholars smuggled prohibited publications into Taiwan from Hong Kong, or were forced to ask friends at the American Embassy to intercede if airport police confiscated their data. As for first-class mail: "Don't bother to seal your letters," advised the chairman of Tunghai University's Political Science Department, "because they'll open them anyway and you may as well save them the trouble." And a Taipei friend warned, in 1964: "Please never write to me again from America, because they [the Nationalists] have lists of suspected natives and foreigners whose letters are to be screened." American diplomats, scholars, newsmen, and tourists visiting Formosa all seem to have been warned by friends on the island not to mail any incriminating letter or publication through the Nationalist Chinese postal system.

Among the many government mass organizations to promote loyalty, the China Youth Corps is perhaps the most effective. Established in 1952 on the occasion of Chiang Kai-shek's 65th birthday by his son, Chiang Ching-kuo, the Corps has branches throughout the island based in senior high schools, most of whose students belong to it. Members of the units practice paramilitary training, study the KMT classics, and are encouraged to spy on other students and teachers. Because the KMT party and its armed forces were patterned after the Soviet party and Red Army of the early 1920's, the Nationalist civil and military branches both sponsor mass organizations for security and propaganda. In addition to the Youth Corps and a Women's Anti-Communist League (headed by Madame Chiang Kai-shek), the central and provincial governments sponsor several other organizations for women, farmers, urban workers, students, and veterans. To rally support for government policies, Taipei encourages such associations as the Friends of the Armed Forces, the Confucius-Mencius Society, and the Asian Peoples' Anti-Communist League, China Chapter. Unlike Communist China, however, the Nationalist regime also permits many private organizations of a non-political nature.

The Pattern of Social Discontents

To an outside observer, the grievances of Formosa's original natives, the tribal aborigines, are probably the most conspicuous. Many of these people have settled in the eastern plains or foothills, but about 160,000 still live in the central mountain ranges. In 1965 the Presbyterian Church, whose missionaries to Formosa are the best experts on these tribes, claimed 67,000 members—approximately one-third of the total tribal population.[31]

Vestiges of nineteenth-century hostility between the Formosan-Chinese and the aborigines are still evident today. Some eminent Formosans spoke of "the shiftlessness of mountain people who won't work beyond the next meal," and Formosan guides along the heavily tribal eastern coast showed obvious paternalism even toward tribesmen who have settled near the main towns. Undoubtedly each group has just complaints against the other; nevertheless many tribesmen took part in the 1947 revolt and have resisted Nationalist indoctrination.

"Do you like the Chinese government better than the Japanese before 1945?" I asked tribesmen in several villages and towns of the east coast. "What a silly question," was a typical reply. "The Japanese gave us better schools and protected us from commercial thievery." Others mentioned that traditional practices such as headhunting had been suppressed by the Japanese.[32] "We still speak Japanese," I was somewhat unnecessarily reminded; in fact, many spoke no Mandarin at all. One evening, in a general store of the small hot-spring village of Chipon near Taitung, I encountered several tribesmen who were on their way back up the mountain. They were quiet until the lights suddenly went out. "*Saa, teiden da!* [Well, it's an electric stoppage!]" I said in Japanese. Immediately, the group laughed and grew more at ease. They spoke of the 1947 atrocities, the higher taxes and poorer services under Nationalist rule, and their hope that the mainlanders might return to China and leave Formosa alone.[33]

Nearby, in their small thatch-roofed house, the aborigine parents of the Olympic decathlon champion C. K. Yang talked to me about their famous son and his life at UCLA in California. "We weren't able to go to the Tokyo Asian Games to see him, but maybe you can persuade the KMT to pay our fare if he is in the 1964 Tokyo Olympics," the father said. "You can see his picture on the wall shaking hands with President Chiang—the government promised us a new house, but all we have are photos for the mud walls." (The Nationalist China Olympic Committee later advised the senior Yang there were no funds for such a trip.) Neighbors of the Yangs told me of the poorer than average living conditions of such tribal families who had settled in towns. "Many were forced to sell their homes after 1946, and even the family of an Olympic star lives in poverty," said the wife of a provincial assemblyman.

Complaints of the Formosan Majority

The many social complaints of the Formosan majority fall into two general categories: those ills visible to the intellectuals or the better educated, and those attracting wide mass dissatisfaction. For example, I found that the increase in crime and poor sanitary conditions drew the most widespread criticism from all levels of society, whereas the "backward trend" of social conservatism (as in the Nationalists' tolerating superstitions and "pai-pai"—folk festivals—while opposing birth control and modern scientific rationalism generally) antagonized the middle class far more than the average farmer or pedicab driver. At the same time, cleavage between Formosans and mainlanders is greater than social class differences among Formosans: *"zoku ga chigau"* ("we're a different people" [than the mainlanders]), was stated by Formosans of all types.

Public health and sanitation are safe targets of popular criticism in Formosa, as frequent editorials and official exhortations attest. The poor sanitation in Taipei streets (some of them lined with uninspected open-air food wagons), restaurants, rivers, and other public places offends not only Western visitors but also the local English-language press: "In most eating places, one cannot find a clean table, to say nothing of clean dishes. Taxi drivers offend customers with odorous apparel or breath. Public latrines have stiff competitors in the form of sidewalks or open lots." [34] Environmental sanitation is mentioned because most Formosans I interviewed claimed that conditions in that respect were better under the Japanese. "We had cleaner parks, safer water to drink, and fewer bugs before the Chinese came over," was a comment made by city-dwellers throughout the island. Whether true or not, the invidious comparison suggests a political dimension behind these cultural criticisms.

Formosan cities bore the brunt of the postwar influx of 1.5 million mainlanders plus the growth of the native population. Taipei grew from 300,000 to 1,200,000 in the twenty years after the war and Kaohsiung, Tainan, Taichung, as well as smaller cities, expanded proportionately. Public services have suffered much more by Nationalist neglect than they did during World War II, according to those who serve in municipal government today. The water and drainage systems were all Japanese-built, and have not been properly maintained (much less rebuilt) since the war, as newspaper reports testify: "Lai Tun-yung, deputy director of the Taipei Waterworks, said 'Don't drink tap water without first boiling it!' . . . many of the water pipes totaling 400 kilometers have become rusty . . . only a fraction of the old pipes can be replaced every year . . ." [35] Older natives in a shop in Taichung said their city had prided itself on safe water before 1945, but "we can't be sure now because the [mainlander refugees build shacks along the canals and the police do not enforce anti-pollution regulations."

Although the Nationalist government claims great progress in its public sanitation and health work, enforcement of health regulations is lax, which many Formosans blame on unhygienic mainlanders. "The nation as a whole seems lacking in sanitary habits," said a *China Post* article in 1962; but Formosans insist they themselves learned good hygiene under Japanese rule and that it is the mainlander refugees who neglect it.

An official in Kaohsiung drove me along the harbor road to the edge of a military restricted area. "Before the war, this was a fine swimming beach, but look at how dirty it is now. Just because the Chinese don't like to swim, they ignore the beach areas unseen by foreigners." He pointed to the hilltop behind us, the site of a Shinto shrine before 1945, now converted to a Chinese military reservation: "It's closed to the public when it could be a fine recreation park rivalling Taipei Lake, which they improved because the Gimo [Generalissimo Chiang] has a rest home there."

Formosans seem to agree with Nationalist editorials urging better restaurant sanitation, such as this one: "In the heartland of Chinese cuisine, Taipei, Japanese restaurants are mushrooming . . . and their customers are mainly Chinese. Lack of sanitation is conspicuous in ordinary Chinese restaurants. Food poisoning has become too commonplace to rate special attention.[36] The inference drawn by many readers is that Japanese are cleaner than Chinese.

Garbage collection "has never gone beyond the primitive stage," admitted the *China News* in 1966.[37] "The Chinese make big claims to have eradicated epidemics of malaria, cholera, and other diseases" said one physician, "but did they invent the cures? The Japanese had stamped out most such diseases, and the regime today should thank American aid for postwar drugs and sprays."

American military health officers often come from Okinawa to inspect villages in Formosa and have commented favorably on their condition. "Do they see just model villages created by the government, like the land reform model near Taipei, or can they really see the island?"one Formosan doctor wondered. Officers at the Foreign Service Institute (FSI) Language School in Taichung reported quite different impressions of the villages they visited to practice conversation, as did the Tunghai University Sociology Department's survey of three villages in the area.[38]

"Before the Chinese came, the Japanese colonials would consult Formosan doctors without hesitation, but the Chinese look down on us and prefer their own men or unlicensed quacks," said a Kaohsiung doctor educated in the Tokyo University medical school. When the central government did crack down on unlicensed doctors in 1967, some legislators wanted to soften the ban to favor retired military doctors. Reported the *China News:* "It is not known how many doctors are practicing without proper license . . . [but] yesterday some even kowtowed to Legislative Yuan members as they submitted their petition." [39] The introduction of modern medicine was not only Japan's major social improvement in Formosa, but the practice of medicine was one field in which native sons could rise without discrimination; and Formosan doctors tend to be the most politically conscious group on the island, respected and consulted for more than medical advice. This is why visiting American Congressmen who ask the U.S. Embassy in Taipei to meet "some spokesmen for the Formosan natives" usually find themselves in doctors' offices. Some doctors play an active political role by running for local office (one was finally able to unseat the KMT mayor of Kaohsiung in 1968); the majority are informal community leaders.

The city park in Taichung, marred by some one-story barracks for retired veterans, was strewn with paper and its little pond was littered with fruit peelings. "Just like a park in Japan or America," I thought aloud in Japanese. "Oh no," corrected the owner of a nearby shop, "this park was much cleaner before the war. Maybe the Japanese police don't enforce laws at home but they surely did here. Now the Chinese don't enforce either traffic or safety laws. Squatters build shacks any place they want, and if they are mainlanders the police look the other way."

Every municipal police department in Formosa is headed by a mainlander army officer immune from local control. "They keep asking me to move my sign in from the street closer to the bookshop," said a bookdealer in the south, "but if I pay them a little every month they don't bother me. That shop down the street is owned by a mainlander, and the police never squeeze him." Middle-class homes in large cities are usually surrounded by a stone wall topped with broken glass or barbed wire like those I had seen in postwar Shanghai and Tokyo. "Under the Japanese, we never had to lock our houses because the thieves were afraid of the police. Now robberies occur in broad daylight and we must protect ourselves as best we can," complained the wife of a pastry shopkeeper. Whether or not the Nationalists are really to blame for such conditions (and they exist in urban centers around the world), many Formosans vent their anti-Nationalist anger on social ills because those can be criticized with impunity.

Typical of incidents that intensify civilian irritation with the military was one involving the husband of my cook who was employed as a delivery man for a local Taichung bank. One day, while driving his bicycle near the railway station, a military jeep struck him down, breaking his leg. "The jeep was to blame," witnesses told me later, "but you can't expect the Chinese army to respect Formosan civilians or pay any compensation."

The debate over birth control in recent years exemplifies the conflict between what Formosans call Chinese conservatism and modern rationalism. Formosa's net population growth rate declined from 3.7 per 1,000 in 1955 to 2.5 in 1968, but remains among the highest in the world. After the influx of mainlanders in 1949, the population rose from 6.8 million then to 13.1 million in 1967, causing many observers to question the effect on economic viability and living standards.[40]

The late Dr. Chiang Mon-lin aroused much Nationalist opposition with speeches and articles urging the regime to face up to the population problem. "Each year we add the equivalent of the population of our second largest city, Kaohsiung . . . which means 52,000 tons of rice . . . $72 million for new teachers . . . $420 million for classrooms . . . and more for clothing . . . and will naturally lead to lowering the living standard." [41] Dr. Chiang, noting the limited resources on Formosa and the temporary nature of American aid, warned that failure to adjust population to economic growth would induce tragic Malthusian remedies. He did not openly advocate government-subsidized population controls, but the implication was clear.

A 1966 Manpower Seminar of the Council for International Economic Cooperation and Development urged reduction of the annual population growth rate to 2 per cent lest large numbers of children "continue to be a heavy burden on the economy of Taiwan for years to come." It noted that illegal abortions were common and that "tacit approval" of birth control measures was promoted by the provincial and local governments.[42] Nationalist Premier and Vice President C. K. Yen avoided comment on the population issue in his speech to the seminar, representing as he did a regime whose Confucian philosophy and "back to the mainland" slogan both demand maximum manpower.

"How can we worry about overpopulation?" asked a mainlander official in 1959. "We will surely counterattack in the next ten to twenty years and . . . if we do counterattack, we shall be worried about the shortage of population due to the demands of war . . . Dr. Chiang's advocacy of birth control . . . assumes no war while my viewpoint assumes we must counterattack." [43]

Three women members of the Provincial Assembly objected to birth control in 1967, asserting that 13 million is not a very large population.[44] But one of the University of Michigan researchers, who assisted the Formosa Provisional Health Department in a two-year intrauterine loop experiment financed by the Population Council of New York, reported that 75 per cent of the Formosan women accepted the loop and paid half the $1.50 cost: "There was behind-the-scenes opposition from central government mainlanders, but cooperation from most Formosans." He told of the Formosan belief that the loop was a prewar Japanese invention, accepted partly for that reason, and predicted wider success as the loop method was made available throughout the island.[45]

Another example of the conflict between mainlander tradition and Formosan social customs is that prostitution is permitted but dancing— at least on college campuses—is forbidden. "China was always a conservative country so it is easy for the government to accept ancient institutions like prostitution. Anything foreign, except those things absolutely necessary, they generally reject. This is why dancing is prohibited while prostitution, which is surely a great social evil, is endured," explained one of my students. To foreigners and to many Formosans it is puzzling that Western-style dancing is restricted in civilian cabarets and totally forbidden to university students, while every community has its licensed quarter and call girls.

The desire to attract and cater to American troops on rest leave from Vietnam and tired Japanese businessmen, and a pragmatic attitude toward sex generally, are strong incentives for continued Nationalist tolerance of prostitution, which the regime planned to suppress from 1969.[46] Some of my Formosan informants suggested the Nationalist mainlanders might also be politically motivated to divert Formosan energies toward sex as a harmless, non-political pastime—an "escape from politics" encouraged by undemocratic regimes that Lucian Pye has referred to as the equivalent of the Roman bread and circuses.

"Hypocrisy is the byword of the Nationalists, who parrot the Confucian ethic but live by their own immoral code," commented a Formosan professor safely in the United States. "Everyone knows that prostitution and blue movies are found throughout the world, even in lands where they are strictly prohibited. We also recognize that the military caste in charge of our island agrees with professional officers elsewhere that commercial sex should be government-approved for troop morale. But we object to the corruption encouraged by the Chinese system, and the contrast with political suppression."

Many Formosan (and some mainlander intellectuals too), stifled by the nature of the regime but unwilling to rebel or unable to escape abroad, take refuge in nihilistic writing or romantic fiction.[47] I noticed that movie theatres were crowded every day in the week, especially with young people evidently seeking relief from boredom.

The gap between the supposedly uplifting slogans painted on roadside billboards (such as "Mainland Recovery" and "Oppose the Communists") and the myriad restrictions on freedom of speech, press, assembly, teaching, and research, annoy Formosan intellectuals, who are particularly sensitive to the regime's hollow ideological sloganeering. "While President Chiang repeatedly preaches government of the people, by the people, and for the people, his regime has been ruling Formosa by martial law under a democratic constitution. It seems to me that both the schools and the army are used by the present regime to keep the young generation under tight control and avoid social tensions," said a Formosan veteran.

The Future of Sino-Formosan Integration

"The process of 'Chinization' of the island is likely to take a few more decades, until the younger generation outnumbers their opinionated elders. In any case, efforts to keep the island Taiwanese [culturally separate] seem now doomed to failure," wrote an American correspondent in 1965.[48] On the other hand, some observers think that, assuming the continuation of the status quo between mainland China and Formosa the Formosan majority will influence and absorb the refugee minority. "In another generation," said a China specialist in the Japanese Foreign Ministry in 1957, "Taiwan will be Taiwanese socially, economically, and politically through natural evolution." A member of the United States Embassy in Taipei who had grown up in China looked forward to a gradual acceptance by the Nationalist elite of their island destiny: "They may be forced into a two-China solution; they have shown great adeptness in concessions and compromise in past history. They will never openly admit this, but might be forced into it slowly over a period of time."

Spokesmen for the Nationalist regime minimize the persistence of native or Japanese customs, whose political significance they deny. "In spite of their differences from other people of the mainland, the Taiwanese are essentially and basically Chinese . . . They are 100 per cent Chinese ethically and culturally [and] would feel greatly offended if they were thought to be otherwise," wrote a Chinese commentator in 1967.[49] Nationalists disagree only on the extent of Formosan "cultural aberrations" and the length of time that will be required to eliminate them. Chinese Communist writers also contend the Formosans are Chinese and would be offended by "American plots" to separate them from the People's Republic.

As we have seen earlier, Japanese businessmen who travel to Formosa often come into close contact with the middle-aged and older natives. "Can you tell the difference between mainlanders and us?" asked a Taipei businessman of his two Tokyo guests—one of whom answered: "The Nationalist regime here says there are no differences because they don't want to recognize any, but we Japanese can tell through your language, customs, dress, and food." The wife of a Japanese-American couple from Brooklyn who spent several months in southern Formosa and came to know local people in Kaohsiung declared: "I was amazed at the depth of emotion and antagonism when native women told me of the mainlanders." Businessmen in their thirties who guided me around Kaohsiung and Taipei were uniformly sure that the two communities would not merge. "We're like oil and water. Even if a few daughters or sons of elite families do marry mainlanders of the same social rank, most of us wouldn't sleep with a mainlander girl, much less marry her." [50] It was reminiscent, in reverse, of two young Chinese officers who in 1957 had said in my presence, with feeling: "We have no family on Formosa and don't like Formosan girls. How long do you think it will be before we can get back to China?"

Americans stationed on the island have sometimes heard Formosan parents scolding their children for using Mandarin. "On the day we visited a local street restaurant, the younger brother was speaking Mandarin to his older sisters, who are in primary school. Then he asked his mother for more rice—in Mandarin—and was promptly scolded by a Taiwanese. . . . in Mandarin loud enough for everyone to hear. The man teased the young brother about speaking Mandarin when he was a Taiwanese! The brother laughed and switched to Taiwanese." [51]

It will be the future parents of Formosa who decide whether their children will blend into the minority Chinese society, and it would be rash to predict their decision. "They're learning all the bad Chinese customs and forgetting the good Japanese ones," snorted one of the few Formosan members of the Legislative Yuan, whom I happened to meet on a train.

An American woman teacher wrote her friends in late 1966: "There are 1,000 students here, about two-thirds of whom are Taiwanese and the rest mainland Chinese who came here at the time of the Communist takeover in 1949. *The uneasy relationship between these two groups is one of the chronic problems of the island.* What, we ask ourselves, is the role of the foreigner with his 'outsider' status, in regard to this problem? Should he attempt to be a force for reconciliation and if so, how?" [52] (Emphasis added.)

Many Formosans think the Nationalists do not expect or perhaps even wish positive reconciliation. After all, most white Americans, British Canadians, and Russians seem content to have the dissident groups in their nations remain quiet. Even if the membership of nine of every ten Formosan social organizations is wholly Taiwanese, is this dangerous to the regime if the members use them for purely non-political activity?

Cultural differences in Formosa will persist for many years to come. The key question will be whether they can serve as the foundation for a political separatist movement. An astute American observer has written: "Certainly the Formosans have a strong sense of common identity and believe that they belong together. Within the narrow confines of the existing totalitarian political structure they have done everything possible to prove that this is so." [53]

4

THE ECONOMIC MIRACLE OF
FORMOSA THROUGH NATIVE EYES

This chapter will survey, first, the overall picture of economic growth in Formosa as seen by Chinese, American, and other commentators, and then discuss in turn the impact of Nationalist agricultural policy—especially land reform—industrial expansion to diversify the economy, and the role of American aid. Formosan economic complaints are included throughout to illustrate the interrelation between these and Formosan nationalism.

Economic failures on the mainland in the late 1940's speeded the decline of the Nationalist regime and helped its Communist rivals win peasant and intellectual support. The third of Dr. Sun Yat-sen's "three principles of the people," usually translated as "people's livelihood," could not be implemented because of internal weaknesses and the Japanese war.[1] After moving to Taiwan in 1949, the Nationalist leaders knew they would be judged by their ability to make that island an economic "model province." Doing so would attract people from the mainland and reconcile dissident Formosans, whose bitter memories of the 1945–1947 period threatened to undermine the Nationalists' political stability in their only territorial base. An economic success would also appeal to the rest of the world, which was highly critical of past Nationalist performance. The newly independent states in Africa and Asia, which were being wooed by Peking, might well support Taipei diplomatically if they saw in Taiwan an "economic model to developing nations."[2]

Perhaps the most decisive impetus to economic development in Formosa was the pressure of the United States. Approximately $1.5 billion in economic aid and $3 billion in military aid supplied by Washington between 1949 and 1969 were predicated largely on the willingness of the Nationalist regime to build up Formosa as a viable economic unit.

Perspectives on Economic Growth

American and Chinese Nationalist spokesmen often refer erroneously to Formosa as second only to Japan in levels of living in Asia. This comparison is invalid to Formosans because they know that their island ranked next to Japan before World War II, but is behind Okinawa today. "Okinawans, Koreans, and Filipinos are all *namakemono* [lazy drones]," commented a Formosan elder statesman in 1963, "but we and the Japanese are the hard workers of Asia, and we should rank much closer to Japan."

When discussing the economic miracle of Formosa, one should not use the 1945–1949 period as the base for a study of recent progress, as the late Vice-President Chen Cheng did in *Land Reform in Taiwan*.[3] "The immediate postwar years were the worst in our history, due to carpetbagger thievery and corruption," said a professor in Kaohsiung. "Comparisons of recent production figures with the peak under Japanese rule are also misleading, because of technology changes," he added. "It's scandalous to say we live in an economic paradise compared with the rest of the Afro-Asian world when we can't even catch up to Okinawa!" scoffed a doctor in Tainan.

Whereas few native Formosans ever saw the mainland or know anyone living there, displaced refugees, who know the poverty they left behind on the mainland but not the prewar conditions of Formosa, are more likely to speak of the better conditions on the island. This helps explain the wide difference between Formosan and official mainlander interpretations of recent economic progress.

Moreover, the Formosan considers himself under colonial rule. "Did the Greek Cypriots or your American colonial forebears stop to think of economic matters when they fought against British imperialism?" asked a provincial legislator from central Formosa. "The Americans may have suffered economically in the early years of independence, as many new Asian and African nations do today, but that was irrelevant to their political aspirations." Nationalism is often irrational to the outside observer. "These people wouldn't know what to do without the large number of mainlander experts in the government," said an American educational officer after six years in Formosa. "The mainlander experts are really responsible for this island's remarkable progress." [4]

The native viewpoint, however, emphasizes the contributions of the Japanese material heritage, American postwar aid, and the hard work of Formosan farmers, workers, and businessmen. "The Nationalists cannot claim credit for those things," insisted an economics student at Soochow University, "and we could do even better under our own system without the incubus of a refugee mainlander government." Yet Formosans tend to stress the seamier side of the island economy, such as underemployment, low wages combined with rising consumer prices, taxes that fall heaviest on the poor, and the burden of a bloated civilian and military bureaucracy. "Go into the villages and you'll see plenty of poverty," advised the first hotel floor boy whom I met in Taipei, "but you can start by touring the slums of the city first."

Most statistical charts and tables on the postwar Formosan economy show steady improvement in agriculture and new industry, and a phenomenal expansion of foreign trade. Tourists are shown the new hydroelectric plants, industrial zones outside Taipei and Kaohsiung, and solid new farmhouses owned by beneficiaries of the land reform. The Nationalist regime publishes voluminous economic data, unlike the Peking regime since 1960, and its figures are usually confirmed by objective experts in Washington, Hong Kong, and the United Nations. Although Formosan nationalist groups abroad tend to discount any evidence of material progress, the average native inside the island has a more balanced view based on personal experience.

"We in America admire what you have done to bring economic prosperity to Taiwan . . . Taiwan's land reform program is outstanding in Asia . . . a model for countries around the world . . . Your people now enjoy one of the highest standards of living in all Asia," said President Johnson to visiting Nationalist Premier and Vice President C. K. Yen on the latter's state visit to the U.S. in mid-1967.[5] When AID announced in 1964 the termination of its Formosa programs in 1965, it lauded the "exceptional growth . . . of more than 6 per cent annual GNP [gross national product] since 1953, agricultural production increase of 4 per cent annually, and industrial production increase of between 10 and 12 per cent annually." [6]

Time magazine, a staunch supporter of the Nationalist regime, welcomed Premier Yen's visit with a feature story describing his nation as a "model for Asian economic development," and using statistics even more favorable to the regime (US$3 billion GNP, 400 per cent industrial expansion over 1952, US$1.1 billion foreign trade, and per capita income of nearly US$200 annually).[7] The *Reader's Digest*, another pro-

Nationalist journal, in a February 1966 article by Keyes Beech and Clarence W. Hall celebrated "Formosa: Asia's Heartening Success Story." [8] Crediting the economic growth to wise government planning which allegedly placed agricultural progress ahead of steel mills, the article used 1945 or 1950 base years in demonstrating production increases. Similar reports have been published in other American newspapers and magazines, all stressing the low ebb after World War II and subsequent spectacular economic growth based on an agricultural-industrial balance, good use of American aid, and political stability under wise leadership.[9]

To spread the word about Formosa's economic miracle, Taipei in June 1967 hosted a Sino-American seminar on the economic development of Taiwan. Economics Minister K. T. Li cited as major achievements since 1952: the 17 per cent annual advance of private industry (compared with 11 per cent for government enterprises); a rise in the industrial share of exports from 5 to 54 per cent; and the decline of dependence on Japan and the United States as export markets. He insisted the economy was still backward, however, with per capita income of US$189—slightly more than one-quarter of that in Japan, and far behind the world leaders. Li also warned the seminar of the low rate of industrial employment as compared with agricultural (20 and 45 per cent, respectively, of the labor force) and a 30 per cent ratio of employment to population.[10]

Formosans look at the official production claims from a more historical perspective. "We had a better per capita income in the late 1930's. Population has doubled, so production must rise even faster if we are to keep ahead," said Formosan economists working for AID in 1961–1963. Table 1 shows that only citrus, cement, electricity output, and fish production increased between 1939 and 1965. The increase is more marked in textiles, small vehicles, electric appliances, and postwar commercial crops like mushrooms. Formosans says the mainlander elite takes an unfair share of the island wealth through heavy taxation, and in 1964 AID officials agreed that the Nationalist regime "overstates the rate of growth in GNP by applying inadequate price deflators" because inflation ate up about one-fifth of the official gains.[11] Even so, indices of industrial production (1953 = 100) rose to an average of 300 in 1963, and to over 400 three years later. Rice and sweet potatoes, the staple foods, totalled 2.3 and 3.1 million tons, respectively, in 1965, while only 9.5 million tons of sugar cane were produced that year, less than half of peak prewar production.

Over 100 countries imported Formosan products in 1966, Japan buying one-fourth of the US $500 million export total (especially perishable

TABLE 1

FORMOSA: PREWAR AND RECENT PRODUCTION *

(*Unit:* 1,000 metric tons unless noted)

	1937–1939	1964–1966
Rice	1,400	2,350
Sugar cane	12,835	9,480
Sweet potatoes	1,770	3,131
Jute	15	13
Bananas	219	412
Pineapples	146	231
Citrus fruits	38	114
Tea	14	21
Fish	120	381
Poultry (1,000)	9,500	17,200
Hogs (1,000)	1,800	2,936
Draft cattle (1,000)	325	376
Chemical fertilizer consumption	389	628
Cement	300	2,443
Coal	2,850	5,040
Electricity (mil. kilowatt-hour)	1,200	6,692
Railway (mileage)	565	609

* *Sources:* Prewar data from Fred Riggs, *Formosa under Chinese Nationalist Rule* (New York: Macmillan, 1952); Han Lih-wu, *Taiwan Today* (Taipei, 1951); and Sasamoto Takeji, ed., *Industrial Structure of Taiwan* [in Japanese] (Tokyo: Asia keizai kenkyujo, 1964). Recent data from the *China Yearbook* 1966–67 (Taipei: China Publishing Co., 1967).

bananas and fresh pineapple). Less developed nations served as markets for the lighter industrial products of the island, such as the 222 million meters of textiles, 700,000 cases of plate glass, and 7 million cases of canned food produced in 1965.[12] Electricity production has an installed capacity of 1.5 million kilowatts, slightly less than half of which is hydro-generated, and the 6.7 million kilowatt-hours produced in 1966 went primarily to industry (4.7 million kwh) rather than to residential consumers who must pay triple the industrial users' rate. Finally, despite the growth of private ownership of industry, the state still controls the sugar, petroleum, fertilizer, aluminum, shipbuilding, mining, and electric power industries.[13]

Among the criticisms voiced by even Nationalist officials, the threat of underemployment looms largest, based on steadily growing labor force. Other common targets of criticism are excessive government interference in the economy, the high tax burden (70 per cent indirect), and low wage levels. The *China News* boldly pointed to these shortcomings on

Retrocession Day, 1966: "In our propaganda, we claim that Taiwan has the second highest living standard in Asia. That isn't true: we are fourth, behind Japan, Malaysia, and the Ryukyus [Okinawa]. Furthermore, we neglect to state that our per capita level is only a third that of Japan's. In seeking to attract foreign investments, we make much of having wages that are among Asia's lowest. That is a mixed blessing. The millions we get from overseas will not be as effective in creating prosperity as the increased domestic consumption resulting from higher wages and salaries . . . skilled workers are making less than US$2 a day . . ." [14]

Land Reform and Agricultural Progress

Formosa, despite the advance of industry and urbanization since 1953, remains predominantly rural, with 54 per cent of all workers engaged in agriculture and only one-fourth of the population living in the urban centers (1965). Until very recently the island depended heavily on exports of rice, sugar, and other farm products, mainly to Japan.

The Nationalists claim that the farmers of Formosa formerly suffered from insecure, unwritten tenancy contracts as well as from exorbitant rentals. Before land reform began in 1950, almost two-thirds of farm families had been tenants or farm laborers, and tenant families paid an average rent of 57 per cent of the harvest, with some occupants of better land paying up to 70 per cent. [15] The first step in land reform reduced rents to 37.5 per cent of the crop for 296,000 families. In 1951, the government required a minimum six-year contract for tenancy and began selling 247,000 acres of public land (inherited from the Japanese) to 203,000 tenant farmers.

The Nationalist reformers' next step, called the "land-to-the-tiller" program, began in 1953. With some exceptions, those owning more than 7 acres of paddy land were forced to sell the excess land to the government for a price equivalent to 2.5 times the main annual crop yield. Payment was made 70 per cent in the form of commodity bonds (usually redeemable for rice over a ten-year period) and 30 per cent in shares of government corporations taken over from the Japanese. Tenants could then buy the land at the same price over the ten-year period, with interest added. By late 1962 when the program was completed, 55 per cent of all privately owned land (about 350,000 acres) had been sold to 194,000 families, or 64 per cent of the tenant population. [16]

"It was a complete success, and neither landlords nor tenants had any complaint," said a Formosan ex-landlord who served as the appointed civil administrator during the first years of the land exchange. "Landlords were treated much better than in the Japanese land reform [begun a year earlier] because we received crops and stocks as a hedge against inflation, while our Japanese counterparts got only worthless money. The Chinese learned from the Japanese lesson, and we had Wolf Ladejinsky to advise us." [17]

There was an increase in owner-cultivated land from 56 per cent of all agricultural land in 1948 to 86 per cent in 1959, while tenancy declined to 15 per cent of all farm families. Most new landlords were small owners; although 106,000 landlord families were affected, only a handful of these were very large landowners who had held high social and political status before the war. One of the latter gave me a two-hour lecture on his view of the "iniquities" of the land reform: "The regime will never tell its real reasons for stealing our land because one was political. They wanted to eliminate the power of landowners because we were the social elite in every community, looked up to by the peasants, and were known to have been active in the 1947 revolt. It was easy for them to implement such a reform here because none of the Nationalist leaders owned land on Formosa. (Back on the mainland, as you know, landlords were a major source of Nationalist Power.) Except for five or six of us, most of the 190,000 landlords affected were small holders, but they were community leaders throughout the island." [18]

This critic denied that the compensation paid to landlords was fair. "If you got stock in a good company, fine, but not all people got such stock, did they?" he asked a friend standing nearby. "You and I got stock in poor companies, whereas Mr. X, who praised the reform, was luckier. Moreover, despite rules to the contrary, much of the farmland near cities was resold later for industrial or commercial use at great profit to the government." Two years later, the same man spoke of the urban land equalization law in scornful terms: "First they stole my farmland; now they want to take the city land too." The urban law compelled owners to assess their own property for tax purposes; if the assessment was appreciably lower than the official estimate, the government could buy the land at the owner's valuation. "It sounds fair," he admitted, "but never look only at the law; under this government you must study how the pigs administer it."

One alleged virtue of the Formosa land reform was that it encouraged the ex-landlords to become industrialists by careful investment of their compensation. Reduction of government ownership was a prime target of the United States aid program, and the sale of public lands, together with landlord compensation in government corporation stock, were steps in that direction. "Much of the good land taken over from the Japanese by the Nationalist government stayed in the hands of the Taiwan Sugar Company," explained a farmer near Taitung. "A lot of the 40 per cent sold to the public were uplands and farms used to settle mainland veterans." A 1952 survey of sixteen rural townships on the eve of the compulsory land sales found landlord influence beginning to decline; 48 per cent of the owner-operators said that "villages are worse off now than in 1937 when the Japanese were here," but 35 per cent disagreed.[19]

At this point it might be well to recall the agricultural record of the Japanese in Formosa. According to one observer, "Japan gets little credit for what it accomplished in parts of the former empire. Japan in fact did a great deal in Taiwan, most particularly, I think, in bringing organized effort to the agricultural economy. The growth in agricultural production in Taiwan from 1920 to 1939 averaged better than 4 per cent a year, nearly twice the population growth rate. . . . Consumption per capita in Taiwan seems also to have gone up by about one-third in those years."[20] Some farmers say they remember that Japan organized farmers' associations, experiment stations, and teams of experts to introduce better quality hogs, draft cattle, rice, and sugar. "Commercial farming began in those years," said a farmer near Changhwa. "The Nationalists cannot take credit for leading us out of the dark ages, as they often pretend to foreigners."

The fragmentation of Formosan farms resulted from land reform and population increase. "Land reform at best tends to fragment land holdings and whatever its benefits to the individual farmer it does not by itself contribute to production gain," wrote the American specialist Joseph Z. Reday. "I doubt that [land reform] has been much responsible for the solid production gains of agriculture in Taiwan."[21] Reday attributes the gains to a 20–30 per cent increase in capital "in the form of equipment —and higher cost but higher return new crops." Natives deny that power tillers and other machines have replaced the ubiquitous water buffalo, except on showplace farms selected to impress visitors.

The Nationalist regime has tried to consolidate scattered farm holdings to make more efficient use of machines. Beginning on a small scale near Changhwa in 1959, the provincial government had consolidated about 100,000 acres by 1964 and plans to straighten paddy field borders, swap adjoining plots, and achieve consolidation of a total of 735,000 acres by 1974,[22] thus permitting deeper plowing, and economizing on farm labor. The average land holding has fallen from 5 acres to less than 2.6 acres since 1949, but better seed, fertilizer, and other improved agricultural techniques raised production.

The Joint Commission on Rural Reconstruction (JCRR), created and sponsored jointly by the American and Chinese governments, deserves credit for the relatively smooth implementation of land reforms and for subsequent improvements in rural economic life. The first chairman of JCRR in Formosa, Dr. Chiang Mon-lin, encouraged sensible programs of village participation by enlisting competent personnel, regardless of place of birth, and achieved excellent farmer cooperation. The JCRR surveys, reports, and other research provide the best picture of Formosan farm conditions during the postwar years, and its joint sponsorship has minimized Nationalist party interference. With a total budget of only US$7 million and the equivalent of about US$98 million in local currency (proceeds of American aid), the JCRR financed over 6,000 projects between 1950 and 1964. Water use and control took one-third of this amount, while other projects ranged from forest conservation and livestock production to rural health and extension programs. American aid supplied a total of $213 million in capital to Formosan agriculture, 23 per cent of all American aid given Formosa between 1951 and 1965, which "financed nearly 59 per cent of net domestic capital formation in agriculture. . . . Relatively more aid could probably have been invested profitably in agriculture [because] the multiplier effects of relatively small outlays . . . were relatively large," wrote Jacoby.[23]

Farmers interviewed on both the populous west coast and the narrow, sparsely inhabited east coast complained to me about the gap between what they receive for their produce and the prices they must pay for their needs. This was also the major complaint of 1,176 rural household heads in the 1952 Raper survey.[24] In addition, the government system of bartering fertilizer for rice has irritated Formosan farmers who think the exchange ratio favors the government. Recently, however, the ratio has been reduced to .86 to 1, as Governor Huang Chieh pointed out in 1967 in defense of the system against perennial critics in the native-dominated provincial assembly.[25] In 1949, when farmers had to barter 1.5 tons of rice worth US$250 for one ton of fertilizer costing the government only US$70, such complaints were more justified than in recent years when the exchange has been more equal.[26] Moreover, Formosa used to import most of its chemical fertilizer from Japan, but has become more self-sufficient since 1964, saving the government $5 million annually.

"The mainlander regime was able to profit by selling or renting the

Japanese lands it inherited. It also took a percentage on the private Formosan land exchanged in the land reform. So we wonder why it cannot
permit a free market in fertilizer and/or rice after all these years," commented a farmer in Taichung. Many farmers smiled when told that experts considered their taxes lower than those of non-farmers.

The government-owned Taiwan Sugar Corporation [TSC] operates
many pineapple canneries, paying women 40 cents for a 12-hour day, or
52 cents for night work. "A TSC official admitted that the women laborers' pay is too low," reported the China News, "[but] he said it is necessary to maintain the wage scale to bring down production cost." [27] Because the legal minimum wage remained less than US$20 monthly in
1967, the cannery girls may receive little sympathy from foreign impor-
ters anxious to sell to their Japanese and American markets. Despite the
depressed world price for sugar, total agricultural exports in 1966 approached $250 million, or about half the value of all exports, but such
statistics do not impress the local farmer.

I had assumed that the retail price of food in Formosa would reflect
its low production cost. Instead, I found the prices of staples equal to
those in Tokyo or Hong Kong, while poultry and meat prices were
higher.[28] In 1961, the Economic Affairs Minister warned that 53 per
cent of the national income was being used for food purchases, "leaving
no surplus savings for investment." "We must pay over 20 per cent duty
on imported feed for our animals," explained one farmer, "and look at
the interest rates we pay—12 per cent a year to Farmers' Associations and
animal husbandry banks, and even more to other sources." [29] Farmers in
the 1952 Raper report paid about 4 per cent monthly interest, while
one-quarter of the sample surveyed paid over 6 per cent a month. Official
publications emphasize the improved facilities for farmers, but very few
natives in the villages were impressed in the early 1960's.

The black market in foreign foods, visible in all major cities during
the 1960's, flourished despite the Nationalist regime's laws against smuggling or the sale of tax-free foods imported by American organizations.
Milk powder, edible oil, and other gift foods imported by religious organizations and then sold by recipients on the local market prompted an
investigation in 1962, but military commissary foods with their United
States prices stamped on them could still be bought at a 150 per cent
markup in dozens of stores in Taipei, Taichung, and Kaohsiung. "Didn't
you realize this is a yami no kuni [black-market country] as much as
a country of baishun [prostitution] and baishu [graft]" asked one of the
shopkeepers.

Several recent surveys of farmer opinion posed general questions about living conditions and a few specific queries having political connotations. Bernard Gallin's study of a rural village, *Hsin Hsing*, for example, notes that "the sweet potato is a standard part of the diet." [30] A Formosan student acquaintance commented: "As you may know, the majority of Taiwanese regard sweet potatoes as pig fodder, so if it is a standard part of the diet one can imagine the people are far from satisfied with their lot." Gallin had earlier concluded, as the result of another study, that "rural Taiwan still has a basically peasant population whose needs are decidedly different from those of the urban segment of the nation, a factor the urban-oriented government planners responsible for the rural educational programs apparently fail to understand." [31] An Okinawan visitor, sent to study sugar and pineapple operations in early 1963, found his contacts eager to have the mainlanders return home because current net income was lower than it had been during Japanese rule: "Our sugar and pineapple production and marketing are far superior to yours in Okinawa, but our farm workers earn less than what yours do," the Formosans told him.

Native Taiwanese in a sample of 1,000 native and mainlander respondents interviewed for the United States Information Service in 1960 were less contented with their livelihood than mainlanders, although fewer than 12 per cent of either group expressed more than moderate satisfaction.[32] Farmers were less convinced of recent improvement in their situation than civil servants, professional men, or industrial workers. They were also less able than urban dwellers to cite examples of United States aid, even to agriculture.

The 1960 village study by Tunghai University students, referred to in Chapter 3, showed 33 per cent of those questioned approving the effects of land reform, compared with 44 per cent who were indifferent or dissatisfied. A plurality said that sanitation was worse than prewar, that rent reduction had had little effect on livelihood, and that taxes were higher than prewar. Farmers in the 1952 Raper survey had given similar replies. In 1962, however, I found my rural informants dissatisfied primarily about the rate and equity of taxation.

Formosan fishermen interviewed in Kaohsiung and along the east coast spoke of the lack of government aid to their industry, and their fear of venturing too close to Indonesian or Philippine territory. "In the old days, our Japanese flags protected us, but Indonesia doesn't recognize Nationalist China and the Filipinos are hostile." [33] Deep-sea fisheries are relatively underdeveloped. "We envy the Japanese fisheries and would like to study their practices and receive the same kind of subsidies they get from their government," said the owner of a small fleet in Kaohsiung. Three-fourths of the 69 fishery associations, which have 200,000 members, were suffering financial losses in 1966, according to the Taiwan provincial government.[34]

E. Stuart Kirby conducted a survey in 1959, under JCRR auspices, as a follow-up to the 1952 Raper report on Formosan farm life, interviewing leaders and farmers in 54 villages within eighteen townships (the original sixteen plus two others, covering all fifteen counties on the island).[35] He found that farmers were enjoying slightly better homes, more credit facilities, and a wider range of consumer goods, but they nevertheless expressed a desire for irrigation, long-term credit, more health stations, agricultural extension programs, and common silage and threshing facilities. While few farmers were aware of birth control methods, most favored their dissemination to reduce population pressure on the land. The survey disclosed that one-third of the persons interviewed were illiterate and fewer than 8 per cent had more than an elementary education; four-fifths of all farm houses had dirt floors; only one in ten had an inside privy; but most houses contained a kitchen water tank, mosquito netting, a wash tub, a wooden bed, and a clock. Fewer than 15 per cent had a radio, electric iron, phonograph, or window screens. The survey directors saw much need for improved sanitation, increased use of chemical fertilizer, and more community participation in elections and social welfare organizations.

The late Vice President Chen Cheng had predicted that after land reform, "liberated" tenant farmers would not only produce more, but take a greater interest in political affairs: "For thousands of years the Chinese farmer . . . had almost no social status. The plight of the farmers on Taiwan under the Japanese administration was even more pitiable than that of those on the mainland . . . Owing to force of habit, few farmers participated in the [Nationalist-introduced local government] which not only has done away with discrimination, but . . . encouraged able native-born leaders to come to the fore. The whole picture changed with the enforcement of land reform." [36] He attributed the greater participation of villagers in social life to the compulsory meetings during land reform. The Raper and Kirby surveys do indeed show a gradual replacement of ex-landlords by younger farmers in positions of village leadership, and a high rate of voting in town headship elections. However, only 63 persons in the 1,350 households covered in the 1959 survey claimed to have held any office in the Farmers' Associations, and only 241 had worked in any government office. Only one-third of male heads of households, and fewer women, had ever participated in elections to the land tenancy committees, very important during land reform; but slightly more than one-half had voted in Farmers' Association elections.[37]

Officials of the mainly Formosan provincial government have often urged emulation of Japanese methods of land reclamation, reforestation, and conservation.[38] Privately, they express envy of Japanese animal husbandry, agricultural experimental work, and the high percentage of national revenues devoted by Japan to economic and social programs: "We cannot legally protest the 50 per cent of total Formosa tax revenues, including 80 per cent of central government income, spent for military purposes. But it is obvious that we could do much for the farmers and fishermen, and their living conditions, by using that money for constructive purposes. Those 40 million rats who do so much damage to our crops would be a good target if only the Communists hadn't been anti-rat," (a reference to Nationalist insistence on avoiding policies advocated by Peking).[39]

Other officials active in the rural areas bemoaned the farmers' lack of political interest, as revealed in the 1960 USIS survey whose respondents having less than eight years of schooling or being under 34 years of age, expressed almost no interest in "politics and government," (although a strong majority of those over 45 or with a secondary education were interested).[40] "The Nationalists, even more than the Japanese colonialists, teach our people that politics is a dangerous business, and they prefer that the farmers think only of work, festivals, and other safe subjects," explained a politician in a rural area.

Industrial Progress and Urban Life

Industrial and urban progress in Formosa under Chinese rule has been more marked than rural progress, perhaps because the fifty years of Japanese rule had laid the foundations for modern cities with transport and communications facilities, and many industries. As mentioned earlier, agriculture accounted for over three-fourths of all Formosan production in 1902, but for only 42 per cent in 1942. "The accelerated Japanese industrialization in the late 1930's and early 1940's was Taiwan's period of greatest material progress . . . Japan's half-century is therefore everywhere evident not only as a background of present-day industrial development, but equally important as a part of the attitudes of the people, whether Taiwanese or mainlanders . . . current conditions are always being compared with those of the Japanese period," wrote Raper in 1954.[41]

A budget for social overhead, such as transport and communication facilities, is vital to both urbanization and industrialization. American aid to the Nationalists included funds to purchase Japanese railway cars, trucks, buses, telephones, and similar items both for replacement and improvement of the prewar equipment. When tourists ride on the express trains in air-conditioned, reclining-seat comfort, few notice the Japanese manufacturer's mark or the clasped-hand insignia of the American aid mission, but every Formosan knows that Japan built the system and continues to supply the parts.

"Japan surveyed the route for a cross-island highway, but doubted its feasibility," explained one Taichung engineer during one of the frequent periods when landslides closed the Nationalist-built US$10 million mountain highway. "It is closed to through traffic most of the year . . . [and] was hurriedly and crudely built in the first place." [42] Troubles with the Taipei-to-Keelung MacArthur Expressway after its 1964 opening were described even by mainlanders as "a mockery of free China's transportation history." [43]

The multi-purpose dams constructed at Shihmen and planned for Tsungwen in the south are genuine accomplishments of the Nationalist regime, though assisted by American and Japanese capital and technical ability. The Taiwan Power Company, a joint national and provincial government concern inherited from Japan, produced over 6 billion kilowatt hours in 1965 (40 per cent being generated from dams) of which 80 per cent was used by industry. The Shihmen reservoir, twice as large as the Japanese-built Sun-Moon Lake, was completed in 1963 at a cost of US$66 million and seven years' work.[44] The Tsengwen project near Tainan was begun in late 1965 and will cost US$94 million over six years to irrigate about 210,000 acres, generate 256 million kwh of electricity, and provide both flood control and water supplies to the relatively dry area of the southwest.[45]

But some experts are concerned about energy problems involving coal. "Where petroleum refining and electric power generation have grown along with industry, coal mining has not," says Joseph Z. Reday. "The coal mines are old and thin-seamed, and the best are owned and inefficiently operated by the government. At something like US$15 per ton on average, Taiwan steam coal costs about twice the world price. Japanese steam coal, for example, is about US$8 f.o.b. and under US$12 delivered to Taiwan . . . compared with US$20 for poorer grade Taiwan coal." [46] The regime charged a 20 per cent duty on imported coal, however, and local businessmen in industries most affected by power costs could only envy their Japanese counterparts.

The American aid mission relied heavily on the J. G. White Engineering Corporation for advice on how best to allocate the one-fifth of its funds used in Formosan industrial projects: partly to rehabilitate and modernize the aluminum, fertilizer, textile, agricultural processing, and other prewar industries; and partly to develop newer labor-intensive industries to make the island less dependent on imports. The pharmaceutical industry, for example, depended on Japanese imports until 1962, but had switched to domestic production by 1964, albeit with the cooperation of many Japanese firms. "We do not earn any more profit under the home production system," said a Taipei druggist in 1964, "but the prices are slightly lower and consumers think we are more self-sufficient. They still respect a Japanese trademark, however, and often consider local products inferior to those from Japan."

Despite Sun Yat-sen's vague advocacy of public ownership of major industries and the tendency of the Nationalist regime to retain control of Japanese properties left on Formosa, Washington supported local demands for more free enterprise. Stock in four government corporations was distributed to ex-landlords as compensation in the 1953 reform, but Taipei resisted pressures to sell other profitable government businesses. 'There isn't enough private capital to buy the firms or expertise to run them," explained Nationalist officials during the 1950's when public industries produced twice the total value of all private production.[47] In 1953, for example, government enterprises accounted for from 50 to 100 per cent of alcohol, tobacco, salt, transport, fertilizer, power, chemicals, sugar, timber, and cement production. By 1967, however, cement, chemicals, plywood, and most consumer and light industrial items were in private hands.[48]

Formosan private businessmen dominate small business and such new fields as electric appliances, artificial-fiber textiles, and plastics, but according to a 1965 cabinet statement the government "has no intention to transfer to private capital those state enterprises vital to either national defense or economic development." [49] That same statement specified the sugar, petroleum, fertilizer, power, shipbuilding, and machinery as those which would remain under national control.

Every developing nation is tempted to acquire a steel mill for reasons of prestige if for no other. "This island needs an integrated steel mill like a hole in the head," commented an American economic advisor in 1962 after many years in Formosa. When the private Tan Eng Iron Works in Kaohsiung fell into government hands after bankruptcy, a friend of the owner predicted: "Now the regime will sink more of our taxes into a steel project rather than buy cheaper and better steel from Japan." After several years of reliance on scrap steel, Taipei invited foreign steel experts from the United States, Germany, and Japan to advise it on the feasibility of a major complex in Kaohsiung.[50]

"Would a US$200 million steel project be justified without first making Kaohsiung's export processing zone system work well?" asked an official of that southern port in 1966. The zone system permits duty-free import of raw materials for processing and re-export, and is successful in many parts of the world where labor is cheap. By 1967, however, Nationalist red tape and poor working conditions in Kaohsiung had caused a number of complaints. According to the China News "Many investors . . . feel that it is too difficult to get entry permits for their overseas technicians. . . . Workers complain that they are not paid adequately, averaging only NT$400 to $500 a month (US$10–$12.50) after being lured to work in the Zone by honeyed promises from their employers. . . ."[51]

Nationalist red tape is the target of many local and foreign business critics, as well as of American officials and economic advisors. A great many citizens, too, agree with the sentiments expressed in a China News editorial attack on "the bureaucratic anchor that now hangs around the neck of legitimate business," which declared: "Our bureaucracy has two faults. First, regulations are too numerous and too cumbersome. . . . Everything takes several times as long as it should. This encourages the iniquitous use of red envelopes [money bribes] to get faster results. . . . Second, our whole bureaucratic system is based on mistrust and unwillingness to accept responsibility. . . . Investors, workers, and their families are to be mistrusted . . . as sharpers and cheats awaiting the smallest opportunity to defraud the government. This is nonsense, of course, yet . . . such an outlook can become a fatal obstacle to economic progress."[52]

In contrast to the suspicious attitude of the regime toward private business, public corporations or those favored by the government (such as the mainlander-owned Yue Loong Motor Company) receive undue protection. "In many government-owned enterprises," says Raper, "there is an excess of management and worker personnel . . . In urban areas the large public enterprises were reported [by community leaders] to have been helped most and the small, private enterprises least [by United States aid up to 1953]." [53] Featherbedding in state industries is a perennial accusation made by natives as well as by some courageous mainlander members of the Control Yuan, who have also accused the regime of absolving the military forces of their debts to state enterprises.[54]

According to several Taipei business informants who were critical of the regime's liberal policy toward "inefficient" firms with a practical monopoly, commercial banks are controlled by the government through both stock ownership and lending restrictions. The Yue Loong Motor Company has assembled Japanese Nissan trucks and cars since 1959, and has sold them locally at double the price quoted in Japan.[55]

Native industrialists often complain about the lack of domestic capital, poor protection of patent rights, and complicated government export and import procedures. Lin Ting-sheng, president of the company that dominates the electric appliance market, described the conflict between "good" and "bad" mainlander officials "who fight each other at our expense . . . and respect military first, scholars next, and businessmen last. Land rents are low because few mainlanders own land and the regime only wants to extract high taxes from it. The government appoints the heads of commercial banks due to its 51 per cent stock control, and is too bearish on extending loans to business." [56] United States AID officials, who praised Lin and his firm as the most progressive on the island, also mentioned the impatience of native entrepreneurs toward the Nationalist bureaucracy. "The provincial assembly, which is locally elected, has little power," said another Taipei businessman, "and there are only a few natives in the Legislative Yuan."

Retail businessmen in the cities were easiest to converse with when no customers were within earshot. One commented that "The mainlanders have crowded into all our cities and prefer excessive competition and haggling to paying fixed prices. Due to their influx, we have too many small shops open almost every day for long hours. The regime is afraid we may organize as our Japanese counterparts do, and the shortage of credit prevents our expansion into larger chains of stores."

The urban merchant and worker are very conscious of the seamy side of postwar industrialization. The cities bore the brunt of the mainlander influx which, combined with simultaneous domestic migration from villages to urban areas, tripled the populations of Taipei, Taichung, Kaohsiung, and other large cities in the postwar decades.[57] When Arthur Raper's survey team asked 1,383 urban households about their biggest health problems in 1953, poor sanitation, undernourishment, and high medical costs ranked in that order; community leaders in nine of the 17 cities said environmental sanitation was worse than before the war.[58]

"Just walk along the riverbanks, canals, railroad tracks, or unused public grounds and you'll see the thousands of illegal shacks that are the blight of our cities," remarked a doctor in Taichung. While statistics prove that the average urban house is better constructed and equipped than its rural counterpart, much urban housing is crowded and unsanitary—like the rows of inflammable shacks along the railroad tracks in downtown Taipei housing some 5,000 persons, mostly poor mainlanders in marginal employment.[59] This Chunghua Road slum was too visible to be ignored, so the government replaced it with a two-story cement shopping arcade and gradually tore down squatters' sheds in other parts of Taipei as well. The China News expostulated: "They [the Nationalists] neglect most slums in the other cities where fewer mainlanders or foreigners reside. The slum shacks are often shops in front and dwelling spaces behind, with refuse thrown into a nearby open ditch or canal. Mayor Henry Kao commented on these problems in his 1966 'State of the City' report to the city council. 'Taipei looks like a prosperous city with its tall buildings, tourist hotels, cabarets, and restaurants . . . but there are not enough jobs . . . classrooms, housing, sewers, wide streets, or grade crossings . . . The sham prosperity has created a serious breakdown in morals,' the mayor said, and blamed these problems on the sharp increase in population." [60]

The urban Raper report of 1953 showed that one-half of the city houses had leaky roofs, and over one-third, dirt floors. Illiteracy in the towns and cities averaged about 25 per cent for men and 60 per cent for women. Ten years later, physical conditions had improved, but urban income remained unevenly distributed and municipal services were far below the residents' desires. The Taipei press reported that one-fourth of Taipei's 1.2 million residents were still living in flimsy wooden houses in 1967—more than before the city tore down 8,000 such houses without providing adequate replacements.[61]

Aside from better housing and sanitation, urban dwellers want more jobs. In mid-1966, according to a provincial government survey, 3.75 million of Formosa's 7.8 million city dwellers over age 12 were employed; that is, excluding housewives and students, 260,000 were unemployed.[62] But other estimates have placed the real unemployment rate at 10 per cent or higher, depending on how one calculates the large number of the partially employed. Labor unions exist mainly to regiment the workers, but are not allowed to strike or bargain like their counterparts in Western countries. "The sizable unemployment rate of 1965 would more probably rise than decline, as a result of huge accessions to the labor force during the next decade from a young population. . . . Independent and militant labor unions were unlikely to develop under the Government of the Republic of China," predicted Jacoby.[63]

"Sure, the daily factory wage is less than in Hong Kong or Japan," said workers during an interview, "but that sounds good only to the government, or foreign investors seeking cheap labor." It makes Formosa "a much more attractive site for labor-intensive manufacturing industries," in the words of Jacoby, but not a more attractive place for native workers to live. The American trade union representative stationed in Okinawa from 1961 to 1963 spoke of the poor condition of Formosan unionists he had met and of their difficulties in organizing workers, pressuring employers, or influencing the hostile mainlander regime. "Wages actually average only about US$11 a month, and the workers have less social security, welfare, or other fringe benefits than here on Okinawa," said an economics professor at Ryukyu University after a survey of Formosa in 1966.[64]

The Nationalist regime claims that local workers need more technical training, and the press either blames "Chinese students' reluctance to go to vocational schools" or says: "Too many of our people still feel that ladies and gentlemen should not work with their hands. They make desperate efforts to educate their children for overcrowded professions and government service." [65] Such comments reflect the mainlanders' ignorance of how much Formosan custom differs from their own.

All of the community leaders interviewed in the 1953 Raper urban survey wanted more industrialization and foreign trade, and my informants in the early 1960's agreed. "But first we must have easier and cheaper credit," said one medium-scale businessman in Taipei, anxious to expand his medical equipment business. "Taiwan was still a capital-deficit country in 1965, offering high rates of return to those with funds to invest," concluded Jacoby.[66] In some degree the credit problem affects all businessmen, from the millionaire industrialist to the corner grocer, but foreign trade is equally important to a people who export about one-sixth of their gross national product (US$500 million out of US$3 billion in 1966). Jacoby noted: "As a small economy with a limited domestic market, [Formosa] would always be heavily dependent upon the expansion of foreign markets. . . . Progressive relaxation of controls on foreign trade and payments must be a keystone of Chinese economic policy . . . also a gradual elimination of protection for infant industries

as they mature . . . It [Formosa] should overcome its fears of investment by Japanese and overseas Chinese firms, whose potential political
influence in Taiwan is exaggerated," Jacoby added.[67]

Objections to taxes have more political overtones in Formosa than in
most other countries. The average rate of taxation over the past decade
has been 20 per cent of national income, with three-fourths of the taxes
being indirect and less than one-fourth direct land or income taxes.
"AID's effort to obtain a shift from indirect to direct taxation would
have diminished development effects, although it would have produced
greater equality of incomes," according to Jacoby. "Genuine reforms
would have required alteration of deeply held Chinese military and political objectives." [68]

Few wealthy Formosan businessmen favor higher income taxes, but
the average citizen objects strongly to the regressive nature of the tax system, and he is supported by some officials. A taxation study group of the
Provincial Assembly complained in 1967 that "ordinary people are over-
taxed compared with the rich ones." It urged consolidation and simplifi-
cation of many taxes and the elimination of surtaxes, such as those for
defense, education, and electric power.[69]

The press announced on May 1, 1962 that the Legislative Yuan had
approved a special 14-month defense surtax at a secret session the previous midnight, in response to an urgent request by President Chiang to
collect more money for an imminent counterattack against the mainland. The vote was unanimous and not even the few outspoken fiscal
critics in the national legislature voiced any objection. The independent-
minded China News surprisingly did not challenge the contention of Finance Minister (later Premier and Vice President) C. K. Yen that the
surtax was needed "to curb inflation while preparing the counterattack,"
but merely questioned the method. Although no surtax was applied to
industrial income taxes, or to import duties and freight taxes on goods of
industrial businesses, all other taxes were raised from 20 to 50 per cent.
The China News quoted three Taipei newspapers to the effect that "the
government itself and ranking government officials should set an example" by reducing their own graft, waste, and corruption: "The austerity
drive is empty talk because the government and ranking officials have
too many feasts, sedans, golf matches, and parties at military hostels." [70]

In the following weeks I questioned Formosans about the tax, its justification, and its effect on their lives. One shopkeeper in Taipei, a week
after the surtax announcement, wondered why the tax increase was necessary: "It helps rather than hinders inflation, and I for one won't raise

my prices." Another merchant reported that the black-market rate for the American dollar had risen to 48:1, or 20 per cent above the official 40:1 rate. A member of the Legislative Yuan, encountered on the train from Taipei to Taichung, smiled when reminded of the speed with which the Legislature had passed the measure: "Oh, we don't really have much power and we seldom draw more than 300 of the 600 members who live here. Anyone who openly criticized the sacred goal of mainland recovery would be punished, so don't ask me any more questions." During the next two months, in Taichung, Tainan, and Kaohsiung, every shopkeeper and professional man interviewed on the subject pointed to the lack of public debate on the surtax before it was rubber-stamped by the unrepresentative Legislative Yuan. A young member of the Provincial Assembly agreed that "we can freely criticize graft, favoritism, and corruption—but not the policy of mainland recovery because that is the national government's excuse for existence."

The Political Connotation of Economic Complaints

It is frequently asserted that because two-thirds of the industrial production comes from Formosan private factories, such growing economic power reduces Formosan political discontent. American officials had assumed that, as living standards rose, and local businessmen enjoyed an increasing share of foreign trade and industrial wealth, economic equality would bring political equality for the majority. In the words of Jacoby: "Efforts to force the pace of political and social change would have created unrest and uncertainty within the Chinese government, and between it and the people of Taiwan. It was wise for the United States to focus upon rapid material progress, based on a vigorous private sector. In this way, American aid helped to disperse economic power and to create new power sectors in society. Indirectly, pressures were built up for political and social changes that are likely to occur in due time." [71]

American officials sought increased Formosan control of the economy, in the hope that it would create a "model province" and a self-sustaining economy when United States aid ended. Formosan businessmen, privately in favor of less military spending but unable to voice their thoughts, expressed similar demands: less government corruption and interference with the economy and more resources devoted to raising consumer income, welfare, and health. Government deficit financing of unbalanced budgets through currency expansion, manipulation of taxes and credit, and other inflationary devices drew severe warnings from some United States aid officials: "China has been living too high off the hog . . . too little private or public thrift. Governmental costs took 20 per cent of GNP and total consumption took 90 per cent, compared with 65 per cent in Japan. . . . Free China needs more domestic savings, private capital, a favorable business environment, and a balanced budget. . . . The defense bite has been rising to 15 per cent of GNP, double the rate in the U.S., and 80 per cent or more of the national budget." [72]

TABLE 2

THE COST OF GOVERNMENT IN FORMOSA, 1957–1963 [*]

(NT$40 = US$1)

	1957	1959	1961	1963
Total population (1,000)	10,099	10,769	11,440	12,115
Growth Rate %	3.4	3.2	3.0	2.9
Per capita GNP (US$)	125	135	148	158
Net government revenue				
(NT$1 million)	10,191	11,349	11,786	13,458
Ratio to GNP %	20.0	19.5	17.4	18.0
Government spending				
(NT$1 million)	9,537	11,714	12,229	13,954
Military spending ratio %	54	58	56	54
Military/GNP ratio %	10	12	10	10
Government spending index				
(1956 = 100)	106	130	135	165

[*] *Source:* AID Mission to China, *Taiwan: U.S. Aid Program Fiscal Year 1964*, Part IV, 1964. See also Neil H. Jacoby, *U.S. Aid to Taiwan* (New York: Frederick A. Praeger, 1966), Appendix C; and Sheppard Glass in Mark Mancall, ed., *Formosa Today* (New York: Frederick A. Praeger, 1964), p. 78. The latter claims that military spending averaged 57% of total government consumption and 83% of central government spending in 1957–1961; AID claims that almost all central government costs were military, with most of the regular budgetary deficits being covered by American aid.

S. Y. Dao, a leading economic expert in the Nationalist government, has pointed out that "the major United States–China disagreement is over defense spending, not the rate of industrialization," and a planning officer in AID agreed that "the major problem is the 50 per cent of all government revenue going to defense." [73] (See Table 2.) Jacoby has argued that the large military budget of the Nationalists was not a deterrent to economic growth. "The U.S. repeatedly, and unsuccessfully, tried to persuade the Chinese to reduce military spending during the latter half of the aid period. . . . The civilian economy provided large hidden subsidies to the military establishment in the form of rice, transportation services, electricity, and other items for which the military paid nothing, or less than market prices. . . . The military burden probably lowered Taiwan's economic growth rate, with [U.S.] aid, by 22 per cent . . . [but it] was not as heavy a drag on Taiwan's economy as generally believed.[74]

Throughout the past fifteen years, however, thoughtful Americans have noted that "programs for economic development in Taiwan operated in a secondary position to those dealing with the political and military situation . . . Most of the Mainlanders want to go back to the mainland and tend to think and plan within this framework . . . hence, the business and industrial plans of this group, which has charge of the government and of the extensive public enterprises, are everywhere conditioned by this primary goal . . . Still others, especially the Taiwanese, seem to be looking forward to the time when they might have a greater degree of local autonomy." [75]

Crucial to this uneasy situation is the reluctance of the Formosans to place the Nationalist goal of mainland recovery above the economic growth of the island. "It's just a dream to think of mainland recovery, but worse to ask our ten million people to sacrifice for such a dream of the mainlanders," said one elder statesman.

Few others would disagree so directly with the regime's military-economic priority ("those who do often become *yukue fumei*" [whereabouts unknown], I was told), but they manage to convey the same feeling nevertheless. It is much safer for Formosans to couch their criticisms in socio-economic terms, implying that the Nationalist central government devotes too much money to unnecessary bureaucratic and military purposes and too little to human welfare, health, wages, and modern education. Formosan mayors are actually raising similar objections when they complain of the lack of funds and policy powers to correct municipal defects.

No Formosan businessman could express his desires more clearly than the writers of a 1964 Agency for International Development report on economic and social trends in Formosa. After a detailed statistical evaluation of recent economic growth and probable future trends to 1972, the AID report spoke of cultural impediments

> First and foremost, the Chinese on Taiwan need to become reconciled to the idea that economic development means change . . . a willingness to suffer social and cultural disorien-

tation in the larger interest of economic growth. . . . The contribution of government, in this effort, can be to stay the dead hand of bureaucracy, on the one hand, and to establish status for the entrepreneur, the innovator, and other exponents of original, analytical thinking, superseded by a belief in man's power to control the forces of nature. . . . Taiwan appears ambivalent regarding the priority of the goal of economic development, relative to other competing national goals. Over-infatuation with things Chinese is a roadblock to exploiting the trial-and-error experience of the West. A stagnation theory tends to view profit-making as iniquitous rather than as an index of services rendered. Replacing inefficient, obsolete technology and equipment is hampered by an aversion to 'breaking another man's rice bowl' . . ." [76]

Formosan economists, many of whom worked for the American AID mission, might, however, have complained more openly of the main-lander political system as the cause of economic problems. "They never had it so good," a popular Nationalist slogan borrowed from the West, has received few echoes from the supposed beneficiaries of Formosa's economic miracle. Throughout this study, I have regarded *perception* of fact as more important politically than supposedly "objective" fact. A Formosan will perceive his economic status under alien political rule as inferior to what it might be under a government of his own choosing, regardless of what outside experts may tell him.

The most pessimistic economic prediction I heard came from a veteran of the Puerto Rican "Operation Bootstrap" who was an industrial development advisor toward the end of the American aid program in Formosa. He compared Taiwan unfavorably with his native island, where "we did without U.S. aid, raised industry with only labor as a resource, reduced sugar mills and acreage but kept the same production level, and have less public ownership and higher income taxes than here." He thought that economics was the whole problem, not politics, and foresaw no solution to the need for more jobs in Formosa: "Where will they find hundreds of thousands of jobs when the current rate of new jobs is only 50,000 annually? One-half are fully employed: 36 per cent underemployed—four hours a week or more—and 16 per cent are unemployed." He saw the Nationalists' goal of mainland recovery as a drive for bigger markets because the island's future is so limited, and wondered why the workers of Formosa had not revolted. "This is a revolutionary situation, worse than in Brazil where riots are occurring now, and this situation would cause revolution in a Latin American context. But these people are very patient." [77]

Finally, an American engineer who had worked on contract to the Chinese government since the last days on the mainland recounted his dismal impressions of the Kuomintang regime. "Expect a major political upset within a few years because the Taiwanese are fed up with inefficiency—my workers are mostly laborers, but they say they prefer the Japanese era to now. The Chinese are good on theory but bad on application, and have too much squeeze. They can't administer any project well, and only want to promote themselves and take money from us. A few top bureaucrats like S. Y. Dao, and local Formosan businessmen like Lin of the Tatung Company, are good men, but are sat upon by the higher government officials." [78]

This opinion expresses what most Formosans appear to believe. Formosan political refugees often ignore the economic accomplishments of the Nationalist regime, but the regime and most of the world press glorify those achievements far beyond native comprehension.

THE MYTH OF POLITICAL DEMOCRACY

Even in the opinion of staunch supporters of the Nationalist regime social and economic progress in postwar Formosa have been greater than political progress.[1] We have seen how native Formosans usually qualify their criticisms of relatively "safe" aspects of their mainlander-controlled government; it is much more difficult to assess the extent and intensity of their strictly political attitudes. Perhaps political democracy is a luxury of low priority to people of material underdevelopment, under a regime technically in a state of civil war with a Communist regime across the narrow Formosa Strait which has been threatening violent "liberation" of Formosa since 1949.

The Formosans have not enjoyed many political rights under any previous regime. Do they agree with ex-Congressman Walter Judd that political reforms must await military security, or with Vice Admiral William E. Gentner, commander of the United States Taiwan Defense Command, that "under President Chiang's leadership, the island has become a showcase of democracy in Asia"? [2]

No national elections have been held on Taiwan since 1948 because the Nationalist regime insists they must be postponed until the mainland is recovered. Essentially the elite in power today on Formosa is the same that sought refuge there under Chiang's leadership in 1949, without benefit of popular elections. Our concern here is less to judge the merits of the political situation on Formosa than to study the reactions of the native majority to what Jacoby has called their "measure of democracy—more than a facade, yet less than a genuine and full structure." [3]

Is it possible to study Formosan political attitudes? "No political research is possible on this island today," said a leading Formosan politician in 1963, "because there are no reliable sources and good men don't run for office." The eldest son of a Taipei businessman warned me that "under KMT rule there is no freedom of speech, so nobody dares to criticize the regime politically." The calling card of a professor of political science was enough to frighten many native informants who felt that the very words "political science" spelled danger. Dr. Pardee Lowe, after his retirement as cultural affairs officer in the U.S. Embassy in Taipei, told a scholarly convention in 1965 that the American authorities gave full cooperation to all researchers in Formosa "except those studying topics opposed by the regime." [4]

On the other hand, as Jacoby says, "the government and party system of the Republic of China is better described as authoritarian rather than totalitarian. In spite of an efficient security system, government and party controls were neither absolute nor total throughout the society." [5] The regime does permit open criticism of corruption and policy methods, if not of policy goals.

To assess the myth of Formosan political democracy, this chapter will briefly describe the Nationalist system of national and local government, explain how the dominant leader and party maintain their position, and report reactions of various Formosans to the political system, ranging from outward support to absolute alienation. Finally, the chapter will show the methods by which the regime, while tolerant of some kinds of criticism, punishes other kinds by economic or physical means.

Dual Government and Local Autonomy

The most salient political fact about Formosa is the existence of both a national and provincial government, with theoretical division of functions but actual unity of decision-making within the central core. "Both the national and provincial governments were throughly dominated by the Kuomintang, with the authority of the Director-General of the Party [President Chiang Kai-shek] close to absolute in those areas where he chose to exercise it . . . the Chinese tradition of authoritarian rule was still dominant," wrote Jacoby in 1966.[6]

The 1946 constitution took effect in 1948 and no elections to the Legislative Yuan or the National Assembly have been held since that time. The Nationalists' entire cumbersome political and military apparatus was transplanted intact from the mainland to Formosa, and operates within the narrow confines of the island refuge. The situation is analogous to what might happen if a hostile power had occupied the United States mainland, causing the administration in Washington to flee to Honolulu and attempt to operate the U.S. Congress, Supreme Court, Cabinet departments, Federal agencies, and party structures side by side with Hawaii's state and local governments.

The organs of the Chinese national government in Formosa exhibit the outward trappings of constitutionalism, but these, says Jacoby, "did not provide a real picture of the actual location and disposition of power . . . [because] it was at the top echelon of Kuomintang leadership that the decisive power relations existed." [7] The National Assembly of 2,961 members originally elected on the mainland and Formosa in 1947, whose number had dwindled to 1,488 by 1966, selects a president and vice president every six years and ratifies constitutional amendments. The Legislative Yuan, a unicameral parliament of 457 survivors of the original 760 elected in 1948, is under strict KMT party discipline and serves primarily as a forum to discuss a limited range of problems. The Judicial Yuan, an appointive body, has dealt more zealously with administrative malfeasance than with violations of civil and political rights, because the martial law still in force—since 1948—provides that any civilian accused of sedition (broadly defined) is to be tried by a military court of the Taiwan Garrison Command.

The Control and Examination Yuans are judicial and personnel management boards, respectively. Like the national bodies just described, they are composed almost entirely of mainlanders who have survived the ravages of time. Cynics have dubbed the entire Nationalist regime a "gerontocracy."

Most administrative power resides in the Executive Yuan whose premier controls all ministries and is the third most important constitutional officer behind the president and vice president. His relationship to the Legislative Yuan (somewhat like that of the French Fifth Republic premier to the French National Assembly) is reinforced by the strong Kuomintang party majority.

The Nationalist presidency, however, is even more potent than its French equivalent under De Gaulle. President Chiang Kai-shek *is* Nationalist China and was elected by the National Assembly in 1966 to his fourth six-year term.[8] Chiang is also supreme director-general of the KMT and commander in chief of all Nationalist armed forces. Like De Gaulle, he possesses wide emergency powers and, under the Temporary Provisions Effective During the Period of Communist Rebellion, may issue wartime orders "to ensure national security" which "need not comply with procedural restrictions." [9] At its session in March 1966, the National Assembly further amended the Temporary Provisions to allow President Chiang to form a new mobilization agency, reorganize the national government, and call for elections to fill vacancies in those central government positions "vacated or added because of population increases in free or newly recovered areas." [10]

In my field research I was struck by the similarity between Formosan references to Chiang, and Japanese references immediately after 1945 to their Emperor or to General MacArthur: "He is above reproach, and of course does not know all the bad things his subordinates do," some Formosans said of Chiang. "We never criticize him, but the men and policies in his administration." In addition to his role as a Confucian mandarin, Chiang built the KMT along the lines of the Leninist model in Russia to serve as a pervasive control mechanism within the civil and military bureaucracy. As long as Chiang lives (he was born in 1887), the structure will probably remain unified, rigid, and loyal; speculation about his successor is one of the forbidden topics in Formosa.

Local autonomy was ostensibly achieved by Nationalist efforts to make the island's provincial and local governments a model of participatory democracy. In 1951, the province of Formosa was granted a "pilot self-government system . . . [whereby] all members of the Provincial Assembly and of city and county councils, magistrates, mayors, chiefs of rural and urban districts, townships and villages are elected by universal, equal, direct suffrage and secret ballot." [11] Under Japanese rule, all local executives and one-half the members of assemblies had been appointed, so the 1951 reform was hailed as a great advance. Almost all these elective positions are held by native Formosans who are KMT members, the reasons for which will become clear later in this chapter.

The national government continues, however, to appoint the governor of the province, who wields great power over the mainlander-dominated provincial executives and assembly. Jacoby has admitted that the Provincial Assembly has only token power, although he maintains "it provided a significant sounding board for . . . local interest groups." [12] The Provincial Assembly has taken strong positions in favor of such measures as birth control and more equitable taxation, and in 1966 more than half of its 74 members signed a petition urging resignation of native members elected in 1947 to the National Assembly, Legislative Yuan, and Control Yuan to pave the way for new elections in accordance with a constitutional amendment just approved.[13] Contested elections that year and in 1968 for provincial assemblymen and mayors demonstrated active voter participation and rivalry among native politicians, enabling the regime to point out that non-KMT candidates often won in such urban centers as Taipei, Tainan, Taichung, and Kaohsiung.

The Kuomintang regime denies charges that it is a one-party state by blaming the absence of strong political adversaries on the ineptitude of the small opposition Democratic Socialist and Young China parties, both born on the mainland and still dominated by non-KMT mainlanders since they were transplanted to Formosa. These two parties together hold 141 seats in the National Assembly, 26 seats in the Legislative Yuan, 7 seats in the Control Yuan, and 2 in the Provincial Assembly.[14]

Goddard claims: "Universal suffrage has operated for years and today Formosa has the government, local and national, that the people want . . . [Party] differences are really matters of mechanics, as all three [parties] share the same basic aims . . . Prior to 1949, the people of Formosa had no political rights." [15] The weakness of the elected levels of government as now constituted, however, lies in their lack of real decision-making power. Such power resides almost entirely with the top, or national, level, for which no general elections have been held in a generation.

In mid-1966 only 38 native-born Taiwanese were serving in the three major organs of the national government elected before 1949 on both the mainland and Formosa (27 in the National Assembly, 6 in the Legislative Yuan, and 5 in the Control Yuan).[16] Native representation in the high levels of national bureaucracy was even weaker, and only a handful of Formosan military officers ranked above army captain although the enlisted ranks were 85 per cent Formosan. In any centralized state, major decisions are controlled by officials at the national level, but Formosa is in addition an example of taxation without representation. Taipei, with 1.2 million people and an active electorate, was placed under the national government in 1967, thereby removing it from the provincial tax rolls and its mayor from elective to appointive status, although incumbents retained their posts.[17] Jacoby suggests: "The Chinese leaders did not want to absorb large numbers of natives from one province into a government intended to rule all of China. . . . Taiwanese . . . naturally resented the fact that they had little national representation of their interests." [18] The myth of mainland sovereignty for the Republic of China, and the large number of mainlanders whom the Chiang regime wishes to reward with government jobs, prevent adequate representation for the Taiwanese in their central government.

Additionally the mainlander-dominated central (i.e., national) government has maintained its supremacy over the elective local government through such other methods as these:

Insistence on the Leadership Principle. The personal influence of Chiang cannot be overestimated because his position as leader of the nation, the KMT party, and the military forces gives him the power to make important decisions by the mere suggestion that he considers a certain policy good or bad. His oracular speeches urging Confucian obedience to a paternalistic state are reinforced by plaudits in all mass media. Frequent ceremonies honor him; statues of him abound; criticism of the leader is interpreted as disloyalty to the state. The rising power of Chiang's eldest son, Ching-kuo, during the past decade presages a smooth transition of authority upon the death of the Generalissimo.

Legalized Political Suppression. In the name of national security, temporary amendments to the constitution have suspended many civil and criminal rights, such as the writ of habeas corpus, "during the period of Communist rebellion." Before moving to Formosa, the National Assembly had also attached conditions to the basic constitution allowing the president broad powers beyond its stated provisions; these powers were extended in 1954 and 1966.[19] The period of "political tutelage," or party indoctrination of the masses, theoretically ended with the 1947 elections —only to be replaced in 1949 by a period of martial law, never lifted, under which the executive branch of the government has continued to postpone genuine democracy and political dissent remains potentially subject to court-martial. Restrictions on freedom of speech, assembly, press, and criminal rights will be described below.

KMT Party Controls. The Kuomintang is far more than a political party in the American sense. It began in 1894 as a conspiracy to oust the Manchu dynasty; grew to maturity under control of the military who wished to unify China, expel the Japanese, and fight the Communists; and has never known effective opposition on Formosa. Moreover, as the relative of a former member of its central committee commented in 1965: "I have more and more felt the similarity between the ruling class in Taiwan and on mainland China in their sentiment and ideology. Except for power struggles, nothing distinguishes them too clearly." My better students at Tunghai University agreed when I abbreviated my lectures on the Communist party of the USSR, explaining it was very similar to their own KMT in its organization and its use of secret police, political commissars, youth corps, labor indoctrination, and dogmatic slogans. KMT party spies appear to infest every local government office, private organization, school campus, and community organization in Formosa. It seems probable, therefore, that even if the elective officers held more power and national administrative posts were opened to direct suffrage, the effects of one-party domination would continue to stifle Western-style democracy.

Factionalism. President Chiang has long been known to play off one faction against another to prevent any from becoming too strong, or any individual from rising to challenge himself. Over the years, he has favored fellow-members of the Whampoa clique (veterans of the Whampoa military academy near Canton, started by Chiang after his return from Moscow in 1924). After the transfer of his regime to Formosa, the mainlander elite tended to gravitate to either Vice President Chen Cheng or the Gimo's eldest son, Ching-kuo. As Chen weakened physically before his death in 1965, Ching-kuo rose in both party and Cabinet rank until by 1968, as the regime's 58-year old Defense Minister, he had placed his protégés in most key government posts and moved less "reliable" persons to innocuous positions.[20] Factionalism within the mainlander elite has grown more diffuse and impotent as Ching-kuo's power has expanded.

Meanwhile the regime has demonstrated adeptness at manipulating the personal ambitions and jealousies of Formosan politicians. In the Nationalists' eyes, one useful function of the election campaigns for local and provincial office is to play off one native group or leader against another. Often the successful candidates are themselves immobilized, as reported by Jacoby: "The Taiwanese who were elected to office, by necessity, were likely soon to reach an accommodation with the Kuomintang. In effect, the Taiwanese politician became a creature of the one-party system; in the process, his responsibility to represent his constituency was considerably compromised." [21]

Rewards for Faithful Obedience. The power of the central government to dispense financial favors to politicians and businessmen who remain politically obedient can be assumed from what has already been said about government control over banks, credit, foreign exchange, subsidies, and finances generally. The KMT is the only well-financed political organization on the island, with unlimited funds to reward its friends. University intellectuals, journalists, and Formosan big-businessmen are acutely aware of both the penalties of dissent and the benefits of political acquiescence. "There's no profit in challenging the regime," sighed a wealthy corporation president as we drove from his office in Taipei to the golf course at Tamsui. Several locally elected Formosans I met were (by local reputation) paid puppets of the central regime.

Formosan Political Attitudes and Behavior

First, let us describe the more general political aspirations which apply in varying degrees to the full spectrum of Formosan society. Albert Axelbank, who was United Press International bureau chief in Taiwan from 1960 to 1962 and later followed Formosan developments from Tokyo, wrote in 1963: "If a poll were taken now to determine what status Formosans want for their island, I am sure that at least a two-thirds majority would favor independence . . . responsible Formosan leaders, both Kuomintang and opposition members, have told me that more than 90 per cent of the people desire the establishment of an independent Formosan republic—shunning both Communist and Nationalist Chinese ties." [22]

Nationalist China forbids open discussion of Formosan self-determination or independence, the topic most sensitive on the island, where pro-independence sentiment is usually cloaked by terms like "equal representation" and "democratic rights." (More political representation and freedom of speech have been cautiously urged on the Nationalist regime by American authorities, who might be expected to support greater democracy within the existing framework more readily than creation of a separate, possibly unstable, Formosan state.)

Most Formosans espouse the idea of political independence only indirectly, since to deprecate or even discuss the Nationalist chances for mainland recovery through the "sacred counterattack," or to suggest that Formosa should be administered as a self-contained island rather than as just another Chinese province, is to exceed the bounds of safe speech.

Formosans inside the island, I found, were vehement in their hatred of Communist China, and mainland events since 1966 probably have disabused the most optimistic of the belief that the "red pigs" would tolerate Formosan autonomy. Among all the Formosans interviewed in Taiwan, Japan, and the United States, I have never met a pro-Communist. "Why should we welcome the red pigs when we dislike the white ones?" asked Taiwan intellectuals and businessmen. "Our bananas, pineapples, and other crops would disappear, and our economy would be dragged down to the mainland level."

There was general agreement among Formosans that President Chiang's death—whenever it occurred—would not bring much change into their political status, although fear of still greater rigidity under

Ching-kuo was lessened by awareness of anti-Ching-kuo sentiment among many mainlander officials, and by hope that the United States would be a restraining influence. While few Formosans thought they could affect the outcome of the power struggle within the Nationalist hierarchy either before or after Chiang's death, they agreed that the attitude of Formosan troops would be important in determining the outcome of a possible revolt if the mainlander military officers fought among themselves.

Formosans interviewed also considered most elected officials of low calibre and under strict control by the mainlander police network. "The 1964 elections in which I was re-elected do not indicate any democratic trend at all," said one local politician. "Who but a fool can expect this regime to tolerate real democracy?" Another who had run as a minor party candidate several times unsuccessfully, but who won in 1968, scoffed at KMT statements that the two small parties offered islanders a genuine political choice. "Mainlanders control those two parties also, and the KMT tolerates them as window-dressing for American visitors. The KMT cannot kill the minor parties without loss of face, but they have never allowed us to grow into political maturity. Even Peking used to allow puppet parties to exist as a sign of its united front."

It seemed to be considered common knowledge that political elections meant little because nominations were controlled; issues could not be freely discussed; campaign speeches were taped for possible use against the speaker; and KMT candidates had unlimited government funds. Moreover, those elected were subject to control by mainlanders in the provincial bureaucracy, the national cabinet, and various police agencies. Formosan incumbents with KMT affiliation admitted their own impotence.

In positive terms, it appeared that most Formosans wanted more emphasis on non-military spending and abolition of secret police, secret political trials, and taxation without debate or equitable native representation. Those in office, however, confined their comments to material needs and introduced non-office-holders to talk to me about political matters because "they are freer to tell the political truth—you can believe those out of office." Despite differences of emphasis and attitude among segments of Formosans described below, and the socio-economic divisions separating them, all appeared to share an overriding sense of political frustration against mainlander rule. The common bond may be more negative than positive, however, as is natural in anti-colonial nationalism.

From Collaboration to Alienation

The "Half-Mountain" Collaborators. The term "half-mountain" is a pe-
jorative expression used by Formosans to describe those who were born
on the island but who left it and served with the Nationalist-regime during its mainland years, and who now continue their loyalty to the KMT
on Taiwan. "This means they are only half-Formosan [because] they
went to China during World War II, where they worked for the Chiang
government. . . . These are the Formosans—virtually all Kuomintang
members—whom the Nationalist government points out to foreign
visitors." [23] The mountainous Fukien coast across the Taiwan Strait,
from which most Formosans' ancestors came to the island in past centuries, explains why those who are considered to have sold themselves to
the Nationalists are termed "half-mountain people": they are thought to
have returned at least halfway over the mountains to China, and surrendered half of their island heritage.

Not all Formosans who served Nationalist China on both the mainland and Taiwan belong in this category, but a record of anti-Japanese
activity followed by KMT service is characteristic of those who do. Interior Minister Lien Chen-tung, for example, when we were introduced in
1962 by a ranking KMT professor, spoke of his father's support for the
Ch'ing dynasty, his own education in both Japan and China while opposing Japanese rule on Taiwan, and his six years as provincial civil administrator before being elevated to the Interior post and a seat on the
KMT central committee. Lien claimed that the provincial government,
not his national ministry, was responsible for such police actions as the
suppression of black markets and illegal prostitution, "because we have
local autonomy at the provincial level, though of course the central regime appoints the chiefs of our local taxation, auditing, personnel, and
police branches." [24]

"Why do you bother to visit such men?" asked several of Lien's
friends who had also spent the war years on the mainland and later held
appointive posts in the island. "They may not believe what they say, but
while they hold office it's impossible for them to criticize the regime."
The collaborators doubtless believe they can serve Formosa best by full
cooperation with the mainlander elite. But the more bitter among native
Formosans regard the half-mountain men as traitors "who will be the
first to die if Taiwan becomes independent." Even those who serve as

KMT politicians in local government regard them as "second-rate men."

Another "half-mountain" Formosan who, like Lien, had been close to the late Vice President Chen Cheng and suffered politically after Chen's death, told a group of overseas Formosan students in the mid-1960's that Formosans should support the policy of counterattack because: "After the successful counterattack, the mainlander will go back and the island's population problem will solve itself naturally. Formosans could also travel freely to the mainland and develop careers there. . . . Because of the Red cultural revolution, this would be a good time to counterattack. But American arms would be needed—and the U.S. only promises to defend Formosa, not to assist the counterattack; and mere reliance on our own strong forces is not enough."

The students then asked him why, if the counterattack were hopeless, he advocated it. "It isn't hopeless . . . but the most difficult problem today is that the United States tries to prevent the KMT government from planning the counterattack, and *the advocacy of counterattack is the only rationale for the KMT's existence.*" [Emphasis added.]

When he was asked to evaluate the prestige of the KMT inside Formosa, he insisted he had always reminded KMT officials "that Formosans' minds are not as recovered as their territory, because they still think there has been no improvement over Japanese rule. The lack of popular support can be seen in local elections where non-KMT candidates were elected. Perhaps the KMT has about 60 per cent support; it would be embarrassing to say it has less than 50 per cent."

To improve this situation, he said he intended to "suggest the reform of one-party dictatorship, and a coalition cabinet of the three parties," and made no further comment when reminded of the failure of previous efforts in that direction. As to his opinion of the Formosan activists for independence, he admitted: "Their enthusiasm is indeed praiseworthy, but experienced people want to wait because, if the government still cannot launch a counterattack after another ten years, Formosa will automatically become independent." [25] This optimistic view is shared by many Japanese observers, but few Formosans.

One of the Legislative Yuan members previously quoted smiled when I envied his security without election worries: "Yes, the government keeps extending our terms indefinitely, but we have little power and less respect from the citizens."

The Insincere Collaborators. Native Formosans fill almost all governmental offices at the provincial, county, and municipal level. It matters little politically, however, that mailmen and railway workers are natives;

nor do the Formosan policemen patrolling the city streets, or bus drivers in the provincial highway system, influence policy.

A city official warned: "Some of the lower echelon native bureaucrats are genuine traitors, whom you cannot trust because they would sell their own brothers to the security police." Paid spies are placed in most local government offices to watch the behavior of the higher officials, and each city's police chief (always a mainlander) also has his own trusted operatives to check on the Formosan spies: "The police chief is really the boss of this town," remarked one mayor.

It is difficult to separate genuine collaborators from self-serving politicians or from Formosans who accept public office hoping to bore from within. "The sincere collaborators are very rare," commented an American diplomat with long experience in Taiwanese affairs, "but so are the anti-KMT activists. Taiwanese in political office are so carefully watched and pressured that even if they wanted to oppose government policy they could not go far. The majority, especially those nominated by the KMT for local office, are in it for personal profit." The men serving as mayor of Taichung and as county magistrate of Taitung at the time of my 1961–1962 research were perhaps typical of the self-serving native office-holders who can be termed "the insincere collaborators." "He'd never be elected if good quality men ran against him," said a Formosan of one such politician. "If we lived in X city with a good KMT native mayor, or Y city with a minor-party mayor, we'd vote for them, but few really good native-born men run for office under this regime."

Formosan informants delighted in stories of reputedly collaborating mayors or assemblymen who were living conspicuously beyond their means. Graft was taken for granted and practiced by many office-holders who expected to be double-crossed by the regime after a few profitable years.

"Under Japanese rule we never had a political party with unlimited access to government funds," said a local politician out of office, "but the KMT can reward its political pets and discriminate against the others." Many quiet collaborators were convivial types adept at local patronage and vote-getting, but privately cynical, arguing: "Under the circumstances, somebody has to hold the offices and it's better if we play their game rather than allow mainlanders to win elections."

Across the island in Taitung, the county magistrate received me in his official residence for two hours' private discussion of every subject except politics. "He's no politician," said a member of the Taitung county assembly, "and he is always being watched, so he fears to talk politics to a foreigner, especially one known to be a political scientist."

Two members of the Provincial Assembly interviewed separately refused to criticize the national government or the KMT, although they freely discussed corruption and economic discrimination. Municipal councilmen often bemoaned their weak position: "We have very little salary and meet about seventeen days three times a year. Local people can voice their complaints to the city, county, and provincial assemblymen, but only a few municipal legislators speak up boldly."

Concerning the national regime's use of intimidation, financial pressures, and wiretapping, one correspondent reported interviews with provincial assemblymen who looked behind curtains before whispering: "Don't mention our names or we'll surely be arrested." Another politician turned up the volume of his radio "so the police won't be able to tape-record our conversation . . ." [26]

Would the insincere collaborators join the more active critics in the event of an internal uprising against the mainlander elite? Most informants thought not. "They would not risk their lives or fortunes unless the outcome were clear. They are like the loyalists in your own revolutionary war who opposed violence and fled to England," said one extreme anti-Nationalist. On the other hand, a leader of the younger Formosan refugee community in Japan was more optimistic: "It is true that factionalism exists, but it can be corrected. Below the surface, most of the outwardly loyal native politicians agree with the outspoken ones." [27]

It seems probable that the quiet collaborators, and perhaps even some of the "half-mountain" people, share the aspirations of their compatriots. But if they are too afraid even to speak privately today, for fear of personal, family, or property dangers, would they behave more bravely in a crisis? It seems more realistic to assume that these men would willingly serve whatever authority ruled them.

The Passive Opposition. This category includes some Formosans within the KMT membership as well as a large percentage of non-KMT politicians. Their expressions of antagonism toward the regime range from verbal attacks in private conversation to public criticism—the latter, however, limited to permissible topics, never including an espousal of Formosan independence or renunciation of mainland recovery. As between the "half-mountaineers" and the "insincere collaborators," there is a gradual shading from insincere collaboration to passive opposition.

The most famous anti-KMT politician in postwar Formosa is Henry

Yu-shu Kao, first elected mayor of Taipei in 1954 and again in 1964. Formosan informants regarded him as their best spokesman in public life. Born in Taipei in 1913, Kao was educated at Waseda University in Tokyo as an engineer and first ran unsuccessfully for the Taipei mayoralty in 1951 but lost (18,000 to 92,000) to Wu San-lien. When Wu failed to keep his promise to join the KMT, he was replaced in 1954 by a more amenable party candidate who lost to Kao, 90,000 votes to 110,000. According to Jacoby, "Kao's three-year administration was an excellent one, though the KMT was disgusted with it . . . and mobilized its military, police, and party units" to elect Huang Chi-Juei over incumbent Kao in 1957. "One of the so-called security measures [during that campaign] was to suspend electric service during the opening of the ballots . . . This election was regarded by Taipei citizens as an illegal and unfair manipulation by the KMT." [28]

Ostensibly because he wanted Taiwan to avoid a situation like "the unfair Korean election of 1960 which provoked the riots leading to the downfall of Synghman Rhee," [29] Kao withdrew from the 1960 Taipei mayoralty campaign, and the KMT's Huang was re-elected. Subsequently Chou Pai-lien, another KMT Formosan, became acting mayor when Mayor Huang was suspended during the settlement of a corruption case. Huang refused to resign, however, and in the next election campaign personal animosities between Huang, Chou, and other Formosan-born KMT leaders splintered the KMT party in Taipei. The unexpected result was that Kao succeeded in winning re-election in April 1964 despite formidable Nationalist Chinese opposition. [30]

The Kao victory coincided with other non-KMT electoral successes in Keelung and Tainan, all of which the regime tried to explain as proof of its democratic progress. "Nonsense," commented the mayor of another city that summer; "personalities played the major role—and maybe some foreign governments warned the KMT not to repeat its pressure tactics of 1957."

Kao had been a leader in the abortive attempt to form the China Democratic Party in 1960, whose fate will be discussed below. In September 1960, the regime threatened to prosecute on three charges of past corruption, and two years later his wife was accused of performing abortions. "With these charges," Kao told Axelbank, "the government has a noose around my neck which it can tighten whenever it wants to." [31]

In the late 1950's, all but a few mayors and county magistrates were Formosan, but secretaries appointed by the mainlander governor "to be their chief assistants" were Chinese. [32] Under such circumstances, the mayor of Taiwan's largest city and provisional capital had to be more careful than any other elected official. In the April 1968 local elections, although the KMT won 17 of the 20 mayoral and county magisterial offices, and 61 of the 71 seats in the Provincial Assembly—independents were elected mayor in the cities of Taichung and Kaohsiung.[33]

Among the passive opposition are a few outspoken members of the Provincial Assembly (including an independent who won 1963 re-election in Kaohsiung city) who are noted for their fiery speeches in support of civilian economic progress, government economy, population control, and election of the provincial governor. A younger member of that assembly, who privately criticized the large number of mainlander bureaucrats serving in the provincial government (including those assigned to spy on the legislators) asked: "Why does Chiang appoint such a man as General Huang Chieh [a mainlander] to be our governor except to make sure we [in the Provincial Assembly] remain his rubber stamp?" Huang previously had served as army commander in chief and head of the infamous Taiwan Garrison Command.

One retired Formosan official limits his present opposition activities to "de-brainwashing" Japanese, American, and other foreign visitors, to correct misleading official reports. "I have seen too many people suffer from the useless protests during Japanese rule and in 1947; violence is no answer to our problems," he said. "Yet the facts of our life must be broadcast to the world, and Nationalist leaders somehow persuaded to follow more rational policies." The speaker of one county council was memorable for his cogent description of both prewar and postwar injustices, especially to the tribal peoples. A local government politician spent hours guiding me around the slums of his city, explaining the ways in which the mainlander police and military command violate civil law and human rights. The mayor of another city confided his many frustrations in the face of party and military controls. He may have been the same man who told an American reporter that "the military 'milked' 80 per cent of his city's budget . . . He said he had hardly any authority in his own city's affairs." [34]

The most outspoken opponents risk interrogation or harassment by the police. A councilman from Yunlin, Su Tung-chi, was arrested and sentenced to jail for "plotting rebellious acts against the government," after which his wife and a mainlander friend who defended the couple in print were also arrested and imprisoned incommunicado. The Su incident was part of the continuing suppression of those affiliated with the China Democratic Party movement of 1960. It is hardly to be wondered that so few Formosan politicians reveal themselves as open opponents.

Based on all available observations, including those of local politicians themselves, my estimate is that about 10 per cent of elected Taiwan officials are "passive opponents," including many ostensibly loyal to the KMT. Another 20 to 30 per cent are "insincere collaborators" on the surface, but beneath it are close personal and ideological friends of the opponents. About 50 per cent avoid any dangerous talk or action, and in a crisis would probably side with whatever faction seemed ahead. This leaves between 10 and 20 per cent who are either genuine collaborators or "half-mountaineers," on whom the mainlander elite can rely.

The Totally Alienated. Some local intellectuals, businessmen, and professionals would never accept government office under the Nationalist regime or work with even liberal mainlanders toward reform. They disparage any Formosan who holds office or believes that collaboration is desirable, and usually refuse to speak Mandarin. Yet many of this relatively small group are qualified to hold public office and should be included as members of the potential elite. They may also be classified among the most politically conscious of the general public. As observers of Formosan society know, a few of these men can be found in any community; it is they who are sought out by foreign embassies when visiting dignitaries ask to meet "native spokesmen." Often, I found that office-holders would know of my having talked with a Mr. X previously and would say "Ah, yes, you can believe him because he is a private citizen. We in government would tell you the same things if we could. Believe what Mr. X says, because he would be a high official if we had our own government."

It is difficult to estimate the number of such people, but somewhere between 500 and 2,000 probably fall into this category. Some, survivors of the 1947 massacre still in hiding on the island, are impossible to locate. Most, however, are business and professional people between 40 and 70 years old. The regime would discount their opinions as embittered by personal experience and narrow vision; but the few I met were better informed than the KMT officials who disparaged them or sometimes denied their existence.

The alienated usually were educated in Japanese universities and held high social or economic status before World War II. Some, however, did not participate in the 1947 revolt and are unknown to the refugee groups abroad today. Most have close friends now serving in the provincial and local governments. In every city I visited, I encountered similar persons who spoke with bitter contempt of the mainlander regime. They expressed the most extreme criticism of Nationalist economic policies, from land reform to social security, and ridiculed the 1962 defense surtax as simply another extortion to pad the payrolls of mainlander officials.

A lawyer and his son gave details of legal corruption whereby money can buy release from any but political prisons. "The judges are all politically controlled, so prisoners expect no justice and avoid the courts. Taipei may say that our economic level is higher than before, but democracy has not progressed." A trained economist, reduced to a shabby-genteel existence in his large mansion, spoke at length of the bad unemployment problem in the island. "No matter how hard we work, we cannot advance far because of the heavy taxes, the Chinese system of squeeze which was unknown in Japanese times, and the ever-expanding population," he explained.

One former landlord felt that "the security police are the main problem because they control everything. Many mainlander officials have good ideas, but the leaders suppress them." One of his friends, who often briefed foreign diplomats, did not anticipate any lessening of Washington's support for the Nationalist regime: "We must look to our own domestic force and not dream of American or Japanese aid to free us from this tyranny." A few of the outsider elite group estimated the number of reliably patriotic Formosan office-holders from 1 to 20 per cent, but none would accept office himself or advise others to do so.

The lawyer spoke most harshly of American complicity in the Formosan tragedy: "If Washington did not supply the regime with so much aid, the Nationalists could not arm our sons for the hopeless mainland recovery project. And the failure of the United States to exert pressure in the realm of civil liberties, free elections, and release of political prisoners is even less understandable to us. Your government sends its troops to fight for Vietnamese freedom and forces Saigon to draft a constitution providing for popular presidential elections even in wartime. Why doesn't it also ask this regime to give us the same rights?"

Few of these extreme Formosans were aware of overseas refugee movements, although some in Taipei did receive copies of Formosan independence journals smuggled into the island. The defection in 1965 of Dr. Thomas Liao, erstwhile chief of the Formosan Provisional Government in Tokyo, stunned many of them although they held him in low esteem: "Even if he couldn't succeed after thirteen years in Japan, why did he sell out to the regime? We, too, lost much money and had relatives imprisoned, but we did not surrender. Now he mouths Nationalist propaganda and is nothing better than a 'half-mountain' puppet." Between 1961 and 1964 I had often quoted Liao's views to persons inside Formosa. "He came from a millionaire family, and that type lacks courage in the pinch," was the opinion of several university students who belonged to an underground association. The youths appeared to regard their fathers, often apolitical businessmen, as "men who always criticize with their mouths, but never *do* anything!" They seemed to take the same view of those I have called "passive opponents," partly because any collaboration or boring from within struck them as naïve at best and traitorous at worst.

Before ending this description of various types of Formosan elite, it is appropriate to mention again the high calibre of political, professional and managerial talent possessed by thousands of Formosans in and out of public office. Well-endowed talents for a future Taiwan could chiefly be observed outside government service, especially in the professions of teaching, medicine, law, banking, and business management. Let no one assume, however, that Formosans lack competence to govern themselves if the opportunity should ever arise.

Needless to say, the top-heavy Nationalist bureaucracy allows Formosans only secondary positions (and a few honorary ones at the top); and Nationalist spokesmen, as well as a few American officials, claim: "These natives haven't the experience or capacity to fill the policy-making posts in the island. The Japanese didn't educate them for politics or higher management, and they need more time to develop." But "if the emerging African nations can provide their own leadership, don't you think we can?" a prominent Formosan asked an American newsman. "The Nationalists know that if they did permit equality of [political] opportunity it would mean their eventual doom, since we are the vast majority." [35]

Prior to Thomas Liao's defection to the Nationalists, he had spent several hours with me defending the capacity of the natives to fill every post now held by mainlanders in Formosa. He even listed the men he would place in his cabinet, and praised the ability of men now in private life to assume public office: "Your own American government brings many executives from General Motors, Ford, and other corporations to Washington, and we also think business is a good training ground for public administration. Professors and university administrators also make fine government advisors if placed correctly, and both the Japanese and Chinese allowed our local leaders to get substantial training in community affairs." The Formosans I interviewed agreed that an independent Republic of Formosa could dispense with thousands of superfluous military and civilian jobs now held by mainlander generals and bureaucrats.

Secret police agencies and spy networks would be the first to disappear, they said, while government monopolies and business interference would be reduced. "The mainlanders don't really believe we couldn't fill their positions: they only want to hold onto them for themselves because they couldn't make an honest living elsewhere," said one of the usually silent collaborators.

A Formosan elder statesman, perhaps the best-informed native on the island, told me in 1962: "The Taiwanese are not inherently incapable, though they do need more experience and training. Some of our best men are in prison; others could fill government posts if the regime only allowed them to rise. A few now in office are figuratively handcuffed, but could do a good job if freed from KMT control. Don't you think most of the postgraduate and other Formosans abroad in Japan and the United States would return if they had faith in the future of Formosa? Never believe anyone who says we lack the men to run our government, our economy, or our society—that's only propaganda, and becomes less valid every year."

Political Attitudes of the General Public

Scientific opinion surveys are so rare in Formosa that a specialist in foreign surveys at the United States Information Agency said in 1963 the USIA had never been able to arrange a Formosan survey on sensitive political topics: "We can use any question we wish in Japan, but inadequate facilities and government censorship hamper us in the Republic of China." The USIA had, however, sponsored at least two previous surveys, dealing with American aid to Taiwan (April–May 1960) and radio listenership (January 1961), each of which contained a few questions of political significance.[36]

The respondents in the 1960 survey were asked whether their general situation was better or worse than a few years before, to which 67 per cent of the mainlanders but only 43 per cent of the Taiwanese reported an improvement. Economic factors accounted for most of the felt progress, whereas fewer than one in ten mentioned political or military aspects. Twice as many of the native as mainlander critics cited the latter but both groups placed more emphasis on "livelihood" and material problems.[37]

The 1961 listenership survey revealed a lack of interest in political affairs (Table 3). Only professional persons, or persons with over 12 years'

TABLE 3

POLITICAL INTEREST ON FORMOSA 1961 [a]

A. *Percentage of Interest in Politics and Other Subjects* (based on 1000-person sample)

	Very Interested	Interested	Not Particularly Interested	Not Interested At All	Net Plurality Interested [b]
Politics & Gov't	11	23	51	15	−32
Asian Affairs	11	28	46	15	−22
World Affairs	16	31	42	11	−6
Music	54	32	11	3	72
Entertainment	50	36	9	5	72
Education	15	43	31	11	16
Medicine & Health	16	41	31	12	14
Cost of Living	19	34	32	15	6
Work Problems	13	31	51	5	−12
Development of Industry	12	28	45	15	−20
Development of Agriculture	7	20	56	17	−46

B. *Percentage Variations in Degree of Political Interest* [b] (N = persons interviewed)

	Politics & Government	Asian Affairs	World Affairs	Entertainment	Music
Taiwanese (N = 566)	−23	−17	2	84	83
Mainlanders (N = 434)	−43	−29	−14	58	59
Students (N = 143)	−73	−47	−26	89	87
Housewives (N = 169)	−93	−28	−85	50	76
Workers; Farmers (N = 141)	−60	−76	−55	69	60
Merchants (N = 238)	−55	−36	−6	62	71
Gov't Workers/Teachers (N = 226)	51	60	65	73	72
Professional Workers (N = 68)	71	79	79	74	72
Age 15–24 (N = 251)	−96	−95	−90	82	90
Age 45–54 (N = 148)	81	74	76	57	61
6–8 Years Education (N = 281)	−77	−76	−29	62	91
12 years or more Educ. (N = 269)	52	66	9	68	28

[a] Data from Radio *Listenership in Taiwan* (Taipei: USIS Office of Research and Evaluation, July 1961) as published by the Chinese Institute of Public Opinion, Taipei, December, 1964. The 1,000-person sample was drawn from a list of registered radio-owners in the five major cities.

[b] The net percentage rating is used in all USIS survey reports, in this case indicating the net percentage difference between those expressing great or some interest minus those in the other two categories.

education, or those over 45 years of age, pressed strong interest in news of politics, world, or Asian affairs. A plurality of every other group showed little or no interest in these topics, but great interest in music and entertainment. The three political categories do not receive much coverage in domestic or foreign radio programs reaching the listeners in Formosa; in my own work I had discovered either apathy or resentment toward the high propaganda content of the domestic news programs. Japan ranked first among Asian countries of interest to both mainlanders and Formosans (23 and 39 per cent, respectively), but the former group was three times more likely to mention other nations as well.

The lack of interest shown by 1961 survey respondents in political affairs as seen in Table 3, belies the claim that political consciousness in Formosa is acute. The three political categories attracted less popular interest than any other subject listed. This confirms the inverse relation of voting participation to political interest I had found in Japan.[38] President Wu Teh-yao of Tunghai University said that those between 25 and 55 were the most discontented with mainlander rule, and that the refugees were also becoming impatient with their delayed return to the mainland.[39]

Arthur Raper, in his 1953 report on rural Taiwan, mentioned the high voting rate of over 75 per cent combined with a realization that "the people's participation in elections can be most meaningful only as elected officials come to exercise an increasingly important role in the overall decisions of the government . . . [and give] larger and larger measures of self-direction to the people." [40] Raper also noted unfamiliarity with party politics in the rural areas: "Interviews with local leaders in all townships indicated the near absence of party-wise thinking, either by the electorate or by the candidates . . . Even at the prefectural level, the percentage of non-party candidates was high, and would in fact have been much higher if the non-party-minded members of the KMT had been classified in the non-party category." [41]

The British scholar E. Stuart Kirby, in his 1960 report, was more sanguine about rural political attitudes at that time: "It is striking that, in comparison with 1953, community leadership has shifted from older persons in the 60–70 age group to a younger generation in the thirties and forties . . . political life in rural Taiwan appears more lively . . . the activities in the present survey were characterized by orderly speeches, responsible utterances, objective judgments and analysis, clear statements, and increased understanding on the part of the local people of provincial, national, and even world affairs and trends." [42] Rural farmers and politicians to whom these remarks were quoted only laughed at them as typical pro-Nationalist opinion. "What else would the government allow the J.C.R.R. to publish? We agree instead with your comments and those of Mr. Raper," they said.[43]

Raper's 1954 report on urban and industrial Taiwan confirmed that "the majority of the executive posts are held by Mainlanders, whereas the majority of the assembly posts are held by Taiwanese . . . The local leaders everywhere emphasize the need for genuinely competitive elections and for a larger measure of responsibility and status for elective officials to safeguard the significance of the new franchise. More than four-fifths of the total [rural and urban husbands] voted. Some of the voting was in response to expectations of officials, and sometimes of other leaders to whom the people are beholden for one reason or another." [44]

Almost all my informants, from the highest-ranking officials to the lowliest pedicab drivers, agreed the average Formosan was either apathetic or fearful of political involvement. "They were taught by their parents for generations not to become entangled with politics," said a Formosan in the United States. "Our ancestors learned by bitter experience under the Manchus and the Japanese that political opposition does not pay. All their pathetic revolts failed miserably and we learned the same lesson in 1947. Those who were not killed were cowed into submission, while the average farmers were too busy earning a living to think of events beyond their villages."

Richard Koo, leader of one group of Japan-based political exiles, thought that "the masses don't want to kill or be killed, and therefore they can be controlled by the KMT police and military. And the old business elite wants only to protect its money." [45] The tradition of obedience to authority seems even stronger, however, among the propertied groups of urban businessmen than among their sons or the poorer workers.

One group of Taipei University students from upper-class families met regularly to discuss strategy for a democratic future. Although they could not organize nor conduct open meetings, they claimed a loose association of about 200 members in various parts of the island. In general, the educated youth from the expanding universities and overseas campus communities appear the most disenchanted of any group except the totally alienated ex-elite. Nevertheless the majority of students both at home and abroad remain afraid to express political opinions, join political clubs, or work politically against the regime.

"Yes, the Formosans are discontented and complain a lot when you have them alone, but they won't do anything violent," concluded an American scholar of long residence in central Formosa. Yet occasionally I came across an exceptionally vocal critic—on the streets, or in a shop after closing time, or on the docks of a port city—who had not received a higher education under Japanese rule or suffered postwar loss of social or economic status. "Did the students in Budapest come from capitalist families, or have to be taught to hate the Russians?" asked the wife of a Hualien shopkeeper. "I was only a girl when the troops came through in 1947 to bayonet women and children on the riverbank, but I have seen enough of the pigs' rule with my own eyes to hate them."

Further evidence of popular sentiment is the heavy vote for known opponents of the regime in local elections. "The island is too small to permit effective underground organization," said a shopkeeper in Kaohsiung. "On the mainland, opponents could always hole up in the mountains far from the cities, and the same is true of Vietnam and other places today, but Formosa is too small and well-patrolled for that." While I am positive that underground political organizations exist, I do not know of any which is large or effective.

Despite the absence of violent domestic challenges to the Nationalist regime, rank-and-file Formosans have taken many risks to assure visiting diplomats and scholars of their political discontent.[46] Although, as previously noted in other connections, the regime professes to welcome social and economic criticism, outright political dissent is often suppressed with such vigor as to attest to the bravery of the dissenters.

The Methods of Nationalist Political Suppression

Formosa has remained under limited martial law almost continuously since 1945, thereby facilitating political controls in the name of wartime security. Goddard is probably typical of apologists for the regime, defending such controls as a necessity to prevent Communist infiltration, while insisting that "the people enjoy freedom: personal, political, and religious . . . Formosa is the one section of Asia that enjoys internal peace . . ."[47] Jacoby has credited most of Formosa's economic progress to its stable government: "[AID] underwrote the stable political framework for economic progress provided by an authoritarian government, and let political reforms come later."[48] Suffice it to note here that few Formosans interviewed agree with either of these statements.

The Nationalists pride themselves on encouraging "constructive" criticism, especially of officials suspected of graft and corruption. "Free China is plagued by five political ills: graft, waste, nepotism, violation of law, and dereliction of duty," said a leading KMT member of the Control Yuan in 1961, citing as one cause the failure to insist on retirement of old officials; a mainlander colleague condemned "encouragement of corruption from the powerful and the influential." [49] The press reports cases of administrative malfeasance, and often urges a governmental housecleaning. "Both leaders and molders of public opinion usually respond with pretty lectures about spiritual integrity," complained the *China News* in 1964; but Nationalist courts did convict fourteen high officials in early 1967.[50]

Several of those bribery and corruption cases were popularly regarded as politically motivated. A procurator of the Taipei District Court, for example, who had once accused the Taiwan Garrison Command of using torture, was sentenced to six years for accepting a bribe.[51] (Anyone heard criticizing the powerful security command is liable to punishment, usually, if he is an official, on a charge of graft—a trumped-up one if need be—or on political grounds if he is a private citizen.) Taipei Mayor Henry Kao's younger brother, Provincial Assemblyman Yang Yu-cheng, was arrested with several others on December 11, 1965 and charged with having misappropriated $74,000 in Taipei city funds intended for the purchase of gravel. In 1966 he was sentenced to eight years in prison, but few of my informants believed him guilty.[52] "Yang is a scapegoat for others and a hostage for the good behavior of Mayor Kao," said an Okinawan political leader.

The use of bribery charges for political suppression of dissident mainlander or Formosan officials is a favorite practice of the regime, partly because corruption is easy to prove when one controls all the evidence and partly because many will assume it is a traditional Chinese offense unrelated to political crimes. "Who can disprove charges after the government has managed the evidence and the witnesses?" asked an overseas Formosan student. "They can't reveal the real reasons, and many officials *are* guilty of corruption, so people believe the false accusations." Whether or not individual suspects are actually guilty of the charges, many Formosans assume there is a political motive behind the arrest of local officials. The latter live in constant fear of finding themselves or a close relative threatened with arrest for "corruption."

"The Nationalists can use many euphemisms when they want to suppress a troublesome official, whereas they can simply whisk an ordinary

person off to prison without trial or publicity," explained one lawyer
with long experience handling such cases. "The fact that many of our
politicians, the poor type, use their offices for personal gain endangers
the honest ones who are politically offensive to the regime." Past mayors
of Kaohsiung, Taichung, and several smaller cities were charged with
graft. Known anti-mainlanders, as has been noted, are not normally appointed to government posts, and are rarely permitted to seek elective office.

Martial law places heavy communication and travel restrictions on
both Formosan and foreigners. Censorship of mail, and the prohibition
of most Japanese books and magazines with political content despite the
widespread pirating of other foreign books in Formosa were cited in
Chapter 3. Every book leaving the island is subject to police scrutiny,
and letters to or from those on the security checklist are carefully
watched. Some Formosans said they were interrogated by the police after
receiving mail from foreigners. When, in 1965, the Taiwan Garrison
Command objected on security grounds to allowing nationals of friendly
states to enter for 72 hours without a visa, the practice was rescinded.
Even in 1962, the American travel editor Horace Sutton objected to
entry procedures: "It took me only some 50 minutes by jet from Hong
Kong to Taipei, but I spent nearly an hour's time at the airport check-
point. The complicated procedures and lack of politeness are seldom
seen elsewhere . . . How could you treat every tourist as an intelligence
agent?" [53]

According to an American student arrested at Taipei airport in 1967
for carrying a Formosan friend's letter to be mailed in Hong Kong:
"They took me back to Taipei where I was interrogated by six men, the
highest-ranking an army general. They read all my correspondence,
notes, and addresses, but refused to let me phone the American Embassy. 'China is a sovereign country with full investigative powers, and
it's illegal to carry a letter for posting abroad,' the general told me." [54]
Other foreigners have been detained at the airport or Keelung harbor
while their baggage was searched for such contraband as transistor radios,
tape recorders, publications from or about Communist China, or issues
of any work critical of Chiang Kai-shek. Formosan businessmen described minutely detailed inspections "designed more to find forbidden
writings than illegal monies." Thomas Liao, when still president of the
provisional Republic of Formosa in Tokyo, spoke of keeping their newspaper small "so it can be carried back to Taiwan in people's shoes." [55]
The American Embassy in Taipei maintained a private library where

visiting Fulbright scholars could read such books as A *Nation of Sheep* by William Lederer, banned from entry or pirating in Taiwan. Slips in Taiwan's censorship occasionally occur because the Nationalist censors cannot read every page of an English book, as I discovered when Andrew Tully's book on the CIA appeared in the local pirate-edition bookstores before the police discovered its chapter on CIA operations in Quemoy.[56] Formosan residents with American diplomatic or military friends could sometimes obtain clandestine copies of forbidden books and magazines. "The *Taiwan Chinglian* [organ of the United Young Formosans for Independence in Tokyo] is a very hot item here," said a Formosan employee of the United States government in Taipei, "and we value it highly for news not printed in the local newspapers."

The Nationalists deny the existence of prior censorship or post-publication penalties for objectionable matter, but objective sources recognize the heavy control exercised by the security forces and the official Central News Agency. "In the spring of 1956," says John Israel, "the Peace Preservation Command threatened the English-language *China Post* for reporting a conciliatory statement from Chou En-lai to Nationalist officials. In December 1957, a [Chinese-language journal's] chief editorial writer was arrested on charges of failing to register his past Communist affiliations." [57] A graduate of one of the large universities in Taipei who went abroad to study journalism said of the Taiwan press: "It was never free under either Japanese or Nationalist rule, and it does not print facts about political arrests or secret suppression of political rights." Several journals, including *Time and Tide* (unrelated to its English namesake), the *Kung Lun Pao*, and the *Free China Fortnightly*, have suffered temporary or permanent suspension for political reasons, while others have been denied a license to begin publication. In some instances, notably Li Wan-chu's *Kung Lun Pao* in 1961, the regime has replaced the offending publisher or editor with more amenable executives. A satirical literary magazine, the *Jen Chien Shih*, was suspended for its treatment of President Chiang, and the regime forbade the convening in Taipei of the Second Asian Press Conference in 1963 because Foreign Minister Shen Chang-huan feared "controversial political statements by delegates from countries such as India and Indonesia." [58]

Probably the most famous denial of Formosan press freedom was the 1960 suppression of Lei Chen's *Free China Fortnightly* (often shortened to *Free China*) as a result of its publisher's arrest on sedition charges. *Free China* had been the bravest opposition journal from November 1949 until September 1960. It had repeatedly criticized the KMT for perpetuating one-party rule under the guise of democracy and for suppressing political opposition on the ground that unity is needed for mainland recovery.[59] The venerable Dr. Hu Shih was the original publisher of the journal, with Lei Chen—a liberal mainlander and former KMT official—as editor; but Hu later retired to the security of the Academia Sinica (the major government-supported research institute in Formosa) and seldom defended the more outspoken Lei Chen. Under Lei, *Free China* published cynical commentaries on the counterattack, military interference in civilian politics, and nepotism in the highest levels of government, and urged cooperation by liberal mainlanders and Formosans to promote democracy. The late Vice President Chen Cheng lent cautious support to *Free China*'s call for a genuine opposition party "that would follow the American example." [60]

It was Lei Chen's role as leader of the China Democratic Party movement whose proponents were mostly Formosan politicians like Henry Kao, Wu San-lien, Li Wan-chu, and Kuo Wu-hsin, that provoked the regime to drastic countermeasures. The Formosan leaders had petitioned the government unsuccessfully in 1958 for permission to organize a "Chinese Local Autonomy Research Institute" to promote fair election practices. After five months, permission was denied on the ground that similar organizations already existed, but the group changed its name to "Democratic Self-Government Study Group" and applied again. "This time," says a Japanese account, "warnings came from the Taiwan Garrison Command and, simultaneously, a list of the founding members was published in the press . . . along with an alleged confession from a Communist agent sent from the mainland to contact those advocating democratic freedoms. . . . This caused the newly proposed group to disintegrate, fearing they might be suspected of sympathy for 'Communist bandits'. . . . It appears that the real reason for the government's rejection was its fear such an organization might become the nucleus of a powerful native opposition party against the KMT." [61]

In May 1960, just after the local spring elections, Lei Chen joined the Formosan liberals, and others who had recently petitioned the government for an electoral reform, to prepare a new political organization. Evidently they were all spurred by irregularities in the April election, such as forced withdrawal of non-KMT candidates; electioneering for KMT candidates by security police, army troops and civil servants; and intimidation at the polling places. A Japanese reporter later wrote: "Chinese members of the *Free China* group, led by Lei Chen, wanted to form an opposition party to legitimize the Republic of China, while the

Taiwanese . . . desired the new party to insure fair election practices and to win political liberty for the Taiwanese. Both, however, shared opposition to . . . the despotism of the KMT and its heavy financial support by the government, and demanded (1) expansion of freedoms, especially for Taiwanese, (2) reduction of military spending, and (3) cessation of military attacks on the mainland." [62]

Lei was arrested on September 4, 1960 and given a one-day military court trial on sedition charges centering around his alleged failure to report an ex-Communist on the magazine staff. He received a ten-year prison sentence, while other mainlander associates were given terms of varying lengths, and both the *Free China* journal and the nascent China Democratic Party were suppressed. Despite pleas for clemency or pardon from eminent foreigners and brave liberals in the island, the regime refused to free the editor and cracked down on many who rose to his defense. Mrs. Lei even found it difficult to hire a lawyer to defend her husband because so many feared retribution against themselves or their children.[63] In April 1963, after publication of an interview with her husband, including a sad poem written in his cell, Mrs. Lei was denied visitation rights for five months and the magazine involved, *Time and Tide*, was suspended for one year.

Li Wan-chu and other Formosans connected with the abortive new party movement suffered either business or personal punishment. Su Tung-chi, who had persuaded his Yunlin assembly to pass a resolution asking President Chiang to pardon Lei, was sent to prison on sedition charges in 1962, and was later reported either to have been killed or to be undergoing "thought reform." Councilman Su's wife was arrested for pleading her husband's case, and a mainlander who protested these developments by writing, in *Democratic China*, that "the people will not forever stand idly by and tolerate such unconstitutional practices," was also spirited away to a political reform camp.[64]

During my Fulbright year in Formosa, I asked both mainlanders and Formosans about the Lei Chen case as an example of political suppression. Many Tunghai University faculty had joined mainlander colleagues on other campuses to ask for Lei's release. At a private carol sing at Tunghai on Christmas Eve, 1961, I whispered, between songs, to university president Wu: "It doesn't seem appropriate to sing Christmas carols knowing that Lei and so many others are sitting in jail." Wu replied: "Oh, don't worry, he's not really in prison, but more under house arrest in a special place." Others contradicted this optimistic rumor, but few would discuss the case. "Whenever the Garrison Command makes an arrest, the victims' friends begin claiming they never knew him, while others fear to be connected with anyone charged with a political offense," said the director of the local United States Foreign Language School.

After the April 1963 local elections, one Sung Lin-k'ang was denied victory in a Taipei city contest when the election office reversed the results as announced by the press, radio, and even on the police radio station, five hours before. Sung's appeal was denied by the court, but mobs turned out in his district of the city when he held an appreciation parade. Mancall states: "Sung's case is simply one example of how the regime can manipulate voting procedures, and judicial appeals, to ensure the defeat of candidates it feels would be in opposition to its policies." [65]

The most famous sedition case against a Formosan was the arrest in September 1964 of Professor Peng Ming-min and two of his former students. Peng, former chairman of the Department of Political Science at National Taiwan University [NTU], was born in Kaohsiung in 1923 and received undergraduate training at Tokyo Imperial University during World War II (when he lost his left hand in the Nagasaki atomic bombing), and later at NTU. After obtaining a master's degree in law at McGill University, he received a doctorate from the University of Paris, and later held posts as a visiting professor at both Tunghai and Harvard while rising to the chairmanship of his department at NTU. An authority on international law, Peng was invited to advise the Chinese United Nations delegation at the 1961 Assembly session and, in a 1963 contest sponsored by the Nationalists, was named one of the ten most prominent young men in the island. Many of Professor Peng's former students spoke of his excellent scholarship and warm devotion to fellow-Formosans. "It was unusual for any native professor to rise so high in Taiwan's biggest university, especially in the law faculty where even more surprisingly, the regime gave Peng several high advisory duties and seemed to trust him as a loyal collaborator." [66]

Peng and his two former students were arrested September 20, 1964, after engaging a local printer to make 10,000 copies of "examination papers" which the printers discovered to be political tracts urging Formosans to unite against the regime. The printers informed the police, who arrested the three men in a hotel rendezvous, seizing the manuscript and all but 300 of the copies. The Taiwan Garrison Command, which handles all security cases, announced the arrests on October 23, but delayed the indictment until January 21, 1965. The contents of the leaflet were never made public by the authorities, but copies were smuggled out of the island, verified by the author's contacts, and published in English by overseas Formosan organizations.[67] The indictment specified only that the three wrote a pamphlet urging violent overthrow of the constituted government.

Between the arrests and the perfunctory one-day trial on March 27, 1965, the prisoners were constantly interrogated. "Mrs. Peng was allowed to see Dr. Peng three days after he was arrested. She was horrified to find her husband's appearance completely changed. You can imagine what kind of treatment he had received." [68] American professors in the island said at first they could not believe Professor Peng would be foolhardy enough to publish a rebellious manifesto for distribution. "Even if they had picked a more secure printing shop, how could they expect to circulate the copies without being discovered?" asked one long-term resident. "Yet we finally were convinced he and his ex-students were guilty as charged."

On April 2, 1965, the military court sentenced Peng to eight years, and his fellow-defendants, Hsieh Tsung-min (then 32) and Wei Ting-chao (age 29) to ten and eight years, respectively. They could have been sentenced to death, but the court "took cognizance of their repentance and full cooperation with investigators and decided to reduce the punishment." Officers in the U.S. State Department reported one year later that mail protesting Peng's conviction was still coming in daily. The international publicity on both the Lei and Peng cases undoubtedly moderated the regime's attitude, and on November 3, 1965, President Chiang Kai-shek announced he had pardoned Professor Peng. The sentences of Tsieh and Wei were cut in half in 1966.[69] According to the Chinese News Service, "Peng attributed his wrong-doings to his misunderstanding of the current situation and his negligence of responsibility . . . 'I am deeply ashamed of myself for what I have done . . . Everybody should do his share of work in the sacred task of national recovery by uniting closely and giving up egotism . . . I will dedicate myself to my country and people in the days to come . . .' " [70] The regime's success in luring back Thomas Liao from Tokyo earlier in 1965, and Liao's advice to his new masters, may have encouraged the leniency toward Professor Peng. However, the regime thereafter tightened its surveillance of overseas students, entry of foreign nationals, and control of domestic dissidents.

Hsieh Shu-chia, brother of one of the defendants in the Peng case, drafted a petition in his brother's defense in April 1965, which was allegedly approved by all NTU Law School graduate students and many undergraduates. "The brother was then arrested and tortured without trial," according to a well-informed Formosan who received a copy of the petition smuggled out of the island in late 1966. The petition tried to refute Nationalist charges of "stirring up mass sentiment" by arguing that in a democratic country one should be able to criticize the constitution and national policies, and that incitement to "bloodshed" could not be illegal since it was praised during Sun Yat-sen's 1911 revolution.

The Nationalist regime found itself accused by the Provincial Assembly in 1966 of railroading people to secret jails without warrant, trial, or legislative approval. The Assembly approved a resolution urging court trials for alleged "rascals," "hoodlums," and "vagabonds," the regime's euphemisms for political troublemakers.[71] According to a Hong Kong report at that time, over 10,000 political prisoners were awaiting trial and there were an estimated 30,000 secret police in 5,000 "guard areas" to watch every Formosan household.[72] Facts on the suppression of political dissidents are naturally difficult to obtain except from ex-prisoners and occasional government releases. For example, the Provincial Police Commissioner reported the arrest of 1,345 "rascals" in the first ten months of 1964, while his superiors in the Justice Ministry listed 203 "security cases solved in recent years," 27 in the latter half of 1965.[73] "I think there are always many such incidents inside Taiwan," commented a veteran of the army political division, "but they are not known to outsiders because newspapers and radios are tightly controlled by the ruling party."

Martial law forbids public assembly of more than seven persons without police permission, as I learned in 1962 while investigating the abrupt police removal of food stalls from the Hualien dock area. The day after observing the police tearing down the stalls, I returned to question the hawkers and their stevedore patrons, who were obviously annoyed by the action. "We'd been paying off the police chief to operate illegal stalls," explained one hawker, "but the new chief wants more money than we could afford, so he ordered us out." A crowd of dock workers gathered around as they overheard our Japanese conversation about political corruption, but, after a few minutes a voice from the rear shouted "Let's break this up! The police won't like so many of us talking in the open."

Formosans returning from study overseas are watched for political subversion and occasionally penalized for innocent association with fellow-Formosans abroad. When a Formosan who was a University of Wisconsin doctoral candidate, Hwang Chii-ming, tried to return to the island briefly in 1966 to gather thesis data under a U.S. Office of Education grant, he was arrested, detained from early September until his military trial in February 1967, and on February 28 (an ironic date) sentenced to five years in prison for allegedly attending Formosan student meetings in the United States.[74] The American Embassy refused assistance, but the president of the University of Wisconsin lodged a strong protest. A retrial in May 1967 brought Hwang a reduction of sentence and parole by July 4, but denied him permission to leave Formosa.

Many veterans of the Nationalist political prisons related their experiences to me while I was in Formosa, and in secret correspondence thereafter. "It is customary to deny bail and keep the arrested person at least four months before trial, with no publicity and few visitors allowed. Then they try to secure a confession by promising good treatment or, if necessary, by threatening arrest of the prisoner's relatives. Finally, mental and physical torture, such as electric shock, pulling out fingernails, pouring peppered gasoline down the nose, and less delicate methods may be used. Only later, after the indictment, can he seek a lawyer, but he may not write or receive letters." Another ex-political prisoner spoke of the practice of mixing all types of criminals in the same detention cell, often including a stool-pigeon to report conversations. "TB patients and other sick people were kept in my cell, and the food was unimaginably poor except the few days before trial or release." A source qualified to know estimated that over 30,000 local leaders, intellectuals, and students were arrested after the bloodbath of 1947, of whom two-thirds vanished without trials. "Between 1949 and 1955, over 90,000 anti-Nationalist elements, by no means all Communists, were arrested and more than half of them summarily executed . . . A man who spent six months in 1965 in one of the military prisons witnessed 8 executions and 90 newcomers; another witnessed 11 executions and 126 new inmates during his nine months' detention in 1964. If these figures, as well as the number of military prisons, are used as a basis for calculation, it would mean about 200 executions and 1,500 arrests of political offenders annually." [75]

Green Island, a small islet of 1,000 people off Taitung on the southeastern coast, is popularly regarded as a major center for political punishment and "thought reform." Formosans always refer to it fearfully, and those in Taitung confirmed its reputation. In 1963, a group of students spent five days on the island, their return trip delayed by the innkeeper whom they suspected of having both financial and spying incentives. Two officers visited them, but refused to allow them any contact with prisoners. The uncle of one of the students, a man who had spent several years on the island for his involvement in the 1947 incident, said the prisoners were classified as either mainland Communists or Formosans engaged in anti-government activities: "Before they were sent to the island, from which only one person has been known to escape, they had been tortured in the prison near Taipei, so their torture on the island seemed no worse to them than their earlier experience." According to one of the students, "Gangsters are imprisoned on another island south of Green Island because Chiang is afraid they are a source of support for anti-KMT politicians, as he himself had relied on Shanghai gangs in his youth. There is much truth to his fear, and gangsters sent to the island usually suffer great physical torture.

Once I was guided to a "political reform" camp near Taitung, but not allowed to speak to any prisoners. "It would be useless for you to take the rough trip over to Green Island," said the guide, "because they're even stricter with foreign visitors there than on Formosa. Moreover, important political offenders are kept in Taipei." Others confirmed the methods of torture used during interrogation, but warned me never to mention their names.

Under these conditions, one can understand why able Formosan youths seek to escape abroad, while those on the island speak cynically of "the myth of Chinese Nationalist democracy."

6

FORMOSAN DEFENSE OR MAINLAND RECOVERY?

The major objective of the Chinese Nationalist regime since its flight to Formosa has been to mount a counterattack against the Communists and recapture the mainland. Anyone on Formosa who questions this policy is accused of defeatism or Communist sympathies and is subject to punishment as a traitor. No debate on the policy is permitted under Nationalist martial law, and devoted sacrifices for the counterattack are considered the duty of every citizen. The schools, the armed forces, and the mass media try to imbue the Formosan majority with sacrificial fervor and officials of the Chiang regime make frequent exhortations to prepare for "liberation" of their 700 million compatriots on the mainland.

Between 1966 and 1968, economic and political disruptions on the Communist-ruled mainland renewed Nationalist hopes. "Suppose that the Nationalists are invited back . . ." asked Joseph C. Harsch in mid-1967. "This may not be as absurd as it first sounds. The Chinese Nationalists on Formosa are not inactive. They are not isolated from the mainland. If they ever had a chance to find their way home someday, now is the moment." [1] The Gimo himself said in 1966 that opposition to the Red Guard and the cultural revolution were "what we have expected . . . [inspired partly] by free China's efforts in the past seventeen years." [2] Much earlier, in 1951, Professor Russell Fifield had warned that the possibility of the Nationalists' return to the mainland, if Peking alienated enough of its army and peasantry, should never be discounted. By 1968, civil strife in mainland China seemed to indicate such an alienation; yet the collapse of the Maoists and the return of the Nationalists cannot be so easily equated. As a young Chinese Communist diplomat wrote after his defection from his post in Central Africa to the United States in 1964: "The younger Chinese don't know anything about Chiang, and the older ones ones think he is an American puppet." [3]

The close relation between the goal of mainland recovery and the maintenance of martial law and military preparedness on Formosa was analyzed by Professor Peng in his manifesto of September 1964: "Why then is Chiang Kai-shek so persistent in demanding the 'Return'. . . . For fifteen years [he has used this empty slogan] . . . justified the enforcement of martial law and held 12 million people under tight military control. . . . It is the only means by which he prolongs his political power and enslaves the people." [4] The attitude of Formosans to the mainland-recovery goal is related to the Nationalists' heavy defense spending, military conscription, and neglect of civilian needs. The *China News* commented on the air-raid shelters required in every new home: "House owners have been complaining that from three to five per cent of the total construction cost have to be spent on the dugouts that are utterly useless . . . To believe in the effectiveness of such protection against a possible air raid is sheer ridicule [sic]." [5] The lavish expenditure on military clubs and hostels for Nationalist officers provoked an earlier accusation in the same paper that they were "actually commercialized establishments . . . [but] do not pay taxes . . . The public is worried by the spending spree of some of the quasi-military agencies . . . when the whole nation is dedicated to one single sacred task of mainland recovery." [6] Every press criticism of preparedness is couched in patriotic terms, but such public objections to military tax exemptions, price discounts, and immunity from many civil laws are frequent and can be taken to indicate resentment against the special privileges of the military class.

The actual size of both the Nationalist military forces and their budget is secret, but can be gauged by data provided me by American, Japanese, and other close observers. It is estimated that the United States has contributed over $3 billion in military hardware and defense support for the Nationalists since 1951.

This chapter discusses, first, the nature of the Nationalist military position, especially the morale of the native troops who constitute over 80 per cent of the enlisted men and perhaps one-fifth of the company-grade officers. The contradictory illusions of many Americans that, on the one hand, the "Nationalist troops are too old to fight" or, on the other, that "Chiang's forces could easily defeat the Communists in China and Vietnam if given American material help" will be viewed here primarily through Formosan eyes. The second part of the chapter concerns the offshore islands of Quemoy and Matsu as bases for the counterattack.

Nationalist military plans include defense of Formosa and the offshore islands, as well as eventual return to the mainland—preferably, Nationalist spokesmen say, without the use of force. When Taipei established a National Security Council in 1967 to plan strategy for mainland recovery, the Nationalist Ambassador to the United States Chow Shu-kai declared on an American television program that "mainland recovery is basically a political operation which may not involve large-scale military operations." [7] His statement re-emphasized claims by the Nationalists that revulsion against Communist misrule would eventually cause the 700 million mainlanders to welcome them back without the necessity of firing a shot. The idea of a peaceful return to the mainland also coincided with United States desires to avoid open conflict with Peking or Moscow on the China issue.

On the issues of Formosan defense and mainland recovery, the Nationalists have been ambivalent, apparently aware that only the problem of defense interests most Formosans. "There is no discernible Taiwanese eagerness to get to the mainland, much less to fight to go there, as many mainlanders still ritually profess to want to do," wrote Tillman Durdin in *The New York Times* in mid-1967.[8] "Most mainlanders want to go back [but] . . . most Taiwanese . . . only wish to be left alone. The natives are not interested in the 'liberation' projects of either the Communists or the Nationalists," a ranking Japanese diplomat had stated ten years earlier.[9]

Reactions to Military Preparedness

The Nationalist military forces are today far better trained and equipped than the motley assortment of illiterate and discouraged troops who arrived from the mainland in 1949. "We couldn't believe our eyes when we saw such slovenly troops," reported witnesses to the arrival of the defeated soldiers. "Many didn't even have shoes and began stealing our watches, as their predecessors had in 1945." [10] By 1954, over half of the 500,000 mainlander troops had been retired; those mainlanders left were mostly veteran non-commissioned officers and higher field and general rank personnel, who continue to form over 80 per cent of the Nationalist officer corps. Since 1954 a tighter military service law has been in effect requiring all youths to serve two years active duty and then stay in the

reserve until age forty-five. By 1963, the director of State Department research on Asia estimated that over 80 per cent of the enlisted men and
perhaps 10 per cent of lower-rank officers were Taiwanese, reflecting the
impact of conscription and compulsory ROTC for college males. The
Nationalist army, navy, and air force were no longer composed of aging
men who had come over from the mainland: young natives and sons of
refugee families began to replace them.

Because the regime publishes no statistics on its armed forces or their
equipment, it has been necessary to rely on various experts for the following estimates, which are remarkably consistent. Twelve different
sources, for example, estimated between 1959 and 1965 that the total
Nationalist armed forces were between 550,000 and 600,000.[11] They require at least 85 per cent of the national government budget, despite the
$3 billion or more in United States military subsidies (mainly weapons)
from 1950 to 1968. In fact, the United States has given Nationalist
China about twice as much money in military aid as for economic assistance, and the former continued after the latter tapered off in mid-1965.
A U.S. Military Aid and Advisory Group (MAAG-China) began operating in Taiwan in 1951 and has trained the Nationalist forces in the use
of American weapons, including Nike-Hercules missiles and jet fighters
with Sidewinder missiles, as well as defensive air and naval hardware.
The adequacy of the United States nuclear striking forces in Okinawa
and the Seventh Fleet is cited to Nationalist officers to explain why they
are not given atomic weapons. "But no matter what we tell them, every
year they keep asking for more and more; they're never satisfied," said an
American colonel after two years' service on a Sino-American planning
committee.[12] Most U.S. officers, however, whether in MAAG [Military
Aid and Advisory Group] or at the several American supply, communications, and air bases, are loyal to the Sino-American security treaty of
1954. "MAAG people won't tell us much of their operations," said an
American member of AID in 1962, "and they associate mostly with their
opposite numbers in the Chinese forces."

The Nationalist army is the largest of the regime's three military services and takes the bulk of Taiwanese conscripts and ROTC officers.
"The Army has a highly mobile force of 400,000 men, of whom about
100,000 live in perpetual underground existence barely a mile and a half
off the China mainland, on Quemoy and Matsu islands. They have
American-supplied medium tanks and Nike-Hercules missiles," wrote an
American correspondent in late 1965.[13] A reliable Japanese source noted
the increasing mobility of the Nationalist army as early as 1953, and the

Japanese Defense Agency estimated that it had 21 infantry, 1 paratroop, and 2 armored divisions in 1961, as well as a missile battalion and the ubiquitous Taiwan Garrison Command to handle subversion.[14] Each year about 200,000 conscripts, mainly Taiwanese, receive two years training (or three in the navy and air force).

The Navy has over 60,000 men, including 25,000 Marines, and about 200 small vessels totalling 140,000 tons. Nationalist naval power, like that of the Chinese Communists, is relatively weak. Japan, for comparison, easily matches Nationalist naval power but has only one-third its ground forces.[15] The hundreds of Nationalist frogmen who paraded in the 1961 Double-Ten celebration are based on the offshore islands to engage in special intelligence and sabotage. The island of Formosa is not well-endowed with natural harbors, but the Japanese developed naval bases near Kaohsiung and at Makung in the Pescadores islands which the Chinese and their American allies have expanded.

The Nationalist Air Force is the pride of the cooperating Sino-American military officers, partly owing to the success of U-2 flights manned by Nationalist pilots to gather intelligence over the mainland, and partly because of the good showing made by Nationalist jets in their dogfights during the 1958 Quemoy crisis. According to a journalist's 1965 estimate, "The Air Force counts some 80,000 men, including several thousand highly-trained pilots who are currently phasing out the F104G fighters . . . replacing them with the F5A, the supersonic jet answer to the Communist MIG-21." [16] The Nationalists possess over 600 planes, but no bombers: they work in close cooperation, however, with the American air forces stationed in Okinawa and Taiwan. United States military forces on Taiwan are mostly Air Force personnel.

Nationalist success in deterring Communist attacks on Quemoy has been attributed to U.S.-supplied Sidewinder missiles aboard Nationalist jet fighters, while Moscow was unwilling or unable to give Peking comparable equipment. Communist Chinese resentment against lack of Soviet support, and corresponding Russian fears of a Quemoy engagement leading to a larger conflict with the United States, played an important role in deepening the Sino-Soviet rift. At the same time, the performance of Nationalist planes in 1958 calmed those Americans who had feared the implications of President Eisenhower's 1955 "Offshore Islands Resolution." [17]

One of my former students at the University of California who later served as a jet pilot in Formosa, told of many secret reconnaissance missions over the mainland by Nationalist and United States planes. The rapid development of satellite and space photography has reduced the need for lower-level overflights, but an American correspondent later wrote: "Chinese pilots have reportedly contributed to Washington's advance knowledge of Peking's atomic developments. These pilots have instructions to destroy their planes, equipment, and themselves in the event of emergency. The Taipei Government claims that these instructions have been obeyed." [18]

Soldiers are visible on the streets of every major city, especially Taipei, headquarters for the Chinese and American commands and a majority of their personnel. Every railway station has military police stationed on the platforms, and passengers on domestic airlines must show identification cards or passports to security guards at the gate. All mainlander officers encountered on military bases I visited were the epitome of high morale, but guided tours never reveal the truth about military bases in authoritarian nations. "I laugh when I see our Congressmen, diplomats, and businessmen being given the grand tour of Formosa," said an American businessman with long experience on the island. "They are shown only what the regime wants them to see." [19]

Formosan troops in an armored regiment who witnessed an abortive revolt in 1963, however, told the following story:

It happened in late 1963 after announcement of the removal of Chiang Wego, younger brother of Chiang Ching-kuo, as commander of the Armor Corps. We and some mainlander troops speculated that the removal was due to Ching-kuo's fear that his opponents in the old Whampoa clique and other groups might rally around Wego as an effective force should anything happen to the "Old Man." According to custom, the senior of the two vice-commanders under Wego should have succeeded him. Before the official announcement arrived, however, there were rumors that the junior vice-commander, a protégé of Ching-kuo, would be chosen. Thereupon, the senior vice-commander decided to revolt.

Orders came from the headquarters of the corps in Taichung in the guise of an emergency military maneuver and all officers were told to assemble near Hsinchu, where one division of the corps was located. The target of the maneuver was to be Taipei, less than two hours' drive north. By the time the senior vice-commander arrived, the corps was ready for any action. A plan of revolt must have been worked out by the vice-commander and his loyal staff officers.

The vice-commander faced the thousands of assembled

troops and began a four-hour speech denouncing Chiang Kai-shek and Ching-kuo. The audience remained patiently quiet, nobody daring either to give support to the disloyal speaker or to shout against him. It was a boring speech to last so long, but somehow sounded exciting to the Formosan soldiers, who were witnessing an example of dissension among their main-lander overlords. Finally, as the vice-commander was bran-dishing his pistol to emphasize his words, a political commissar standing nearby rushed over and disarmed him. That dramatic move ended the story and the political officer was promoted from lieutenant colonel to major general as a reward.

Meanwhile, the authorities had learned of the plot during the speech. Nearby infantry divisions were moved to the area and artillery units near Taipei readied for combat. The air force was instructed to destroy the two bridges south of Taipei, but other rumors about bombs being dropped and rebel tanks advancing on the capital were very dubious. If the vice-com-mander had been wiser and not made his long speech, he might have led his 30,000 troops to an attack on Taipei. In other words, it would have been a successful *coup d'état* if the corps had actually been moved. The fact that a political com-missar risked his life to thwart the plot shows how important the political commissariat is in protecting the regime. The event also taught us that, despite such close security surveillance over the armed forces, a revolt is not impossible.[20]

The regime punishes those who reveal dissension in the armed forces or between the military and civilians. For example: in July 1966 a 50-year-old newspaper deliveryman was sentenced to one year in prison "for spreading false rumors that an Air Force unit and the Taipei Seventh Police Station were involved in a serious brawl." [21]

On Quemoy, Formosan officers witness friction between the privileged mainlander officers and their homesick poor, and discontented enlisted men: "Some of the veteran Chinese soldiers would go to the top of the mountain to look at the mainland with tears in their eyes . . . [Diversions limited to] gambling, drinking, and the 'paradise houses' made me pity the Chinese troops who had no relatives in For-mosa. The animal-like existence in the Nationalist army is little known to the world because people hear only about the military elite, not the depressing story of the rank-and-file. Thus, any thoughtful Formosan who sees the seamy side of Chinese military life realizes that KMT rule involves suppression and injustice toward Chinese too and cannot be treated purely as a racial matter of Chinese versus Formosans," wrote a Formosan veteran.

The command system of the Nationalist armed forces is patterned after that of the Soviet Red Army, which Chiang Kai-shek studied in Moscow as the model for the KMT forces. Formosans often consider the system of parallel military and political chains of command "peculiar" until they learn in foreign universities that a similar military dualism is also used in Communist China and the Soviet Union to insure the loyalty of the professional soldiers by placing political officers in all units. A veteran of the Political Staff College explained that although the Ministry of Defense and the Joint Chiefs of Staff are the top military echelon, "in fact the headquarters of the Political Commissariat exercises independent authority over the political officers and men who represent the KMT in the armed forces."

In each company there is usually one political commissar and an assistant who are beyond the jurisdiction of the military commander. Their duties include (1) organizing political cells with one political soldier for every ten to twelve men, (2) conducting political indoctrination sessions, including self-confession meetings, (3) maintaining various recreational programs to boost morale, (4) reporting the thought of all members of the company, including the company commander, and (5) preventing subversive activities by recruitment of KMT members and punishment of those guilty of "dangerous thoughts." The regime claims that the political officers are merely Chinese equivalents of the information, education, and welfare officers in the United States armed services.[22] While they do resemble the latter in some respects, the Chinese political officers' main duty is to control the military in the name of the ruling party, a function quite alien to their American counterparts.

Formosans are seldom admitted to the Political Staff College, which trains political commissars, to the Fengshan Military Academy or the Tso-ying Naval Academy; the regime distrusts them as professional military men and in any case it appears that few Formosans wish a military career. Occasionally, however, a Formosan college graduate will be sent to the Political Staff College near Taipei as part of his compulsory service.

The Political Staff College, the political commissar school, enrolls three types of students: regular commissars who have been returned for three to six months' re-education; those who enrolled for the full four-year course; and ROTC graduates sent for three months' training as temporary political officers during their year of compulsory active service. Of the 1,500 to 2,000 total, about one-third were in the latter category as of 1962. Between 1961 and 1964, when Nationalist dreams of actually regaining the mainland were beginning to revive, students at the school were told they would be the prime agents to establish order in recovered mainland areas. With that objective, courses included geography of the mainland coast, the psychology of people living in coastal provinces, military administration, guerrilla warfare, party operations, and the work of political commissars.

"The students' attitude toward the school's staff officers was very hostile, partly because of the instructors' superiority attitude and a tendency to treat college graduates harshly," said a veteran of the school. "But more important was the students' established hatred of military men in general and political commissars in particular, stemming from their previous ROTC training, when the KMT instructors had tried to recruit them for the party and to control their political thoughts and behavior.

> One day at lunch, some students talked a bit too loudly and the officer-in-charge ordered the dining hall cleared. Ten minutes later the students were allowed to re-enter the dining hall but the students moved their chairs noisily, and were ordered to stand upright at our tables. Then, when they told us to sit down to eat, 90 per cent of the group walked out. Such incidents happened frequently. Students accused of leading others in any disrespectful action were punished by being sent to the offshore islands or other undesirable places.
>
> While we were at the staff college Formosan-Chinese friction was subordinated to our common fear of the officers. But many of the Chinese were KMT members, whereas only about one-third of the ex-ROTC students had joined the party. Through bribery, persuasion, and threats late at night, they raised the proportion of party membership among the ex-ROTC group to over one-half, a rather small percentage considering the pressures applied. The school's courses were extremely poor in content and reading materials, and we learned mostly the operations of the KMT party and Ching-kuo's plan to dominate the government.

Another Formosan youth explained how the ROTC had operated at all universities in the island prior to 1966, when the system was revised to channel most students into the regular two-year military training program:

During the academic year, ROTC cadets underwent training similar to that of their American counterparts, but with the addition of strict political indoctrination. After their junior year (or the sophomore year for some engineering students), they were expected to undergo three months' summer training at a camp near Taichung. In addition to four hours a day of basic training and another four hours spent in gunnery practice, the students were required to devote at least two hours to a study of Chiang Kai-shek's moral, political, and military instruction. Sometimes on weekends they had to engage in small group discussions very similar to the 'self-criticism' practiced in Communist nations. Students were urged to make an 'honest criticism' of themselves in thought and behavior, and tell what they had learned from reading the Great Leader's works. If we wanted to avoid punishment, we had to praise the Great Leader [Chiang Kai-shek] once in a while. Constant meetings of this type really exhausted the ROTC students. At the end, you began to hate everything the authorities wanted you to believe.

One Nationalist goal for the ROTC training was Formosan and Chinese integration—provided that Chinese dominance was unchallenged. "The impact of ROTC training lets the two groups get together for a period of time," said another Formosan veteran. "Psychological friction between them is reduced because they struggle against the military command and the incessant political nonsense, but it would be a mistake to assume that short periods of togetherness lead to significant ethnic integration. Their relationship remains on a superficial level. Once they go back to school again, the ethnic division will reappear. But if we take a long-term view perhaps the experience in the camps does lead many Formosan cadets to think of the injustice they resent as more political than ethnic. Military service, in other words, is one of many experiences of younger Formosan and Chinese tending to strengthen their integration against the KMT dictatorship."

Few local officers rise above the company grade level, because the ROTC alumni serve their one- or two-year duty and then return to civilian life. Formosans who attended high school are qualified as corporals or even sergeants. Those who never went to high school form the bulk of the Nationalist forces, while most commissioned officers are mainlanders. "Such a clearcut distinction naturally produces a psychological gap between the two ethnic groups," said a Formosan enlisted man. "We perform the bulk of the manual labor in the Nationalist military services, such as building bridges, repairing highways, or other civilian chores when we are not needed for military labor. And without the Formosan backbone, where can the Nationalist officers go?"

A veteran from southern Formosa who had been an instructor in the air force said that "many Formosan college graduates in the service are assigned to teach English, mathematics, natural sciences, and other subjects in the military schools. The presence of such Formosan officers pleases the Formosan soldiers, most of whom are fearful of their Chinese officers." The regime employs the same political indoctrination for all its officers that it uses in the Political Staff College and summer ROTC courses, based on Chiang's works on mainland recovery, military strategy, morality, and every other topic on which the "Great Leader" has written or spoken.

The political commissar in the company where a certain graduate of Soochow Law School spent his required year of post-graduate service "called a self-examination meeting every month, requiring the attendance of all who were not on special duty." The Soochow graduate recalled these meetings as very unpopular with the officers and men. "They were supposed to force us to criticize ourselves honestly and sincerely, to criticize our colleagues, to accept and admit errors publicly. We were also expected to suggest ways of improving living conditions, and to make our other wishes known to the commissar. The original motive might have been to win the soldiers' wholehearted support, but the meetings became so superficial that soon they functioned only to trap and control soldiers with undesirable opinions. Therefore, most of the men who understood this design refused to express anything. The commissar used to have his agents in the company speak up during any embarrassing silences, and we would usually play along with the game by making innocuous self-criticisms. Such deception and superficiality are common parts of military life in the Nationalist armed forces."

Many veterans referred to the behavior of Hungarian soldiers in 1956 as an example of what might occur if Formosan troops were asked to fire upon their own compatriots: "Would they rely on us to suppress a Formosan revolt or attack mainland villages? Our outward obedience is bought cheaply today, but mutual distrust makes genuine loyalty impossible. The KMT cannot count on our loyalty to regain the mainland because whatever it can promise its own mainlander refugees in the event of a successful overthrow of the Communists remains totally irrelevant to us."

The official Nationalist position is that the large number of Formosans in military service proves the regime trusts them as loyal Chinese. "They could turn against their officers at any time and revolt, but they do not. This shows their patriotic loyalty and integration as Chinese," wrote the Nationalist ambassador in Tokyo.[23] Foreign observers, such as the American correspondent Albert Axelbank, are closer to the truth when they report "the police are extremely watchful for any stirrings of revolt . . . About half of the Formosans in Chiang's army are stationed in Quemoy and Matsu—far enough away so they could not cause any trouble on Formosa. And on Formosa, very few soldiers, incidentally, are given live ammunition." [24] Such precautions suggest grave and probably well-founded doubt by the Nationalists on the reliability of the Formosan troops. "If we were sent to Vietnam, as the government claims it would do if requested by Saigon, we would shoot our Chinese officers at the first opportunity," said a young corporal in 1964. Axelbank quoted a ranking U.S. naval officer as saying, "I want to be miles away from this island when Chiang dies," implying fear of either a mainlander or a Formosan military revolt.[25]

Japanese and Okinawan observers who are permitted to visit Nationalist military bases are seldom allowed to talk with Formosan officers or troops, but a few have managed to speak with them privately. "No native servicemen like their Chinese officers," said one such observer in 1962, "because they are arrogant and consider Formosans only as cannon fodder or labor battalions." An American who was a MAAG officer in the 1950's said his colleagues had little respect for the Nationalist officers, who were then "in discouraging disarray," while Formosan troops were afraid to express their obvious discontent: "The few Taiwanese in the military with whom I came into contact felt they were being used as cannon fodder . . . and their grievances were real and justified."

Formosan civilian views of the Nationalist military budget and conscription include such complaints as: "Taxes are too high for a useless military force with so many mainlander officers and noncoms," (from a food dealer in Tainan); and "The defense surtax in 1962 proved how the government extracts money from the ordinary people to pay its generals and retired veterans." Many Formosans were resentful that Nationalist China exempts all imports for military use from customs duties; gives servicemen cut rates on public transportation and many recreational facilities; and often allows the military to delay payment of utility bills.

Even such a sympathetic observer as Jacoby admitted that the Nationalist military burden, in terms of percentage of GNP and manpower, exceeded that of "the rich and advanced economy of the United States . . . The civilian economy provided large hidden [not budgeted] subsidies to the military establishment in the form of rice, transportation services, electricity, and other items for which the military paid nothing, or less than market prices." [26] Jacoby concluded that the $2.5 billion U.S. military assistance between 1951 and 1965 benefited the civilian economy through local procurement orders, skilled training experiences useful in civilian life, and encouragement to new civilian industries. Recognizing that U.S. aid officials had failed in constant efforts to persuade Taipei to lower its defense budget, Jacoby nevertheless thought that the experience of Taiwan refuted the view that a semideveloped country "cannot simultaneously maintain a powerful military force and also finance rapid economic growth. The case of the Republic of China suggests that both National purposes can be achieved simultaneously . . . provided that major military hardware is supplied by an external source." [27]

No Formosan whom I have met at home or abroad has shared Jacoby's view of the benefits or minimal damage of defense spending to the economy. "The army takes more land for bases than the Japanese ever did," commented a former landlord as we drove around the perimeter of the Chinese air base near Taichung: "The Chinese officers inside that base may say they get along well with the farmers, but ask the farmers and you'll hear a different story." Knowing that over 80 per cent of national taxes and 10 per cent of the island's GNP support the 600,000-man armed forces, Formosans in all walks of life envied the Japanese, who pay less than 2 per cent of their GNP for defense. "Formosa's economic development is hampered by two grave problems: a huge military budget and rapidly increasing population," wrote the authors of the Declaration of Formosans in 1964. "We advocate reducing armaments to the level of self-defense and guaranteeing the position and livelihood of retired soldiers." [28] If Japan can be defended by 250,000 of its own troops, about 40,000 U.S. forces, and an American defense treaty, Formosans wonder why their smaller island needs more. Again we approach the forbidden topic of mainland recovery, because to challenge the need for defense spending is to question the Nationalists' fundamental *raison d'être*.

"If Washington wants to give us defensive weapons, fine, but why give them to a government whose sole ambition is to fight a war on the mainland? Couldn't the Seventh Fleet, the Far East Air Force, and other U.S. units defend us without 600,000 armed forces, most of whom are Formosans kept in the Army to be indoctrinated and brainwashed?" asked a lawyer in central Formosa. Businessmen who handled procurement orders and others who benefited indirectly from the military buildup as laborers would nevertheless have preferred to deal with less military hardware and more civilian goods. "We know how few Formosan troops are given weapons," said one local politician, "and we wonder if all the conscription and armaments are not really designed to keep us cowed into submission." [29]

The Offshore Islands and Mainland Recovery

After their flight from the mainland in 1949, the Nationalists managed to retain a few groups of offshore islands within sight of the Communist coast. "They are the only bits of real Chinese territory the regime controls," said a Formosan in the underground, "because those islands were always governed by whoever controlled the coastal provinces, whereas Formosa seldom enjoyed the dubious pleasures of effective mainland rule." After a period of Communist bombardment in late 1954, Taipei, under pressure from the United States, evacuated the Tachen island group (far north of the Quemoy and Matsu islands), "which had come to be regarded in Washington as a military liability." [30] Thereafter, the Nationalists strengthened their garrisons on Quemoy and Matsu, with the assistance of American weapons and advisors.

"Kinmen [Quemoy] and Matsu are shields to the defense of Taiwan. Without them, the control of the Taiwan Straits would be imperilled. And Taiwan would be constantly under threat of Communist air attack without an effective warning system. The strategic importance of these islands, therefore, lies chiefly in denying the enemy the advantages to be derived from the islands if they were in enemy hands," wrote the author of a Nationalist pamphlet in 1960. [31] The Nationalists also claim that their possession is a symbol of hope to the "enslaved millions on the mainland," a useful staging area for guerrilla and reconnaissance raids against the mainland, and a logical forward base for the eventual counterattack. Moreover the Nationalists assert that their bases on the Kinmen group, which lies within the outer approaches to the Chinese coastal port of Amoy, bottle up that harbor and force the Communists to deploy up to 500,000 troops along the Fukien coast to guard against a

Nationalist attack. "Kinmen is the West Berlin of the Far East," declared Kaya Okinori, one of the few pro-Nationalist leaders in the Japanese governing party.[32]

During the heavy Communist shelling of Quemoy in late 1958, in which American Sidewinder air-to-air missiles gave the Nationalist jets a great advantage over their MIG opponents, the extent of United States support for the offshore islands was hotly debated in Washington. Neither the Sino-American defense treaty of 1954 nor the 1955 "Formosa Resolution" mentioned Kinmen or Matsu specifically. Secretary of State John Foster Dulles, during the 1958 crisis, expressed doubt in the wisdom of Nationalist military build-up on the offshore islands and said the United States' attitude was one of "acquiesence . . . not of approval."[33] A few weeks later, however, he flew to Taipei to reassure Chiang Kai-shek that the offshore islands were "closely related" to the defense of Taiwan, even if military force should not be the principal means of restoring freedom to the mainland. As A. Doak Barnett has written: "The sequence of events and statements during 1958 highlighted the dilemmas, ambiguities, and uncertainties in the United States' policy toward the Taiwan area."[34]

The Nationalist regime has maintained continual aerial surveillance, propaganda drops, and guerrilla campaigns against the Communist mainland. Despite occasional claims by President Chiang that "military victory is of secondary importance," and "our war of national recovery is essentially a war of ideology [because] only a victory in the field of culture and education is final,"[35] the regime has had many military encounters on the mainland. Taipei claims to have agents in 27 mainland provinces, arousing the anti-Mao forces to rebel and assist an invasion force, as Premier (later Vice President) C. K. Yen said in late 1966 while reaffirming his government's intention to retake the mainland.[36] Yen also approved the bombing of Peking's nuclear installations suggested by Madame Chiang in an American television interview the same year.[37] In 1965 the Nationalist Foreign Minister, Shen Chang-huan, contended that the Nationalist forces were "tying down one-third of Peiping's land force, one half of its air force, and almost its entire navy," thereby preventing the Communist regime from sending more aid to Vietnam and deterring it from aggressive acts on other frontiers.[38] But these and similar claims by other KMT leaders were defensive, less relevant to the Nationalists' goal of mainland recovery than their military probings of the coastline.

The mildest form of Nationalist counterattack is the radio and leaflet campaign designed to persuade those on the mainland to oppose the

Communists and welcome a Nationalist invasion. In addition, almost every foreign visitor to Quemoy is asked to release a few balloons carrying messages or relief parcels. "We are very annoyed" State Department officers told me in 1963, "at all the publicity photographs showing our Fulbright grantees releasing those balloons." [39]

The Quemoy garrison uses the balloons to send soap, toothpaste, biscuits, and toys on the many Chinese holidays, especially the Dragon Boat festival commemorating the death in 295 B.C. of Chu Yuan, a poet-statesman who drowned himself after the government ignored his pleas for reform. During the 1966–1968 civil strife on the mainland, the Nationalists increased their psychological appeals by radio and leaflet.

The Nationalists beam 16 radio transmitters in a concentrated attempt to spur revolt against the Maoist regime, and claimed response was greater in 1967 than in the previous seven years of the radio campaign: "We tell them to mail their letters to a post office box in Singapore or Hong Kong, avoiding political comment but asking for rice because they do not like to eat [Poorman's] cabbage," said the president of the Broadcasting Corporation of China.[40]

In early 1967, the *Central Daily News* of Taipei reported over 1,000 propaganda and relief flights to the mainland since 1949, involving an annual average of 100 million propaganda sheets up to 1960, after which the Nationalists focused on only key areas with 12 million leaflets dispersed annually, mainly by balloons.[41] A Formosan who served on Quemoy in the early 1960's doubted the effectiveness of the balloon drops: "The mainland areas were under strict control of the Communist regime, and the leaflet messages usually repeated the poor, sentimental praise of Chiang as a savior of the world. The Communists have used similar propaganda devices which struck me as more effective—but only to arouse homesickness among the old Chinese soldiers."

Nationalist military missions against the mainland are cloaked in greater secrecy, but they include frequent overflights by U-2 and other planes for intelligence purposes. Chinese Air Force headquarters announced a record number or reconnaissance missions in 1966 and 1967, but did not give details, except for the claim that two Nationalist pilots had downed two MIG's without injury to their own planes.[42] According to the *Japan Times* of January 14, 1967, the incident occurred when 12 MIG-19's allegedly jumped on 4 Nationalist planes near Quemoy; but a Nationalist military spokesman told reporters in Taipei that he would not take advantage of the "victory" to announce an invasion of the mainland because "we are waiting for the right moment and it is better

to leave the Chinese Communists guessing." [43] Sporadic air and sea battles have occurred, such as the sinking of 4 Communist (PRC) gunboats in May 1965 near Matsu and four more later the same year.[44]
Again, however, the Nationalist claims must be viewed cautiously in
the light of an eyewitness account by a Formosan naval officer who contradicted a newspaper headline that proclaimed "Heroic ROC [Repub-
lic of China] Vessels Scuttled Themselves after Sinking Five Red Ships"
in August 1965: "No sea battle occurred at all, but the two largest
ROC ships were sunk by the PRC navy, and the Nationalist Navy
commander-in-chief had to resign." [45]

The Nationalists' record in guerrilla landings along the mainland coast
is more impressive, because they can use their offshore island bases
whereas the Communists cannot send their agents easily into Formosa.
The Nationalists claimed to have killed at least 15 Communist soldiers
in a mid-1967 commando landing to deliver weapons, ammunition, and
advisers to anti-Communist guerrillas on the Shantung Peninsula of
north China. They also implied that sabotage by anti-Maoists on the
mainland proved the efficiency of their agents. Several dozen Communist soldiers, including a few pilots and Red Guards, went over to the
Nationalists in highly-publicized "flights to freedom" in the past few
years for personal, financial, or political reasons. They were rewarded in
gold and then vowed to help the Nationalists "liberate their enslaved
compatriots" unable to flee the mainland.[46]

Do the island-born soldiers in the Nationalist forces share the enthusiasm for the recovery of the mainland? The Nationalist regime answers
unequivocally: "They most certainly do, for they are also
Chinese . . . They realize that Taiwan is an integral part of China and
that their families would not be safe unless the Chinese Communist regime is overthrown. They were battle-tested on Quemoy." [47] Our concern here, however, is with the direct response of the Formosan troops.
The Nationalist garrisons on Quemoy and Matsu are heavily Formosan,
and I spoke with many after their tours of duty on Quemoy.[48] The following accounts of military life on that island are drawn from some of
their diaries:

> Quemoy, or Kinmen in Chinese, includes the large Kinmen
> island and a much smaller island of the same name between it
> and the mainland. Both used to be part of Fukien province,
> and the Nationalists still govern them as Fukien, not Taiwan,
> province. The 45,000 to 50,000 native inhabitants speak Fu-
> kienese, which is very similar to the dialect spoken on Formosa.

Even after years of Communist bombing, those buildings looked beautiful; some were used as offices of the military administration. A military committee rules the islands' non-military affairs and leaves purely military work to the Kinmen Defense Command.

Most Quemoy islanders live by agriculture and commerce, importing rice from Taiwan because the Quemoy soil is not suited to rice culture. Economically, the population seems indispensable to the Nationalist army as laborers, farmers, and merchants, so the army forbids departure from the islands. Of course, security always occupies a key place in official justification, and the islands are under tighter martial law than Taiwan itself. One can enter or leave only by military transport, but we believed rumors that Communist frogmen in rubber boats enter rather easily at night.

Geographically, the islands seem too close to the mainland to be defended, and during the daytime one can see houses, military fortifications, and even human activity by using a medium-power telescope. Many fishing boats approach within a few hundred yards of Kinmen and both the Communists and Nationalists have an informal agreement not to harm each other's civilians. I used to go to the top of the mountain near our quarters to watch the mainland boats, partly for fun, partly to breath fresher air than in the caves where we had to live. Occasionally, a veteran mainlander soldier would come up to look across the water: Homesickness has been the most serious morale problem for the KMT mainlander troops on the offshore islands, resulting in numerous attempts to swim to the mainland at night. At night, when one can see lights flickering on the opposite side, the distance appears much less, and political commissars are ordered to pay special attention to those affected by the sight.

The Nationalists often invite foreign friends and overseas Chinese to visit Quemoy, and we used to wish the visitors could be shown the truth. Instead, they were led routinely to the Defense Headquarters, selected villages, the radio station which broadcasts to the mainland, and the psywar center where they could release propaganda balloons and have their pictures taken. A highlight of the guided tour is Tai-wu Mountain, from whose peak they could look over at the mainland through a powerful telescope (about 15 power). I am sure the visitors gained a favorable impression of the vast underground installations, impregnable to anything but a direct bomb hit. But they never had a chance to look at the situation deeper in the minds of the Quemoy-based troops. It is dangerous to assess the Nationalist strength on the offshore islands simply by seeing the relatively impressive military constructions.

Quemoy is very well developed in its highway system, which reaches every corner of the big island. The exact number of troops is not published, but a friend in the supply unit of the Combined Service Force headquarters estimated it at 110,000 in early 1962.[49] There were at that time six or seven army divisions, one MP battalion, one Air Force regiment, plus smaller units of frogmen, marines, engineers, and security troops. Small Kinmen island has another army division. Troops are rotated to Taiwan every two or three years, but symptoms of poor morale could get a soldier back to Taiwan in one year's time.

Most military headquarters are located underground in tunnels; and the main headquarters is located at the bottom of Tai-wu Mountain opposite the mainland. Its conference halls, offices, theatre for entertaining higher personnel, and other facilities could hardly be reached by a mainland bomb. We were told the underground units could survive up to two months if supplies from Taiwan were cut off. The part of the subterranean network occupied by the American MAAG officers is even air-conditioned.

Naturally, all of this cost a lot of money, but we were told every day that Quemoy was vital as a jumping-off base for mainland attack (hence a threat to the Communists) and as proof to the world that the regime will pay any cost to defend even an inch of territory. We native Taiwanese, however, thought the biggest reason was to control more than one Chinese province.

According to another informant who had spent over a year in the Kinmen garrison:

The mainland coast is well-guarded and very few civilians, except fishermen, are allowed to live there. Occasionally, the fishermen clandestinely exchange goods with Nationalist troops at night, and some of those goods can even be found in the streets of Taipei. The Communists have demonstrated no real intention to take over the offshore islands under the present circumstances. I personally think they do not fear the presence of the KMT troops, perhaps because they know how much of a drain the occupation is on the Nationalist budget. Since 1960 they have not shelled the islands on a large scale, only every other day at predictable night hours. When I was on Quemoy the Communist shells contained mostly propaganda leaflets similar to the ones dropped on the mainland by the Nationalists, telling of the happy life and "socialist construction" under their regime. Many of our soldiers disobeyed the rules and picked up the leaflets, and many mainlander troops grew homesick if they found leaflets with pictures of their home province.

During the winter when the winds blew from the northwest, the Communists broadcast to us in various languages, causing the Nationalists to increase their counter-propaganda by radio and balloons. The KMT told us they had an effective underground on the mainland, using frogmen as liaison. Of course, they did send frogmen to the mainland for sabotage and intelligence duties, but we never thought they could operate on a large scale against the well-guarded coastal areas. For liaison work, the radio stations in Taiwan could broadcast to mainland agents just as easily.

The Communists sent a lot of their frogmen to Quemoy, trying to set up an underground there and bore from within. I was officially told that these frogmen come in rubber boats, three to a team, at midnight when the weather is poor. Two would land, sending the third man back with instructions to pick them up again after a few days. The two who remain have orders to collect information and contact pro-Communist agents on the islands. They wear KMT military uniforms and carry forged ID cards and enough rations for two days. It is not difficult for them to find places to hide, and while I served on Quemoy I heard occasional rumors that Communist frogmen had murdered KMT soldiers on the shore, chopping off their heads to carry back for a reward. We tended to believe such rumors, which might have been planted to scare us. No troops were allowed out of their own area after ten o'clock at night, except in case of emergency when they used a password to the trigger-happy Nationalist guards.[50]

A third veteran of military service on Quemoy agreed that few troops wanted to venture outside their caves at night. "Most of the Chinese soldiers stay in their area to gamble. During the Lunar New Year period, Chinese custom allowed gambling, so the authorities at first permitted it but then found they could not keep it within bounds. Gambling has become one of the most serious and troublesome problems in the Nationalist armed forces. Losers often become irritated and kill people after a mahjong or poker game, but officers also gambled, though more quietly. The most notorious story I heard was that of a soldier who won NT$150,000 (US $375) and two MP's protected him for a week after the game." A former officer added:

> Drunkenness was another serious problem. Most men drank Kinmen *kaoliang* which runs up to 160 proof, and wines were relatively easy to obtain. During the cold winter months, drinking became more widespread especially among the non-Formosans.
>
> But the most sickening of all were the pitiful prostitution habits of the troops on Quemoy. Isolation made the problem even worse on the offshore islands than inside Taiwan, especially for the many soldiers who had followed the KMT willingly or unwillingly for so many years. They had never had a taste of normal human life in their youth so, without women, money, freedom, social respect, or hope for the future, they depended on the officially-sponsored houses of prostitution for an occasional sexual release. Prostitution on the offshore islands is run by the military, who take a certain percentage of the income from what is called, officially and euphemistically, "military paradise." Enlisted men paid about US $.40 and officers enjoyed prettier women for US $.60 in a different place. Apparently there were about 2,000 prostitutes. Some of the older ones had been sent there after being arrested in Taiwan; others were "volunteers" recruited either on Quemoy or in Taiwan. They all seemed able to earn a fair living from the thirty or so patrons every day.
>
> Very few of the Formosan troops dared to go to such places, or were smart enough to secure their own entertainment. VD has been a serious problem because the regime lacks enough medicines and prophylactics. Almost every Chinese soldier in my company had VD in various stages, so that I wondered about their combat effectiveness. One of my sergeants had VD symptoms but continued to patronize the prostitutes twice a month. The week after the monthly payday was the worst to handle, and headquarters often asked each unit to discourage the troops' use of prostitutes unless they took penicillin or other medicines. But they never gave us enough medicine.[51]

One of the Formosan ROTC graduates who spent seven months on Quemoy in 1962 was struck by the economic advantages of Formosan officers and men compared with most of the Chinese forces on the island:

Formosan families send their sons money to buy better food. This caused the Chinese to be very jealous, so we would sometimes bribe them with good meals. The game we played of inviting the "right" officers and the latter's maneuvering to secure invitations was a peculiar type of politicking symptomatic of Chinese-Formosan relationships in society as a whole. But maybe because some Formosans could afford to bribe, those who could not were embittered by the system.

The Quemoy command made us all read selections from Chiang Kai-shek's works between rising at six a.m. and breakfast at seven. Without electricity in our caves, we worked and read by gasoline lamps, then sang the party anthem and listened to the company leader's orders for that day.

My artillery bases were scattered on Tai-wu Mountain and I walked around them every week to see the seven or eight men at each base, commanded by a Chinese. The ratio of Formosans to Chinese was about 60–40 in my company, and the Formosans always greeted me with special warmth, complaining in whispers about their mistreatment. I sympathized with them, but had to avoid being accused of "regionalist" favoritism, a very dangerous charge. Most troops on Quemoy had to spend much time in manual labor, such as highway construction, bridge repair, the digging of caves or tunnels, and constant short-distance marches. They were warned never to listen to Communist radio broadcasts on penalty of being charged with Communist sympathy. The Reds used four powerful stations, in Mandarin, Shanghai, Cantonese, Amoy, and Formosan dialects, which were much stronger than any radio from Taiwan except that of the Taipei Central Broadcasting Service. The Voice of America from Manila was also audible in Quemoy, but the Communist stations came in strongest on the 20 radios in our company.

American informants who had taken the one-day guided tour of Quemoy all confirmed its strong defenses, and regretted they could not speak privately with the troops. MAAG officers and men with experience on the offshore islands between 1959 and 1965, whom I interviewed either in Taiwan or after their return to the United States, were reluctant to challenge the statements of the Nationalist regime concerning the loyalty of Formosan troops, but few felt the garrison was capable of offensive operations against the mainland. "Both sides seemed to fire their artillery more for show than real," said and Air Force sergeant. "The Nationalists need all the ammunition they get from us, but we won't give them offensive weapons. Those Sidewinder missiles sure saved Quemoy in 1958, but the Reds have Quemoy ringed on three sides and could probably take it if they really wanted to." [52]

An American colonel with high-level consultation duties complained that every year the Nationalist generals demanded more of the latest United States weapons: "They're never satisfied, and expect us to finance all their military ambitions even if we do not share them," he said. Another colonel, after his transfer from Formosa to West Point, was even more contemptuous of the Nationalist military elite: "We'd all be better off if Japan still held Formosa."

The Dream of Mainland Recovery

The consensus among Formosans interviewed for this book was that the Nationalists hoped to return by embroiling the United States in a war with Communist China. One of Axelbank's informants said that "Chiang wants to lead America into a war with Red China. That is the only way he will ever get back to the mainland." [53] "Why . . . is Chiang so persistent in demanding the 'return'?" asked Professor Peng in 1964. "Because this slogan is the only means by which he prolongs his political power and enslaves his people. . . . Indeed, his scheme of 'Return to the Mainland' is the greatest act of deception of the 20th century." [54]

Postwar-educated Formosans often echoed the opinion of one student who wrote to a friend at Stanford: "Recovery of the mainland is not my problem. Most of the soldiers from the mainland are too old to fight, and the young Taiwanese don't like to fight for them." [55] Formosans on active military duty must be particularly cautious in expressing their true opinions to foreigners because surveillance is even stricter in the armed forces than among the civilian population.

After completing military service, however, Formosans often go abroad where they can report their honest opinions more freely: "President Chiang is only a normal person, not the 'saving star of China' as [he is] called by those who came from the mainland," wrote one of those now in the United States.

The Chinese Opinion Survey Association in Taipei reported in 1966 that 30 per cent of Formosans and 70 per cent of mainlanders among its 1,200 respondents wanted to go to the mainland after it was recovered. [56] We have noted earlier the unreliability of political polls in

Taiwan, all conducted by mainlander groups associated with the regime, but even so, these figures suggest the gap between mainlander and Taiwanese enthusiasm for the recovery objective. Formosans to whom I talked had no interest in "returning" to a mainland they had never seen, much less in fighting to go there or in defending the offshore islands. "Don't bother to take the official trip to Quemoy," advised several shopkeepers and students in Taichung when I had the opportunity to accompany other Fulbright scholars on a tour there in late 1961. "Those people on Quemoy aren't like us, and your guides wouldn't let you speak to them anyway. You can learn more by questioning native troops after they come back or go to America."

The Chinese Nationalists and their Communist enemies both have "liberation" projects: the former to liberate the mainland and the latter to liberate Formosa. One day in January 1966 a Communist agent reportedly dropped boxes into Sun Moon Lake which later rose to the surface exposing such slogans as "Liberate Taiwan!" and the Nationalist police promptly dragged the lake to search for other subversive boxes.[57] "The only kind of liberation we want," commented a group of Formosan students overseas when they read this story, "is liberation from *any* Chinese rule."

A Formosan veteran summarized his view after seeking the safety of the United States. "As long as the KMT continues to advocate the counterattack, the loyalty of its Formosan troops is very doubtful. They serve quietly only because they fear reprisals against their families. Can obedience under such conditions be called support of the regime? If the regime ever loses control, the local troops will reject its norms and policies . . . Due to ethnic differences and mutual distrust, genuine Formosan loyalty to the KMT is impossible. Formosans have all their property in Formosa, so they would gain nothing from mainland recovery. To them, such a goal appears only the mainlanders' dream for which they are forcibly drafted and taxed."[58]

7

THE POLITICS OF FORMOSANS ABROAD

Intellectuals of many ex-colonial nations learned the meaning of freedom when they studied overseas, then returned home to lead the anti-colonial struggle or assume key roles after independence. On the other hand, those who emigrate for economic reasons are less likely to participate in political movements abroad. The familiar pattern applies to Formosa. Under Japanese rule, Formosans who attended Japanese universities usually returned home and were active politically, whereas the larger number who went to Japan to seek jobs generally remained but have, in any event, not played any political role. Since 1946, most Formosans seeking education abroad have gone to either Japan or the United States. This chapter discusses the political activities of Formosans in those two countries.

One of the more liberal Nationalist policies has been to admit Formosans in large numbers to island universities and permit many graduates to emigrate for graduate study—although the Nationalist regime often speaks of the "brain drain" caused by thousands of scholars and professional men refusing to return after once being allowed abroad. One Formosan who came to the United States in 1951 said he had been among the 80 permitted to leave that year, but that over 2,000 annually have come to the United States in recent years. The Institute of International Education reported 6,271 Formosan students in the U.S. in early 1967.[1] The Nationalist Economic Minister, K. T. Li, admitted that only "five out of every 100 local college graduates who went abroad" between 1963 and 1966 ever returned, and thought economic lures might induce up to 20 per cent to come back.[2] "More than 80 per cent who leave go to the U.S. and very few ever return," lamented the president of National Taiwan University to an American reporter.[3]

The regime recognizes the economic appeal of the United States, and even Japan, but ignores the political motives of many mainlanders and Formosans who stay abroad. "As long as the KMT rules that island, I prefer to live in a democratic country," said the relative of a high Nationalist official. Probably a higher percentage of Formosans than mainlanders remain abroad for political reasons, but the anti-KMT attitudes of mainlander intellectuals, whether at home or overseas, should not be underestimated.

Formosan Activities in Japan

Japan, which contains more Formosan émigrés than any other country, saw the beginnings of the postwar independence movement led by refugees from the 1947 incident, and now has a broad cross-section of Formosan residents, activist and otherwise.

Most of the approximately 25,000 Formosans living in Japan during the 1960's had migrated before 1945 for economic reasons. They take little interest in the political life of their homeland or the conflicting appeals of their pro-Nationalist, pro-Communist, or pro-independence compatriots. Very few have opted for Japanese citizenship (a rather difficult process), so the majority retain the ambiguous "China" on their alien registration cards.[4] Perhaps as many as 1,000 are men who escaped after 1947, including almost all the pro-independence activists over the age of 45. Another 4,000 or so are students or, if their student visas have expired and they have antagonized the Nationalist regime, stateless persons subject to deportation.

My first contact with Formosans in Japan was a series of talks in the summer of 1961 with the one-time Foreign Minister of the Provisional Government of Formosa in Tokyo headed by Thomas Liao. "I fled Taiwan after the 1947 massacre, first to Hong Kong, then here in 1949 to make appeals to the U.S. Embassy," he told me. "After Dr. Liao followed me here from Hong Kong under an assumed name, the [U.S.] Occupation allowed him to remain on condition he make no political speeches. However, Liao couldn't resist holding a press conference in the Tokyo YMCA building. American MP's broke in and arrested Liao as I escaped through a rear window. Liao was put in Sugamo prison with the Japanese 'war criminals' for six months, but was later released and given considerable protection by Japanese authorities." [5]

Liao, born in 1910 to a wealthy rural family in southern Formosa, had become the self-proclaimed leader of Formosan refugees in Japan by 1955. His excellent English, learned during graduate studies in the United States, (M.S., University of Michigan, and Ph.D., Ohio State University), helped him in pleading his cause to Americans. Moreover, the effervescent Liao had the bearing of a Theodore Roosevelt as described by Richard Hofstadter: a man who wanted to be "the bride at every wedding and the corpse at every funeral." Liao and his elder brother Joshua formed the first overseas League for Reliberation of Formosa in mid-1948 in Hong Kong, and Thomas created the Formosa Independence Party on his 1950 arrival in Tokyo.[6] He dominated the "Provisional Government" after its foundation in September 1955, and was long regarded as the leading expatriate Formosan by Chinese Nationalists, Japanese, and Americans. It is appropriate to begin this discussion with Liao's philosophy and activities before he renounced his past to fly back to the Nationalist fold in 1965.[7]

Colleagues and close friends of Thomas Liao have told of his frustration over the apathy of most Formosan residents toward his political movement: "This may explain Liao's high-handedness toward inferiors and colleagues, which the latter naturally resent . . . We got little sympathy from the American government, which refused to allow Liao to accompany his American wife when she came to Tokyo en route to New York in 1951. He always had great faith in eventual American support, but on the one occasion when Washington permitted him to cross the United States on a world tour they gave him only a transit visa good for one night in New York and a change of plane in Los Angeles. . . . Liao was over-confident, but that is his personality and it must have required many disillusionments over the years to embitter him," said a friend in 1963.[8]

One who had been active in Liao's group before deserting politics for business spoke of organizational problems. "We can sell very few copies of Liao's newspaper, perhaps 4,000, and not many visitors from Taiwan will risk carrying back copies in their shoes. We appealed to the U.N. at the time of the Korean War, but without effect. Most Japanese are indifferent to our cause, although they may favor it in theory, and the average Formosan businessman here is as reluctant as his Japanese counterpart to contribute money."

The Provisional Government elected Liao its president in 1955, a post he held until his defection ten years later, but during that decade several other officers resigned from the movement or created splinter parties. It is safe to say that every leader of an anti-Liao group had once been an associate of Dr. Liao. "I couldn't stand Liao's ingratitude and egotism," explained one in 1966. At the 1963 Provisional Government memorial service to honor the 1947 revolt, only about 30 Formosans attended and no member of any dissident group. The attendance was a sad commentary on both the apathy of the Formosans in Japan and the factionalism which had separated the small number of activists into the Democratic Independence party, the Freedom Independence party, the Young Formosan Association, and several smaller groups.

"Factionalism? Everyone has a different explanation and they are all partly right," said a close friend of Dr. Liao in 1963. "The Chinese Nationalists have spies in Japan to harass our movement and encourage splits. They won over two ex-officers of the Provisional Government who had worked with the Wang Ching-wei regime of Japanese puppets during World War II, luring one back to Taiwan while the other became an agent of the Nationalist embassy here. Others left the movement for personal reasons, either to take care of their wives and children or to protect relatives still in Formosa. Many of us, perhaps half, have married Japanese women who are often impatient if we spend time or money on independence work. Only a few activists deserted the movement because of Communist propaganda." [9]

An American expert on Formosan history has ascribed disunity among overseas Formosans to the long period from 1600 to 1900 when "the old curse of Formosan factionalism [was] bred into them . . . when every village and clan was on its own." [10] Other causes parallel those that plague émigrés from nearly any authoritarian regime—among them, as listed by Dr. Joyce Brothers; "Lack of clearly defined authority for leaders—each uncertain of his power; lack of group-defined goals and tactical priorities; and lack of good leg-work with each committee given a separate task." [11] Historic diversity inside Formosa, Nationalist efforts to disrupt and suppress overseas movement, and honest differences over strategy all have promoted dissension.

Thomas Liao spent several hours in early 1963 explaining his movement to me. "I don't worry about the split in our movement here," he said. "It's only natural among émigrés and nothing to fear. Koreans divided into many groups before 1945, and it may even benefit us to have several groups able to collect funds and make appeals to diverse people . . . KMT spies record names of Taiwanese who are active in Japan, so that deters students from joining us. Many of the 80,000 who were here in 1945 returned home after the war and those who stayed on seemed to lose their identity as Taiwanese. Many belong superficially to the pro-KMT Overseas Chinese Association [Kakyo Sokai]; a few are ideologically Communist; others hope for trade with the mainland." [12] Liao spoke of friendly assistance from the Japanese police, but said he had received no financial aid from Japanese businessmen or politicians. "Most Liberal-Democratic Dietmen agree with me privately, as you discovered in talking with them, but the Socialists are as bad as the Japanese Communists in parroting the Peking claim to Formosa."

In Liao's views, the United States was aiding the Nationalists now but was likely to sell out Formosa to the mainland later. "Washington's support for Chiang indirectly buttresses Peking's claim that Taiwan belongs to China," he said. He also believed that "the Pentagon controls Asian policy and places anti-Communist security above human liberty, even though [the Department of] State, AID, and USIA are far more sympathetic toward our cause." Turning to strategy, Liao thought that "blood is necessary to make our cause succeed: we must expect to pay for independence," but he criticized such acts as defacing the Nationalist consulate in Osaka or throwing stink-bombs into a Nationalist meeting. "We also think it bad to criticize publicly either Japanese or American leaders who praise Chiang. It's better just to applaud those who agree with us."

What would Liao do if he could move his regime to Formosa as the legal government? "Neutralism is impossible, so a free Formosa would need American as well as U.N. guarantees," he replied. Tax reform, reduction of military spending, withdrawal from the offshore islands, acceptance of those mainlanders who wished to be citizens of an independent Formosa, and promotion of the Taiwanese language were some of Liao's other plans. He did not think the KMT would permit gradual evolution toward native political power and, like most activists I interviewed, he was more concerned with the road to independence than with post-independence policies.

The following week, we met again at the 1963 anniversary of the 1947 uprising. Club Oslo near the Ginza was decked out in Taiwan flags and pictures of Koxinga as two dozen Formosans and three Japanese guests entered for the meeting.

The meeting consisted of a series of speeches, first by Liao and his colleagues, then by two Japanese involved in the movement. World developments favorable to the Formosan cause, such as the gradual loss of support for the Nationalists in the U.N., cheered the audience. One speaker reported on internal events, such as the arrest of Councilman Su Tung-chi (described in Chapter 5). An alleged cancer operation on President Chiang (later discounted by the Japanese Ambassador in Taipei) was interpreted in terms of presaging an early end to his regime. Liao in his speech urged: "We must work peacefully to arouse public opinion here and abroad. Today is our July 4—America makes a holiday of a date seven years before she was actually independent and we can use 2-28 even if it takes us 25 years or more to reach our goal."

Two years later, in the spring of 1965, Liao was visited by Nationalist emissaries who persuaded him to renounce his "treasonous" work and return to Taiwan.[13] The exact nature of the threats and appeals they made to Liao is unclear, but evidently political and personal motives both played a part in his subsequent decision to defect. Politically, Liao had alienated many of his former colleagues and, to judge by the statements of those who thereafter took over the Provisional Government, he had been expelled by his own Congress five days before his defection on May 14, 1965. Rumors that Liao was returning with undercover support from the American CIA to bore from within must be discounted as fully as Nationalist claims that his return signalled the demise of all overseas independence movements.

Reliable evidence exists that several of Liao's relatives had been imprisoned in Formosa, where one of them was already rumored to have been executed, and that Liao was told they would be freed if he returned. "After Liao's defection, his brother, niece, and sister-in-law were released as promised," wrote a close relative, "but the sister-in-law soon died from illness contracted in jail . . . One of his nieces and the rest convicted in March 1965 are still in prison." [14] After flying back to Taipei, Liao claimed he had come to see his 91-year old mother, who died there the following year.

On his return, the Nationalists pardoned Liao and returned his properties, which had been confiscated in 1964.[15] The prodigal son paid calls on many high KMT officials, including Premier C. K. Yen, who had been his friend in 1947, and voiced support for President Chiang, mainland recovery, and every other symbol of the regime he had fought against for 18 years. "Blood is thicker than water, and nobody in the world can ever create dissension between us by any means . . . I would do anything that may help promote the nation's anti-Communist cause and the well-being of the Chinese people on Taiwan," he told the Taipei press.[16] Liao praised President Chiang for the social and economic progress on the island and announced that his colleagues in Hong Kong, Macao, and Japan were all following his order to disband.[17] Later, Liao was named by President Chiang to the post of deputy chairman of the new Tsengwen Dam Commission, for which his engineering background ideally suited him.

Since his return, Liao has performed notable propaganda service for the Nationalists, who claimed that the Taiwan independence movement was dead. Before his defection, the regime had minimized Liao's importance, implying that nobody followed him or believed in him. After May 14, 1965, however, it exaggerated Liao's role in the émigré movement. Liao meanwhile told Taipei reporters he had received "no support from the Japanese or American governments," an admission of failure as pleasing to his Nationalist hosts as it was painfully true, with a few minor exceptions. In early 1966, after publication of a laudatory review of George Kerr's *Formosa Betrayed* in the January 23 *New York Times* by Robert Trumbull, the *Times's* Tokyo correspondent, Liao wrote a bitter attack: "Mr. Kerr does not even speak our language, nor does he read Chinese. His contention that we are not Chinese . . . cannot be further from the truth. The fact is that the people on Taiwan are ethnically, historically Chinese . . . I was wrong before, but I believe that I did the only right thing in returning to my homeland . . . In the last eight months I have seen with my own eyes the miraculous transformation of Taiwan . . . a government can only be judged on what it has accomplished for the social and economic well-being of its people . . ." [18] And yet three years before Liao had praised Kerr to me as the American best informed on Formosan problems.

Cheng Wan-fu, ex-leader of the splinter Democratic Independence party in Japan, also returned to Taiwan in April 1966, and the vice president of Liao's former government in exile, Dr. Wu Chen-nan, a Yokohama physician who had been in Japan since 1927, flew back in October 1966. "For all purposes," commented United Press International, Wu's return "marked the end of the Taiwan independence movement, which had little hope of success when it was founded nearly 20 years ago." [19]

The return of Liao to the Nationalist fold was a shock to his more devoted followers, some of whom had warned me not to make contact with anti-Liao groups because they were "agents of the KMT." [20] For Chinese Nationalists, the return of high-ranking Formosan nationalists compensated somewhat for the defection to Peking later in 1965 of Li Tsung-jen, the former Vice President of Nationalist China who had spent the years between 1949 and 1965 in the United States.

The exiled provisional government, both of its splinter parties, and a few smaller independent groups cooperated more fully than before to disprove Nationalist claims of their demise, and condemned the defectors as traitors to the Formosan people. "We are ashamed of how weak Dr. Liao was to fall from our line of revolution, yet we consider it due mainly to personal reasons," declared the provisional government newspaper, *Taiwan Mimpo*.[21] "Liao's father and elder brother died young and Liao, who is now 56, worried about attaining his political goal before he died." The same paper urged renewed efforts in the face of KMT duplicity: "The main reasons for disagreement among our independence groups are our mutual distrust, cultivated by the colonial powers among Formosans and [by] our subjection to the enemy's cunning tricks to divide us." New leaders were chosen who held several joint talks with members of other factions—a departure from the practice under Liao.

Liao's successors ascribed his action to personal worries over his family, property and future. They thought the world-wide publicity given by the Nationalists to such defections, after years spent denying their significance, helped make the world aware of the Formosan cause. The *Taiwan Mimpo* blamed the major rival group in Japan, the Formosan Association (later United Young Formosans for Independence), for its part in driving Liao to defect by its attacks.[22]

Liao's original associate in Japan was "astonished by the news. . . . I never doubted Liao's loyalty and fidelity to the nation, but after hearing the news I could only feel that a human being can stand only so much. . . . It's almost 20 years since Liao and I initiated the basic theory of Formosa's status and began the independence movement . . . nothing happened. . . . The answer was and still is not very promising, so can we blame anyone for his misfortune but fate? Too much criticism of Liao without constructive action is irresponsible. . . ."[23]

One consequence of the Liao defection was that Formosan student leaders were inspired to work harder for the cause. The older activists abroad, who had tended to follow Liao, lost face and allowed younger men to assume leadership of the movement. One American-based student group distributed a letter to Formosans in Europe, Canada, Japan, and the U.S., urging all groups to "encourage one another and cooperate closely for a free and democratic future Republic of Formosa." The letter expressed dismay at Liao's statements after surrendering to the Nationalists, but focused on future positive action rather than criticism of Liao's past errors. A relative who knew Liao's personal problems "regretted the shameful act of an old man" but said he was thereby inspired to devote himself wholeheartedly to the independence movement—much

as sons of Formosan businessmen said they had been fired with greater
zeal for independence by their fathers' fear of opposing the Nationalist
dictatorship. Who can say Liao's defection will not have a similar boomerang effect on thousands of young Formosan intellectuals? [24]

Factional Offshoots of the "Provisional Government"

About 25 Formosan activists I met in Kobe, Osaka, Yokohama, and
Tokyo all claimed to be friendly with Liao, but had worked along lines
that crossed or conflicted with his between 1961 and 1966. At no time
did I gain the impression that any of the groups received substantial
funds from any source. "Money is our biggest problem," said Ryo Mei-
yo, later speaker of the Provisional Assembly, in 1963. "Most Taiwanese
who could help financially think first of themselves, and the big businessmen inside Taiwan think they can make money under present conditions, so they don't risk upsetting the status quo." [25] An activist in
Osaka agreed that "few Japanese or Taiwanese businessmen give us direct or indirect help, and the KMT has not only lots of money but better public relations skill." Others added that wealthier Formosan residents of Japan usually had business connections requiring trips to Taiwan: "Whenever I've asked for contributions, the Japanese say they fear
visa denial and the Taiwanese claim their business comes first," reported
a leader of the Democratic Independent group in 1962.

After hearing some of these Formosans speak among themselves of financial problems for several hours, I decided they were telling the truth:
"People say they favor our goal, but fear to help in any way. Is selfish-
ness the rule among individuals as it is among nations?" They could not
quite bring themselves to give up hope of receiving American aid, although aware that, as a Nagoya activist said, "We must rely on ourselves
first and try to mobilize more of the thousands of Formosans in Japan."

"Japan's language, customs, and political freedom make it the best
place for Taiwan refugees," said an Osaka businessman. A Tokyo-based
activist, however, asked me to appeal to Washington for logistical supplies in 1964 because "Japan wouldn't give us arms, but your CIA did
that for the Cuban exiles—and I have enough volunteers to man landing boats if we could get $150,000 worth of weapons." [26] He insisted
that if only 100 of his men landed on Formosa's east coast, sympathizers would rise up in every major town and city. "The Japanese have

insular feelings and won't help unless America acts first. It would be over very quickly because native troops in Taiwan know where the ammunition is stored. They may seem to be quiet, but when the time is ripe they will do anything to win freedom."

Some Formosans in Japan expressed neutralist desires, or even preference, for mainland rule. "If we had to make a choice between Mao and Chiang, Mao would be better because there might be some chance for a change under his rule but never under the KMT . . . ," said a Tokyo radical. "My father was killed by the Communists while we were living on the mainland between 1947 and 1950, so I hate Communism, but Taiwanese independence must have the Chinese Communists' consent. Liao and his group are too pro-American, so I quit and took a neutral position. All the old men here and in Formosa are too conservative and out of touch with reality; a younger leader will arise as Nasser did in Egypt or the young colonels in South Korea." [27] Many activists in Japan hoped for close ties with the United States and Japan after Formosan independence had been won, and thought that American military guarantees would be better than unarmed neutrality. Several were convinced that prematurely raising post-independence issues would only divide their factions further.

Far more, however, seemed to fear that the United States might eventually acquiesce in a deal with the Nationalists to turn Formosa over to Communist China. "Some KMT diplomats in Japan are more pro-Communist than we Formosans could ever be," argued a former chief of the pro-KMT *Kakyo Sokai* in Nogoya who had become an activist. "The KMT fears U.S. support for an independent Taiwanese state and would hand the island over to the mainland before accepting that idea. Both regimes are Chinese above all, as in their views of Tibet, Mongolia, and the offshore islands." [28]

The story of Kaku Ko-yu is illustrative of the problems of a Formosan activist in Japan. Seeking refuge in Japan after the 1947 massacre, Kaku married a Japanese girl and for most of the next two decades was a small bar owner in Kobe, then a restaurateur in Yokohama and Tokyo. "My wife and daughter sometimes ask me to stop running around and spending our scarce money on the Formosan movement, but I can't help myself," said he when interviewed in a ramshackle bar-residence under the railroad tracks in downtown Kobe.

Kaku became locally famous for the Osaka consular incident of 1961, when he and a friend placed their own "Consulate of the Republic of

Taiwan" sign over the Chinese Nationalist door plaque. They did this after notifying Japanese newsmen, and were quickly arrested for desecration of official property. The case dragged on for years until the Japanese Supreme Court rejected their appeal. Kaku went to jail from May to November 1965, under the strictest type of Japanese prison rules.[29] He resented such a severe penalty: "Why should they penalize my political act, which caused no injury, when they don't punish American GI's who commit murder or other Taiwanese who do worse acts than I did?" he complained after his release.[30]

Shi Mei, an older Formosan writer, talked at length in 1966 of his postwar experiences in Communist China and Japan. "I spent the war years in Japan, then helped teach Taiwanese prisoners for the Chinese Communists before returning to Taiwan in 1949 and then fleeing here in 1951," Shi explained in a tiny room above his Tokyo restaurant.[31] He despaired of help from foreign governments or wealthy Formosans and hoped that more overseas Formosan students would return to work within the island. "The educated youth are the best hope for a free Formosa; they should go back and even join the KMT," he declared.

Kyu Ei-kan, who had written occasional articles in the Japanese press but usually remained aloof from organized groups, entertained me at his luxurious Tokyo home in August 1966. "I am not a politician by personality," he said, "so I could never lead a movement, but I try to mediate among the various groups and write as a spokesman for my people . . . Liao received my help for many years, and also got money from a few Liberal Democratic Party (LDP) politicians, but he was too egotistical and lost his supporters. Richard Koo [president of the Formosan Association] comes from a very good family whose ancestors guided the Japanese troops into Taipei in 1894 and was rewarded with land and a membership in the prewar House of Peers, but he is also a businessman type." [32] At that time Kyu was pessimistic about the future chances of the Formosan movement, but later there were indications that he, Shi Mei, and others who had formerly abstained from organized action were working more closely together; they began publishing a new magazine, *Dokuritsu Taiwan* [Independent Formosa] in mid-1967.[33]

Only time will prove whether it is more durable than earlier journals and whether Liao's former associates could work with the United Young Formosans for Independence, first organized in February 1960 by the Formosan scholar Ong Jok-tik.

The United Young Formosans

Ong's organization, called *Taiwan Chinglian* [Formosan Youth Association] after a prewar Formosan student organization in Tokyo, consisted mostly of students who considered Liao and his provincial government too old and conservative. "I had taught some of [them] when they were in high school on Formosa. . . . Believing that steady propaganda and secret organization were the most important activities at the time, the Association began to publish [the periodical] *Taiwan Chinglian* in Japanese and the *Formosan Quarterly* in English." Ong wrote in 1963.[34] He claimed that 800 Formosan students belonged to the association, "which receives moral and economic support from some 25,000 Formosan businessmen in Japan." In 1966, the name was changed to United Young Formosans for Independence, partly because students in the United States used a similar name.

At our first interview in early 1963, Ong had not claimed such exaggerated support for his organization but instead criticized the division of the independence movement in Japan and the political indifference of most overseas Formosans. "Some of the exiles want a neutral Taiwan without American bases, but this is unrealistic," he said.[35]

In February 1963 we had a lengthy discussion at Ong's home with several student leaders of the Association. "We oppose Liao because of his personality, and also because we feel it is too early to have a provisional government or a 'president'" some of them said. "It's more efficient to operate informally and secretly to evade KMT spies, persuade the timid majority among us to give money or other help, and avoid a rigid organization." Of American military aid one of these young men said: "The United States should help train us because our 500 members have all had recent KMT military service and are young enough to become guerrillas if only we were given Ranger-type training." Although Ong evidently objected to any plans for violent action, whether advocated by his own followers or by those connected with Liao's group, he did not comment on his more militant colleagues.[36]

Everyone attending that discussion expressed disappointment that President Kennedy dropped his criticism of offshore island defense after becoming President. When I reminded them that in 1952 the Republican party had campaigned on other issues, such as "unleashing Chiang Kai-shek," which also had been soft-pedalled after the election, they only continued to insist: "But withdrawal from Quemoy and Matsu is the first step needed; then after that some kind of military training for us and better American controls on weapons given to the Nationalists." [37]

Claims by some of Liao's followers that the Formosan Association contained KMT spies were vehemently denied in 1963, but early the following year one of the members was caught giving information to the Nationalist Embassy. I was told in August 1964:

> We began to suspect a spy when a friend told us there was a leak to the embassy. The spy had been threatened that his family would suffer if he did not cooperate, so finally he agreed. He was around our office a lot, offering to carry messages (which never reached their destination), and running for election to our board of directors. At election time he demanded an open counting of the ballots and left, thinking he had been elected. But after he was gone I asked the others to remain and help trap him by altering the list of successful candidates and eliminating his name. The next day, when we heard that the embassy had the original list of winners, we knew that only he could have been guilty.
>
> When we called him to appear at an executive meeting, he first denied any spying and one of our leaders got mad and knifed him in the shoulder. He broke down and confessed, promising to reform and asking forgiveness for what he had done because of the KMT threats to his family in Formosa. He agreed not to mention the knifing incident, but later he told the Nationalist Embassy, which bypassed the Tokyo police and complained directly to the Japanese Justice Ministry. Seven of us were arrested a month later, held in various police stations for 25 days, then released pending trial. . . . We kept secret data out of the office or private homes, to avoid spying or police searches, but this was our first internal spy case.[38] [At their trial in October 1964 the seven men involved were given suspended sentences.]

Ong Jok-tik attributed the spy danger to membership expansion of the Association, which he had opposed, and perhaps to its consequent militant trend's having aroused Nationalist curiosity. The KMT appears to have feared it more than other Formosan groups in Japan, and cited my contributions to its journals as the official reason for denying me a transit visa in 1966.[39]

Richard Koo, who succeeded Ong as chairman, toured the United States in 1965 to encourage greater unity among Formosan groups abroad. "The causes of factionalism in Japan," said Koo, "included Liao's personality and the lack of his appeal to younger, recent émigrés from Formosa. The masses inside Formosa have no violent spirit so they can be cowed by the KMT police and military. Older Formosans on the island want primarily to protect their money while they send their sons overseas. . . . [Among émigrés] the Liao group were mostly concerned with their past experiences, such as 1947, and their wealth. They wanted to reminisce about the past, whereas our group attracts the younger Formosans who think of the future." Koo denied the possibility of gradual democratization under Nationalist rule: "The trappings of local elections mean nothing as long as mainlanders rule Formosa, nor can economic progress compensate for political suppression." [40]

In the summer of 1966, Koo and some of his colleagues explained their recent strategy. "We just returned from a sit-down demonstration near the Kyoto site of the Japanese-American ministerial conference . . . ," they told me. "Many former Liao supporters joined us in Kyoto and during the 2-82 street march in Tokyo last February, so I think there is more cooperation among the Formosans in Japan than ever before." [41] On the other hand, one of Koo's associates claimed there were ten Formosan activist groups in Japan, all without financial aid, and still divided. Refugee Formosan organizations and their publications continued to remain separate through 1969.[42]

We must remember that the Japanese Justice Ministry has been under Nationalist Chinese pressure for many years to suppress Formosan political activity and, in some cases, to deport activists to Formosa for trial as traitors. Minister of Justice Kaya Okinori, one of the most pro-KMT members of Japan's governing party, was succeeded in that post by Ishii Mitsujiro and others equally sympathetic to the Chinese Nationalists. The Japanese immigration authorities never permit foreigners to live in Japan as "political refugees," as Japan has no political asylum law; but in practice Formosans who entered before the 1952 Sino-Japanese peace treaty have been allowed to remain as stateless persons. But in 1967, two members of the Formosan Association who had overstayed their student visas were arrested for deportation to Taiwan. They refused food and drink in their cell while their colleagues staged a simultaneous hunger strike outside the Justice Ministry, and a large number of Japanese and American friends appealed for leniency.[43]

As Japan's Prime Minister Eisaku Sato prepared to fly to Taipei for an official goodwill visit in September 1967, the Association accused the Sato regime of "bartering the lives of helpless Formosan refugees" for the sake of better trade with Formosa. The two men were released in early September 1967, but the incident made all Formosans in Japan more fearful than before to engage in political activity. The tightening of immigration restrictions had already caused one illegal immigrant to hang himself in the Yokohama deportation center rather than be forced back to certain death in Taiwan.

The most serious deportation incident occurred March 26, 1968 when Liu Wen-cheng, a member of the United Young Formosans for Independence was arrested by order of the Justice Ministry for overstaying his student visa. The next morning he was rushed aboard a Chinese plane at Tokyo airport despite his attempt to commit suicide and the efforts of ten Formosan friends to wrest him from the police at planeside. The forcible deportation aroused widespread protests and led to the formation of an Association to Protect Human Rights of Taiwanese in Japan whose founders included 55 Diet members, numerous scholars, and other public figures.[44] "Another similar case may happen at any time," wrote Ng Yu-zin, a leader of UYFI. "This is just the beginning of our tragedy."

Members of the UYFI and friends had demonstrated peacefully against the 1967 visit of Chiang Ching-kuo, after the Tokyo District Court revoked a previous ban on their approach to the Nationalist Embassy area, ruling in an historic decision that foreign residents in Japan "have the same right of freedom of expression as any Japanese." [45] The fact that ten times more pro-Peking demonstrators than non-Communists separately demonstrated against his visit enabled Ching-kuo to accuse them all of Communist sympathy.

While the United Young Formosans for Independence and all other activist groups in Japan continue to face problems of leadership, tactics, financial support, and the elusive goal of unity among themselves and with similar groups abroad, the majority of their fellow-Formosans in Japan remain aloof from political activity. "Politics is bad for business, and I am only concerned with my *pachinko* [pinball] parlor," explained one apolitical Formosan, who made occasional visits to Formosa and, typically, wanted to preserve both business and personal ties with the homeland.[46] "This means we cannot criticize the Nationalist regime even if we dislike it," said a Formosan official of the *Kakyo Sokai* [Overseas Chinese Association] who had noted the lack of freedom on his visits to Formosa. Those few apolitical Formosans in Japan willing to speak with me seemed to confirm the activists' opinion of them. One doctor who had been in Japan 20 years explained that he never wanted to return to Formosa. "I may change my mind later, but Japan has been so good to me," he explained.[47] His younger brother who was on a student visa and planning to return home eventually, said apologetically: "I agree with your impressions of my homeland, but cannot take any active political role here because of my student status."

Despite Nationalist blandishments, recurring reports of the arrest of Formosan students who do go home have naturally discouraged others from returning. In mid-1967, several Formosan students who had returned from Japan, at least two of whom were enrolled at Tokyo National University, were arrested inside the island and held as suspected political activists. Nationalist officials stationed in New York denied any such arrests had been made.[48] A friend of one of the victims, however, wrote: "In 1967 there were two 'security sweeps,' one in August and one in October . . . purportedly to locate wanted criminals but actually to take into custody those who are suspected opponents, real or imaginary, to the Chiang regime." [49]

The Nationalists deny the existence of any independence sentiment among Formosans in Japan, attributing all demonstrations (such as those against Chiang Ching-kuo's 1967 visit) to a small group of Communist-paid agents. Yet the Nationalist regime's pressure on Japan to deport Formosan activists or restrict their activity inside Japan, and its increasing tendency to arrest returning Formosan students of questionable politics, show its real concern about the growth of independence sentiment.

Formosan Activities in the United States

In June 1963, I began a systematic program of interviewing students, businessmen, and other Formosans in the United States. By mid-1968, I had spoken with over 600 Formosans in New York, Boston, Philadelphia, Los Angeles, and on university campuses across the country, and had corresponded with many others. Some were activists; others were willing to talk at clandestine meetings even though they refused to participate in organized groups because they wished to return to the island or feared pressure on their families. Based on the five-year study, my conclusions are that about 10 to 20 per cent of the Formosan students and teachers on any campus are politically active; over 80 per cent join only in Formosan social affairs; and almost all the latter would say privately that they shared the beliefs and aspirations of the activists.

There were very few Formosans in the United States before 1949; most had come as postwar students. They could provide valuable information on the Nationalist armed services in which all male students had served before being allowed to emigrate. In one case, a student had been regarded as very pro-Nationalist by American professors who knew him as an undergraduate in Formosa. After coming to the United States, however, he explained that he avoided giving an anti-Nationalist appearance in order to get his passport and be able to return after earning his American doctorate. I met others who began with similar intentions, but changed their plans after the Nationalists arrested some of their compatriots.

Early in 1963 I had been struck by the amount of factional rivalry among activist groups in the U. S., resembling that in Japan. Edward Chen, then the leader of the Philadelphia-based United Formosans for Independence, claimed in a February 1963 letter that his was "the only organized Formosan group," and denied knowledge of a smaller group in New York which called itself the Formosan Readers Association. In truth, the leader of the FRA had split off from the UFI in an attempt to appeal to incoming students more successfully than the pro-Liao UFI group of older members. "Don't worry too much about the divisions in our ranks," advised Alfred Choy, a Formosan businessman in New York and perhaps the leading activist in that region. "I've seen so many Formosan student groups rise and then disintegrate as their members left their campuses. A solid organization cannot be based on graduate students." [50]

Most factional disputes among Formosans in the United States, as in Japan, arose over personalities and tactics rather than basic goals. For example, one issue that divided many activists was the role to be assigned to anti-KMT mainlanders either before or after independence. Should any such mainlanders be considered revolutionary allies, allowed to vote in a plebiscite, or welcomed in the governing of a future Republic of Formosa? "It is a shame we must reveal to you our differences, which only serve to divide us in the face of the Nationalist enemy," wrote one Philadelphia student.

The divisions among American-based Formosans result partly from generation gap and partly from tactical differences among their leaders, but mostly from the inherent difficulty of financing and staffing a large and transient organization. Moreover, most Formosan students must work while they study and can rarely spare the time or effort to be active politically.

Evolution of the UFAI (United Formosans in America for Independence)

Alfred Choy said he had become disillusioned as he saw "many generations of students scatter and disappear because they wanted to seek a permanent life in the United States." He added: "Formosan students here should return to work within the island, even joining the KMT to bore from within. Our ancestors always told their children to avoid politics: this created the apathy, lack of trained political types, and the social differences you saw in Taiwan. The same spirit pervades most of the overseas Formosans who fear involvement in our activist movement, and won't attend anything but purely social events. They flock by the hundreds to a New Year's party, but prefer to live as apolitical businessmen after leaving college." Yet Choy and his colleagues who came in the 1950's instigated a political movement which inspired others, such as Edward (I-te) Chen, to form the United Formosans for Independence (UFI).

In early 1963, the UFI struggled to publish two magazines: *Ilha Formosa*, a quarterly in English to appeal to Americans which lasted only a year, and *Formosagram*, a bilingual monthly newsletter exclusively for the Formosan students which continues as an excellent channel of communication for the nationwide student community. Chen edited both journals originally but after 1966 the reorganized UFAI edited the *Formosagram* and the *Independent Formosa* quarterly (transferred from Tokyo).

Centered in the Washington-Philadelphia-New York-Boston area of the northeastern United States, the UFI sponsored social events which sometimes attracted as many as 1,200 participants. Not surprisingly, political demonstrations—at the United Nations, for example, or in front of the Chinese Nationalist Embassy in Washington—brought out much smaller numbers who often masked their faces. Nevertheless, the UFI public demonstrations attracted local attention and inspired many incoming Formosan students to consider more deeply opportunities for political expression which were not available in their native island.

"On February 29, 1964, about 50 Formosans took part in the demonstration in Washington. It was a dramatic scene, unexpectedly large, covered by over a dozen reporters including four Japanese. The police prohibited us from marching within 500 feet of the Chinese Embassy, so we were 7 or 8 blocks away and quite a few passersby were confused about our purpose," wrote Chen. In the early 1960's the UFI had perhaps 200 active members and another 500 sympathizers among the Formosan student community. Most members were between 35 and 45 years of age; few were graduate students.

In late 1965, a small conference with representatives from several sections of the United States and Canada met in the Midwest to plan a more effective and unified Formosan Independence organization. Richard Koo, alluded to earlier as leader of the most active Formosan group in Japan, had visited several American cities the previous summer to urge coordination of groups in the United States and Japan. The younger activists in America chose UFAI (United Formosans in America for Independence) while Koo's group became the UYFI (United Young Formosans for Independence).

At Yale in 1965, fifteen Formosans out of about forty on that campus assured me that the others were equally devoted to the common cause but were afraid to be associated with it publicly. In Manhattan, Kansas, about 40 Formosans and 30 Nationalist Chinese students at Kansas State University attended a university-sponsored lecture I gave based on Chapters 4 and 5 of this book. "What are the Formosans in Tokyo paying you for writing in their journals?" asked one of the Chinese. "You are not a scholar, but a propagandist! An ugly American!" said another after the lecture. None of the Formosans spoke up, although many had defended the Formosan cause in the university newspaper.[51] Mainland Chinese students on most U.S. campuses are politically neutral, however, and seldom interfere with Formosan student clubs.

Formosan students expressed their political feelings in letters to me and to campus newspapers. A Formosan student in Oklahoma wrote: "The Formosan people are one of the most miserable people in the world, yet not many people outside the island pay attention to them . . . I strongly believe that without struggle the Formosans cannot have their liberty and independence . . . I appreciate very much your speaking of the truth about the situation in Formosa." [52] A Formosan at the University of Kansas wrote: "My studies impress on me that only a rebellion back home can push the Formosan issue into the process of a U.N. solution. I feel frequently that most Formosan students abroad are too theoretical but not practical; too idealistic but not revolutionary." [53]

A Syracuse University student and another enrolled at the University of Iowa expressed similar sentiments, and a few others wrote anony-

mously for fear of Nationalist retaliation: "It is encouraging and heartening to find that not all Americans belong to the China lobby. There
are a few like yourself who really understand the agony and tragedy of
Formosa. You will be remembered by 10 million Formosans. . . . Let
us never lose hope that one day there will be true freedom and democracy in Taiwan." [54]

Very few Formosan students go home after obtaining a graduate degree in the United States. One of that brave minority wrote before his
return: "Being the only child of my parents from a poor family, I never
expected to get an education above high school . . . After receiving a
master's degree in the Midwest, I went to New York and held many
talks with older Taiwanese there. I argued and even quarreled with them
about ways to solve our problems. I advocated a course of cooperation
between young Formosans and mainlanders to overthrow the KMT dictatorship rather than to create Formosan independence. Then they converted me to the independence cause. Now I go back to do my best to
serve this cause, very aware of the dangers involved. . . . I believe that
more Formosans should go back to penetrate the KMT and to bring
them down by all means, while others work abroad." [55] It is a path requiring great skill, patience, and luck.

Pressures against Formosan Students in America

How does the Nationalist regime exert pressure on overseas Formosan
students? It cannot easily deny the right to study abroad, as all the island
students are careful to behave properly in order to get their passports for
study in America or Japan. Moreover, a few Nationalist consular officials
in the United States privately sympathize with Formosan students who
apply for extension of their passports after engaging in mild political activity: "The vice-consul I approached seemed very indifferent politically
and approved my passport extension even though he knew I'd been active in my campus Formosan Club," said one graduate student. The few
efforts by Japanese immigration authorities to deport Formosan activists
have had no counterpart in the United States, where authorities have
not deported Formosans who overstayed their visas.

One of the most active leaders of the Formosan independence movement in the United States reported KMT use of parental dissuasion:
"The mother of my brother's fiancée was sent [over here] to break up
the engagement because of my reputation. . . . We must expect that

kind of KMT pressure—they even sent one of my parents to America to dissuade me from political activity." Strong Formosan family loyalties are likewise exploited. "Last year the KMT refused my parents an exit visa for the United States to see me, my wife, and our baby. So my father died, later the same year, without having seen my wife or his grandson. My mother is desperately trying to reach the U.S.A., but I feel it is hopeless unless I surrender to the Nationalists. The nearest Chinese consulate even refused to verify my name-stamp which would allow my mother or brother to inherit my property," a Formosan student in the United States wrote in 1967.[56]

One of the most serious Nationalist attempts to punish a returned Formosan student occurred in 1966. Chii-ming Hwang returned in March 1966 to spend two months gathering Ph.D. dissertation material for a thesis supported by a grant from the U.S. Office of Education. He was arrested in early September 1966, held in jail without benefit of habeas corpus or a lawyer, and was sentenced to five years for sedition. News of the trial was printed in *The New York Times* the following week: "A 35-year old native of Taiwan was convicted . . . by a secret military court . . . Arrested September 2 by the Taiwan Garrison Command [after] unsuccessfully seeking an exit permit . . . The indictment asserted that Mr. Hwang had attended a meeting of the Taiwan Independence Federation in Chicago and said he had met with a Taiwanese independence leader in Tokyo on his way to Taiwan . . . Mr. Hwang was given a closed two-hour trial on February 7 . . ."[57]

President Fred Harrington of the University of Wisconsin sent the following telegram to Secretary of State Dean Rusk, on March 17, 1967: "Urgently request your intervention case Chii-ming Hwang, Republic of China graduate student at the University of Wisconsin, now imprisoned by Chinese government on Taiwan. . . . Formosan Affairs Study Group was officially registered UW student group with the required faculty advisor. Such groups freely debate issues. Faculty participation in such meetings assures us no ground for charges sedition in such meetings. . . . No free university worthy of its name can tolerate this kind of political interference with legitimate research. If students from Republic of China not free to participate in discussion programs in this country, we believe will be impossible to accept further such students. Will advise other graduate schools accordingly. . . . Believe most urgent representations must be made to Republic of China in this case, including our intentions with respect to future students from that country."[58]

The Department of State and the U.S. Embassy in Taipei disclaimed any responsibility for Hwang. "He is not an American citizen, and has broken the laws of his country against political activity abroad, so what can we do?" was the view of several Washington officials in late 1966. Meanwhile a military appeals court granted Hwang a retrial on May 16, 1967 and he was released in early July on "insufficient evidence," but not permitted to leave the island.[59]

Three inferences can be drawn from the case of Chii-ming Hwang. First, other Formosan graduate students in the United States feared to return home as a result of Hwang's fate. Second, those Americans in Washington who had helped Hwang obtain an Office of Education grant were disturbed by his arrest, imprisonment, and release under surveillance, but powerless. "We, too, have been concerned about Chii-ming Hwang," wrote an officer of the United States National Student Association in Washington. "A former member of the NSA's National Supervisory Board happens to have been his program officer in the Office of Education, the person responsible for Hwang's grant to go to Asia . . . He was outraged by the action of the Nationalist government, but alas, we knew of no course open to USNSA which could assist Hwang." [60]

Third, the cautious attitude of American officials in Washington and Taipei indicates that Formosa is not an American colony, as Peking charges, but that Washington seems in some ways a captive of the Chiang lobby. Every State Department official whom I reached in late 1966 denied that the Embassy in Taipei could give Hwang asylum "unless he ran through the gate with police chasing him, like Cardinal Mindzenty in Budapest during the 1956 Hungarian revolt."

In mid-1967, the *Central Daily News*, an official Nationalist in Taipei, attacked a Formosan law graduate of Yale University for publishing an anti-Nationalist book, *Taiwan, China, and the World Community*, co-authored by Professor Harold Lasswell of the Yale Law School.[61]

To sum up the attitudes of the 6,000 or more Formosans in the United States: the vast majority hope to remain abroad until their home island is a democratic republic safe from either KMT or Communist rule. Most would prefer to avoid direct confrontation with the Nationalists, because they value their own lives or the security of their parents back in Formosa. "It is shameful to admit that our people don't have the same militant spirit of self-sacrifice as the Cuban refugees, the South Koreans, the Greek Cypriots, or other peoples with less reason to revolt," was a typical apology of several overseas Formosans. The influx of more young Formosans to American campuses, however, probably presages a more militant generation not so likely to be satisfied with the "Politics-no-touch" attitude of their parents. Debate over "freedom and self-determination" aspects of American policy in Vietnam and the black power movement inside the United States have combined to persuade many newcomers of the importance of Formosan efforts to secure their own goals.

What do the more numerous (about 200,000) Chinese residents of the United States think of Formosan nationalism? Although overseas Chinese are usually both anti-KMT and anti-Communist, I had assumed that most would be antipathetic or apathetic and would not understand or approve the Formosan separatist view. Yet Formosan student leaders in the United States often suggested the large "third force" among overseas Chinese as a good source of information and possible support. For example, the aged publisher of a New York Chinese journal attended the 1964 benefit dinner of the UFI in New York. "Isn't he Chinese?" I asked my seatmate at the speakers' table. "Yes, but he supports our Formosan cause," he replied. From that time, I tried to make contact with as many overseas Chinese as possible to ascertain their views on the Formosan issue.

"There *is* a nationalism in Taiwan. Not talking about it wouldn't help solve the problem," a Chinese professor who had been a personal advisor to President Chiang wrote from Michigan State University in 1967. A nephew of a former Nationalist official wrote in 1965: "I don't think my opinion is representative as a mainlander student. Few of them are concerned about the political, moral, or intellectual issues in Taiwan. Still fewer are anxious to go back to the Far East. I am pessimistic about the U.S. giving fuller support to a free Taiwan: I think there is greater probability for the U.S. to render Taiwan back to mainland China for various considerations. If I can do anything in this country, perhaps it is to exert my opinion against this 'return of Taiwan' to China. But, ultimately, would it be worse for the Taiwanese to live under the Communists than to live under the demoralizing and de-intellectualizing KMT regime? . . ." [62]

The chairman of the Department of Political Science in a state university wrote in 1966, before my banishment from Taiwan: "I certainly hope you will be better welcomed in Taiwan than last time . . . and that you can see Professor Peng and his other colleagues released from prison." [63] Another mainland Chinese professor wrote from South Dakota that he was forced to flee from China to Taiwan and was neither "pro-KMT nor pro-Taiwanese . . . my main intention is to pursue the academic truth." [64] Henry Pan, editor-publisher of the Chicago *San Min Morning Paper* (now defunct but which was founded by Sun Yat-sen), held two meetings with me in 1967. "I may not agree with your pro-Taiwan views, but you have every right to express those opinions," he said. "I have refused several Nationalist government invitations to return to Taiwan, because of its authoritarian habits." [65] The major Chinese-language newspaper in New York is pro-Communist, and those on the West Coast more pro-Nationalist; Pan's paper was the most objectively critical of both regimes.

The majority of overseas Chinese are apolitical, as I discovered when speaking to Hong Kong businessmen about conditions on Formosa. "Why do you ask me about Chiang and the Formosans?" one shouted angrily. "I'm not interested in either Chiang or Mao, and know nothing about the Formosans." One exception was an older woman selling beaded handbags in her small Hong Kong street stall in late 1966. When I wrote for her, on a pad in Chinese, of having been blacklisted by both Chinese regimes for my writings, she nodded and said "Same, same!" On the other hand, Chinese faculty and students at the two major universities in Hong Kong showed little interest in the Formosan issue.

Formosan Activities in Other Countries

Outside of Japan and the United States, there are active Formosan organizations in Canada and Western Europe. The Formosan Association of Canada is composed primarily of students on university campuses and has the same social purpose as the Formosan Clubs on American campuses. More politically conscious Formosans in Canada formed the Committee for Human Rights in Formosa, headed for several years by Robert Y. M. Huang. In late 1965, Huang said there were about 200 Formosan students in Canada of whom less than one-fourth belonged to the Committee.[66] "We chose the human rights name to emphasize basic issues, appeal to the majority of Canadians who have no sentimental attachment to the Nationalists, and avoid the factionalism that plagues other Formosan groups," Huang explained after the 1965 unity conference. Formosan students created a Union for Formosa's Independence in Europe (UFIE) in 1966 with headquarters in Paris. The Canadian Committee and the UFIE co-sponsor the *Independent Formosa* quarterly with their compatriots in Japan (UYFI) and the United States

(UFAI), but are much less active than the latter in conducting meetings and organizing demonstrations among either fellow-Formosans or the public. All overseas Formosan activists tend to pin their hopes on the U.S. as the only nation capable of influencing the fate of their homeland.

"One of the greatest failures in American foreign policy is her blind support for dictators such as Chiang and Franco. American prestige and the significance of her domestic democracy will certainly be reduced by half as long as she keeps on such a wrong policy. It seems to me that the U.S.A. can do much more to influence the KMT in Taiwan in exchange for military and economic aid. . . . The CIA should support Taiwan independence activities abroad . . . If we asked Russia for aid, then Washington might listen to us. I think the U.S.A. needs some stimulus to take the Taiwan problem seriously. You know as well as I do that the majority of Taiwanese are both pro-American and anti-Communist." [67] This was a Formosan student's rebuke to United States indifference toward Formosan aspirations while it was spending $28 billion a year on the war in Vietnam. The wealth and lives which America has spent to defend West Europeans, South Koreans, and South Vietnamese seem to many foreign-based Formosans relevant to their own cause: "If Washington committed itself to those fights for freedom," they reason, "it should also recognize our right to self-determination."

8

AMERICAN VIEWS OF FORMOSAN
NATIONALISM

United States policies during and after World War II have had the major influence on the course of Formosan nationalism. They led to the island's being virtually handed over to the Nationalist government, which has ever since been able to count on America for diplomatic, military, and economic support. And, as a consequence of those policies, Chinese leaders in Taipei and Peking have come to regard the U.S. as their principal ally and enemy, respectively, while many governments have been inhibited from dealing flexibly with the China problem by their reluctance to antagonize America's pro-Nationalist leadership.

For their part, Formosans look to the U.S. for help in achieving at least economic and political equality with, if not actual independence from, their mainland rulers. In the words of the Formosan scholar Peter P. C. Cheng, "the United States, being the leader of the free world in the Western Pacific, has most deeply committed herself on the entire affair. Positive steps at an early date on the part of the United States are necessary to ensure unimpeded progress to Taiwan independence . . ."[1]

The American government and people became emotionally attached to the Nationalist regime during the Sino-Japanese war of 1937–1945 and their own Pacific War. Later, although disillusioned by Chiang's inability to defeat the Communists, they were committed to defend the Chiang regime on Formosa by the logic of the post-Korean War policy of containment of Communist China. Both Washington and the American public remain divided on the complex issues of their alliance with the Nationalists and on the future of Formosa itself.

This chapter examines official United States policy toward Formosa as background to its principal focus on the attitudes of government officials, scholars, journalists, and the general public. As throughout the book, the emphasis is on Formosan nationalism, rather than on attitudes toward Communist or Nationalist China in United States policy, since many other books deal with the latter topics.[2]

The Evolution of Official American Policy

David Schoenbrun, an American correspondent with experience in Southeast Asia, likes to tell a "bitter joke circulating among diplomats in Paris. It began with the question: Who was the worst American Secretary of State, Acheson or Dulles? Answer: Dulles. Reason: Acheson gave China to the Reds but Dulles gave America to Chiang Kai-shek." [3] The first half of the reason is, of course, false (although many Nationalist Chinese would agree with it), but the second half is true in Formosan eyes.

Until Pearl Harbor, Americans scarcely knew of Formosa's existence. More Canadian and British than U.S. missionaries had served there before and after the island's transfer in 1895 from Chinese to Japanese rule. Washington had merely maintained a consulate in Taipei as recognition of Japanese sovereignty; and U.S. Navy plans to invade the island in 1945 were discarded in favor of the Okinawa campaign.

The Yalta Agreement of 1945, affecting Eastern Europe, Manchuria, and Japanese interests in the Kurile islands, received much postwar criticism. The less publicized Cairo Conference transfer of Formosa, however, revealed an equal ignorance of historic facts and lies at the root of the United States' China problem today. The Cairo commitment, and subsequent United States support for the Nationalist refugee regime on Formosa after 1950, can be cited by any mainland Chinese government as evidence of official American approval of their claim that Formosa is an integral part of China. The commitment began what George Kerr has termed the "American betrayal of Formosans."

Relatively few Formosans blame the United States for collusion in the 1947 massacre, and about half the present Formosan population was born after that incident. Formosans complain most about what they consider American indifference to their plight, U.S. support for the Chiang regime as an anti-Communist ally, and possible U.S. willingness to trade Formosa for a future settlement with mainland China. "You [Americans] think of our island as a pawn," said the son of a lawyer in southern Formosa. "After the record of Washington's past policies here, can we be blamed for being cynical about American motives?"

The Truman administration began its reappraisal of China policy with the famous "White Paper" of 1949 and Secretary of State Acheson's indirect exclusion of Formosa from the Pacific defense perimeter in January 1950.[4] Later that year, after Peking had occupied Hainan island in mid-May and prepared to mount an invasion across the Formosa straits, President Truman suspended aid to the Nationalists and denied any U.S. intention of "utilizing its armed forces to interfere in the present situation. The United States will not pursue a course which will lead to involvement in the civil conflict in China . . . Similarly, the United States will not provide military aid or advice to Chinese forces on Formosa." [5]

Chiang's forces, ironically, were saved by the June 1950 invasion of South Korea. Immediately, Washington placed South Korea and Formosa within its defense perimeter and ordered the Seventh Fleet to patrol the Formosa Straits. "In these circumstances," Truman stated on June 27, "the occupation of Formosa by Communist forces would be a direct threat to the security of the Pacific area and to the United States performing their lawful and necessary function in that area." [6] He added: "The determination of the future status of Formosa must await the restoration of security in the Pacific, a peace settlement with Japan, or consideration by the United Nations."

Truman's action amounted to a moratorium on Formosa, but he did not explicitly recognize the Chiang regime's sovereignty over the island (which Japan had surrendered in 1945 to all the Allies, not just China); nor did he accept Chiang's offer on June 29, 1950 of 30,000 troops to help in Korea. A month later, however, on July 31, General Douglas MacArthur flew from Tokyo to Taipei for an overnight visit to assure Chiang that American advisors and weapons would soon arrive.[7]

In 1952, Nationalist Chinese rejoiced when General Eisenhower was elected U.S. President, assuming that his administration would "unleash" their forces to counterattack the mainland. The Republicans in Congress had condemned the Truman administration for "losing China to the Communists" and not giving more help to the Chiang regime on Formosa, but campaign slogans are a poor guide to actual intentions. Eisenhower ended the Korean War without the total victory demanded by the MacArthur wing of his party, but included in his State of the Union message in 1953 the promised "de-neutralization" of Formosa to permit

Nationalist operations. No counterattack occurred, however, because the United States still opposed it in practice.

John Foster Dulles, soon to become the Republican Secretary of State, interpreted the 1951 Japanese Peace Treaty renunciation of Formosa and the Pescadores, without naming a beneficiary state, as merely taking "Japan out of the Formosan picture, leaving the position [of Formosa] otherwise unchanged." [8] During the ratification of the Mutual Defense Treaty between the United States and the Nationalists, Dulles went even further by claiming that "technical sovereignty over Formosa and the Pescadores has never been settled . . . the Japanese peace treaty merely involves a renunciation by Japan of its right and title to these islands. But the future title is not determined by the peace treaty which was concluded between the Republic of China and Japan [in 1952]. Therefore, the judicial status . . . is different from [that] of the offshore islands which have always been Chinese territories." [9] Moreover, in giving its consent to the Nationalist China defense treaty, the Senate declared in February 1955 that "it is the understanding of the Senate that nothing in the treaty shall be construed as affecting or modifying the legal status or sovereignty of the territories to which it applies." [10]

Secretary Dulles and Nationalist Foreign Minister George Yeh agreed in an official exchange of notes dated December 10, 1954 that "offensive military operations by either party from the territories held by the Republic of China would be undertaken only as a matter of joint agreement." [11] The Nationalist regime has chafed under that restraint ever since.

By the time of the Communist 1958 offshore island bombardment, Washington was committed by treaty to defend Formosa and the Pescadores while the 1955 Formosa Resolution approved any use of American forces to protect "such related positions and territories" as necessary to defend Formosa. Neither the 1954 treaty nor the 1955 joint resolution mentions Quemoy or Matsu by name, apparently because Eisenhower and Dulles wanted a "predated check" to keep the Communists guessing which offshore island might be defended.[12] After the 1958 crisis subsided, Dulles said that the Nationalists would be foolish to keep a large garrison on the offshore islands, "if there were a dependable cease-fire." His deputy (and later successor) Christian Herter called the Nationalist attachment to the small coastal islands "pathological." [13]

A year before the 1958 Quemoy incident, an American sergeant killed a Chinese prowler in his Taipei garden, precipitating the only postwar riot against the United States Embassy in the Nationalist capital. The sergeant, acquitted by an American military court three days after the shooting, was flown home. The victim's widow shouted for justice outside the embassy gates, attracting a large mob which sacked the building, tore down the flag, and injured a few employees. William Lederer claimed that the riot was staged by Chiang Ching-kuo to embarrass the United States and possibly uncover secret files in the embassy.[14] Formosan informants told me in 1961 and 1962 that the demonstrators had been Chinese, not Formosan, organized to dramatize Nationalist demands for a status-of-forces agreement permitting Chinese trials for American servicemen committing off-base crimes. Washington had signed such agreements with NATO nations and Japan, but delayed giving such privileges to other Far Eastern allies until 1966.

During the Kennedy-Nixon presidential campaign of 1960, Senator Kennedy questioned the wisdom of the American position on Quemoy and Matsu. He said he doubted the strategic value of those islands and feared that the vagueness of the American commitment to defend them would entangle America in the Chinese civil war. However, when accused by Nixon and others of "softness" toward Communist China, Kennedy drew back from advocacy of any offshore island disengagement.

When the Nationalists threatened to use their Security Council veto to bar Outer Mongolia from the UN in 1961, Secretary of State Dean Rusk asked President Kennedy whether U.N. Ambassador Adlai Stevenson could be authorized "to inform other delegations discreetly that a study committee might recommend for the consideration of the General Assembly in 1962 an essentially 'two-China' solution based along these lines. [Kennedy] then expressed his own sympathy with Stevenson's position: 'You have the hardest thing in the world to sell. *It really doesn't make any sense—the idea that Taiwan represents China.* But, if we lost this fight, if Red China comes into the U.N. during our first year in town . . . they'll run us both out . . . I am going to send a new letter to Chiang Kai-shek, based on what is good for us . . . We'll have to get [Henry Luce, Roy Howard, and Walter Judd] to make it clear to Chiang that he can't expect to make a domestic political issue out of our strategy in the U.N." [15] (Emphasis added.)

Kennedy's impatience with Chiang was reminiscent of President Truman's similar comments on December 5, 1950: "I gave [Prime Minister] Attlee a short summary of the kind of trouble that Chiang presented for us. I pointed out that his friends, especially in the Senate, kept up a running clamor on his behalf. Yet all of Chiang's actions suggested that he was not interested in improving the conditions of the territory he controlled but rather that he hoped to get us involved on China's mainland." [16]

Kennedy made good use of the unofficial ambassadorial-level talks with Communist China in Warsaw as reported by Kenneth Young: "An even more dramatic signalling of intentions and lessening of tensions came in 1962 when the Chinese Nationalists gave the appearance of preparing to harass and invade coastal China and Chinese Communist forces began to build up opposite Taiwan. In this grave confrontation, President Kennedy used the Warsaw channel to tell Peking that the United States would not support any such undertaking by the Chinese Nationalists, but on the other hand would defend Taiwan if Peking mistakenly resorted to force. The signal went through, for the crisis abated. This may well have been the most valuable single consequence of the Ambassadorial talks." [17]

When President Johnson denied any American intention to overthrow the Communist regimes in Hanoi or Peking, despite his escalation of military efforts in Vietnam, he also predicted that Communist China would one day "take a respected seat" in the family of nations.[18] The China News of Taipei dismissed the prediction, but warned its readers that "the Republic of China cannot relax in certitude that the United States will never make an approach of any kind to Peiping. The United States has made gestures in the past; the Warsaw talks are one such. Washington no doubt will make others while the Peiping regime survives . . . The United States is looking out for its own interests, just as is the Republic of China. We cannot presume that the American alliance automatically guarantees the fulfillment of all our hopes and aspirations . . ." [19]

Peking is wrong in claiming that the United States occupies "China's territory, Taiwan" against the wishes of Formosans who want only to be liberated by their mainland comrades. It would be more correct to say that Chiang occupies a preferred position among American allies in the Pacific. When Lyndon Johnson was Senate majority leader, he agreed with Adlai Stevenson's 1954 warning against going to war over Quemoy and Matsu ("such miserable real estate," in Stevenson's words). Johnson thought Stevenson "correct in asserting that the only real solution lies in due regard to the realities in Asia, rather than saber-rattling and blustering." [20] However, as President, Johnson after 1963 openly embraced the Nationalist regime as a free world ally and an economic model for developing nations, while maintaining the equivocal attitude of his predecessors toward a Nationalist counterattack. President Richard Nixon is unlikely to promote a counterattack, despite his reputation as a warm friend of Nationalist leaders, but he is even less likely to advance the cause of Formosan self-determination.

Diplomatic and Military Officers' Views

Few active-duty diplomats or military officers with experience on Formosa wish to be quoted as sympathetic toward the cause of Formosan nationalism, but State Department and USIA officers are more likely to be pro-Formosan in their personal views than military officers or AID personnel, perhaps because of their closer association with the Formosan natives or their focus on political and cultural issues.

Military personnel worked most closely with their Nationalist counterparts, both during the struggle against Japan and the Maoist rebellion and the later years on Formosa. By training, they are taught to follow orders, respect Allied governments, and place security above all other considerations. As a group, therefore, military officers with experience in Formosa distrust their civilian colleagues and avoid even private disagreement with official policy. "He may be a bastard, but at least he's our bastard" is likely to be their strongest criticism of the Chiang regime. One Navy captain, active for many years in the Naval Medical Research Unit in Taiwan, said, "Our work would be jeopardized by any expression of political sentiment critical of the governments with which we must work." An Army officer with wide experience in Asia, questioned about aid for Formosan political prisoners replied: "Both State and Defense are clear about the undesirability of members of a MAAG or other military officers initiating queries concerning persons held for political purposes . . . One of the prices for political activity against regimes such as the Republic of China is a lack of complete freedom."

Officers stationed near the Taichung Nationalist military bases who shopped in downtown Taichung, and occasionally stayed at the same hotel that I did, sometimes mentioned mainlander-Formosan differences, including the cultural and social gap. Once, when an Air Force pilot stationed at the Tainan air base overheard me speaking in Japanese to one of the hotel clerks, he said, "I was in Japan and Okinawa before I came here. Those were better people than we have to work with here, but the Formosans are okay. They'll tell you the truth about Chiang Kai-shek's gang if you get to know them—but you speak Japanese so I don't have to tell you anything."

Occasionally, at the Taipei Officers' Open Mess where Fulbrighters were allowed limited privileges, American officers at the bar would speak very frankly after several drinks on Saturday night. "You're for the Formosans? Have a drink on me!" was a common attitude, although one in three would defend the Nationalist regime as more reliably anti-Communist. Their contacts had been with mainlander officers almost exclusively, and not many of the Formosans they encountered, such as drivers and maids, spoke English well enough to communicate political ideas.

Veterans organizations, with their tradition of support for all anti-Communist regimes, cannot be expected to favor the idea of Formosan independence. The editor of the American Legion magazine wrote me a very long defense of a pro-Nationalist article in the May 1966 issue: "The so-called native Formosans today are largely, like Chiang's refugees, mainland Chinese who came to this island at various times in the past. . . . The major fact remains that on Taiwan the Free Chinese have made an Asian bastion of major significance in the world as it is today. . . . Certainly they can occupy no other place off the mainland with more justice than Formosa . . . I trust you are not so naive as to believe that the island would long remain untrod by the mainland Reds . . . or that the island situation would not retrogress to what it was when the Nationalists arrived." [21] He referred at length to the strategic importance of Formosa as an anti-Communist base and compared the Formosans to American Indians.

Friends in the AID office in Taipei reported that MAAG officers seldom shared information with them, and seemed aloof from the civilian operations in Formosa. "All they're interested in is the military hardware and training mission, not the economic or political problems on the island," said an AID planning officer. Perhaps in consequence, Formosans were likelier to seek employment in the United States diplomatic, economic, or informational services than in the military units.

It was natural, perhaps, that American diplomats in the 1950's expressed very pro-Nationalist attitudes. Less than one year after my first visit to Formosa in 1957, the State Department sent a memorandum to all its missions abroad explaining the policy of non-recognition of Communist China. After denying that its policy was inflexible, the memorandum catalogued all its complaints against the Peking regime: "The United States holds the view that communism's rule in China is not permanent and that it one day will pass. By withholding diplomatic recognition from Peiping it seeks to hasten that passing." [22] Graham Parsons, then assistant secretary for Far Eastern affairs, told the Wisconsin Bar Association in 1960 that a "two Chinas," or "one China, one Taiwan" policy was unrealistic because both Chinese regimes bitterly opposed it. "On the other hand, by means of the joint communiqué issued by President Chiang and the late Secretary John Foster Dulles on October 23, 1958, the Republic of China made it clear that it would pursue its policies in the area primarily by political rather than military means. . . . [To question our China policy] is almost to deny faith in the capacity of free peoples to build their own lives under a free system." [23] However hollow these words sounded to Formosans, they represented diplomatic policy in the Dulles era.

Paul M. Popple, the State Department Republic of China affairs officer in 1963, wrote from Washington that "if we were to adopt such a policy [of denying aid to undemocratic allies], we would not only lose many friends and allies, but we would withdraw support from many countries that need it in order to maintain their independence. The Communists would be quick to exploit such a policy . . . The Republic of China is under the constant threat of attack from Communist China. For decades it has been forced to cope with civil wars, invasion, and other disorders that would have caused most governments to crumble. It is not surprising that it has adopted certain measures limiting the freedom of action of its citizens. Nevertheless, there is an important degree of freedom of action, of press criticism, and of participation by the people in elections for the provincial government." He then listed the many economic advances benefitting the Formosans, especially land reform, which "stands in sharp contrast to the economic conditions and political oppression in Communist China." [24]

Between 1963 and 1968 I interviewed Popple and several of his colleagues. Said one: "If we pressure the Nationalists too much, some criticize us; if we don't use enough pressure, others complain. We had to cut economic aid to a loan basis to convince them we meant business about moving to an autonomous economy. We believe in greater use of Formosans by the Nationalist government, but many in the regime don't see it that way and fear the consequences." Another China desk officer in 1965 admitted: "The Department continues to receive letters protesting Professor Peng's sentence, but he did try to distribute anti-government leaflets so they had to crack down. Ching-kuo must be a competent administrator because he eliminated graft from the army and uses the secret police to limit native resistance smoothly. See how he praised Formosans in the army . . ." After several such pro-Ching-kuo comments from State Department officers, I concluded that the Nationalist Defense Minister was not only the heir-apparent inside Formosa but also the choice of Washington to succeed his father.

American diplomats inside Formosa were more prone to sympathize with the Formosan cause. One, who had spent several years in the island, was widely known among native activists as a friend of Formosan nationalism. Another Embassy officer, born in mainland China, was sanguine about eventual Nationalist acceptance of an autonomous Formosa: "They usually managed to adjust to reality in the past, so I think the Nationalist minority on Formosa will gradually accept the reality of 'one China-one Taiwan' even though that may require a long time. They are realists, after all."

One must remember that the American Embassy in Taipei is far smaller than the Consulate in Hong Kong, where a competent staff of several hundred keeps watch on mainland China. "We have so little to do in Taipei, other than attend parties and parades, that we travel throughout Formosa observing the local scene," commented one diplomat. A junior officer has usually been assigned to the "Formosa desk" in the Embassy to handle research on local affairs, although the very knowledge that such a desk existed would offend the Nationalist regime. "Every officer here compiles a wealth of data on what the local people think," one of them told me in 1963. "We follow the local election campaigns, interview people all over the island, and travel frequently. Washington must have rooms full of reports sent from here in the past years." Officials in Washington agree, but naturally such data are classified material. "They are full of native complaints," a young diplomat at the Taichung Chinese Language School told me, "confirming what you found in your own field studies." [25]

The Foreign Service Institute maintains a Mandarin and Taiwanese language school in the city of Taichung, attended by an average of twenty FSO's and USIA employees, where I sometimes lectured and talked with the students. "We make regular tours around the nearby villages for conversation practice, but most farmers prefer to speak the Taiwan dialect rather than Mandarin. Those of us who know that dialect hear a lot of anti-government stories." [26]

In private, American diplomats on the island seldom parrot the State Department line that "on Taiwan, they have a successful system in every sense of the word." [27] Rather they are likely to admit the wide gap between mainlanders and Formosans, the complaints against political suppression, and the passive desire for independence, but insist that Defense rather than State controls American policy toward "Free China." "George Kerr knew too many Formosans when he taught there in the prewar years," commented a diplomat who served in Taipei during the 1947 incident. "He allowed his personal emotions to interfere with his official duty to be neutral in the revolt, and diplomats must not be swayed by their personal feelings." Officers who hoped to remain in the Foreign Service kept their personal emotions in better check.

Higher-level diplomats spoke more openly. For example, Averell Harriman, a former Assistant Secretary of State for the Far East and later a roving Ambassador for the Kennedy and Johnson administrations, told a Formosan student after a 1965 public lecture at Madison, Wisconsin: "The United States is going to support the inhabitants of Formosa in their struggle for independence. Even if they choose to join Communist China, we will support them in accordance with the principle of self-determination." [28] George Ball, former Undersecretary of State, wrote: "Today the Nationalist government is like something from *Alice in Wonderland* . . . [It is] anything but an example of a virile and militant democracy since the Taiwanese have little more voice in shaping their destinies than the citizens of the District of Columbia . . ." [29]

George Kennan, former U.S. Ambassador to Russia and Yugoslavia, and one of his country's most eminent scholar-diplomats, made the following comment about the future of Formosa in early 1964: "The United States should submit this problem to the United Nations for solution, with these three conditions: (1) a U.N. plebiscite giving natives all possible alternatives; (2) permission for anyone to leave the island after the vote; and (3) removal of all offensive weapons from Formosa to neutralize the island after the vote." [30] Early in 1965, a ranking member of the Nationalist Control Yuan wrote that Kennan's demand for a reduction of the Nationalist armed forces and a solution of the Taiwan issue in accordance with the feelings of the inhabitants "can only lead to confusion and skepticism about the United States and its China policy." [31]

Chester Bowles, twice U.S. Ambassador to India, wrote in a 1960 article that "Formosa's political status is founded on a myth . . . in the long run it is the 8,000,000 native Formosans who will shape the island's fate. We hear very little about their wishes, hopes and fears." [32] Bowles urged neutralization of the offshore islands, development of a Sino-Formosan state, and defense of the latter against a Communist attack or an internal *coup d'etat* designed to hand the island over to the Communists.

Edwin O. Reischauer, Harvard Professor and United States Ambassador to Japan (1961–1966), testified in early 1967: "There is, of course, a completely viable unit on Taiwan with a population of between 12 and 13 million . . . We have the actuality of an independent political and social organ living there." [33] In his 1955 book, *Wanted: An Asian Policy*, Reischauer had written, "We should be working for the development of a democratic Formosa with all the economic and political tools at our disposal . . . The Nationalists will first have to redirect their interests from military conquest to political growth; they will have to turn their backs more decisively on the totalitarian methods they learned from the Communists . . . and, most important, they will have to integrate the native population with the ruling regime until the Formosans themselves have their rightfully preponderant place in the government." [34] After Reischauer's 1967 Senate testimony, the *China News* concluded that "Senator Fulbright has ideas similar to those of Reischauer. Whether they know it or not, both are hell-bent on turning Asia over to the Communists." [35]

Dr. Allen Whiting, another Asian scholar who entered State Department service in 1961 as director of Far Eastern research and moved to the Hong Kong consulate in 1966, wrote in an article co-authored with Robert Scalapino in 1962: "In all probability, most Taiwanese would regard independence in some form as their ideal. Pro-Communist sentiment at present is negligible; Nationalist support fairly limited; and nostalgia for the Japanese period, while rather widespread, is strongest among the older groups . . . The dominant Taiwanese population is starting to absorb the refugee minority." [36]

Legislators' Views

Members of Congress have spoken and written with extreme candor, pro and con, concerning policy toward Formosa. William P. Knowland, Senate majority leader in the early years of the Eisenhower administration, became widely known as "the senator from Formosa" because of his strong devotion to Nationalist causes.[37] (However, not only articulate pro-Nationalists but virtually all members of Congress approved the 1954 treaty with Nationalist China, the 1955 Formosa Straits resolution, and the perennial resolutions urging the President not to recognize Peking or permit its seating in the United Nations.)

Representative Walter Judd of Minnesota, even after his departure from Congress in 1962, was a leading advocate of Nationalist China. "We should never put reform—particularly political reform—ahead of security," Judd testified before a House Foreign Affairs subcommittee in 1967. "The people of a developing nation are interested first in security and a sense of national pride with freedom from foreign control. Secondly, they want improved living standards, and third—only after the others are achieved—is there an irresistible pressure for democracy and a voice in the government." [38]

Paul Douglas of Illinois, one of the senators who joined the Committee of One Million Against the Admission of Communist China to the United Nations (the most effective pro-Nationalist lobby in the United States), remained on its steering committee after his defeat in the 1966 congressional elections. Queried about the compatibility of his domestic liberalism with his support of the Nationalist regime, Douglas replied: "It is not so much that I am in favor of Chiang Kai-shek. In fact, I am somewhat dubious about him. But I am opposed to the admission of Red China to the United Nations and to its recognition by the United States." [39] Other Congressional members of the Committee of One Million probably allow their anti-communist feelings to determine their attitude. In fact, Marvin Liebman, secretary and leader of the Committee, has said that his organization "takes no position on the question of Taiwanese self-determination—one way or the other." [40]

A few Senators make non-political criticisms, such as Allen Ellender, in his 1961 report, after a study trip to Taiwan: "The people seem to be happy under [Chiang's] able leadership . . . A graduated, well-balanced income tax should be imposed and everyone should be made to pay proportionately . . . All industries now partly owned by the state should be put in the hands of private enterprise [excluding for the time being] transportation, communication, and electric power." [41] This type of mild economic criticism can be found in almost every Congressional report on Formosa, but relatively few Congressmen espouse political reform.

Former Senator Wayne Morse, a persistent critic of recent American policy in the Far East, voiced the harshest criticism of Formosa policy: "How many Americans know that their military aid program enables Chiang's soldiers to rig and control elections? . . . The demise of

Chiang Kai-shek is going to bring a struggle for power . . . the military dictatorship we have built up there will last only as long as it can maintain its rule by force . . . Let us not forget that the native Formosans never had a word to say about the imposition of a U.S. puppet over them, which we have maintained these long years . . ." [42] Earlier, Morse had advocated reduced military spending in Taiwan because "Red China is forestalled from attacking Taiwan by the U.S. 7th Fleet, and not by any Chinese and Formosan army on Taiwan . . . Taiwan would be saved by the American Navy and the American Air Force." [43]

Senator J. William Fulbright, chairman of the Senate Foreign Relations Committee, has been far more vocal on the Vietnam war and Communist China than on Formosa. His interest in the latter seemed peripheral and derivative, but in an interview with a Japanese reporter in March 1966 the Senator was quoted as saying "Giving independence to Taiwan is the best course. We can't allow Red China to occupy it." [44] Shortly thereafter, however, the Senator spoke at Johns Hopkins University on his favorite theme, "The Arrogance of Power," and suggested that Taiwan might be able to "work out some arrangement" for self-government under Chinese Communist sovereignty. [45]

Senator Mike Mansfield, in a Senate speech at the time of the 1958 offshore island crisis, stated: "I cannot see how [the United States] can accept the doctrine that Formosa is a province of China at this time . . . I question it first on the ground of elementary justice to the people of Formosa. They had nothing to do with the Chinese civil war and I see no justification in subjecting them to the bloodbath which may still ensue as a result of that conflict. I question the Chinese view, too, on the grounds of the security rights of the United States . . . To permit extension of that war to the island would obviously constitute the gravest possible danger to world peace." By 1968, however, Mansfield had adopted a pro-Peking view. [46] Senator Stephen Young of Ohio voiced strong sympathy for the Formosan cause: "I have been in Taiwan and I completely agree with you and wish you and your associates success in accomplishing your objectives," he wrote to me in 1965. [47]

Congressional views of Formosa range from total support of the Nationalist cause to total opposition, but almost every member of Congress is far more concerned about Communist China and his view of Formosa usually depends on his degree of hostility toward the mainland regime. Most Congressional critics of Chiang's regime wish only that Chiang's Republic of China would abandon its mainland recovery aspiration and settle down to become "The Republic of Formosa" without American military aid.

Judges' and Lawyers' Views

In the judiciary, Supreme Court Justice William O. Douglas has spoken most vehemently against United States policy toward China. On January 26, 1967, Justice Douglas remarked that the United States cannot prevent Peking's domination of Asia and that "Taiwan belongs to the Chinese Communists in the same way that Long Island belongs to the United States." [48] The Nationalist press naturally agreed that Taiwan belongs to China, but not to the Communists.[49] Few federal judges express political opinions as often as Justice Douglas, but occasionally a deportation case arises. In 1959, District of Columbia Federal Judge Alexander Holtzoff ruled that two deportable Chinese could not be sent to Formosa. "Formosa has not been legally regarded as a country by the Government of the United States . . . Formosa may be said to be a territory or an area occupied and administered by the Government of the Republic of China, but is not officially recognized as being part of the Republic of China. Expressions of the State Department are drawn with care and circumspection to refrain from such recognition . . ." Judge Holtzoff accepted arguments that neither the 1951 Japanese Peace Treaty "nor any other agreement thereafter has purported to transfer the sovereignty of Formosa to China . . . The situation is, then, one where the Allied Powers still have to come to some agreement or treaty with respect to the status of Formosa." [50] To my knowledge, confirmed by the State Department China Desk officer in 1968, the United States has not forcibly deported anyone to Formosa. In this respect, Washington has been more considerate of politically dissident overseas Formosans than Tokyo.

Quincy Wright, a leading scholar of international law, based his advocacy of self-determination on a 1958 visit to Formosa and other research: "I agree that the people of Formosa should have the right of self-determination. This would accord with the purposes of the U.N. Charter to which the U.S. and the other parties to the peace treaty with Japan of 1951 are committed. My visit to Taiwan in 1958 convinced me that the Taiwanese generally wanted to govern themselves in preference to government by mainland Chinese whether Nationalist or Communist. In any case, they should have the opportunity to choose." [51]

Public Opinion on the Formosan Problem

Like most government officials, the American press and public usually speak of "China" as the Communist-controlled mainland and "Formosa" as the territory controlled by Chiang Kai-shek, and are far more interested in the former.

TABLE 4

AMERICAN VIEWS OF NATIONALIST CHINA [a]

(in percentage)

1. INFORMATION ON CHINA: "Do you happen to know what kind of government most of China has right now—whether it is democratic, or Communist, or what? [If answer uncertain:] Do you happen to know if there is any Communist government in China now?"

	Knows	Does Not Know	Total	(Number)
Total Sample	72	28	100	(1,501)
Men	81	19	100	(647)
Women	66	34	100	(854)
Grade School Education	46	54	100	(396)
High School Education	83	17	100	(497)
College Graduates	97	3	100	(167)

a) [If knows about Communist China:] "Have you happened to hear anything about another Chinese government besides the Communist one? [If respondent has not mentioned the Nationalists, Republic of China, Chiang Kai-shek, Formosa, or Taiwan, go on:] Do you happen to remember anything about this other Chinese government—like what it is called, who its leader is, or where it is located?"

	Knows	Does Not Know	Total	(Number)
Total Informed Sample	60	40	100	(1,088)
Men	71	29	100	(520)
Women	50	50	100	(567)
Grade School Education	49	51	100	(183)
High School Education	56	44	100	(415)
College Graduates	86	14	100	(162)

2. *ATTITUDE TOWARD COUNTERATTACK:* [Asked only of those knowing both Chinese governments:] "Some people say we should give the Nationalists all the help they need to attack the Communists on the mainland of China. Other people say we should protect the Nationalists from a Communist attack, but should not help them attack the Communists. Do you have an opinion about this? [If 'yes':] How do you feel about this?"

AGAINST helping the Nationalists attack the Communists		62
Multiple Reasons: Might involve us in war	45	
Attack wouldn't succeed	25	
Wrong to be aggressor	10	
Let them fight battles	9	
Other reasons	18	
No reason or don't know	8	
FAVOR helping the Nationalists attack the Communists		10
Favor protecting Nationalists; no other opinion		7
No opinion or other		21
		100 (N: 656)

a Taken from A. T. Steele, *The American People and China* (New York: McGraw-Hill, 1966), Appendix, pp. 257; 263; 271–273.

As already noted in Chapter 1, the findings of a 1964 national sample itemized in Table 4, show that 28 per cent of the sample did not know that "most of China" was under Communist rule, while only 60 per cent of those aware of that fact—informed group—knew anything about "the other Chinese government." [52] In other words, fewer than 4 in 10 Americans could identify the Nationalist regime, its leader, or its location. Of that small group, only 10 per cent believed the United States should help the Nationalists attack the Communist mainland, while 62 per cent opposed the idea. Americans between ages 18 and 24 were less aware of the Nationalist regime than older ones, but A. T. Steele, who arranged the survey, found that "overwhelming opposition to an attack on Communist China is fairly consistent throughout the population . . . among those with different political affiliations, among both men and women across all regions of the country, and for all age groups." [53]

In reviewing American opinion on Nationalist China, Steele cited a 1949 Gallup Poll wherein 50 per cent of those questioned had approved the withholding of further aid to the collapsing Nationalists, and only 20 per cent had disagreed. After the outbreak of the Korean War in 1950 however, those figures were reversed, and 58 per cent favored defensive aid to the Nationalists on Formosa. By 1955, almost three-fourths of another Gallup sample applauded that year's Formosa Resolution.[54] On the other hand, a Gallup Poll in September 1958 during the Quemoy crisis showed that 91 per cent favored a United Nations solution to the Formosa Straits problem "before we get more involved in a military way over these two islands," and 61 per cent agreed with the suggestion that "Formosa be neutralized, that is, put under the protection of the United Nations." [55]

Between 1963 and 1965 Steele interviewed hundreds of academicians, businessmen, legislators, and other Americans on China policy, concluding that "few Americans in leadership categories take seriously, nowadays, Chiang's periodic pledges to fight his way back to the mainland . . . Chiang's strongest American support today comes from the military and naval brass, active and retired, and the two major veterans' organizations . . . In the main, American thinking on Taiwan is fluid, confused, and uncertain, except on such basic propositions as the following: (1) We cannot abandon Taiwan; (2) We must honor our treaty obligations to the Chiang regime; (3) We must give full consideration to the wishes of the Taiwanese people in any discussion of their political future. On these matters we have found wide agreement and very little dissent among Americans." [56]

Among the few Steele found with strong opinions about Formosans were a Yale professor, a retired Navy captain, and a California scholar back from Formosa, all of whom feared a native uprising after Chiang's death. A Protestant mission official told him: "Today more than three-fourths of the Christians in Formosa are native-born Taiwanese. Almost to a man they are anti-Chiang. They do not feel they are free. Yet they are strongly anti-Communist. Many feel that the Chiang regime will eventually disintegrate and come to terms with the Communists." Steele concluded that "The internal inponderable in Taiwan is not whether the native-born Taiwanese would like self-government—they would hardly be human if they did not—but rather the intensity of their feeling on the matter." [57]

Thousands of American businessmen, tourists, and students visit Formosa annually, but most remain only a week or two and take no interest in the island's politics. Hamilton Wright Jr., partner in his father's firm which handled Nationalist Chinese public relations in the U.S. until 1963, wrote me that "We are very much aware that our 1957 NBC radio tape referring to Taiwan as 'the temporary home of 10 million Chinese who fled the mainland . . .' was incorrect . . . I do understand the desire of those people who have lived under external domination for so long to be recognized [and] anticipate that the Taiwanese, who already play the major economic role on the island, may suddenly find themselves thrust into the political spotlight for which they now clamor." [58] A Japanese-American business consultant who spent a year in Kaohsiung reported hearing consistently anti-Nationalist complaints from Formosans with whom he and his wife could speak in Japanese: "We don't want to hear any more sorrowful tales because we feel so helpless." [59]

Occasionally students and tourists whom I met inside the island or in the U.S. after their trips had seen beneath the superficial prosperity and political calm. One student observed a group of Chinese in the Taipei Friends of China Club following the 1960 American presidential election returns: "There was deepening glumness among the Chinese as it became evident that Kennedy would beat Nixon; only a Taiwanese medical student present was happy." [60] Another wrote: "Behind the blackout, or inside the shuttered windows, we found a sick society," while a middle-aged woman from New York spoke in Hong Kong of "recovering from the shock of seeing intense poverty combined with the so-called wonders of Chiang's regime . . . If Taiwan is a sample of what went on in the mainland prior to 1949, I can understand why the Communists were able to overrun China." [61]

Press Opinions

Among American newspapers, The New York Times and Washington Post have most often commented editorially on the desirability of Formosan self-determination. "Any future settlement of the China problem must include self-determination for Taiwan," declared a Times editorial in 1964. "If, as evidence suggests, the Taiwanese want independence, their island republic should have membership in the General Assembly of the United Nations, while the seat of mainland China would be occupied by whatever Chinese group actually ruled the mainland." [62] Walter Lippmann voiced his support for an independent Taiwan after noting the possibility of a political deal reunifying the two Chinas. Lippmann wrote in a 1965 column that "the only hope in the near future" lay in U.N. recognition of Peking as China and Taiwan as Taiwan: "[This] would recognize the independence of Taiwan which has not been under the rule of the Chinese mainland since 1895. It would amount to treating Taiwan, which was conquered and colonized by the Chinese from Fukien in the 17th century, as so many other former colonies, now independent U.N. members, have been treated

. . . In principle, an independent Taiwan, neutralized under a U.N. guarantee, would be in the spirit of the age." [63]

The Lippmann opinion was shared by several other commentators. Robert Elegant, who became Hong Kong bureau chief for the *Washington Post-Los Angeles Times* News Service in 1965, wrote me that year: "I believe that time's wastage, assisted whenever we can do so by slight prods will take care of Taiwan's self-determination. The Taiwanese are, after all, a long way toward economic self-determination—and the withdrawal of American aid as a major economic factor in the country would, it seems to me, deprive the mainlanders of their last strongpoint. The Taiwan matter is, at the moment, best left for time to resolve." [64]

David Schoenbrun quoted Sosa Rodriguez of the Venezuelan delegation to the United Nations as having urged self-determination for Formosa because there were "powerful historical, juridical, political, and simply human reasons" why the natives "should decide for themselves whether they wish to be annexed by continental China or to set themselves up as an independent state." [65] In a letter to me, Schoenbrun confirmed his support for a "Free Formosa as the only way to break the absurd deadlock caused by those who say 'we can't throw Taiwan out of the U.N.' Fine, then let's pull Taiwan out from under Chinese imperial domination!" [66]

Lederer, co-author of *The Ugly American*, wrote a less popular book in 1961, *A Nation of Sheep*, with one chapter devoted to denunciation of the Nationalist regime.[67] "The present situation is and can be even more harmful to U.S. interests," Lederer wrote me in 1967. "The myth of a 'great fighting army' on Formosa represents one of the great hoodwinking jobs which has been done on the United States. The military there may be beautifully trained and have magnificent equipment, but about ninety per cent of the young people in the military are Formosans, not Chinese." [68]

On the other side of the argument, *U.S. News and World Report*, *Reader's Digest*, and the *Time-Life* magazines usually take a strongly pro-Nationalist stance. Clarence Hall on "Why We Must Never Abandon the 'Offshore Islands'" (April 1961) and a Keyes Beach-Clarence Hall collaboration on "Formosa: Asia's Heartening Success Story" (February 1966) are among several laudatory accounts published by *Reader's Digest*. The latter article candidly admitted that "Chiang's control at the top national level is complete and inflexible . . . while the Chinese press lacks complete freedom," but insisted that "tensions between native Taiwanese and Chiang's mainlanders have lessened considerably . . . And Free China achieved this through adopting precisely the opposite means the Communists used to impose their tyranny on 700 million Chinese."

The *Saturday Evening Post*, before its demise, occasionally straddled the fence. In a remarkable editorial in 1964, the *Post* advocated a new policy toward Formosa: "[Our China policy] must decide, once and for all, that Chiang Kai-shek's government cannot claim to be the government of mainland China, which none of his officials has even seen for 15 years. Instead of maintaining this legal myth, rather like the Count of Paris' claim to being the King of France—we should concentrate on protecting the freedom and self-determination of Chiang's stronghold, Formosa. That land must not under any circumstances be handed over to Red China." [69] The *Wall Street Journal* took a similar position in 1967: "It is inconceivable that the United States would acquiesce in handing over [Formosa] to the Communists against the will of its inhabitants. It is almost as inconceivable that any other solution would be likely to satisfy any Red Chinese government any time soon." [70]

On balance, the American press has focused on mainland China more than Formosa, but credits the Nationalists with considerable progress even while doubting their ability to capture the mainland. The Formosan identity is seldom mentioned, probably because no riots have occurred to contradict Nationalist claims of internal harmony.[71]

Academic Views of Formosa

In the American academic community, attention is also on the mainland rather than on Formosa. Since American scholars cannot enter the mainland they often carry out mainland studies from Hong Kong and Formosa, where they hesitate to criticize the regime lest they or their students be denied re-entry to the island. "We do not know of any American scholar before you refused a visa by the Nationalists," said a State Department expert in 1966, "even if he signed petitions favoring Communist China: one fellow who signed the 1966 Committee of 198 Asian Scholars' statement was given a two-year visa." [72] That committee's statement, as published in *The New York Times*, urged the U.S. to take steps toward recognition of Peking while continuing relations with Taiwan, and to end the American trade embargo against goods from mainland China.

Among scholars favoring the Formosan cause, those who have worked in the island during the past decade are particularly persuasive. Maurice Meisner, Mark Mancall, and John Israel did pre-doctoral research in Formosa, and gathered data on Formosan political sentiment peripheral to their main studies. Mancall told me about various Nationalist police interrogations of his Taipei hosts when his *China Quarterly* issue on Taiwan appeared, and later pressures against its publication in book form.[73] "I welcome the opportunity to do whatever little I can to inform others of the situation in Taiwan and the nature of Taiwanese aspirations," wrote Maurice Meisner, "and do not share the reluctance of many in the field of Chinese studies to express a view on these matters." [74] John Israel, whose Taiwan research was on the prewar mainland student movement, told of Nationalist police harassment of a few Americans in 1960 and 1961 whose research notes were inspected, books confiscated, or native assistants arrested.[75]

A political scientist in Vermont reported that in 1957 "we discovered Taiwanese approaching us with their stories on an increasing scale. Sometimes total strangers would take us aside, in the obvious hope that by some miracle, an exposé of the situation related to an American might produce wiser, more sensitive U.S. policies and pressures. The stories we were told add nothing to what you say . . . I'm not convinced by the occasional rumors I hear that the Taiwanese mainlander relations are improving—this is what we were told by the U.S. Embassy when we arrived 12 years ago." [76] "After two years of study and research in Taiwan," wrote another young academician, "I am enjoying a short vacation in Japan, breathing deeply of the clear, fresh, free intellectual atmosphere . . . all the things I'm not accustomed to feeling in Taiwan . . ." [77]

John K. Fairbank is perhaps the most eminent China scholar in the United States to write sympathetically about Formosan nationalism: "The latent American sentiment is for the continued independence of Taiwan on the basis of self-determination. This makes sense in the American political vocabulary, but not in the Nationalist. . . . The sense of Taiwanese (or Formosan) national identity is still expressed by refugee groups in Tokyo, even though its expression is kept down by the police and a widespread informer network on the island . . . [But] recognition of the independence of Taiwan as a state [bigger] than two-thirds of the members of the U.N. is an idea thinkable only by Taiwanese or by non-Chinese who are 'anti-Chinese'. . . . The Nationalist government cannot be changed or controlled by Taiwan politics . . . the door is still not open for organized political opposition . . ." [78]

Another eminent scholar, Robert Scalapino, author of the Northeast Asian section of the 1959 Conlon Report for the Senate Foreign Relations Committee, has frequently urged greater sympathy for the Formosan cause: "The future of Taiwan should be determined by the people of Taiwan. . . . The United States . . . should make it emphatically clear that our defense commitment pertains to the Pescadores and Taiwan, not to the offshore islands which are integrally a part of the mainland. . . . The above policies, taken together, might be labelled a One China-One Taiwan policy; but this is based on the assumption that the people of Taiwan want a separate identity from the mainland, an assumption that is undoubtedly true but should be tested under conditions that make possible a free choice." [79]

The *China News*, upon learning that both Fairbank and Scalapino had been appointed to a State Department advisory panel on China in 1966, editorially deplored their advocacy of " 'two Chinas' or worse," and also criticized another panel member, Professor A. Doak Barnett of Columbia University, as seeking "reversal, not growth, of traditional U.S. policy." [80] Barnett had written in 1960 that "it is both possible and desirable for the Taiwanese to participate in their government and to identify their loyalties with it and for the mainlanders to become increasingly 'Taiwanized' by identifying their interests and sentiments more and more with Taiwan rather than their former mainland homes . . ." [81]

The views of Edwin Reischauer are relevant here even though they have been discussed previously, because he has been a professor as well as Ambassador to Japan, and remains primarily a scholar. His New Year's message to Japan in 1967 expressed hope that "the United States would take further steps to open doors to Communist Chinese contacts with the U.S. and the outside world in general. These should include a redefinition of our stand for the self-determination of the people on Taiwan . . ." [82]

On the pro-Nationalist side of the American academic community are Professors George Taylor of the University of Washington and David N. Rowe of Yale, who testified in the 1966 Senate hearings. Taylor's testimony fully agreed with the late ex-Congressman Walter Judd's defense of the political restrictions on Formosa.[83] Professor Rowe, who received the Nationalist Order of the Brilliant Star after his 1954–1956 service as a visiting professor and Asia Foundation representative in Taipei, called any "two-China" suggestions political suicide, and castigated critics of the Committee of One Million, on which he serves.[84]

Some academicians object to the idea of Formosan nationalism because they think it is not desired by the majority of native-born islanders, or is inconsistent with the American anti-communist crusade. Harold Quigley, a leading prewar Asian specialist, wrote in 1962: "In the absence of a plebiscite there is no sure basis for a judgment upon the views of the Taiwanese people as a whole. Evidence that they would prefer not to be ruled by the present regime is considerable. They might prefer the status of an autonomous region under Peking to the indefinite continuation of the threat of an attempted military conquest. Whether Peking would offer that status, and whether the Taiwanese would trust any of Peking's promises are questions unanswerable today . . . There is no reason to believe that the United States desires to treat Taiwan as a permanent military base . . . Nor would the American people wish to stand in the way of a fair settlement between Peking and Taipei." [85]

Professor Harold Hinton of George Washington University wrote in 1966: "The United States should continue to protect Taiwan and to discourage the Republic of China from invading the mainland, except in the unlikely event of a Communist collapse. The United States should be prepared, however, for the unpleasant but not disastrous possibility that the leaders of the Republic of China may decide some day to reach an accommodation with [Peking]. It would be better for the United States to be abandoned by the Republic of China than to abandon it, for instance by adopting a *de jure* 'two Chinas' policy." [86]

O. Edmund Clubb, a Columbia University professor who spent eighteen years in China as an American diplomat, also saw a future rapprochement between the two Chinas. Citing a series of rumored agreements between representatives of the two Chinas, an Italian interview with ex-Nationalist President Li Tsung-jen in 1963, and other evidence, Clubb wrote that "there exists no proof that an agreement between Taipei and Peking is actually in being—but the potentialities that exist for such an agreement are clear to the view . . . the Nationalists are Chinese, too. If events are simply permitted to take their course, it is entirely possible that at some not distant date the United States will see the successors to Chiang Kai-shek on Formosa reach an agreement with their brother Chinese in Peking. For both the Chinese Communists and the Nationalists are determined that Formosa's future shall be linked to that of the mainland—regardless of Washington's wishes." [87]

Donald Ray of the National Institute of Social and Behavioral Science in Washington D.C. insisted that "Taiwan nationalism is but a shaggy-dog story . . . Taiwan-born resentment is not particularly rational [and] those to whom I talked referred to themselves not as native Taiwanese but Chinese . . . Certainly an independent Taiwan would [become] Peking-dominated. . . . This impractical future dream is in fact a nightmare, both for the free world and the Chinese of Taiwan: I don't think our government supports it even covertly." [88] One or two Columbia University faculty members expressed related fears that "a separate Taiwanese state would not be viably anti-Communist and we shouldn't take such idealistic risks as to support it or the reversion of Okinawa to Japan." [89]

A Catholic teaching priest who returned from Formosa in 1966 insisted: "Apropos the situation in Taiwan today, your views are not at all accurate. . . . There are free elections on the county and city levels of government, and many of the elected officials are non-KMT men. As in most democratic governments, there is political freedom for all except anarchists. . . . There is no question in my mind that Chiang Kai-shek has both the allegiance and affection [of the Taiwanese]." [90] But a leading Protestant missionary teacher in the Far East, Andrew Roy, wrote in 1962 that "because of the 1947 conflict and present differences, even changes in the weather are blamed on the Nationalists. . . . One charge, however, can be laid against the Nationalists: they claim credit for maintaining a high living standard in Taiwan yet request more international aid . . . The Taiwanese say this [anti-mainlander friction] will last as long as political power is retained by a minority; that their children soon learn in society that the basic interests of the two groups are different. They realize that the mainlanders cannot share power for if they did they would be put out of power . . . [President Chiang] has never understood the political value of opposition in the practice of democracy. . . . Americans have an emotional and moral interest in supporting a former ally in a period of hardship, and a military and political interest in having Taiwan part of a cooperative system of defense against Communist expansion. However, we have an equal interest in representative government . . ." [91]

Such differences among American churchmen on what should be done with Formosa only reflect the division in government and academic circles. The dogmatic anti-Communists or emotional adherents of the Chiang mythology can see no alternative to continued American support for the Nationalist cause; the more numerous liberals approve Formosan nationalism or wish it were a more realistic goal; while some who seek accommodation with Peking would welcome a deal between the two regimes over the heads of the Formosans.

9

JAPANESE VIEWS OF FORMOSAN
NATIONALISM

Having noted in earlier chapters the impact of Japanese colonial rule and continuing Japanese influence on Formosa, as well as the role of Formosans in Japan, we shall deal here with relations between Japan and Nationalist China since 1952; the views of Japanese leaders toward the Formosan problem as expressed in personal interviews; and the attitudes of the Japanese public and various special-interest groups.

Japan has attempted to separate trade from politics in her post-treaty relations with the "two Chinas," giving full diplomatic recognition only to the Nationalists but promoting trade with both regimes. The Peking government, knowing how many Japanese yearn for a broader mainland market, periodically tries to extort political concessions from Tokyo. Taipei, on the other hand, enjoying Japanese diplomatic support, opposes Tokyo's efforts for normal trade or exchange of semiofficial missions with Peking, or recognition of Outer Mongolia. Both Chinese regimes seem to suspect that a "One China, One Taiwan" policy, which is anathema to them both, might be secretly desired by Japan.

More than other nations, Japan needs and wants trade and peaceful relations with the two Chinas. As to Formosan independence, a Japanese Foreign Ministry specialist on China predicted in 1957: "Just wait another generation and Taiwan will evolve into a separate nation." [1] Until that time arrives, however, Japan will be walking precariously to gain maximum economic profit with minimal political risk in her dealings with both Chinas.

As Japanese relations with mainland China have been treated in many other works they will be mentioned here only as they bear directly upon the issue of Formosa.[2] Most Japanese regard the mainland as the "real" China and, like Americans, are far more interested in it than in Formosa. Unlike so many of their counterparts in the United States, however, Japanese intellectuals believe that satisfactory solution to the China problem will require prior settlement of the status of Formosa.

The Evolution of Official Tokyo-Taipei Relations

Japanese Prime Minister Sato's official visit to Taipei in September 1967, and that of Nationalist Defense Minister Chiang Ching-kuo to Japan two months later, were hailed by both nations as helping to strengthen their friendly ties with each other. "I was most touched by the noticeable Japanese gratitude for the magnanimity of President Chiang immediately after V-J Day," reported Ching-kuo.[3] Japanese trade with its former colony reached almost $500 million ($160 imports and $300 exports) in 1967, close to the level of her mainland China trade, while tourism and investments increased the importance of Formosa to Japan. "Today Japan is our biggest customer and we buy more from Japan than from any other country," said the *China News* of Taipei on the 22nd anniversary of Formosa's 1945 retrocession. "It is appropriate to point out that the Japanese government and people have had a considerable role in the building of the new Taiwan . . . Japanese investment is not large, but it is pervasive. Technical assistance agreements are numerous. Japan's know-how is playing a big role in Taiwan industrialization." [4] Meanwhile, Prime Minister Sato had denied that his visit, which was opposed by leftist student mobs at Tokyo Airport, would alter his policy toward Peking: "Japan will continue to maintain trade and cultural interchange with Communist China under our basic principle of separating politics from economics." [5] It is precisely that principle to which both Nationalist China and its rival in Peking object in theory, but tolerate for practical reasons.

Because of Allied disagreement over which was the "real" China, neither the Communist nor the Nationalist Chinese government was invited to the 1951 San Francisco conference on the Japanese peace treaty —which, as a result, included Japan's renunciation of "all right, title, and claim to Formosa and the Pescadores" without specifying a beneficiary. The April 1952 bilateral treaty of peace between Japan and the Republic of China, which had the strong blessing of the United States, reiterated Japan's earlier renunciation of claims to Formosa, but limited the area of Nationalist sovereignty to those "territories which are now, or which may hereafter be, under the control of [the Republic of China] government."

After the Korean truce in 1953, Japan's Yoshida government looked favorably on the first two postwar private trade agreements signed by Japanese businessmen with Peking. Hatoyama, the conservative politician who unseated Yoshida in December 1954, was even more eager than his predecessor to improve relations. On the eve of his retirement, two years later, Hatoyama told the Japanese Diet that he was meditating between the two Chinas by sending messengers to impress them both with "Japan's desire to see them find some way of coexisting and avoiding frictions." [6]

Japanese leaders are well aware of the Nationalists' determination to retain their present U.N. status, which includes one of the five permanent seats on the Security Council and, even more important, U.N. recognition as the only legitimate government of China. Thus Japan's perennial support in the General Assembly voting on admitting Communist China is extremely important to the Nationalists (whose delegates "always appear forlorn and lonely" in the U.N. chambers, according to an American observer). Japan served as one of the co-sponsors of the 1961 resolution that designated the China representation issue as an "important question" requiring a two-thirds rather than a simple majority vote, and has done the same every year since.

In all such decisions favoring the Nationalist regime, Japan has closely followed the lead of the United States, its major international partner. Many Cabinet members of the Liberal Democratic party (LDP) have told me: "We cannot change our China policy until Washington makes the first move." Other conservative Japanese politicians have said: "If we remain friendly with South Korea and Nationalist China, and send aid to South Vietnam, then maybe America will return Okinawa sooner and won't restrict our exports to the U.S."

"If you think Washington does not put pressure on us to restrict our trade with Communist China," said Foreign Minister Ohira in 1962, "you are very wrong, because they do—behind the scenes." [7] Ohira then described how the Nationalist Embassy in Tokyo protested every private Japanese trade and cultural agreement with the Chinese Communists. "I try to tell the Nationalist Ambassador we are a democracy, so we must allow private trade and travel to mainland China as long as it does not involve us officially . . . Let our businessmen burn themselves, I tell him, and they will learn the limits of the China market—just as a young boy does who thinks he can dive into a swimming pool filled with only a little water."

After Japanese private trade with China had expanded to over $300 million under the sympathetic eye of the Hatoyama Cabinet and Peking's "soft" line of 1954–1956, a dozen Japanese groups (among whom were many conservative politicians and businessmen) succeeded in persuading Tokyo to allow a permanent Communist Chinese trade mission in Tokyo. In 1958, Peking charged the new Kishi Cabinet (far more conservative than that of Hatoyama) with failure to protect the Chinese flag at a Nagasaki trade fair; unwillingness to let the Chinese Communist trade mission fly the Chinese flag over its Tokyo office; and refusal to exempt members of that mission from Japan's alien registration fingerprinting system.[8] Taipei threatened an anti-Japanese boycott if Tokyo did not refuse these demands, whereupon Peking cancelled all private trade agreements with Japan in May 1958. Kishi's firmness in the face of pressure from Peking earned him a high place in the affections of the Nationalist regime, second only to that of ex-Prime Minister Yoshida, as a friend of "free China." The Japanese press, which grew increasingly hostile toward Kishi between 1958 and his forced resignation in 1960, regarded them both as members of the Japanese "China lobby."

The most serious rupture with Taipei occurred in late 1963 and early 1964, after conclusion of a new five-year trade pact with Peking (the Liao-Takasaki agreement). Takasaki, a former cabinet minister, predicted that trade with mainland China would rise from $80 million in 1963 to $300 or $400 million by 1967.[9] In August 1963, Tokyo permitted the export of a $20 million textile plant to China with credit supplied by the quasi-governmental Export-Import Bank, and moved to approve similar plant sales to compete with West European credit exports to Communist China. Taipei objected that use of a quasi-governmental credit agency to finance sales to its arch enemy was too close to de facto recognition.

When Prime Minister Ikeda, who had succeeded Kishi in 1960, told a group of American newspapermen that the prospect of a Nationalist counterattack on the mainland was a "rumor . . . perhaps a dream," and implied that the status of Formosa was indefinite, Taipei grew more apprehensive.[10] The Nationalists withdrew from the 1963 Tokyo International Sports Week because its organizers used the designation "Taiwan," following the 1960 Olympic decision,[11] rather than "China." Allegedly "popular" anti-Japanese feelings erupted in Taipei late in 1963. A 44-year-old Chinese interpreter with a Communist trade group to Japan, after first having defected, briefly, to the Soviet Embassy in Tokyo had then applied for a Nationalist passport before finally changing his mind later the same day about defecting at all. The Nationalists thereupon accused Japan of having allowed pro-Communist groups to influence the man to return to the mainland. In Taipei, while small groups of organized rioters battered the door of the Japanese Embassy and the Japan Air Lines office, the Nationalist regime suspended Japanese imports; accused Tokyo of "callous indifference to human freedom;" [12] withdrew its ambassador from Tokyo; and urged its people to boycott Japanese goods.

Yet an American scholar who was living in Taipei from September 1963 to August 1964 wrote that "except for the newspapers, I would not have been aware of any anti-Japanese demonstrations . . . They were short-term affairs involving only a small number of people, and the boycott had little effect. Shopkeepers did not discourage the sale of Japanese goods and [anti-Japanese] signs on walls and telephone poles were few and far between. My distinct impression was that none of this was spontaneous. It was not a reflection of native Taiwanese opinion." [13]

Official Tokyo was more concerned with the reactions of official Taipei than with Taiwanese public opinion, however, and Ikeda dispatched the vice-president of his party, Ono Bamboku, with former Prime Minister Yoshida, and other pro-Nationalist envoys to calm Taipei. Ikeda himself made several speeches reaffirming Japanese determination to support the Republic of China in the face of French recognition of Peking and denying any intention to pursue a "two-China" policy. Months later it was revealed that Yoshida, after his return to Japan, had sent a letter to President Chiang promising that no further exports to Communist China would be financed through credit sales guaranteed by the Japanese Export-Import Bank. The "Yoshida letter" solved the 1964 crisis but annoyed many members of the LDP and large sections of the press and public. Ikeda, his successor Sato Eisaku, and members of their cabinets tried to assure their critics that "the Yoshida letter is not binding on the government," but in practice they adhered to it.[14]

By April 1965, commented the *China Yearbook*, "relations between China and Japan have become cordial and friendly," since the signing of a $150 million Japanese loan for economic development.[15] Bilateral trade with Taiwan, usually in Japan's favor, rose to over $357 million in 1965 and to $500 million in 1967.[16] The Nationalist regime has tried to diversify its foreign trade to reduce dependence upon Japan, but this is not easy to accomplish. Cessation of United States economic aid in 1965 and other factors beyond Taipei's control led to even greater reliance on Japanese loans, technical assistance, and joint financial ventures. Moreover, tourists from Japan outnumbered those from any other country between 1966 and 1968, and investments by Japanese firms have steadily increased because labor costs less in Formosa than in Japan.

The Sato Administration, which succeeded Ikeda's in late 1964, is perhaps the most friendly yet toward the Republic of China. More devoted than his predecessors to economic diplomacy and anti-communism, Prime Minister Sato took Japan into the 1966 Asia and Pacific Council (ASPAC), most of whose members were committed to the American Vietnam policy.[17] Conservative Japanese leaders, however, including Deputy Prime Minister Kawashima, told me in 1966 that Japan would never consider ASPAC a prelude to the Asian military alliance desired by Taipei. Meanwhile the Nationalist press chides Japan for not taking a stronger anti-Communist position, which it wrongly claims would have majority Japanese support.[18]

It was just before the Sato visit to Taipei in 1967 that the Japanese Justice Ministry tried to deport two Formosan activists whose cases were discussed, among others, in Chapter 7. Such examples of recent Japanese governmental action against Formosan political refugees, after so many years of toleration and even covert assistance by some Japanese leaders, suggest a desire to appease the Nationalist regime.

Attitudes of Japanese Leaders Toward
Formosan Nationalism

Between 1961 and 1968, I interviewed hundreds of Japanese public officials, especially those with prewar or postwar experience inside Taiwan, to discover their personal opinions—which often differ from what they can say or write publicly.

Japanese diplomats, including those with experience in postwar Formosa, are usually unwilling to criticize the Nationalist regime. "We have to tread carefully here," said one of the Japanese diplomats in Taipei, "because the Nationalists suspect us of having undercover contacts, and sympathy with the Taiwanese." The Japanese Ambassador to Taipei in 1957 believed his desire to open a Japan Cultural Center similar to the USIS Library system (which has been mentioned in earlier chapters) was disapproved by the Nationalists "because they are trying their best to stamp out Japanese influences." His successors in 1961 and 1964 told me of their failure to enlarge the import quota for Japanese films, so popular among Formosan audiences. Probably because of the $150 million loan in 1965, the Nationalists did allow Japan to open a consulate in Kaohsiung; but they banned the Japanese language on the television system established with Japanese aid.

Ambassador Iguchi Sadao discussed a number of subjects with me in a July 1962 interview: "Japan must be very circumspect in pushing for an information office here, because Chinese officials would regard that as an invasion. It's better to work through our Japan Air Lines and commercial channels. Britain has a very interesting two-China policy, but the Nationalists wouldn't permit that arrangement to other nations." [19]

Iguchi's successor in Taipei was Ambassador Kimura Shiroshichi, who in 1966 was transferred to Seoul as Japan's first postwar Ambassador to Korea, the other former Japanese colony. On the eve of his transfer, Kimura said that he "hoped for closer ties among Japan, the Republic of Korea, and the Republic of China to meet the Communist threat." [20] Kimura's comments to me in the summer of 1964 were cloaked in the diplomatic caution surely desirable for a Japanese envoy to either Taipei or Seoul.

The late former Prime Minister Yoshida had been a career diplomat before his rise to political leadership under the American occupation. In a 1964 interview soon after he had made the fence-mending visit to Taipei, the Grand Old Man of Japanese postwar conservative politics was flanked by two friends who fended off every question related to Formosa. "The Prime Minister wishes you to know that he tried to improve relations with the Republic of China after the unfortunate misunderstandings related to our trade with mainland China, and he was satisfied that he accomplished that mission," said one of the friends. Yoshida himself appeared far more anxious to discuss the imminent reconciliation of Japan with South Korea, but admitted, "Yes, Taiwanese do like us better than the Koreans do." [21]

One diplomat usually considered a Yoshida protégé told me in mid-1961: "Chiang is stupid not to prepare now for a Taiwan Republic. Afro-Asians would be willing to accept a separate Taiwan in the U.N., but not a Taiwan which is part of either China. Why does Chiang persist in his fantasy of mainland recovery? If Ching-kuo succeeds his father, as most people predict, I fear he will make a deal to turn Taiwan over to the Communists. Japan did a good job in prewar Taiwan—the people there are different from Koreans—so Taiwan, too, should be regarded as a newly independent state like other ex-colonies in Asia and

Africa. It is silly to think of Taiwan in terms of a 'successor state' [i.e., that two Chinese governments succeeded to the original one in 1949] as proposed by some people . . . the United States and Japan both desire above all to keep Taiwan out of Communist hands, but we cannot do that if it continues under the Chiang regime." [22]

Another high-ranking Japanese diplomat reported in 1963: "People won't speak freely in Taiwan. . . . They were in favor of return to China in 1945, but were later disillusioned. Taiwanese would have resented our prewar colonial rule even if it had been better because they wanted to rule themselves. Many imprisoned natives are friends of mine, and gave me first-hand evidence of the Nationalist suppression of minor parties, such as the abortive party movement of Lei Chen, whom I knew very well. As for the Taiwanese businessmen in Japan, they don't see any profit in financing the independence groups here, whose members are small in number and apt to be less admirable than their compatriots inside Taiwan. They profit too much by trading with Taiwan to jeopardize their profits by supporting the independence cause." [23]

On another occasion, the same diplomat said, "I doubt that many Japanese give money to the independence groups, though Fujiyama [Foreign Minister in the Kishi Cabinet] was raised in Taiwan and knows many natives. For that matter, most American diplomats are pro-Formosan, but wouldn't lift a finger to help them. I think the occasional acts of violence, such as painting up the Chinese consulate in Osaka or throwing stink-bombs into a Double-Ten Nationalist celebration, are more useless to the activists' cause than annoying to my government. They don't accomplish anything worthwhile . . ." In mid-1966, the same diplomat spoke again of the difficulty likely to be faced by any Japanese official who wanted to assist resident Formosans, especially those imprisoned or threatened with deportation: "It's the top Cabinet ministers who make policy, and they bend over backward to avoid offending the Nationalists." [24] A friend of the two men just quoted thought that "most Foreign Office people as well as the ordinary Japanese agree with the ideal of Formosan independence, but it is an ideal hard to realize." [25]

A high officer in the Asian Bureau of the Japanese Foreign Ministry in 1966 who was aware of various academic proposals for a peaceful merger of Formosa into mainland China, doubted that the American government would oppose such a merger effectively: "The Nationalists may indeed combine with the mainland after the Gimo's death, and even a plebiscite on Taiwan might lead to a merger if the military police controlled the election, as they control everything today. For how could the mainlanders be satisfied to remain within Taiwan? They might produce a quiet revolution, possibly one led by their ex-servicemen of low status, to demand a merger with the mainland. Then what would the United States do? What could it do—does it have the power and the will necessary to prevent it? If the natives of Taiwan revolted—they lack such power today—would America help them? We Japanese sympathize with the Taiwanese, but we wonder what America will do, because she has the power to influence the future of Taiwan and Japan does not." [26]

A consul-general in Hong Kong who had previously been stationed in Taipei told me in 1962 that "the American diplomats here and in Taipei underestimate the degree of Taiwanese-mainlander friction and we Japanese think that is the main difference in the American and Japanese views of Taiwan. I used to serve as chief of the Asian Section in the Japanese Foreign Ministry and met with many Formosan activists and Nationalist diplomats to pass on complaints which each had about the other." [27] An American diplomat in Hong Kong, who had served many years in Taipei, Tokyo, and Seoul, agreed: "Japanese do see more friction than we Americans do, and they are closer to the Formosan refugee groups in Japan. Some conservative Japanese leaders may give money to those groups as 'triple insurance,' but never directly or with real expectation of their success." [28]

In late 1962, I interviewed the Japanese Ambassador to Canberra, who had been a prewar protégé of the late Foreign Minister Shigemitsu. "Many Japanese sympathize with the Formosans," said Ambassador Ohta. "Your government's 'permission,' in effect, for the Nationalists to evacuate to Taiwan in 1949 was worse than the Cairo Declaration of 1943. They should have gone to Hainan Island instead." [29]

Like most of their colleagues elsewhere, Japanese diplomats in Washington were reluctant to criticize the Nationalist regime or express support for Formosan independence, but one information officer, in speaking of his youth in Taiwan, remarked: "After the war, I was the first 'Formosan-born' among postwar Japanese officials to reach the island, but I had to be careful in my contacts because in their skin the Nationalists don't trust us Japanese." [30]

Among ex-military officers who had served in prewar Formosa was Vice Admiral Hasegawa Kiyoshi, the island's last Japanese Governor-General, who said in recalling his five years in Taiwan: "Of course they [the Formosans] wanted independence from us, and most would prefer to be free of Chinese rule today. The Formosan groups in Japan are divided, including a few pro-Nationalists or pro-Communists. Formosans always liked Japanese customs, especially the mountain tribes, whom we protected. They appreciated the benefits of our higher culture, mainly agriculture and health. Chiang is a formidable leader, but they have no good replacement. I have no faith in his son, Ching-kuo." [31]

Said the late Admiral Takahashi Sanroku: "Several Taiwan independence men used to visit me, and I think independence would be the best solution for the island and for all concerned." [32] Retired Admiral Nomura Kichisaburo, prewar ambassador to Washington and a postwar conservative member of the upper house of the Diet, expressed similar opinions in 1957. Former Field Marshal Hata Shunroku, Commander of Japanese forces in South China at the end of World War II, recalled his earlier duty as military commander of Taiwan: "The customs and manners of Taiwan are entirely different from those of mainland China . . . partly because Japanese policy there was a success in contrast to out failure in Korea." [33]

None of the former military leaders expressed a desire to see Formosa again under Japanese rule, but several criticized the pacifist sentiment in Japan which prevents any defense commitment to neighboring nations. A few said: "If our people do not want heavy rearmament, they should at least support the willingness of their United States ally to defend Korea and Taiwan."

In the attitudes of Japanese Diet members, there is a wide divergence of opinion reflecting the factionalism in both the Liberal Democratic (LDP) majority and its principal opposition rival, the Japan Socialist party. "I have found that most LDP members privately hope for an independent Taiwan, even if some are reluctant to say that to you," commented the editor who arranged most of my interviews with Dietmen. On the China issue, the LDP is informally divided into three groups: the rightist faction that usually supports the Nationalists; a smaller liberal wing mainly concerned with mainland trade; and many factions in the middle which favor either a de facto "two China" or a "one China, one Taiwan" policy but seldom take a public position. [34]

Probably the most pro-Nationalist leader in the LDP has been Kaya Okinori, a wartime Cabinet minister who returned to high position after having served a prison term imposed by The International Military Tribunal (Far East). "Japan is under great indebtedness to Generalissimo Chiang, that is, the present Taiwan administration . . . The Japanese Government sticks to the policy of absolutely disapproving the denial of the existence of Taiwan," he insisted. [35] "Quemoy and Matsu are the

West Berlin of Asia and must be defended at all costs," he said in 1963. "Kennedy was wrong in 1960 to downgrade the importance of those offshore islands. After Chiang dies there is danger of either a Communist takeover of Taiwan, or a native revolt because the natives don't like the Nationalists and want their own regime; but I think a Communist takeover is the bigger danger, which few Japanese appreciate." [36]

Another LDP leader closely associated with the Nationalist cause is ex-Prime Minister Kishi Nobusuke, elder brother of Prime Minister Sato. In Taipei as Japan's special envoy to President Chiang's fourth inauguration ceremonies in 1967, Kishi praised the Gimo as a "farsighted statesman who is held in high esteem by the Japanese people . . . a fighter for world peace and freedom." [37] It was Kishi's fourth trip to postwar Taiwan; as a leading member of various Japan-Nationalist China friendship committees, he has returned frequently to the island.

Kishi's comments to me in early 1963 were surprising in view of his public statements and reputation.

> Oh, you are interested in Taiwan . . . Do you realize there are 2 million refugees and 9 million natives there? Historically, and racially, Taiwanese are different from mainland people and have no interest in the mainlanders' urge to return . . . Our Socialists and Communists say that Taiwan belongs to Communist China, and both Chinese regimes insist there's only 'one China'. We should ask the native Taiwanese: they would prefer their own regime! If the United States supports one or another contender for power after Chiang passes, there will be great instability, but the Taiwanese may rise with their own leader . . .
>
> You ask why Taiwanese like Japan but Koreans do not . . . One reason may be, as Marshal Hata told you, the better Japanese colonial rule in Taiwan, but I think a more basic reason is the different personality of the Taiwanese: they would be easier for anybody to govern—no long tradition of nationalism, and so much politer than Koreans. Their perspective is different from Chiang's regime. For example, they wouldn't oppose Okinawa's reversion to Japan as the Nationalists do so unreasonably.[38]

Was Kishi more sincere in these remarks or in his lavish praise of the Nationalist regime on visits to Taipei? It may be that it suits the interests of the Japanese government to have some LDP members appear

pro-Nationalist while others, such as Matsumura Kenzo, engage in negotiations with Peking.

Kishi's brother, Sato Eisaku, spoke more diplomatically: "I know less
about Taiwan than my brother Kishi, so you'd better ask him," said Sato
in 1963. "The future of Communist Chinese development will be the
most important factor determining Taiwan's future. The Formosans are
not likely to rise in revolt, but they are easier to understand than Koreans. Taiwan isn't a democracy, is it? What will happen after Chiang
goes?" [39] The following year Sato again said that Taiwan was not a
democracy, so that its government did not reflect public opinion: "It's
probable true, therefore, that the natives of the island do not share the
Nationalist ambition to recover the mainland." [40]

As Prime Minister, Sato relied heavily on Deputy Prime Minister Kawashima Shojiro and Foreign Minister Miki Takeo. "Taiwan isn't a democracy but only Chiang's bailiwick, so who will succeed him?" Kawashima had wondered in 1962. "Unlike the Koreans, the Taiwanese liked
Japanese rule and there must be differences between the natives and
mainlanders today. Chiang keeps talking about mainland recovery, but
what do the Taiwanese think? I don't think it's possible without American aid, which is unlikely. There is a general opinion in Japan that there
should be two Chinas—really one China and one Taiwan. Both Chinese
regimes dispute that, but in reality we have two today and most Japanese
approve this as a good idea for the future." [41]

Four years later, as deputy Prime Minister, Kawashima said: "The Republic of China is a member of the free world, supported by the United
States and part of the United States Pacific defense network, so Japan
must support it politically. We cannot agree to any 'one China, one Taiwan' policy [Communist mainland and a Taiwan Republic], but the
United States seems to be trending toward a 'two China' approach [the
present de facto regimes] which we also support. That is realistic, to preserve the status quo and avoid war. Japan cannot follow the warlike policies of the Seoul and Taipei regimes which want to reunify their divided
countries by civil war, because we have no such problem and want to
separate trade from politics." [42]

Miki was secretary-general of the LDP at the start of the Sato Administration. Later he became Minister of International Trade and Industry
and, in December 1966, Foreign Minister.[43] In a luncheon interview in
1961, Miki had said: "We cannot envisage any definite solution to the
Formosa issue and cannot support or predict a 'two China' future. There
might be many possibilities, such as part of China, a UN trust territory,

or independence. It's too soon to say which will happen, but I only hope for a peaceful settlement in contrast to the current militaristic confrontation between the two Chinese regimes." [44]

One of Miki's predecessors as Foreign Minister, Ohira Masayoshi (who has been quoted earlier in this chapter) was deputy secretary-general of the LDP in 1964 when he told me: "I visited Taiwan this year and explained to President Chiang that Japan could not take a 'down with Communism and China mainland trade' line if the public disagreed. Taiwanese businessmen are acquiring more and more power, but the central government and party are still held tightly by KMT mainlanders and I don't anticipate any great change." [45]

Two senior LDP members had prewar experience in Formosa: Fujiyama Aiichiro and Ishii Mitsujiro. Fujiyama grew up there when his father headed the major sugar company in the island. In a 1962 interview, Fujiyama asked me: "Don't most Taiwanese want independence as their ideal? I think so, from what I remember of my youth in the island and my many friends there. Taiwanese are all anti-Communist and don't want to be ruled by Peking: that's absolutely certain." [46] In recent years, Fujiyama has opposed the Sato China policy as too rigid and has led one of the more liberal "anti-mainstream" factions in the LDP.

On the other hand, Ishii, who had been a secretary to the last Japanese governor of Taiwan, worked closely with Sato and became speaker of the lower house in 1967. "I served in the Japanese administration of Taiwan years ago," he said in 1962. "I visited Taiwan again in 1956, and again this spring on a trade mission. The Nationalists do expect Japanese economic aid because of Nationalist leniency on the reparations issue, and Prime Minister Ikeda seems well-disposed toward granting them economic credits. The Nationalists expressed great worry about the independent Taiwan movement in Japan. They didn't want it to receive any aid from the Japanese government or private groups, and I doubt if it did." [47]

The LDP maverick, the late Kono Ichiro, was known for his blunt tactics and aversion to the bureaucratic background of most party leaders. One of my Japanese students had heard him speak favorably of Formosan independence in the privacy of his home. To me, however, Kono expressed neutral opinions: "Japan should join hands with all friendly neighbors, including Taiwan . . . A Japanese politician should not express opinions on issues like Taiwan under present conditions. American policy is the most important there; Japan has little power to effect a solution and must await other nations' decisions. So I cannot express an opinion on Formosa nationalism—tensions must first be reduced. Japan did have more experience in China and Taiwan than the United States, and Japan is also closer culturally and geographically, so we are vitally interested in good peaceful relations. Our position forbids our intervening as a major force in solving such a complex problem as Taiwan." [48]

In Osaka, a major trading port for mainland trade, almost every LDP member of the city and prefectural assembly who was interviewed in 1953, 1957, and 1961 wanted a more flexible China policy, and maximum trade with the mainland even at the cost of displeasing Taipei. One Osaka councilman, chief of his assembly's Export Promotion League, spoke up strongly for Taiwan's independence: "If Chiang goes, the U.S. should make Taiwan an independent island because its people do not like the regime. If the opportunity arises, America should lead and Japan would follow to keep Taiwan out of Communist hands." [49]

Among the LDP Diet members most sympathetic to mainland China, Matsumura Kenzo travelled many times to Peking on trade and cultural exchange negotiations, especially after the Liao-Takasaki agreement of 1963. What did Matsumura, the LDP factional leader whom Peking and many Japanese regarded as the chief exponent of Japanese-People's Republic of China reconciliation, think of the future of Formosa? "Oh, I think it's logical for Taiwan to become an independent state as India, Burma, and other former colonies did after World War II. But this cannot be expected too soon." [50] Other LDP Dietmen active in private trade and cultural negotiations with Peking, such as Furui Yoshina (a lower house member from Tottori Prefecture) were more circumspect in their comments. "We only hope for a peaceful solution to the issue. Some say two Chinas or one China. The people of the two Chinas must decide this dilemma in the United Nations and in Sino-American dialogues. Taiwan's future cannot be settled first, only after other issues are solved," said Furui. [51]

The late Takasaki Tatsunosuke told reporters: "Manchuria was restored to China, and I do not think Peking will believe in the independence of Taiwan . . . In Taiwan, there are five or six million [sic] people from the mainland. They may well be sad in their hearts for their brethren in the mainland who are having a hard time." [52] Ikeda Masanosuke, another LDP advocate of closer ties with Peking, gave replies equally strange, but of an opposite nature, to the questions of Japanese reporters: "Japan owes very much to Chiang Kai-shek for his benevolent attitude at the end of the war . . . Japan and Taiwan have recognized each other as friendly nations so Japan must do as much as possible for Taiwan, which is a small but comfortable land . . . [However] Japan is the only country which will buy so much of Taiwan's rice, bananas, and sugar, even if the Nationalist regime is displeased about our trading with Communist China." [53]

Of Japanese opposition parties, only the Democratic Socialists (DSP) have openly espoused a "one China, one Taiwan" policy. Nishio Sue-hiro, senior statesman of the party, told me in 1961 and 1963 that "Tai-wan is both a domestic and international question, whereas the Socialists [JSP] agree with Peking that it should be only an internal question to be decided by the two Chinas themselves. The U.N. has a right to inter-vene because of the threat to world peace. Taiwan should be kept as a separate member of the U.N., and many Japanese scholars even think Taiwan should be considered separate from China historically." [54] In 1966, Nishio favored a "one China, one Taiwan" policy in order to pac-ify the Taiwan Straits and exclude Peking's claim to Taiwan; and, in an awkwardly translated magazine article, he suggested that the natives of Taiwan decide their own future: "The 'one China, one Taiwan' idea is favored by the Socialist International, though it has not definitely ex-pressed so. I think that is the world trend . . . You know the expression 'racial self-determination' . . . I believe that almost all non-Communist countries are also of the opinion that Taiwan should remain [in the U.N.] . . . Is it not after all that a one China, one Taiwan conclusion must be reached?" [55]

The other centrist opposition party, the Kōmeitō (a party sponsored by the Buddhist Sōka Gakkai), favors Peking's recognition and accept-ance into the United Nations and mainland control of Taiwan. "The problem of the two Chinas will be regarded as a problem of the domes-tic politics of the two countries and the party will take an attitude of non-intervention," said the Kōmeitō's international bureau chief in 1968.[56]

The leftist Japan Socialist party (JSP) also favors incorporation of Taiwan into mainland China, preferably after peaceful negotiations be-tween the two Chinese regimes. It wants Japan to suspend all relations with the Nationalists in order to recognize Peking as the one China dip-lomatically and in the United Nations. "Our party line is clear," said Matsumoto Shichiro, one of the party's younger foreign policy leaders, in 1961. "We think Taiwan is part of China, as the Cairo Declaration stated, and that China today is mainland China. Taiwan is an interna-tional problem only because the United States supports the Chiang regime and keeps bases there." [57] The late JSP chairman Asanuma (who was assassinated in 1960) made a famous 1959 joint statement with his Peking hosts denouncing American imperialism as the "Common enemy of the Chinese and Japanese peoples" because it prevented the return of Formosa to China and of Okinawa to Japan. The JSP has never repudiated the statement.

Hozumi Shichiro, another JSP member, said in a public speech telling of his six trips to Communist China: "Let us join together and fight American and Japanese imperialism! It is the Formosan question that stands in the way of good relations between Japan and China. We are absolutely opposed to American and Japanese policies of imperialism that obstruct the absorption of Taiwan into China." [58] Wada Hiro, the late chief of the JSP International Bureau, confirmed in 1961 that his party considered Formosa to be "an internal problem of China so no outside power should interfere or try to solve it." He added: "We favor direct talks between the two regimes and, though this seems difficult now, it will come eventually." [59]

Wada's successor as the foreign policy chief of the JSP, Sata Tadataka, asked me many questions about internal conditions on Formosa and seemed to understand the natives' desire for independence. "Our party position is that Taiwan should have a special autonomous status within Communist China, as its people and customs differ from those on the mainland. We recognize those differences, but do not favor any plebiscite," he said. When pointedly asked, "Should Formosa have the autonomous status of Tibet?," Sata smiled and nodded his head, obviously embarrassed by the question. In mid-1966, Sata's colleague Katsumata Seiichi, then the party's foreign policy chief and soon to be named JSP chairman, said, "China policy is very delicate now, and we really cannot say anything about the mainland turmoil or Taiwan." At that time the party had just undergone a serious debate on China policy in which the pro-Peking faction lost strength, yet one Socialist member of a bipartisan parliamentary goodwill mission to Formosa was censured for having made the trip without party approval.[60]

The Japan Communist party was also divided on the China issue because of Peking's charges against the party mainstream, which once followed the Peking line in the Sino-Soviet debate but switched to a more independent position in 1966. Local Communist assemblymen interviewed before 1964, however, took a purely Peking approach to the status of Taiwan: "Only Japanese support Taiwan independence, and a few Americans like you; the natives would prefer to be united with the mainland. Do you really think they'd vote for independence?" asked Kanzaki Yoshio of the Osaka City Assembly in 1962.[61]

But Shiga Yoshio, who was expelled from the Japanese Communist party in 1964 for approving the Nuclear Test-Ban Treaty in the Diet, told me that "most Taiwanese today probably do want independence, as you discovered in your research there—but they will prefer mainland rule later. I don't say this because Peking wants to 'liberate' Taiwan: I'd never parrot anything Peking says; but from my own perspective I think Taiwan will eventually become part of the mainland one way or another. This assumes that Mao's successors will be better than Chiang's successors, and that Peking pursues more peaceful policies. Feeling in the mainland runs very high about liberating Taiwan, as I saw on my last three visits." Shiga compared the viability of Okinawa and Taiwan as independent nations: "Of course, Okinawa is pro-Japanese and isn't able to stand on its feet economically, but Taiwan is a bigger island with better agriculture, so it could be independent. Its population is bigger than that of many nations in Europe and Africa . . . I had some Taiwanese classmates in college, and our late leader, Tokuda, was born in Okinawa so he also knew a lot about Taiwan." [62]

Public Opinion on the Formosan Problem

Table 5 reveals great Japanese support for normalization of relations with mainland China, reflecting the geographic, cultural, and other factors which have led even conservative Japanese to advocate closer ties with their huge neighbor. Dislike of Communist Chinese policies has increased over the past several years, but as late as mid-1967 only 3 per cent of respondents to a *Kyodo* news agency poll opposed diplomatic recognition of Peking, although one-fourth thought recognition would pose a threat to the "peace and security of Japan." (The same sample voted 34 per cent for "immediate recognition," 27 per cent for "delayed relations," 3 per cent for no diplomatic ties; the remaining 36 per cent did not answer.[63])

My own findings were that a plurality of every demographic and opinion group favored recognition, including those few who feared an attack from nuclear-armed China (Table 5). Even those approving Nationalist rule of Taiwan were 5 to 3 in favor of a change in Japanese policy by giving recognition to Communist China. On a related question, 61 per cent of the 1968 sample discounted the possibility that Peking might

TABLE 5

JAPANESE ATTITUDES TOWARD RECOGNITION OF COMMUNIST CHINA *

(in percentage)

	Recognize	Keep status quo	Don't know	Total	Plurality Index [a]	Number of cases
National (1958)	54	30	16	100	+24	2,422
National (1962)	42	18	40	100	+24	2,003
National (1966)	44	14	42	100	+30	2,258
National (1968)	47	17	36	100	+30	2,445
1968 Subgroups						
Male	59	20	21	100	+39	1,095
Female	36	15	49	100	+21	1,350
Under 30	47	21	32	100	+26	579
Over 50	42	16	42	100	+26	704
Elementary education	25	16	50	100	+9	313
University education	74	16	10	100	+58	191
Liberal-Democrats	36	22	42	100	+14	936
Socialists	57	13	30	100	+44	462

1968 Party Subgroups (indices)	Conservative voters [b]	Opposition voters [b]	Number of cases Conservative	Opposition
Male	+27	+58	546	383
Female	+16	+34	586	407
Under 30	+16	+43	208	233
Over 50	+24	+50	406	134
Elementary education	+10	+33	159	57
University education	+30	+80	73	83

Pro-recognition Indices by Attitude on Related Questions

Fear future attack by China	+23	Favor Japan nuclear arms	+29
Don't fear attack by China	+39	Oppose Japan nuclear arms	+37
Favor Formosan independence	+52	Favor U.S. defense of Formosa	+26
Favor Communist Formosa	+69	Oppose U.S. defense of Formosa	+42
Favor Nationalist rule of Formosa	+14		

* All data derived from the writer's surveys in February 1958, December 1962, November 1966, and December 1968, conducted by the Central Research Services, Ltd., of Tokyo, using the question: "Today our government has diplomatic relations with the Nationalist Chinese government on Taiwan, but not with Communist China. Should Japan establish diplomatic relations with Communist China or is the status quo satisfactory?"

[a] Plurality indices derived by subtracting the percentage opposed ("status quo" in this case) from the percentage approving recognition. Such indices are used in USIA reports and are a convenient way to present subgroup opinion concisely.

[b] "Conservative" includes Liberal-Democrats and those who claimed to have voted generally conservative; "Opposition" includes those who said they supported the Socialist, Democratic-Socialist, Kōmeitō, and Communist parties, and those who claimed to have voted generally against the Liberal-Democrats.

use her military power to attack Japan in the near future, compared with 6 per cent who feared such a danger. (Admittedly, when the 1967 *Kyodo* survey cited above used Prime Minister Sato's phrase, "Communist China poses a threat to our peace and security," three times as many agreed.) On the seating of Peking in the United Nations, responses in Japanese surveys, although preponderantly favorable, have shown less enthusiasm.[64]

TABLE 6

JAPANESE SUPPORT FOR RECOGNITION OF BOTH CHINAS *

(in percentage)

	Recognize both	Cancel Taiwan	Don't know	Total	Plurality Index [a]	N sub-total
National (1966)	76	6	18	100	+70	1,000
National (1968)	85	3	12	100	+82	1,135
1968 Subgroups						
7 biggest cities	83	4	13	100	+79	249
Other cities	84	4	12	100	+80	585
Rural areas	86	2	12	100	+84	301
Male	85	5	10	100	+80	649
Female	84	1	15	100	+83	486
Age 20 to 29	84	3	13	100	+81	274
Age 50 to 59	84	4	12	100	+80	170
Elementary education	86	2	12	100	+84	443
High school education	85	4	11	100	+81	474
University education	81	6	13	100	+75	141
Liberal-Democrats	87	2	11	100	+85	414
Socialists	85	3	12	100	+82	261
Democratic-Socialists	83	6	11	100	+77	53
Farmers; fishermen	84	1	15	100	+83	211
Merchants; professionals	88	3	9	100	+85	167
Office workers	84	7	9	100	+77	215
Factory workers	83	3	14	100	+80	174

* Question asked only of those who favored Japanese recognition of Communist China in my 1966 and 1968 surveys: "In that case, what should Japan do about relations with Taiwan: continue or cancel them?"
[a] Plurality index is derived by subtracting the percentage favoring cancellation of Taiwan relations from the percentage favoring maintaining relations with the Nationalists after recognizing Communist China.

Table 6 shows that most Japanese who favor recognition of Communist China also wish to retain diplomatic ties with Formosa. Fewer than one-third of any subgroup advocated their cancellation; between one-half and nine-tenths preferred to have diplomatic relations with both Peking and Taipei.

Supporters of the Liberal Democratic majority party were as inclined toward a two-China approach as their Socialist compatriots. The leaders of both major parties deviate far from the voters' preference, although LDP Diet members often told me they knew the majority of Japanese would applaud such a diplomatic shift if only Peking and Taipei permitted it. Only among the few who would turn Formosa over to Communist China (the official line of the Japan Socialist and Communist parties) were there as many as one-third who desired to cancel relations with the Nationalists.

Clearly, almost all Japanese who advocate establishing diplomatic relations with Peking wish to remain on friendly terms with Formosa too. Lest this imply Japanese support for Nationalist rule on Formosa, a separate question was asked on the status of Formosa. Do Japanese favor continued Nationalist rule of the island, transfer to mainland control, or Formosan independence? Table 7 shows the response in 1962, 1966, and 1968.

In late 1962, one-third of the sample thought Formosa should become independent of both Chinas; about 20 per cent favored the status quo; and 6 per cent wanted Formosa to be ruled by Communist China. By late 1966, a plurality of 27 per cent still favored independence, while 18 and 3 per cent, respectively, approved Nationalist and Communist rule. In December 1968, the pattern of 1962 reappeared as the three alternatives attracted 34, 23 and 3 per cent. Many of my colleagues and students wondered why 4 or 5 in every 10 Japanese could give no opinion on this question, but the "Don't know" rate was almost as high on recognition of Communist China and other complex issues in postwar Japanese surveys. If we focus on the "attentive public" (the males and the better-educated, for example), only one-fifth failed to express an opinion.

Of the 28 subgroups shown on Table 7, 25 gave plurality support to Formosan native independence over both alternatives presented. (The possibilities of rule by Japan or by the United Nations were not mentioned as alternatives because they seemed so unrealistic and because I never heard any Japanese or Formosan express a desire for a return of Japanese rule.) The less-educated conservative voters, those who opposed Japanese recognition of Peking, and those favoring U.S. military bases in Japan were the only groups with a slight plurality for a Nationalist rule. No group in the sample, even the few Japanese Communist voters or those who opposed American defense of Formosa, contained more than 20 per cent who favored Peking rule.

A slight majority of Japanese university graduates, male opposition

TABLE 7

JAPANESE ATTITUDES TOWARD THE FUTURE STATUS OF FORMOSA *

(in percentage)

	Native Independence	Communist Chinese rule	Nationalist Chinese rule	Don't know	Total	Index [a]	Number of cases
National (1962)	33	6	20	41	100	+7	2,003
National (1966)	27	3	18	52	100	+6	2,258
National (1968)	34	3	23	40	100	+8	2,445
1968 Subgroups							
Male	44	4	28	24	100	+12	1,095
Female	26	2	19	53	100	+5	1,350
Under 30	36	3	23	38	100	+10	579
Over 50	29	3	22	46	100	+14	704
Elementary educ.	21	1	18	60	100	+2	333
University educ.	53	5	26	16	100	+22	191
Liberal-Democrats	36	3	25	36	100	+8	936
Socialists	39	4	22	35	100	+13	462

Pro-independence Indices of Selected Subgroups

Conservative males	+6	Favor Peking recognition	+22
Opposition males	+22	Oppose Peking recognition	−13
Conservatives 20–29	+14	Fear attack by Peking	+30
Opposition voters 20–29	+6	Don't fear attack by Peking	+14
Conservatives 50–59	+3	Favor U.S. defense of Formosa	+14
Opposition voters 50–59	+10	Oppose U.S. defense of Formosa	+14
Elem. educ. conservatives	−1	Favor U.S. bases in Japan	−1
University educ. conservatives	+14	Oppose U.S. bases in Japan	+14
Elem. educ. opposition voters	+24	Favor Japan nuclear arms	+14
Univ. educ. opposition voters	+31	Oppose Japan nuclear arms	+10

* Data derived from my Japanese national surveys of December 1962, November 1966, and December 1968, using the question: "Would it be good for Formosa in the future to be a Formosan independent country, to come under the control of Communist China, or to have Nationalist Chinese rule as now?"
[a] Index derived by subtracting the percentages favoring Communist or Nationalist rule from that favoring independence.

voters, and those who either favored recognition of Communist China or feared it might attack Japan in the future wanted Formosa to be a native-ruled island. Among both LDP and Socialist voters, the better-educated were most likely to favor independence, but the net impression one gains from Table 7 is the very low level of popular Japanese support for Communist liberation of Formosa, and less support for the Nationalist position than Taipei would wish.

Two main factors help explain these Japanese attitudes toward Formosa: The first is a deep devotion to peaceful diplomacy, which auto-

TABLE 8

JAPANESE OPPOSITION TO U.S. DEFENSE OF FORMOSA AND THE
OFFSHORE ISLANDS *

(in percentage)

1. "As you may know, Quemoy and Matsu are now in the possession of the Nationalist Chinese government on Formosa headed by Chiang Kai-shek. If Communist China should attack these islands, do you think America should oppose the attack by armed force or not?"

	Should	Should not	Don't know	Total	Number of cases
National (December 1958)	11	48	41	100	676

2. "If Communist China should attack Formosa, do you think America should oppose the attack by force or arms or not?"

	Should	Should not	Don't know	Total	Index a	Number of cases
National (1956)	33	25	42	100	+8	1,291
National (1958)	15	47	38	100	−32	676
National (1968)	13	43	44	100	−30	2,445
Subgroups in 1968						
Males	21	49	30	100	−28	1,095
Females	7	38	55	100	−28	1,350
Under 30	11	51	38	100	−40	579
Over 50	18	32	50	100	−14	704
Elementary education	14	24	62	100	−10	313
University education	14	58	28	100	−44	191
Liberal-Democrats	19	41	40	100	−22	936
Socialists	9	52	39	100	−43	462

Indices of anti-Formosan Defense of Selected 1968 Subgroups

Conservative males	−15	Favor recognition of Peking	−40
Opposition males	−45	Oppose recognition of Peking	−24
Conservatives under 30	−36		
Opposition under 30	−51	Fear Peking attack on Japan	−9
Conservatives over 50	−11	Don't fear Peking attack on	
Opposition over 50	−22	Japan	−38
Conservative white collar	−34		
Opposition white collar	−58	Favor Formosan independence	−36
Primary educ. conservatives	−12	Favor a Communist Formosa	−54
Primary educ. opposition	−5	Favor Nationalist rule of	
University educ. conservatives	−26	Formosa	−29
University educ. opposition	−62		

* Data derived from U.S. Information Agency surveys of January 1956 and December 1958, as reported in Trends in Japanese Attitudes toward Communist China and toward Defense of Formosa and the Offshore Islands (Washington: USIA FE-20, May 1959, declassified August 20, 1963), pp. 1–3; and my survey conducted in December 1968 asking the same question on Formosan defense.
a Derived by subtracting the percentage saying "should not" from that saying the U.S. "should" defend Formosa from a Communist attack.

matically produces an aversion to the civil-war militancy of both Chinese Communists and Nationalists. Every bellicose statement from Peking or Taipei causes the Japanese to fear the outbreak of another Asian war into which they might be drawn involuntarily. Civilian Japanese reactions to the 1965–1969 Vietnam war policy of the United States indicated fear of the war's escalation beyond Vietnam, and a desire for United States withdrawal.[65]

The most striking evidence of Japanese aversion to the use of armed force was embodied in a late 1958 USIA survey inspired by the heavy Communist shelling of Quemoy and in my survey in 1968 (Table 8). Only 15 per cent of the sample queried at that time wanted the United States to defend either Formosa or the offshore islands, while about 40 per cent indicated they would object to such defense even if no Japanese bases or nuclear weapons were used. The percentage of the 1958 sample favoring American defense of Quemoy and Matsu declined from 11 to 3 per cent when the question involved United States use of Japanese bases, to 2 per cent when it was a matter of the United States attacking mainland targets, and to a mere 1 per cent when the interviewer mentioned the possibility of using nuclear weapons against mainland targets. My 1968 survey showed an equal hostility to American defense of Formosa, without a single subgroup on Table 8 supporting that proposal regardless of their views on related questions. Conservative voters were slightly less opposed to defense of Formosa than those who supported anti-LDP parties.

One may agree with opposition to American defense of the offshore islands (the position taken by the late John F. Kennedy in the 1960 presidential campaign debates), because, as noted earlier, these islands are not traditionally part of Formosa. Defending the 13 million people of Formosa is a far different issue. The magnitude of Japanese hostility toward *any* use of force even to defend its former colony reveals the extent of postwar conversion to pacifism.[66]

The second factor is Japan's postwar desire for trade with mainland China, which had been an important prewar trading partner. An international poll in 1958 showed 82 per cent of the Japanese sample favoring increased trade with Communist China, a far higher percentage than in Britain, Australia, or the nine continental European nations included in the survey.[67]

It is thus difficult to escape the conclusion that the Japanese people, whether from pacifist or commercial motives, want no part of the Formosan defense problem. At the same time, reluctance to endanger profitable trade with Formosa is an equally important influence on the Japanese Cabinet and its business supporters.

The Views of Journalists, Scholars, and Businessmen

"You can ask a Japanese national sample what they think of Chiang Kai-shek, the future of Formosa, and defense of the offshore islands because Japan is a democracy," said a Japanese correspondent with Formosan experience, "but anyone who tried to ask such questions inside Formosa would be expelled or jailed." [68]

There are seldom more than three Japanese correspondents stationed in Formosa because Japanese newspaper publishers regard Hong Kong as a better source of news from both Chinas. "Why should we waste money having a man in Taipei when all he gets is government propaganda we can obtain free in Tokyo?" asked one editor in 1962. "The Nationalist regime usually trails Japanese visitors and objects to their contacts with Formosan natives."

"It's unfortunate but true that most Japanese politicians and scholars have little knowledge of, or interest in, Taiwan," commented an *Asahi* newsman, a co-author of his paper's two-volume study of Formosa, who had visited mainland China for three weeks in 1965. "Peking always claims it will liberate Taiwan, but it might better agree to a really free Taiwan." [69] Another Japanese newsman, who had served in Taipei from 1954 to 1958, was pessimistic about the chances for an independent Formosa because "the people don't talk much and are less violent than Koreans or Cubans." He discounted the likelihood of much Japanese support for Formosans in Japan unless the independence movement were visibly advancing toward success.[70]

An editor of the influential *Sankei* newspaper who had visited Formosa thought that independence was the major goal of the Formosans and that it would be good for Japan and the world.[71] The president of a major news association (which is considered very conservative and hence pro-Nationalist) hesitated to talk to me about Formosa, suggesting instead that I fend for myself: "You are very competent to write on that subject, as your Japanese language opens more doors to native opinion than most foreigners could find . . ." [72]

Several reporters, including a few stationed in Okinawa who had made brief trips to Formosa, remarked on the friction between Formosans and mainlanders, the native admiration for things Japanese, and the difficulty of conducting political research there. Hosono Akio, whose *Taiwan no Hyojo* (Conditions on Taiwan) is one of the best accounts of the island, wrote that the "Taiwanese masses acutely feel the burden of supporting two million Chinese, especially the weight of huge military expenditures . . . We were often embarrassed by Taiwanese who spoke to us in friendly tones saying 'How good were the Japanese days here!' . . . The friction between the Taiwanese and the Chinese cannot be explained away by the fact of provincial consciousness alone. More pertinent is the Taiwanese discontent with Nationalist rule and their aspirations for their own free society." [73]

As for Japanese academics' views of Formosa, it appears that most scholars focus on mainland China, preferring to ignore Formosa (as well as Korea) even if they had lived there before 1945. "Neither my colleagues nor my students are much interested if I talk to them about Taiwan, and the editors of magazines are even less interested," said one Tokyo scholar. However, a Fulbright educational administrator spoke in 1963 of several visits to Formosa: "There are two types of Chinese on that island. Wouldn't it be better to have a neutral, peaceful Taiwanese government after all?" [74]

Probably a majority of Japanese academicians support the Socialist and Democratic Socialist parties, while very few follow the ruling LDP. When Averell Harriman asked to talk with a group of representative Japanese scholars in Tokyo, the Embassy introduced him to a dozen, all of whom said they voted Socialist. When Harriman asked their opinion of Formosa, however, all but one admitted they disagreed with the Socialist party line: "When we travel to mainland China, we try to persuade any officials or scholars we meet to approve Formosan self-determination," they explained.[75]

A former president of Tokyo International Christian University, Dr. Ukai Nobushige, spoke favorably of the "successor state" theory under which there would be two Chinese regimes. "Taiwan independence is very improbable," he declared in 1963, but added that separatist sentiment did seem to be stronger in recent years. One of his friends, an advisor to the Democratic Socialists and several government commissions who apparently wanted to know more about Formosa remarked: "'It's a police state, isn't it? What a horrible fate for the Formosans after decades of our colonial suppression."

Professor Eto Shinkichi of Tokyo University, who has written extensively about mainland China, is a friend of the Formosan cause but dubious, as he has explained in magazine articles, that Peking would tolerate independence: "It is theoretically possible that Communist China's attitude toward Taiwan can change if there emerges a problem of fundamental importance whose solution requires abandonment of Taiwan . . . but we can safely contend that no such problem has emerged . . . [Therefore] Communist China's stubborn attitude toward Taiwan will last for a long time to come." [76]

The American consul in Fukuoka introduced me to a Japanese professor who said he had spent over 30 years in Formosa until the 1947 uprising: "I was one of the few Japanese allowed to remain after 1945, and witnessed the entire 1947 incident when Chinese troops mowed down the natives with machine-guns, even hitting my house as they passed by . . . Formosa must be kept out of Communist hands above all else, and I agree the natives prefer self-rule but are afraid to talk politics." [77]

Professor Ohira Zengo, a specialist in international law and politics at Hitotsubashi University, wrote in 1961: "The most that anyone can claim is that the ultimate status of Taiwan is still undecided . . . It is quite obvious that any settlement of the status of Taiwan must take into account the will of the Taiwanese. On this point it is important to keep in mind that the ten million Taiwanese abhor the idea of being under Communist rule and cherish the hope of someday establishing an independent Taiwan . . . From the point of view of basic human rights, it is absolutely imperative that the countries of the free world make every effort to guarantee the right of eventual self-determination to the people of Taiwan." [78]

As noted in Chapter 3, thousands of Japanese businessmen visit Formosa annually: Japan is the island's biggest trading partner and source of tourists. But most of those interviewed claimed it was bad business to involve themselves with politics when they dealt with their Formosan colleagues: "Politics and business do not mix because the Nationalists watch us carefully and our friends warn us to stick to either business or pleasure."

There were some exceptions, however. Two banana traders who commuted between Tokyo and Taipei told me in 1961 that both mainlanders and Formosans mixed well in public but never in private. Another Japanese acquaintance who had grown up in prewar Taipei spoke of complaints by visiting Formosan classmates about the KMT military budget, secret police harassment, and social discrimination. Perhaps the most knowledgeable Japanese businessman I met, who had spent 20 years in the island before and after the war, said in 1964: "I could never tell you anything when we met in Taipei. Japanese firms warn the men they send to Taiwan not to talk politics, and our Embassy in Taipei reinforces that warning . . . Most Japanese I knew in Taiwan would agree with the Taiwanese about the desirability of independence, but both groups are afraid to speak openly." [79]

On the other hand, Okazaki Kaheita, ex-president of the All-Nippon Airlines and chairman of the Japan-Communist China Trade and Friendship Association which negotiated the Liao-Takasaki private trade agreements with Peking, opened an interview by saying that "Chiang Kai-shek is one of the great heroes of this century and I've admired him since before the war . . . His successors may accept Peking's offers to return to high position on the mainland without penalty or purge. I think they will. As for Taiwan, we shouldn't support its independence as that is beside the point . . . it will merge with the mainland eventually." [80]

Two businessmen in southern Kyushu, both active in local politics, took opposite positions on Formosa. The Socialist mayor of Kagoshima advocated Communist Chinese control of Formosa, but the ex-mayor of nearby Kumamoto City, who had lived in Taiwan from 1923 to 1945, disagreed violently: "I served as governor of Kaohsiung, then Taipei, and later head of the unified Taiwan press during World War II . . . There is no reason to hand over the Taiwanese to Red China as the Kagoshima mayor advocates, because they are very polite, hard-working, and wonderful people who deserve their freedom." [81] A group of Japanese Junior Chamber of Commerce leaders who toured Formosa in late 1962 told me their impression was that the Nationalists suppressed Formosans in all walks of life.[82]

An elderly Japanese who had served as a semi-official agent in mainland China from 1937 to 1945, reporting to Foreign Ministers Hirota Koki and Togo Shigenori, told me: "I learned the truth [about mainland peasant attitudes] by talking with many Chinese natives who hated our invasion forces, just as you talked with ordinary Formosans and a few government leaders. It is not easy to master the facts about the island by merely discoursing with senior Nationalist officials and politicians." [83]

Some Views From Okinawa

The island of Okinawa, with the other neighboring smaller Ryukyus, is just north of Formosa, where thousands of Okinawans used to work as government officials or in private business while Formosa was a Japanese colony. The contrast in Nationalist Chinese attitudes toward Okinawan and Formosan independence is marked.

"The will of the people of the Ryukyus should be respected in settling the status of those islands in accordance with the principle of self-determination," claimed Nationalist Chinese Foreign Minister Wei Tao-ming in early 1968, echoing his regime's consistent objection to any reversion of Okinawa to Japanese control.[84] "China was once sovereign in the Ryukyus. It has made no new claim to the islands . . . But how can anyone claim that the people of the Ryukyus will inevitably want to return to Japan 10 or 20 years from now? . . . Most Chinese are of the view that the interests of the Republic of China should be considered when the permanent future of the Ryukyus is decided." [85]

Later, after President Johnson had promised Japanese Premier Sato to return the Bonin Islands and Iwo Jima during 1968, the Nationalist press again objected to such "appeasement" of Japan, especially if it should lead to the reversion of Okinawa. "It could be a dagger aimed at continental China, Taiwan, the Philippines, and even Korea . . . Asia would rather wait a while, a good long while, before seeing Okinawa returned to the Japanese," claimed the China News.[86] "Why should Chiang Kai-shek espouse the independence of Okinawa, which we do not want, when he ignores the right of the 11 million Taiwanese to independence or even a vote on the question?" was the typical retort of Okinawan politicians.

The 900,000 Okinawans have lived under American military control since 1945, and many have travelled to Formosa for study, business, and technical assistance.[87] One, who had been born in prewar Taipei and returned there in 1962 to help establish the Taipei television station, reported: "My classmates from the prewar high school seemed resigned to their sad fate under the Nationalists. They don't want a return of Japanese rule, as we all do here in Okinawa, but they would like to see their local election candidates able to espouse independence. The American authorities permit such freedom of expression here, but the Nationalists are afraid to allow it in Formosa." [88]

Several Okinawan reporters and editors who had visited Formosa on guided tours commented on the friendly reception they had received when they spoke Japanese. "We had little chance to travel alone, but we could sense the friction between Formosans and mainlanders," said one newsman. "The Taiwanese felt better under Japanese rule and are *fuman* [dissatisfied] politically . . . They have more economic freedom today [1966] but no political rights even to the extent we have under American rule," added a publisher.[89] A visiting *Asahi* correspondent, a Taipei resident from 1929 to 1946, said in a 1966 interview: "Whenever I return to Taipei, my local friends refuse to talk politics, but their lack of freedom is obvious." [90]

The leader of the major opposition party in Okinawa, who had lived in Formosa for 16 years before World War II and had returned there occasionally after 1949, confirmed many of his fellow-Okinawans' observations: "From my wide acquaintance with Formosans over the years, I know they hate the KMT regime, although they surely hate Communist China more. They should be given a free choice, which we Okinawans also deserve. Both our peoples live under semi-colonialism, but in Formosa there is no free criticism of the regime such as we have here. When I went to Formosa to watch the provincial assembly election in 1963, nobody would talk politics. A few Formosan mayors I know are anti-KMT independents, but they are subject to harassment, with the fear of facing trumped-up charges if the regime thinks they misbehave. The Formosans like the Japanese better than the Chinese Nationalists, and in a plebiscite some might vote for a return to Japan—but not the prewar type of Japan." [91]

Japan is unlikely to change its basic policy toward Formosa, despite the widespread sympathy in Japan and Okinawa for Formosan independence, unless Washington first supports the "one China, one Taiwan" policy now opposed by both Peking and Taipei. The evidence in this chapter indicates, however, that a large proportion of the Japanese public, political elite, and opinion leaders would welcome a policy based on recognition of the mainland as China, with Formosa as a separate entity.

10

THE FUTURE OF
FORMOSAN NATIONALISM

Predictions are always risky in the field of international politics, perhaps especially so in the case of Formosa, where external factors are more likely than domestic developments to decide its fate. "It may be impossible for America ever to interpret foreign countries correctly," wrote an American foreign aid official with long experience on Formosa. "Most of our [government] information [about Formosa] comes from 'contacts,' and I have never been sure who is doing the manipulation, we or they." [1]

One future possibility is the conquest of Formosa by mainland China, either through armed force or by peaceful merger. Another is maintenance of the status quo under Nationalist rule, with perhaps greater political freedom for the majority but no genuine Formosan independence. A third would be foreign intervention, by the U.N. or a group of powers, to force the Nationalists to hand over political control to the Formosans. We should also consider the prospect for a Formosan uprising against the mainlander elite, whether initiated by local groups or precipitated by some external attempt to change the island's status.

Communist Chinese Incorporation of Formosa?

Future military incorporation of the 13 million people of Formosa into Communist China does not seem likely. The United States is clearly committed, by treaty as well as in its own national interest, to defend Formosa (although not necessarily the offshore islands), while Communist China's naval and air strength might be effective against Quemoy but almost certainly not against Formosa.[2] "Do you think they can walk across water?" said a Soviet diplomat of Communist Chinese threats to "liberate" Formosa and incidentally defeat the United States. Even those few nations which support Peking diplomatically could be expected to oppose her use of force to capture Formosa, and the majority of the United Nations would censure such a military adventure.

A genuinely free Formosa would be even more immune to Communist attack than it is now because the present "civil war" rationale would disappear. As long as Formosa is held by a claimant to mainland sovereignty, Peking retains a theoretical right to defeat its rival and occupy its territory.

What has been the Communist Chinese policy on Formosan separatism? "The Chinese people are resolved to liberate their brothers on Taiwan. Until this is done our national sovereignty will not be complete, peace in Asia will not be secure, and the brave people of Taiwan will not enjoy the freedom for which they fought so long," wrote a Communist official in 1955 at the end of an article claiming that Taiwan is historically Chinese.[3]

The Chinese Communists in early 1956 scorned American proposals to renounce the use of force in the Formosa Straits because "this internal affair of China cannot be a subject of the Sino-American talks . . . [America is attempting substantially] to confuse the international dispute between China and the U.S. in the Taiwan area with the domestic matter between the Chinese government and the Chiang Kaishek clique and a demand that China . . . give up its sovereign right to liberate Taiwan."[4] Chen Yi, later Foreign Minister, agreed that "certain countries are trying to turn the Chinese province of Taiwan into another China, or another country with an independent existence . . . Such plots to interfere in the internal affairs of China constitute an encroachment on the sovereignty of our country . . ."[5] Peking has published several books and pamphlets to denounce the alienation of Taiwan from the mainland, always agreeing with the Nationalist claim that the island is historically Chinese, citing Allied commitments in World War II, and insisting that every Formosan eagerly awaits Communist liberation.[6]

In 1964, I corresponded with the China Publications Centre in Peking, requesting an informal meeting with mainland representatives in Hong Kong later that year. The Centre regretted that as a bookstore it was unable to arrange such meetings, but assured me I would be able to revisit China "when your government gives up its aggressive and war policies." [7] After I pointed out the limited, defensive nature of American policy during the Korean War and the 1958 offshore island crisis, the Centre responded in typical Maoist style:

We strongly protest your letter of September 16. Taiwan has been China's territory from ancient times. But the U.S. imperialists have occupied it, interfered with China's internal affairs, made trouble in the Taiwan Straits, and schemed 'two Chinas': all this is absolutely intolerable to the Chinese people. Your views on this question are sheer nonsense: they only show that you are not in the least a friend of the Chinese people. Those who assume a hostile attitude towards the Chinese people will meet with nothing but an ignominious defeat . . . While you seem to admit that the Chinese people are peaceful, you assert that our Government is not so. That certainly is the most absurd logic! The Chinese Government is the people's government. Have you not even these rudiments of common sense? [8]

Edgar Snow's interviews with Chou En-lai produced strong criticism of any American proposals to create a "Sino-Formosan state" or interfere in any way with a complete "liberation" of Formosa. Chou insisted that his government would refuse to participate in any international organization alongside the "Taiwan clique . . . under whatever form and in whatever name." Snow himself thought that Chiang would not compromise with Peking, but that a future rapprochement would be probable if encouraged by the United States and other powers: "As time begins to run out on the exclusion of mainland China from the United Nations, the bargaining power of Taiwan may be expected to weaken. For this reason, periodic rumors of Kuomintang-Communist negotiations may have to be taken more seriously than in the past . . ." [9]

A leading Osaka businessman said that Chou En-lai told his 1958 trade mission that "China would close one eye to Japan's trading with Taiwan," but insisted on China's right to liberate that island.[10] A *Yomiuri* correspondent who was among the first 12 Japanese newsmen admitted to Peking in 1964 and, while there, had many opportunities to discuss Taiwan, said: "Peking wants Taiwan as a territorial right, not because it fears an American or KMT invasion. It expects most of the old KMT men to return, as Li Tsung-jen did recently [in 1965], because Chinese traditionally want to go home to die. I saw slogans about liberating Taiwan all over China and the people accept their government's stories about the situation in Taiwan. They'll never give up their claim to that island, although I agree the Formosans don't want rule by either China. Older KMT men will inevitably be attracted back to the mainland, so there is a good prospect for a peaceful amalgamation." [11]

"Taiwan is a province of China and the Taiwanese are Chinese, just as Cantonese are Chinese and Texans are Americans," Dr. H. C. Ling, manager of the *Global Digest,* a Hong Kong-published magazine regarded by the United States and Japanese consulates as a mouthpiece for Peking, wrote to me. "Autonomy or no autonomy for Taiwan is a question of Chinese internal affairs, just as autonomy in Texas is a question of U.S. internal affairs. I wonder how you can conceive of a 'neutralized autonomy' in Taiwan and Tibet when they are part of China?" [12]

Peking had welcomed a few Formosan political refugees after the 1947 massacre (notably Miss Hsieh Hsueh-hung of Changhua who was mentioned in an earlier chapter); a small group of mainland-trained Formosans operate a Communist front in Japan; and a few Formosan students in other countries may voice pro-Peking sentiments out of frustration. But for the most part it appears Professor Cheng is correct in stating: "Peking realized that Formosan Communists were more Formosan than Communist." [13] A Japanese expert on both Chinas has written: "Taiwanese have had more than enough of foreign rule and are anxious for their independence. This is why they are annoyed by the Communist promise of liberation . . . Why was Miss Hsieh, who had been the darling of the CCP and praised by that party as a woman fighter for liberation of Taiwan, purged so suddenly? She had said 'the Taiwanese do not understand the CCP nor do they feel warm toward Communist China . . . Even if Communist China succeeds in liberating Taiwan, there will be more 2-28 incidents' . . . Miss Hsieh was, after all, a Taiwanese who understood the feelings of her compatriots. This feeling is an unchanging fact." [14]

As noted earlier, Peking radio beams Japanese language news and music programs to Formosa every night during the KMT propaganda broadcasts, obviously hoping to attract Formosan listeners; but Formosans may be immune, having been indoctrinated with two decades of anti-Communist propaganda by the Nationalist regime after a previous half-century of Japanese suppression of left-wing movements in the island. More important, many Formosans are aware of Peking's rough treatment of Tibetans and other minorities inside China, and of the probability that Communist rule would drain Formosa's rich natural resources for the benefit of the 750 million Chinese on the mainland. "I cannot believe that Peking would allow us to trade or exchange students and visitors with the outside world, least of all with Japan and the United States, so if it came to a choice between the Nationalists we have and the Communists we don't want, the status quo is better," said a Formosan economist in 1962.

The USSR has always supported Peking as the rightful representative of China in all United Nations bodies and has refrained from any public refutation of Chinese claims to Formosa. On the other hand, Moscow aided India against Chinese incursions along the Sino-Indian frontier and has fought Chinese demands for the return of land the Czars acquired from China.

The 1950 Sino-Soviet treaty had pledged mutual assistance in the event of an attack by "Japan or states allied with it," which meant the United States. It is logical to assume that Russia did not wish to risk war with the United States over the offshore islands, much less Formosa, and began to reduce its military and economic aid to China after the 1958 crisis.[15] By the same token, China presumably realized she could not rely on Russian help: "The Soviet leaders, both Khrushchev and the present ones, have betrayed us many times . . . They cannot be trusted. In 1960 they withdrew their technical experts from China to strangle our economy. Their propaganda is not aimed against the United States but mostly against China," said Foreign Minister Chen Yi to a group of Scandinavian newsmen in 1966.[16]

Diplomatic historian George Kennan told me in early 1964 that Russia would never aid a Chinese attack on Formosa unless the Nationalists had launched a prior invasion. "Russia would probably give tacit support to any plan for Formosa which would remove American bases and neutralize the island," [17] Kennan predicted. "In recent years, the Mao regime has been taking adventurist and big-power policy lines at home and abroad," complained Victor Maevsky of the *Pravda* editorial staff to a Japanese correspondent in 1967. "This is a great loss to the Chinese people, but we believe China will eventually return to the original policies of socialism. Consequently, the Soviet Union does not feel the threat of China . . . If China had really been planning to . . . resort to armed strength, Taiwan would have been its target a long time ago. However, as a practical matter, it did not attack Taiwan, and it will probably not attack Taiwan in the future either." [18]

Few expatriate Formosans live in Communist areas outside mainland China, and the smaller Communist nations follow Moscow or Peking on the Formosan issue. Small third-force Communist states using the Sino-Soviet dispute to assert their own autonomy are probably uninformed and apathetic toward the future of Formosa. They avoid official comment but they seem to be more anti-Nationalist than pro-Peking and might well view a neutralized, independent Formosan state favorably.[19]

Communist China has alternated aggressive threats against Formosa with peaceful overtures to the Nationalist refugees, as in a *Hsinhua* news release of 1956: "Our compatriots in Taiwan have always been an inseparable part of the Chinese people. We not only have constant concern for them and support them in various ways in their struggle against foreign rule, but also stand ready to welcome them at any time to participate in the socialist construction of the mainland and share the glory of our nation." [20]

In 1962, the London *Observer* reported that agents of the two Chinas had secretly negotiated the future of Formosa. "Taiwan would become an autonomous province of China but would remain under Nationalist control," according to reports of the alleged agreement in Hong Kong. "Neither regime would launch an attack against the other during Generalissimo Chiang's lifetime . . . After Chiang's death, his family would implement an accord under which Taiwan would become an autonomous province of China with a status similar to that of Tibet . . . Ten to twenty years later a referendum would be held to determine Taiwan's future as an independent state or part of China proper . . . The Nationalist-controlled offshore islands of Quemoy and Matsu and the Communist port of Amoy on the mainland would be integrated into a buffer administrative district . . ." [21] The Nationalists have denied every such rumor as groundless.[22]

Most Washington observers agree that high Nationalist officials would not trust Peking's promises of amnesty regardless of the welcome accorded former Nationalist Acting President Li Tsung-jen, then 74, on his return to mainland China in July 1965. Li had broken with Chiang Kai-shek in 1949 after his unsuccessful effort to negotiate peace with the Communist forces, and had lived in the United States for the sixteen years prior to his flight to Peking.[23] Later, Li accused the United States of having attempted to persuade him to help overthrow the Chiang regime in 1955, but said he had refused. "I sternly rejected this proposal on the spot . . . Formosa is an inalienable territory of China and the Taiwan question is China's internal affair . . . If Mr. Chiang sincerely wishes to settle this internal question, I will not hesitate to go through fire and water." [24]

A chillingly dramatic novel by an American official with experience in Formosa (*The Jing Affair*, by "D. J. Spencer," published by Funk and

Wagnalls, 1965) predicts an attempted deal by high Nationalist officers to turn over Formosa to the Communists. The book suggests that someone like Chiang Ching-kuo might mislead the Gimo by turning a supposed secret invasion of the mainland into a surrender of Formosa, but ends on the happy note of joint efforts by Americans and Taiwanese to thwart the scheme and produce an independent Formosa. The author of the book admitted that "in government circles mine is a rather lonely if no longer a dangerous point of view . . . I can think of no other way [to defend the Formosan cause] . . . in the framework of the U.S. national interest . . . We would be better off with Formosa as the southernmost province of Japan than as the easternmost province of China, and I believe even the Taiwanese would reluctantly concur." [25]

It should be recognized that a secret coup in Formosa by a small number of Nationalist officers could indeed permit a takeover by the Communists, confronting the rest of the world with a *fait accompli* difficult to reverse. "Generalissimo Chiang is in his late seventies," wrote Warren Unna in 1964. "When he dies, his successor might decide to accept one of those long-proffered 'deals' by which Communist China would grant protection and perquisites to those who hand over Taiwan . . . Who then would the United States be protecting as it stood by its commitments to the Nationalist China government on Taiwan?" [26]

Early in 1966, I arranged through Vice President Humphrey's office to interview a Pentagon officer with Taiwan experience. He denied the probability of any "secret deal" between Ching-kuo or other Nationalist officers and the successors to Mao on the mainland, as rumored in the London and Hong Kong press. "Even if Ching-kuo wanted to make such a deal, the bulk of the ChiNat military wouldn't go along," he said. "From my experience there, I doubt that many Nationalist top-rank military would trust Communist promises if they did make a deal. They know what happened to others who surrendered to Peking, and they have too much to lose." [27]

The assumption in *The Jing Affair* that Formosans would revolt to thwart such a secret deal is less tenable than its author's corollary, that the United States would intervene effectively. But if the mainland regime at that time were willing to deal with the United States, the latter might well accept the incorporation of Formosa as part of a larger arrangement, as urged by some of the Americans quoted in Chapter 8. Dennis Bloodworth, a British journalist-expert on China, wrote in 1967 that "a Chinese Communist feels closer to a Nationalist Chinese than to a foreign Communist. And sooner or later . . . Peking and Taiwan will reach some sort of accommodation, discovering that they have not been really enemies but just bad friends." [28] The director of Asian affairs at the Japanese Foreign Ministry in 1966, who knew of the rumors, told me: "I agree with your strong opposition to any such deal, but Japan is in no position to prevent its realization and I doubt that your government would act in time." [29]

Spencer's further contention that both the United States and native Formosans would approve Japanese rule over Taiwan, perhaps by trusteeship, needs to be clarified. As long as independence is an ultimate possibility, it is fairly certain no Formosan would want the return of Japanese rule except as an alternative to Nationalist or Communist Chinese colonialism; and few Americans would favor it. The major reason for its impracticality, however, is the strong antipathy of most Japanese to overseas commitments. Surveys (such as cited in Chapter 9) indicate few Japanese even wish to take over the defense of Okinawa or protect their own nationals' fishing boats in the Sea of Japan, and that far more would accede to a merger of Formosa into mainland China despite Peking's 1964 accusation that Japanese leaders favor self-determination for the Formosans.[30]

Evolutionary Nationalism on Formosa?

A Japanese diplomat predicted in 1957 that Formosans would gradually assume political power after a generation of increasing economic power and American pressure on the mainlander minority. Many American officials in the island shared this belief in the gradual growth of Formosan political power, but felt it justified support of the status quo. Their attitude was similar to that of Frank Morello in *The International Legal Status of Formosa*—acknowledgment that Formosan natives have some justifiable complaints, but insistence that these could be remedied within the Nationalist legal system.[31]

The Nationalist regime claims that it always "welcomes criticisms that are constructive and are made for the cause of freedom," as a Nationalist diplomat assured me: "We would be the last ones on earth to claim that our government or its record on Taiwan is perfect. The important thing is, we feel, that we have honestly tried to improve the standard of living for the people, and offer our system as the alternative to oppressive Communist rule to the people of the mainland." [32] The Nationalists point to rising economic standards and local elections as proof that progress is being made, although some of its own editors complain of the slow pace: "Partly because of taxes, but also because of economic development, our country shows a tendency for the rich to get richer and the poor to have an increasingly difficult time." [33] On the eve of the Nationalists' twenty-first "Constitution Day" (which coincides with Christmas) the China News editorialized: "Under wartime conditions, the record on Taiwan is not perfect. In general, however, our people are free in the exercise of their personal rights and most of the civil rights extended by the Constitution. They cannot be Communists and they cannot advocate overthrow of the government by force and violence . . . [but] They can criticize the government and organize political parties to oppose the ruling Kuomintang. As yet we have not passed on political power to an opposition party. Although such an occasion has not yet arisen, we are confident that it will . . ." [34]

A minority of the Formosans I interviewed preferred political evolution to revolution because "the KMT will be forced to concede political power to the majority when it recognizes it cannot return to the mainland." Some submissive types, especially in the business community both at home and abroad, echoed the words of a young businessman in 1964: "Most people favor improvement in living conditions, water supply, housing, and other conditions for our people regardless of whether you call it independence or not. Independence is less desired than improvements in livelihood." [35] Those who said they were satisfied with non-political progress tended to place economic factors above political freedom, or to question whether Formosan leaders would treat them any better than the more enlightened variety of KMT mainlanders.

We are concerned here with the prospect for a peaceful transition to full democracy on Formosa, rather than just socio-economic improvement within the Nationalist colonial system. One of the more liberal Nationalist Chinese scholars admitted in 1967 that "Politically, the regime in Taiwan is neither a totalitarian dictatorship nor a truly democratic government. It has been fairly described as ultra-conservative." [36] As Richard Koo, chairman of the Young Formosan Association in Japan, remarked on his 1965 American visit: "There is no possibility of democratization as long as the mainlanders rule us . . . the situation is different from most other colonial situations because the ruling elite has no other place to go." [37]

One of the most thoughtful overseas Formosan scholars saw Chiang-kuo as the future ruler of Formosa, enjoying United States support and suppressing Formosan nationalists: "The future situation will be that

America continues to support whoever is in power, and American intellectual sympathizers with our cause will continue to blame us for failing
to create an obviously hopeless revolution . . . The only hope is for the
overseas Formosans to keep the independence ideal alive until the day
that the KMT must come to terms with them." [38]

If, as so many foreign and native observers predict, Defense Minister
Chiang Ching-kuo, and his brother Chiang Wei-kuo, assume the reins of
power in Formosa, they would have the reluctant support of the United
States, Japan, and other pro-Nationalist powers. These two sons of the
Generalissimo are the least likely of the mainlander elite to approve
peaceful political evolution. "He admits that he has more than once
been approached by representatives of Mao Tse-tung through intermedi-
aries," wrote an American reporter of Ching-kuo in 1964. "His detractors
accuse him of stubbornness, arrogance, and an uninhibited disregard for
democratic processes." Formosans I interviewed agreed that Ching-
kuo was not anxious to allow them a greater share of political power:
"More powerless positions, yes, but never more actual power," as one of
the Formosan politicians elected on the KMT ticket expressed it.

If the more liberal, civilian wing of the mainlander elite should gain
control of the KMT, it would be more likely to give the Formosans a
meaningful share of power or permit them to rise through an opposition
party. However, such liberals are in a weak position today and, even if
they should emerge in the future, they would still, as Chinese be tempted
to treat Formosans as junior partners in any political collaboration. The
best hope for an evolution toward Formosan nationalism lies in the
younger, less innately prejudiced mainland refugees accepting their minority status on the island and working with Formosan youth for political democracy. Strong pressures by the United States and perhaps the
U.N. might be necessary to encourage this kind of peaceful transition.
"The Chinese have shown great adeptness at compromises and concessions to reality . . . they may be forced not only to admit a permanent
'two-Chinas' [the status quo today] but, even more painfully, a 'one
China, one Taiwan' [a native-ruled republic] with more real authority in
the hands of elected native officials," said an American diplomat in 1961.
The latter prospect, however, has begun to look less probable than mild
concessions within the status quo of mainlander dominance.

Increasingly since 1960, the Nationalist press has spoken of long-range
economic plans for industrial and social improvements in Formosa, as if
the regime would be there for decades to come. Unlike the refugee tem-
perament of the regime between 1949 and 1960, when few of the Na-

tionalist leaders would invest in the island or consider the future except in terms of return to the mainland, a large number have begun to seem reconciled to indefinite residence on Formosa.

Status quo as used here does not mean, of course, that the Formosan position will remain static. The growing economic prosperity of the island benefits the native majority as well as the refugee minority and the Formosan role in the business world will continue to expand with United States and Japanese support. Socially, Formosans may intermarry more with mainlanders, but cultural differences will probably remain for decades. Formosans may be able to elect an island governor and a higher percentage of the Legislative and Control Yuan members, but mainlanders of the present generation are unlikely to trust them with real political authority. This is the crux of the Formosan nationalist demand and the reason why continuation of the status quo is here defined in political terms, regardless of social and economic concessions and improvements affecting the local majority.

Even if the Nationalists were able to return to the mainland the provincial status of Formosa would remain unchanged. Like the Tibetans, Formosans realize they would be denied genuine autonomy under either Chinese regime because Nationalists and Communists alike agree on the traditional concept of the "Middle Kingdom" as a single China embracing all ethnic Chinese loyal to one central government.

United Nations Aid to Formosan Liberation?

The most optimistic prediction of U.N. aid to Formosan nationalism has come from a young Formosan legal scholar at Yale University, Lung-chu Chen, in his 1967 book, *Formosa, China, and the United Nations,* co-authored by Professor Harold Lasswell. Its central hypothesis is that a U.N. vote to seat Peking as China and a future Formosan regime as a separate member would trigger a revolt inside the island or force the Nationalists to turn over power to the Formosans through the pressure of world opinion. "The passage of a U.N. resolution authorizing and outlining concrete measures for a plebiscite . . . might provoke the Chinese Nationalist regime into withdrawing from the United Nations and attempting to resist U.N. involvement in Formosa's internal process . . . If, as is likely, U.N. personnel were prevented from entering Formosa, the strong support of the world organization would inaugurate a series of chain reactions, both within and outside Formosa, that would most probably culminate in the disintegration of the Nationalist regime and in the establishment of a new Republic of Formosa." [39]

As early as 1950 a group of refugee Formosans in Hong Kong had petitioned the United Nations to administer Formosa by disarming the Nationalist troops, releasing all political prisoners, and conducting a plebiscite to determine whether the natives wished independence, union with mainland China, or retention of the KMT status quo. "Since only those who had been citizens of Formosa before V-J Day will be entitled to vote," wrote the petitioners, "we are absolutely sure an overwhelming majority of our people will vote for complete independence." [40] Later, the Formosan Provisional Government in Tokyo sent similar appeals to the U.N., but no U.N. member ever championed the cause openly.

The outbreak of the Korean war and Peking's involvement in it assured the Nationalists a long period of United States-sponsored delays in U.N. Assembly debate on the problem from 1951 through the 1960 session. On the other hand, the effects of the 1953 truce in Korea, the Bandung conference of 1955, and the admission of 65 new member nations to the U.N. since 1955, has drastically changed the Assembly's membership and perspective. Whereas before 1955 there were only 60 U.N. members, many of whom tended to side with the United States, the new nations often consider themselves uncommitted.

The margin of pro-Nationalist votes dropped annually from 1952 to 1960, when the Assembly voted only on a moratorium on debate. The 1960 vote was 34 against and 42 in favor, with a large group of abstentions, so the United States persuaded several allies to co-sponsor a 1961 resolution classifying any change in Chinese representation as an "important question" which by definition would require a two-thirds vote under the U.N. Charter. The "important question" device worked well in the early 1960's to allow some members first to vote for a two-thirds majority, then safely support a change in representation knowing it could not pass. In 1961, 1965, 1966, 1967 and 1968, the vote approving the "important question" resolution was always greater than that favoring the status quo on Chinese representation. The latter vote was a 47–47 tie in 1965, but pro-Peking votes dropped thereafter to 58–44 against Peking's seating in 1968. [41]

The Assembly never really had a chance to vote on a "two China" or "one China, one Formosa" formula, because both concepts were opposed by both Chinas and by their respective partisans in the United Nations. Italy proposed creation of a U.N. study committee to investigate ways of breaking the Chinese representation deadlock, but the Italian proposal was defeated, 34–62, in 1966 and by 30–67 in 1968. The Nationalist press interpreted the Italian move, supported by Canada, the United States, Japan and a few other "friendly" nations, as a "two Chinas booby trap . . . the most dangerous proposition ever laid before the United Nations." [42]

Professor Urban Whitaker of San Francisco State College, who made a detailed study of United Nations delegates' view on the China representation issue, concluded that "The role of the United Nations is likely to be minimal . . . It is unlikely that the U.N. will take any action on the future of Formosa." He warned: "The Formosan revolution will have to be exactly that—a purely native Formosan revolt against all outside domination . . . An independent Formosa may be sought more successfully through revolution than through international intervention." [43] Even Chen later conceded that Formosan self-help would be the best method: "It is to be underlined afresh . . . that the self-help of the Formosan people, their willingness and capacity to take destiny in their own hands, is the key to any hopeful future change. Only when the Formosan people can demonstrate to the world that Formosa's independence is neither a personal affair of Chiang's nor an artificial outcome of U.S. strategy . . . [will] more elements of the world community be favorably disposed to acknowledge Formosa's new status in the world arena." [44]

Western Allies' Views of Formosa

Since in the past century Britain and her partners in the Commonwealth, especially Canada and Australia, have had closer contact with Formosa than other Western nations, their recent policies and attitudes toward the status of Formosa deserve attention.

The British Labor Cabinet extended diplomatic recognition to Peking in January 1950 and, despite the humiliation of many British merchants and diplomats during the Cultural Revolution of 1966–1968, Britain continued to support the seating of Peking in the United Nations. On the other hand, Britain has managed to retain a consulate in Formosa accredited to the provincial rather than national government of the Republic of China, largely because both Chinese regimes have economic reasons to overlook Britain's *de facto* "two China" policy.

British Prime Minister Clement Attlee had told President Truman in

November 1950 that the question of Taiwan should be settled by peaceful means "in such a way as to safeguard the interests of the people of Formosa." And in 1965 a former Far East correspondent for *The Times* of London wrote: "If a common British viewpoint were defined, it would probably be that the people of the island should be independent and detached from China. Most accounts of Taiwanese opinion agree that this status is what they want. But to bring it about while the Nationalist government still exists is beyond British power or British interests, and there the matter rests."

According to the same source, the British Labour Party in 1961 favored a neutralized Taiwan under U.N. administration: "not two Chinas but China and a freely chosen Formosan Government if that should be the people's wish." [45] Members of the British consulate in Formosa, usually as reticent in discussing politics as their counterparts in Hong Kong, privately admitted their sympathy for Formosan nationalism to me in 1962. "This island is mainly an American and Japanese problem," they said, "and Britain has only economic interests to protect here, as on the mainland." Foreign Secretary Michael Stewart was quoted in Tokyo in 1965 as saying that "in settling the China question, the wishes of the people in Taiwan must be respected." [46]

Both the Nationalist and the Communist Chinese have diplomatic missions in London, but "there are no British pro-KMT organizations [and] only a few KMT organizations for Chinese only," according to a member of the British Friends of Free China Association, a group which, my informant said, "supports the efforts of the Chinese people in their struggle against Communism." But, he added, "many members do not support the ideology of the KMT all along the line . . . I personally support the KMT insofar as it is conducting the struggle against Communism because, as you say, 'the red pigs are worse than the white pigs' . . . I personally believe that Formosa has a right to independence if its people desire it." [47]

The *Economist* editorialized in 1966 that Mao's successors might look upon a genuine native regime in Formosa more favorably than it does today on the island's occupation by the Chiang Kai-shek clique: "Then perhaps Taiwan can reenter the U.N. and the policy of 'one China, one Taiwan' will begin." [48] *The Times* of London, however, predicted a future acceptance of the status quo by Chiang Ching-kuo: "Latterly the view has been that he could stomach more easily than his father a 'two Chinas' solution that would insure continued American backing . . . Both island and mainland might before long face new rulers and new policies. In neither case is outside pressure likely to influence the changes that will come." [49]

Canada kept its Shanghai consulate until early 1951 but did not follow Britain in recognizing the new Peking regime until Prime Minister Pierre Trudeau's efforts in 1969. Instead, influenced by American policy and Communist Chinese militancy toward neighboring states, Ottawa—in the words of a Canadian diplomatic expert—"maintained diplomatic relations with the Nationalists and almost always voted with the United States on Chinese representation in the United Nations . . . Canada has always preferred what is generally called a 'two-China' policy but which Mr. [Paul] Martin [former External Affairs Minister] calls a 'one-China, one-Formosa' solution . . . If some formula could be found for recognizing both the Peking regime, as the government of mainland China, and an independent government of Taiwan and seating them both in the United Nations, there is little doubt that the Canadian government would accept it and that the Canadian public would overwhelmingly approve." [50] In the wake of French recognition of Peking in 1964, a Gallup Poll showed 51 per cent in favor and 33 per cent opposed to Canada following suit.

On the issue of Formosan nationalism, there is wide sympathy. To quote again the same Canadian expert: "Few Canadians . . . can accept the idea that unwilling Taiwanese should be handed over to the Communist regime . . . This attitude is based not on an obligation to the Nationalists but on the right of self-determination. Canadian concern is for the people of Taiwan rather than the Nationalist government." [51] Paul Martin, speaking at the U.N. General Assembly as his country's External Affairs Minister in late September 1967, told the delegates that Canada still wanted two Chinas: the People's Republic in the U.N. General Assembly and Security Council, and "Formosa" in the Assembly, under that name. When Taipei protested and cancelled plans for Vice President Yen to visit EXPO '67, Martin expressed surprise that Taipei should be offended: "Canada has had the happiest relations with Formosa . . . our policy is a one Formosa, one China policy." [52]

Australia, the other Commonwealth nation with strong trade interests in mainland China but without diplomatic ties to Peking, opened an embassy in Taipei for the first time in 1966. According to a University of Sydney professor, "Vague memories of the 1947 massacre on Taiwan and uncertainties as to how far the 'mainlanders' are accepted willingly by the Taiwanese . . . tended to produce a degree of reserve concerning the American commitment to the Nationalist regime . . ." [53] Prime

Minister Robert Menzies clearly dissociated his nation from any defense of the Chinese offshore islands in the 1958 crisis, declaring them "not worth a great war" and insisting that the ANZUS pact did not apply to the Taiwan Straits.[54]

The most outspoken support of Formosan nationalism by an Australian which I encountered came from a retired army general, Sir William Cawthorn, who had served on MacArthur's staff between 1945 and 1947 and later as Australian High Commissioner to Pakistan and Canada: "An independent native-run state of Taiwan is the best solution to the two-China problem, both for those not now recognizing Peking and to save the peace. The 9 million should rule the 2 million; the KMT army leaders are aging and have little hope of mainland recovery. I've heard a little about the Formosan provisional government in Tokyo and, although it is difficult for outside powers to help the Formosan nationalists, I approve their cause from all standpoints." [55] Early in 1968, an Australian graduate student at the University of Kentucky wrote that "by talking with students from Formosa I have readily confirmed all that you have written . . . The Formosans here are really very frightened of any political connections whatsoever and avoid discussion of Chiang Kai-shek . . ." [56]

France under President Charles de Gaulle made a dramatic switch from Nationalist to Communist Chinese recognition in early 1964. Edgar Faure, former Premier of France, had visited Peking in 1957 and returned to champion French reconciliation with mainland China. He thought it might be wise to extend recognition to Peking while offering to retain a chargé d'affaires in Formosa, but realized that neither Chinese regime would permit such dualism. The French newsman Robert Guillain credited Edgar Faure with the 1964 solution: to offer a "one China" recognition to Peking and force the Nationalists to break relations with France.[57]

West Germany, on the other hand, has been far more solicitous of keeping American approval: "In Germany, the United States is regarded as the mainstay of the defense of Europe . . . [and Germany does not wish] to imitate France's action." [58] Since the Bonn government is not a member of the U.N., it takes no part in the China representation debate and recognizes neither regime, while West Germans trade with and travel to both Chinas. A West German businessman in Hong Kong said in late 1966 of his frequent trips to Taipei: "The native Taiwanese connected with our company are all pro-independence, but afraid to speak openly. We Germans are suspect in both mainland and Nationalist

China but they accept us as long as we stick to our business." [59] Italy and Belgium, however, moved toward recognition of Peking in 1969.

Views of the Non-aligned Nations

Both Chinas view neutralism as basically immoral but compete vigorously for the political approval of neutralist African and Asian states. India, Indonesia, and the United Arab Republic have been the leading exponents of nonalignment, and all have supported the seating of Communist China in the U.N. regardless of their disputes with Peking. Taipei, however, has succeeded in winning recognition from several of the new states of Africa, including a few which were alienated by the behavior of Chinese Communist envoys; and Malaysia and Indonesia have welcomed Nationalist trade and aid missions in recent years.

The Nationalists pride themselves on technical aid to the African nations, especially in agricultural fields, and of the more than 20 nations with which they had signed technical assistance agreements by late 1966, 14 were in Africa.[60] Congressman Otto Passman, an inveterate opponent of United States foreign aid, charged that Taipei had used the proceeds from American food shipments to finance their African programs, and this was admitted by United States officials, who claimed the fact had never been a secret. Significantly, Nationalist Vice-Minister of Foreign Affairs Yang Hsi-kun said "the Africans in effect hold the key to barring Communist China membership in the United Nations." [61]

During a student meeting at the University of Wisconsin at Madison on May 2, 1965, however, the United Nations General Assembly president, Alex Quaison-Sackey, was asked by a Formosan student why the United Nations avoided a "one China, one Formosa" solution, and why the Formosan provisional government in Japan should not be recognized, inasmuch as the Nationalist regime in exile is considered the government of mainland China. Quaison-Sackey reportedly "assured the large audience that the African bloc would support the principle of self-determination of Taiwan if that question ever comes up." [62]

Conversations in Cairo and elsewhere with experts on African affairs have led me to believe that few African leaders are informed about Formosan nationalism or even the existence of a Formosan identity. Most African leaders think only of Peking as China, while others are willing to accept aid from the Nationalists without committing themselves to more than a pro-Nationalist vote in the United Nations.[63]

Most Arab states have been anti-Nationalist, although their trade and cultural ties with either Chinese regime are minimal and their interest even less, according to observers in Cairo.[64] Among the Malay peoples of Southeast Asia, only the Filipinos have kept formal relations with Nationalist China despite their anti-Chinese sentiments; while Indonesia was officially pro-Peking until President Sukarno's eclipse in 1966.[65]

To sum up, we can only agree with the pessimistic conclusions of Urban Whitaker quoted above. Many governments give lip service to the ideal of Formosan self-determination, but claim they are unable to implement its realization, while the majority of peoples around the world have no knowledge of Formosan nationalism.

Independence Through Revolution?

It is important to reiterate that the people and territory of Formosa are fully capable of supporting a viable state. Strategically, Formosa and the Pescadores are far more defensible than any small nation adjoining a hostile power, such as South Vietnam, Cambodia, or Laos. Politically, the 12 million natives are more educated, socially unified, and emotionally committed to defend their island against external threats than most of the newly-independent nations. Judged on any basis, Formosans are far better equipped to manage their own affairs than almost any group which has attained independence since 1945. If they have not held high political office, it is only because the prewar Japanese and postwar Chinese regimes have excluded them from such positions.

Is a violent uprising of Formosans, with or without aid from overseas, probable in the near future? Violence was part of the Formosan tradition under the Manchu rule for two centuries before Japan took over the island in 1895, and sporadic revolts continued for the first decade of Japanese rule. We have already noted the causes and effects of the 1947 revolt against Nationalist misrule, especially the reluctance of older Formosans to risk another bloodbath. Under the political conditions existing on Formosa, the question is one of the Formosans' capacity and inclination to resort to violence.

"Formosa is an isolated island and, without substantial foreign aid, it is impossible to conduct any effective large-scale revolt with a hope of success," wrote an overseas Formosan student activist in 1967. The excellent transport and communications systems of the island would help the regime against a rebel force. The mountainous interior, where some 1,947 rebels still live in hiding, might make a good refuge but not a base for the kind of guerrilla operations employed by Castro in Cuba. Topographically, Formosa is more compact than, for example, the Philippines, and easier to patrol. More important, the pervasive network of KMT intelligence, police, and secret operatives, makes any organized revolt extremely difficult to plan, much less to carry out. A rebellion of dissatisfied mainlanders in the armed forces would be far more probable, since mainlanders, but not Formosans, have access to the arsenals.

When overseas Formosan activists speak of their ability to trigger a widespread uprising by landing a few hundred guerrillas on the east coast, they are speaking from years of frustrated wishful thinking. The activists within the island do have a loose communication system but they would need much better underground organization to stage a successful uprising with or without the landing of Formosan commandos. As noted above, the regime has squelched several abortive movements in their early stages.

The young Formosans who constitute over 80 per cent of the army's enlisted ranks and perhaps 20 per cent of its officers (mostly in junior ranks) would be the core of any rebellion. If the mainlanders split over the succession issue, the Formosan troops might have an opportunity to seize control. A palace revolt which did not extend down to the junior officers would be simply a change of mainlander elites; but if the dissatisfied mainlander troops revolted, their Formosan colleagues might have a chance to join the revolt and to rally civilian support. In such an event, the morale of the Formosan troops, their access to weapons, and the response of the civilian majority would all be decisive. Much would depend on circumstances, timing, and on the reaction of the United States, whose Seventh Fleet and forces in Okinawa could decide the issue.

The United States would probably move to thwart a mainlander coup aimed at turning the island over to Communist China, but it is far less certain that Washington would intervene on the side of the Formosans in an internal revolt. Forces on Okinawa are very close and, if Washington felt the security of Taiwan endangered, could be used to help either the Nationalists or their opposition. Robert Elegant, an American journalist with long experience in Asia, advised in 1965 that "since the Nationalist regime is in no wise a useful instrument of American policy . . . I believe we should allow the natural desires of the 11 million native Formosans to be realized . . ." [66]

Self-help is the best method for any national liberation movement. Symbolic acts to arouse the attention of the more apathetic islanders and the outside world would be a useful first step. A demand for a freely conducted referendum on the future status of the island, such as Britain offered the people of Gibralter and the United States held in Puerto Rico, would seem the best approach to use.[67] Underground activists have learned that their pamphlets and leaflets disseminated in Taipei are quickly suppressed, while Nationalist censorship and martial law limit other means of peaceful protest. More ingenious methods would be needed, if only to answer foreign apologists for the Nationalist regime who claim the fact that "no riots occur in the streets" proves local contentment.[68]

How many Formosans would risk involvement in overt acts of political resistance? The revolutionary potential of Formosans is much lower than that of South Koreans, Greek Cypriots, or Vietnamese, and the power of the incumbent regime is far greater than in those territories. Probably no more than a few thousand would initiate even symbolic actions and only a few hundred would be likely to risk violence. If a mainlander split disrupted the surface stability of the regime, up to 100,000 native Formosans might well join the anti-KMT wing of the mainlander minority. If a significant group of Formosan troops revolted, they could expect 500,000 civilian compatriots to assist them, after which foreign support could rally a majority of the 12 million Formosans. It would be unrealistic to predict a major Formosan revolt in the absence of a mainlander rift or assurance of outside assistance. Disunity in the ranks of the Nationalist armed forces is almost a prerequisite to a native show of force, and perhaps only American help, preferably combined with some U.N. action to deter Communist intervention, could turn the domestic tide against the regime.

In summary, the future of Formosan nationalism lies mainly in the hands of the majority itself, which has shown little willingness to fight for the freedom it clearly prefers in theory. The same conclusion applies to the 35,000 Formosans living abroad, most of whom avoid direct participation in the political groups, although one overseas student wrote to me: "You love Taiwan so much, how can I love it less? I have to show my gratitude to you for your great affection to my homeland. Others will do so too someday." [69] In the harsh world of power politics, Formosans at home and abroad will have to demonstrate more unity, sacrifice, and devotion to their ideals if they wish to impress either the power-conscious Chinese elites or the outside world. As one American scholar wrote in 1963, "I'm afraid nothing much is going to change our present policy until the Taiwanese take things into their own hands or until Chiang dies." [70]

The real test of nationalism is a people's willingness to fight for it. Until and unless the Formosan nationalists demonstrate that a majority of their compatriots share their ambitions, the status quo of Nationalist rule is the most probable future for the island. Some reform will continue under the KMT, but economic development is likely to proceed faster than political democratization. Much improvement is possible within the present political framework to alleviate Nationalist police repression, tax inequities, and social discrimination. Mainlander leaders more sympathetic toward the Formosans may well overcome the security phobias of the extremists, and one should not underestimate their influence after the passing of the present leadership. However, no genuine Formosan nationalism could hope to flower under mere modifications of the status quo, which preserves mainlander political dominance.

APPENDIX

A DECLARATION OF FORMOSANS

This declaration was written originally in Chinese by Professor Peng Ming-min in collaboration with his two associates, Hsieh Tsung-min and Wei Ting-chao. On September 20, 1964, they were arrested by the Taiwan Garrison Command on charges of "treason." On November 2, 1965, Professor Peng was released after strong pressure was brought to bear upon the Nationalist Government from influential friends in the U.S. and Canada. Hsieh and Wei, however, were still behind bars in 1969.

At the time of their arrest Peng was the Chairman of the Department of Political Science at National Taiwan University; while Mr. Hsieh was an editor of a Chinese magazine and Mr. Wei was employed by *Academia Sinica*, the highest academic institution in Nationalist China.

A copy of the declaration was smuggled to the U.S. via Japan. Readers are reminded of the fact that it was written specifically for the people inside the island.

A powerful movement is rapidly developing inside Formosa. It is a self-preservation movement of the island's 12 million people who are willing neither to be ruled by the Chinese Communists nor to be destroyed by the Chinese Nationalist regime. Riding high the universal current of awakening peoples, we dedicate ourselves to the overthrow of the Government of Chiang Kai-shek and to the establishment of a free, democratic, and prosperous society. We believe it to be the privilege as well as the responsibility of every one of us to take part in this great movement and help realize our supreme goal at the earliest possible date.

I

That there are one China and one Formosa is an iron fact. In Europe or in America, in Africa or in Asia, whether or not one has already accorded diplomatic recognition to the Chinese Communist Government, the entire world accepts the fact of one China and one Formosa.

Even in the U.S. which finds herself isolated from the rest of the world in her Asian policy, there is only a small number of reactionary politicians who toy with the idea of "non-recognition." The mainstream of American public opinion, particularly that of intellectuals, demands *de jure* recognition of one China and one Formosa as the [ideal] solution for the Chinese question. America's foreign policy is evolving toward that direction. Why then does the U.S. continue to support the Chiang regime, at least verbally, as the sole and legitimate Government of China? It is because the U.S. wants to use this [recognition of the Chiang regime] in her diplomatic bargaining with Communist China so that a compromise favorable to her may be attained. The U.S. has conferred with Communist China several hundred times in Warsaw. Throughout the meetings she has emphasized that if only Communist China relinquishes her demand to "liberate" Taiwan, America's door will forever remain open to China.

The Chiang regime depends on the Seventh Fleet for its survival. We must not be blinded by the myth of the "Return to the Mainland" and be led down the path of destruction. Once the Seventh Fleet is withdrawn the collapse of the Chiang regime is just a matter of a few hours. Indeed, "Return to the Mainland" is merely a pretext whereby Chiang maintains his illegal regime and suppresses its people.

II

"Return to the Mainland" is not even remotely possible! Any person with a minimum of common sense will come to such a conclusion without a moment's hesitation. The troops under Chiang's control are, at best, a defensive force; they cannot sufficiently be an offensive force. Their existence depends entirely on American military aid and the aim of American aid is to maintain America's defense perimeter in the Pacific. For this reason Chiang's troops cannot obtain any weapons beyond the need for defense. Chiang's navy has no ability to wage warfare independently because it has neither battleships nor adequate shipyard facilities. Chiang's airforce is composed chiefly of short-range fighters. The number of transport planes and long-range fighters which are indispensable to launching an offensive is so miserably small. Chiang's army, as always, has only a lightly equipped infantry for its main force. Mechanized troops and heavy artillery are only for window dressing.

Formosa is economically unable to support a counterattack. Even though Chiang may try to support his troops with every means available, including military expenditures which amount to over 80% of the national budget, it is much too great a burden for such a small island to support several hundred thousand troops even in peace time, let alone war time. And what about the human resources needed to replace casualties?

Thus the reason for war no longer can be justified. Nonetheless, while preaching freedom and democracy Chiang Kai-shek violates basic human rights at will, monopolizes political power and through the use of secret police imposes dictatorial rule. Some people say the Chinese mainlanders are eager to return to their homeland and therefore readily accept Chiang Kai-shek's enslavement. The truth of the matter, however, is that the growing prestige of Communist China has given pride to the nationalistic Chinese who feel that their country has for the past 100 years been subjected to foreign humiliation. They are convinced that the corrupt and inefficient Chiang Kai-shek regime could not possibly have made China what she is today. For whom then are we to fight? For what are we to fight? Who is foolish enough to sacrifice his life for Chiang Kai-shek now that the dictator has failed to present his people convincing reasons for war?

Chiang Kai-shek's officers and soldiers have devoted their entire lives to their master. But what has been their reward? Once they grow old they are retired with no guarantee of financial security and are cast into the civilian population only to roam the streets for their living. This kind of situation naturally creates bitterness among retired soldiers. Their resentment is best expressed in the often heard sarcasm: "Just as it was the retired soldiers who toppled the Chiang regime on the mainland so will they again topple it in Formosa."

Life for the active officers and soldiers is even worse. They often complain: "Mao Tse-tung has severed us from our ancestors, but Chiang Kai-shek has severed us from our descendants." Some who are daring risk their lives; others who are less daring let their resentment smolder. More and more officers and soldiers violate military regulations. Commanders seek to appease their soldiers instead of disciplining them. As a result soldiers become more arrogant than their officers.

As for those Formosan youth drafted into the Nationalist army to replace the retired Chinese soldiers, the dreadful memory of the 2-28 Incident in which 20,000 Formosan leaders were massacred by Chiang Kai-shek still lingers. Daring not to speak out, they nevertheless remain Chiang Kai-shek's "silent enemy." Dressed in military uniforms, they reveal no evidence of their inner thoughts. It is not difficult to assume, however, that under no circumstance will they acknowledge "a thief as their father" and accept Chiang Kai-shek's enslavement.

The system of political commissars interferes in the performance of the military and reduces its efficiency. The characteristic of any military activity lies in the accomplishment of its mission through quick movement of manpower and material. The system of political commissars on the other hand, emphasizes political doctrine and surveillance of military personnel. Under the system the political aim is emphasized more than the military aim and political responsibilities restrict military efficiency. Many an enlightened officer in the Nationalist army such as General Sun Li-jen protested the system, but he was falsely accused of harboring Communists and to this day has not been acquitted. Both officers and soldiers say: "If the order for mobilization should come we want first to execute the political commissars."

Imagine an army with no ability to wage offensive warfare, with no economic resources to support war operations, with soldiers' morale flagging, with low military efficiency and with no justifiable objectives of war trying to confront a powerful army of Chinese Communists. This war is called "Return to the Mainland." Thus the stubborn 5-star General Chiang Kai-shek can be compared with Don Quixote comically raising his worn-out broom challenging a windmill to a fight.

III

Why then is Chiang Kai-shek so persistent in demanding the "Return"? Because this slogan is the only means by which he prolongs his political power and enslaves his people. For 15 years using this empty slogan like a bad check which is bound to bounce later he has justified the enforcement of martial law and held 12 million people under tight military control. Indeed, his scheme of "Return to the Mainland" is the greatest act of deception of the 20th century.

Needless to say, Kuomintang officials themselves realize that such deception cannot last much longer. On the one hand, they send abroad their children and the wealth which they have plundered from the people in full preparation for emergency escape. On the other hand they act like "doctors" keeping alive their dying patient, Chiang Kai-shek, by giving him the life-prolonging drug of "Return to the Mainland."

Let us examine what magic power this slogan has yielded:

First, by taking advantage of the psychological weakness of the people, it has prolonged the life of the Chiang regime which would otherwise have lost its *raison d'être*. Some Chinese mainlanders are very homesick and have supported Chiang Kai-shek out of the illusion that they may one day return to their homeland. Even some Formosans have been led to believe in the slogan because of their hope that Chiang's return to the mainland would remove from them political pressure and lighten the economic burden.

Secondly, in the name of national emergency it has been used as a pretext to suspend normal enforcement of the constitution and other laws, to persecute those who out of patriotism and a sense of justice criticize the regime, and to enforce such repressive policies as control of speech and thought and censorship of press.

Thirdly, by insisting to attack Red China, the Chiang regime has enhanced its position in diplomatic bargaining with the U.S. It has been used as a tool to extract more aid from the U.S. When negotiations between the U.S. and China are stalled or when the U.S. applies too much pressure on Chiang, he immediately releases the rumor in Hong Kong that negotiations for peace between Peking and Taipei are in the making, thus confusing the U.S. who has been suffering from acute neurosis over Red China.

In summary, the slogan of "Return to the Mainland" enhances the position of the Chiang regime externally by proposing to attack Red China and enables it internally to enforce dictatorial rule and prolong the regime's life.

IV

Whom does the Chiang Kai-shek regime represent?

The Nationalist regime claims to be "China's sole and legitimate government." It insists that the representatives of the National Assembly, members of the Legislative and Control Yuans are all elected from the people. They include representatives of both the Chinese mainland and Formosa. We all know, however, that elections for those representatives were held 18 years ago (1947). We also know that in less than 2 years (1949) the Chinese people on the mainland had disowned the Chiang regime because of its corruption and inefficiency. Chiang was quickly kicked out of the Chinese mainland in spite of the fact that he commanded millions of soldiers. Clearly the people on the mainland had already selected their own government. If the Nationalist Government could not represent the people of the mainland of that time how can it claim to represent a new generation of people 18 years later? Clearly Chiang cannot represent the people on the mainland today.

Can the Chiang regime represent the people of Formosa? Out of some 3000 representatives of the National Assembly the Formosan representatives occupy only 10 or so seats. Out of 473 members of the Legislative Yuan only 6 are Formosans. Their terms expired 12 and 15 years ago respectively. They certainly have no right to represent Formosans today. What is more, in the 2-28 Incident Chiang massacred 20,000 leading Formosans (at that time Formosa had only 6 million population). Although Formosans have not since raised their voice they remain always Chiang Kai-shek's "silent enemy."

Speaking of Formosans and mainlanders we must point out that when the Chiang regime proposes that the two groups must cooperate, it does not really mean it. On the contrary, it is very much afraid of cooperation between the two groups and has, in fact, employed every means available to divide them. This policy can most clearly be observed in the elections. The Chiang regime wants to make sure that Formosans and mainlanders are divided and made mutually suspicious and independent from one another so that they can be manipulated and controlled. Therefore, the Chiang regime has deliberately prevented Formosans and liberal mainlanders from cooperating in their attempt to overthrow Chiang's dictatorship and establish a true democracy. When Lei Chen sought to unify Formosans and mainlanders, Chiang finally removed his disguise and imprisoned the liberal magazine editor after falsely accusing him of being Communist in outright disregard of protest both at home and abroad. Chiang Kai-shek knows clearly that the day Formosans and mainlanders achieve cooperation will be the day his government will collapse.

Some argue that the Chiang regime represents the Kuomintang; and since the Party and State are traditionally one, it, therefore, represents China. In truth, however, the Chiang regime cannot even represent the Kuomintang. The Kuomintang itself is a symbol of dictatorship. There is no democracy whatsoever. Its members have no freedom of speech. In their conventions their representatives can only listen to their leader, nodding, bowing and applauding. They simply are a group of yes-men capable only of approving the proposals presented by their leader. They neither want nor dare to attempt to question the content of proposals.

Moreover within the Party there are many factions. In their struggle for power the so-called Lian-kwan faction (from the provinces of Kwang-tung and Kwang'si) as represented by Hu Han-ming, Chang Fa-kwei, Li Tsung-jen, etc. has already been liquidated. Other factions which have not been able to gain the personal confidence of Chiang are not permitted to be a part of the nucleus of the Party. Needless to say, those members who are excluded from power are resentful of Chiang's leadership. The clever members either resort to silent protest by not expressing any of their opinions or actively agitate their followers to form the mainstream of anti-Chiang forces within the Party.

We can only conclude that the Chiang regime is composed of a small minority of the Kuomintang. It cannot represent China much less Formosa, and not even the Kuomintang itself.

V

Formosa's economic development is hampered by two grave problems: a huge military budget and rapidly increasing population. They are the traps of self-destruction created by the irresponsible Chiang regime under the false slogan of "Return to the Mainland."

According to Chiang's statistics issued this year (1964) military expenditures account for more than 80% of the national budget. This amount does not include every military expense. Two hundred thousand tons of rice provided annually by the Food Bureau for the military are priced far below the market value and even below the official value set by the Bureau. Expenses for transportation, electricity and other services provided for the military by publicly operated enterprises are never revealed. Income from military industry and from the resale of American aid all go to the military. Thus actual military expenditure is far in excess of the island's productivity.

The rapidly increasing population also has the effect of hindering the growth of the economy. Its chief effect is unemployment which grows worse every day, particularly in the villages. Formosa's labor population is estimated at 4,000,000 of which at least 1,000,000 are unemployed—one-fourth of the entire labor population. Every square mile of arable land is crowded with an average of 1,230 persons. Every year one after another thousands of elite youth graduated from colleges and universities are forced to go abroad. The Chiang regime is afraid to face this reality and seeks its solution in the self-deceiving scheme of the "Return to the Mainland." Even though some intellectual persons give warning to the seriousness of the problem it is all to no avail. Those who advocate birth control are labeled defeatists. Instead the Chiang regime encourages the population growth and pins its hope on the newborn babies, expecting that 20 years later their generation will take up arms and fight back to the mainland.

Many a person believes that the land reform in Formosa has been the result of the virtuous policy of the Chiang Government. The truth is, however, that the purpose of the land reform is to weaken or even eliminate the potential strength of its opposition. Since the days of the Manchu dynasty Formosa's political leaders traditionally came from the landowner class. Chiang Kai-shek is keenly aware that the rise of local leadership is detrimental to the success of his dictatorial rule. For this reason he first eliminated 20,000 Formosan leaders during the 2-28 Incident of 1947 and then in 1950 enforced the so-called land reform policy aiming at overthrowing the traditional political leadership class. The fact that the Chinese mainlanders themselves are not landowners is another reason why the land reform policy was so smoothly carried out. As a result of Chiang's steadfast effort to eliminate the landowner class the local strength was greatly reduced. On the other hand, the farmers, suffering under artificially deflated farm prices, inescapably heavy taxes and exploitation due to the unfair ratio of exchange between crops and fertilizer, spend every day working for a living, leaving no energy for other activities.

Any economic policy should have a consistent long-range development plan. Yet what the Chiang regime has made is a blind investment in total disregard of fundamental economic principles. Its aim is superficial and temporary, designed to meet a one-time need. In order to maintain military food allotments they even resort to plundering of farmers just as foolishly as one would kill a chicken to obtain an egg. They are afraid that any attempt to reform the present taxation system will result in a temporary suspension of their military budget, so instead of admitting the need for reform they let it continue to deteriorate. In order to consolidate their power they collaborate with the rich and oppress the poor masses, thus creating an extremely insecure society where rich and poor are poles apart.

Let us take a look at the final phase of the Chiang regime which has been pushed into a desperate corner. On the one hand Chiang places his henchmen in various important posts to tighten his dictatorial rule. On the other he uses public bonds of 1.2 billion *yuan* derived from the enforcement of urban real estate reform policy and from the sale of public enterprises and several times has sent his number one economic henchman, Hsu Po-yuan, to Central and South America for wholesale purchase of land there.

VI

Can Formosa be an independent country?

A state is only an instrument through which people may pursue their happiness and prosperity. Any people who live under the same circumstances and share common interests may form a country. For more than 10 years Formosa has been an independent country in reality. On the basis of population, area, economic productivity and cultural standards Formosa ranks about 30th among the more than 110 UN members. In fact, people of many small independent countries enjoy an even higher degree of social welfare and cultural advantage; for example, the Scandinavian countries, Switzerland and South America's Uruguay. We should stop imagining ourselves as a "big power" and instead face reality and establish a small but democratic and prosperous society.

Some people say Chiang Kai-shek has become a "naked emperor"; therefore, we'll just wait until the day he passes away. But we must not overlook the possibility of desperate Chiang handing Formosa over to Red China. Nor should we for even a moment forget that Formosa may become the victim of international power rivalries. We, therefore, must not just simply wait.

Many intellectual people are still obsessed by the idea of "peaceful transfer of government" and "progressive reform." We must point out that if we will review the history of the Kuomintang we will at once discover that so long as an arrogant and despotic Chiang is alive any form of compromise with him is either an illusion or a deception designed especially to trap the intellectual appeasers. Therefore, we must not even dream of "peaceful transfer of government" and accept compromise.

We wish to take this opportunity to earnestly warn those who have been collaborating with the Chiang regime:

"You must immediately repent of your sins and pledge not to collaborate any more with Chiang in oppressing the people of Formosa. Or else history will pass judgment on you and the people one day will make you pay the severest penalty possible."

VII

In a region such as Formosa which is still in the process of being developed, economic development requires revolutionary changes in social, economic and political aspects. Among them politics is the fountainhead of power that motivates every change. Although Formosa has a good foundation for modernization, we are still far from such a goal so long as the corrupt and inefficient Chiang regime exists. Consequently, we must not depend on the so-called "progressive reform."

Having recognized this fact we set forth the following proposals and express our firm determination to fight for the realization of them even to the last drop of our blood:

A. *Our Objectives*

1. To affirm that the "Return to the Mainland" is absolutely impossible and by unifying the strength of 12 million people, regardless of their place of birth, to overthrow the Chiang regime and establish a new country and a new government;

2. To rewrite the constitution which will guarantee basic human rights, and to establish an efficient government responsible to the congress and to enforce true democracy; and

3. To participate in the U.N. as a member of the Free World, and to establish diplomatic relations with other peace loving countries and together strive for world peace.

B. *Our Principles*

1. To respect the principle of democracy and elect the head of state from the people, who should not be an idol to be worshipped nor vested with absolute power nor immune from criticism, who being only a public servant should dedicate himself to the people under the supervision and control of the congress;

2. To guarantee freedom of assembly, freedom of organization and freedom of expression and to enforce a system of political parties by granting an opposition party a legal position;

3. To eliminate special privileges, clean up corruption and graft, tighten political discipline and improve the treatment of soldiers, teachers and public employees;

4. To establish a healthy civilian system, enforce scientific supervision of the government, raise efficiency of administration and enforce clean and just politics;

5. To guarantee the independence of the judiciary, abolish laws which encroach upon basic human rights and forbid illegal arrest, interrogation and punishment;

6. To abolish the secret police system and regulate the positions and functions of police officers according to the principles accepted by democratic countries and to cultivate among the people a law-abiding spirit;

7. To guarantee the people's right to communicate both at home and abroad and to guarantee freedom of movement and travel and to maintain an open society; and

8. To reduce armament on the basis of self-defense and guarantee the position and livelihood of retired soldiers.

In the field of economy, because of greatly reduced military expense, we should be able to establish a long-range plan and by fully utilizing manpower as well as material resources promote the development of the economy. We shall by democratic means distribute our economic gains and abolish exclusive privileges enjoyed by any individual or class and guarantee equal economic opportunity. We shall establish a system of direct taxation, adopt a progressive income tax and an inheritance tax and eliminate the gap between rich and poor. We shall plan to increase the national productivity, reduce unemployment and raise the living standard of the people. In this way can the respect of mankind and the freedom of individuals be said to have true meaning.

We shall improve the traditional method of agricultural production, strive for the economic self-sufficiency of villages and establish a scientific mechanized and modernized agricultural society. In the past the Chiang regime has blindly invested its capital, interfered in the operation of economic enterprise, supported the capitalists by supplying low-wage laborers, deprived the farmers of their harvest through the so-called fertilizer-crop exchange program and enormously increased the burden of the public through the increase of indirect tax; e.g., sales tax and household tax. For these problems created by Chiang's economic maladministration we shall seek fundamental solutions.

We are convinced that the purpose of our society is to maintain the dignity of individuals and promote the welfare of the people. We are, therefore, opposed to the policy of terror, exploitation and such other measures aimed at hindering the unity of the people and the normal development of society. We shall dedicate ourselves to establishment of a benevolent society where people can trust and help each other and each individual may pursue a life which will bring him the greatest happiness.

VIII

For many a year the Chinese people have been given two extreme ways of judging values: Kuomintang way of judgment on the extreme right and Communist way of judgment on the extreme left. They have never been given an opportunity to exercise judgment on the basis of truth. We must free ourselves from the yoke of these two extremes. Even more urgently we must abandon the psychology of trying to settle our future by depending on either of the two extreme regimes. Outside the Kuomintang and the Communist Party we must seek the third alternative of self-assertion in Formosa.

Let us put an end to these days of darkness! Let us call upon all those people unwilling to be ruled by Communists or to be destroyed by Chiang Kai-shek to unite in the strife to overthrow Chiang's dictatorial regime and establish our own free country.

Dear compatriots who love democracy and freedom, let us not be discouraged and abandon our hope just because what we see today is dark. Conditions both at home and abroad are turning steadily in our favor. The strength of our movement is rapidly expanding. Our men have already penetrated inside the government, various local organizations, the armed forces, commercial enterprises, newspaper companies, schools, factories and villages. Our organization has already established close contact with our compatriots in the U.S., Japan, Canada, France and West Germany and has obtained their enthusiastic support. Once the time is ripe our men will appear at every corner of the land and together with you they shall fight for freedom.

Dear compatriots, victory is already in sight. Let us rise and be united!

This declaration is the symbol of our struggle. From today on it will appear before you wherever you are or may go. Remember, while you are reading it our organization is continuing to expand and our movement powerfully developing.

Please circulate.

Please reproduce.

Please quote.

Translated and originally published in the United States by the United Formosans for Independence, Philadelphia, Pennsylvania, May 1966.

NOTES

Introduction

1. For assessments of mainlander opinion, I have relied on the work of others and accounts of the famous treason trial of the mainlander publisher, Lei Chen, in 1959. See the chapter by John Israel in Mark Mancall, ed., *Formosa Today* (New York: Frederick A. Praeger, 1964), pp. 59–67.
2. Interview in Tokyo, July 27, 1961.
3. Interview in Taipei, July 6, 1962. Dr. Chiang, a 1912 University of California graduate and a Columbia Ph.D. in 1917, served as chancellor of Peking University from 1930 to 1945.
4. See Mendel, *The Japanese People and Foreign Policy* (Berkeley and Los Angeles: University of California Press, 1961), especially chapter 9.
5. A. T. Steele, in *The American People and China* (New York: McGraw-Hill, 1966), identified none of his informants, although they had far less to fear than the men and women quoted in this book.

Chapter 1

1. For the physical and demographic facts about Formosa, see Hsieh Chiao-min, *Taiwan: Ilha Formosa, a Geographic Appraisal* (Washington, D.C.: Butterworth's 1964); Norton S. Ginsburg, *The Pattern of Asia* (Englewood Cliffs, N.J.: Prentice-Hall, 1958); and the *China Year-Book, 1966–1967* (Taipei: China Publishing Co., 1967), pp. 89–102.
2. A. T. Steele, *The American People and China* (New York: McGraw-Hill for the Council on Foreign Relations, 1966), pp. 257 and 263; available separately from the Council as *The American Public's View of U.S. Policy Toward China* (1964).
3. See Rupert Emerson, *From Empire to Nation* (Cambridge: Harvard University Press, 1960), pp. 102–131, for his complete analysis.
4. Maurice Meisner, "The Development of Formosan Nationalism," in Mark Mancall, ed., *Formosa Today* (New York: Frederick A. Praeger, 1964), p. 161. Language will be discussed further in chapter 3.
5. See, among others, Chong-sik Lee, *The Politics of Korean Nationalism* (Berkeley and Los Angeles: University of California Press, 1963); Ong Jok-tik, *Taiwan* (Tokyo: Kobundo, 1964), pp. 102–103; and Edward I-te Chen, "Japanese Colonial Rule in Korea and Taiwan," unpublished Ph.D. thesis, Department of Political Science, University of Pennsylvania, 1966.
6. "On Facing the Reality of Israel," *Time*, June 23, 1967, p. 24.
7. A. T. Steele, *op. cit.*, p. 50.
8. W. G. Goddard, *Formosa, a Study in Chinese History* (East Lansing: Michigan State University Press, 1966), p. 51.
9. The Dutch period is covered in James W. Davidson, *The Island of*

Formosa (Shanghai, 1903, available in a recent reprint from the Cellar Book Shop, Detroit), pp. 9–48. Written by the first American consul in Taiwan after eight years' residence, it is a remarkable work on all aspects of pre-1903 Formosa.

10. Statement of a Formosan graduate student in the United States, typical also of the view of many inside Formosa. Davidson's account of the Koxinga period is in *op. cit.*, ch. 4.

11. Goddard, *op. cit.*, pp. 98–99. He adds: "Government was corrupt in every sense of the word . . . squeeze [officials' demand for bribes] was the order of the day . . . Each man took the law into his own hands . . . Family feuds were common as Formosa rapidly became a battle field on which each clan fought to maintain its own rights, thus constituting itself into a king of an independent kingdom."

12. Shinkichi Eto, "An Outline of Formosan History," in Mark Mancall, ed., *Formosa Today, op. cit.*, pp. 43–58.

13. Davidson, *op. cit.*, p. 67.

14. *Ibid.*, p. 69, quoting an unidentified foreigner who wrote during the Ch'ing period.

15. *Ibid.*, p. 100, quoting from the notes of British consul Swinhoe.

16. George MacKay, *From Far Formosa* (N.Y.: Fleming H. Revell, 1896), p. 105.

17. Meisner, in Mancall, *op. cit.*, p. 148.

18. Ong Jok-tik, "A Formosan's View of the Formosan Independence Movement," in Mancall, *op. cit.*, p. 163. Dr. Ong (O Iku-toku in Japanese), a lecturer at Meiji University, Tokyo, revived the prewar Taiwan Youth Association in 1960. See also Sia Su, *"Taiwanjin ishiki* [Formosans' consciousness]," *Taiwan Chinglian*, December 1964, pp. 44–49.

19. Davidson, *op. cit.*, p. 247. Ch. 17 is devoted to Davidson's mixed evaluation of Liu.

20. William Thomas, an American Foreign Service expert on Formosan economic development, is one who thinks late Manchu improvements in Formosa have been underrated. See also Samuel C. Chu, "Liu Ming-ch'uan and the Modernization of Taiwan," *Journal of Asian Studies*, 23, 1, November, 1963, pp. 37–53.

21. See John K. Fairbank, *The United States and China* (Cambridge: Harvard University Press, rev. ed., 1958), chapters 7–9, and Joseph R. Levenson, *Confucian China and Its Modern Fate* (Berkeley and Los Angeles: University of California Press, 1958).

22. "No further evidence is needed to prove that the opposition in Formosa . . . is directly attributable to the duplicity of the Chinese government." (*Ibid.*, p. 366.) The president and vice-president of the short-lived Republic fled to the mainland. On the other hand, says Davidson, "the victors behaved splendidly . . . No shops were broken into; no one was molested" (p. 320).

23. A contemporary Japanese account quoted in Ong Jok-tik, *Taiwan, op. cit.*, p. 98.

24. *Ibid.*, p. 99, quoting P. H. S. Montgomery, *The Customs Report of of Tainan, Taiwan: 1881–1891.*

25. See George Beckmann, *The Modernization of China and Japan* (New York: Harper and Row, 1962); the *Studies in the Modernization of Japan* series, 6 vols. (Princeton, N.J.: Princeton University Press) edited respectively by Marius Jansen, William W. Lockwood, Ronald P. Dore, Robert E. Ward, Donald Shively, and James Morley; and Mendel, "Japan as a Model for Developing Nations," in *Monumenta Nipponica* special issue: *Japan's Modern Century* (Tokyo: Tuttle, 1968), pp. 191–207.

26. Hsieh, *op. cit.*, p. 205.

27. One of the best Western sources on the Japanese period is George W. Barclay, *Colonial Development and Population in Taiwan* (Princeton, N.J.: Princeton University Press, 1954). Japanese sources include Takekoshi Yosaburo, *Japanese Rule in Formosa*, tr. by George Braithwaite (London: Longmans, Green, 1907); the more critical Yanaibara Tadao, *Teikokushugika no Taiwan* [Taiwan Under Imperialism] (Tokyo: Iwanami, 1929); Tsurumi Yusuke, *Biography of Goto Shimpei* [in Japanese] (Tokyo: Taiheiyo Yokai, 1943); and such publications of the Japanese Government-General, Taihoku, as *The Progress of Taiwan for Ten Years, 1895–1904* (1905); annual volumes of the *Population Register of Taiwan, Statistical Tables*; and *Yearbooks*. The Nationalist regime published *Taiwan Province: Statistical Summary of the Past 51 Years* (Taipei, 1946) based on Japanese sources. Formosan accounts of the period include relevant sections of Ong Jok-tik, *op. cit.*, and Shih Ming, *Taiwanjin 400-nen shi* [400 Year History of the Taiwanese] (Yokyo: Otoba Shobo, 1962).

28. Hsieh, *op. cit.*, p. 165.

29. *Ibid.*, p. 166.

30. *Ibid.*, p. 237.

31. *Ibid.*, p. 178.

32. *Ibid.*, p. 170.

33. *Ibid.*, p. 306.

34. Neil H. Jacoby, *U.S. Aid to Taiwan* (New York: Frederick Praeger, 1966), pp. 73–74.

35. Hsieh, *op. cit.*, p. 173. See Andrew J. Gradjdanzev, *Formosa Today* (New York: Institute of Pacific Relations, 1942), pp. 54–56 for reasons why farmers earned less from the Ponlai rice.

36. Calculations provided in early 1962 by Formosan economists who were employed by the AID mission in Taipei before its demise in 1964. Per capita income declined in the 1941–1945 war years and fell still lower in the 1946–1950 period, but rose to $113 in 1960 and almost $200 in 1968. See Hosono Akeo and others, *Taiwan no Hyojo* [Conditions on Taiwan] (Tokyo: Kohin Shoin, 1963), pp. 45–126.

37. Meisner in Mancall, *op. cit.*, p. 159.

38. Interview in Taipei, December, 1957.

39. Davidson, *op. cit.*, p. 594. For a retrospective view of early Japanese

rule, see George H. Kerr, "Formosa: Colonial Laboratory," *Far Eastern Survey*, February 23, 1942, pp. 50–55.

40. Ong, *Taiwan, op. cit.*, p. 115. Liang thought China would be helpless to assist the Formosans for the next 30 years.

41. *Ibid.*, p. 115.

42. See Ong, *Taiwan, op. cit.*, pp. 104–136, for details on both armed and political opposition during the Japanese occupation.

43. Goddard, *op. cit.*, p. 164.

44. Ong, *Taiwan, op. cit.*, p. 119.

45. The 1928 platform of the Taiwan CP, an affiliate of the Japanese CP rather than the CCP, is given in Ong, *Taiwan, op. cit.*, p. 127.

46. Yanaibara, *op. cit.* (note 27), pp. 251–253.

47. Barclay, *op. cit.*, p. 33. Agricultural production trebled in value and industrial output rose from 37% of GNP in 1914 to 48% in 1938. By 1930 more than a third of urban Formosans were white-collar and professional workers.

Chapter 2

1. U.S. Department of State, *Occupation of Japan: Policy and Progress* (Washington, D.C.: Government Printing Office, n.d.), pp. 51–52. This and many other relevant documents, plus analytical commentary, can be found in Theodore McNelly, ed., *Sources in Modern East Asian History and Politics* (New York: Appleton-Century-Crofts, 1967).

2. George F. Kennan, *Russia and the West under Lenin and Stalin* (Princeton: Princeton University Press, 1961), pp. 376–377.

3. See George H. Kerr, *Formosa Betrayed* (Boston: Houghton Mifflin, 1965), chs. 1, 2, and 3. Admiral Chester Nimitz first favored an invasion of Formosa, but President Roosevelt, General MacArthur, and others preferred Luzon (pp. 28–33).

4. Interviews with Frank Lim, Tokyo, June 23, 1961, and Dr. Thomas Liao, Tokyo, February 27, 1963.

5. George H. Kerr, "Some Chinese Problems in Taiwan," *Far Eastern Survey*, October 10, 1945, p. 287. China inherited some $2 billion worth of Japanese properties, yet "had no funds for education, public works, or subventions to local government," according to Fred W. Riggs, *Formosa Under Chinese Nationalist Rule* (New York: Macmillan, 1952), p. 107.

6. *United States Relations with China* (often called the "White Paper") (Washington, D.C.: Department of State Publication 3573, 1949), p. 308.

7. Interview with Professor Shioya, Kyushu National University, Fukuoka, Japan, April 5, 1963.

8. George H. Kerr, "Formosa's Return to China," *Far Eastern Survey*, October 15, 1947, p. 206. This was the first of Kerr's two articles on

Formosa after his March 1947 departure from Formosa (the second was published in the same journal November 5, 1947).

9. *Ibid.*, p. 207.

10. Russell H. Fifield, "Formosa in Transition," *The World Today* (London: Royal Institute of International Affairs), May, 1948, pp. 213–214. Dr. Fifield was in the U.S. Foreign Service in China and Formosa during the 1945–1947 period.

11. "Memorandum on the Situation in Taiwan," submitted by Ambassador John Leighton Stuart to President Chiang, April 18, 1947, as reprinted in *United States Relations with China, op. cit.,* p. 924. Kerr, who wrote the original 52-page draft of this document, claims it was edited drastically (*Formosa Betrayed, op. cit.,* p. 323).

12. Kerr, "Formosa's Return to China," *op. cit.,* p. 206.

13. *Ibid.*, p. 208.

14. "Memorandum," *op. cit.,* p. 925.

15. Interview with P. S. Lim in the Grand Hotel, Taipei, December 19, 1961.

16. "The major causes [of Formosan unrest] . . . were the stripping of factories of equipment and of capital goods, the drain on the treasury to pay off the hordes of carpetbaggers, the dismissal or bypassing of competent, trained Formosans, and nepotism." (Kerr, "Formosa's Return to China," *op. cit.,* p. 207.)

17. The most detailed sources in English on the 1947 affair are Kerr, *Formosa Betrayed, op. cit.,* and Kerr's two articles cited above. Ambassador Stuart's memorandum to President Chiang, *op. cit.,* relies heavily on first-hand reports from Taipei including issues of Taipei newspapers on file in the Hoover Library of War, Revolution and Peace at Stanford University. Two reports by native observers, printed in Chinese, are Lin Mu-Shun, ed., *Taiwan erh-yueh ke-ming* [February Revolution in Taiwan], 1948, and Huang Ts'un-hou, *Erh-erh-pa shih-p'ien shih-mo-chi* [An account of the 2-28 Incident], (Taichung: Sao-tang Weekly Corp., 1947). The first is very detailed and generally confirmed by other sources, although the editor was a member of the underground Taiwan Communist Party. The second is a short diary by a pro-Nationalist. The *Taiwan Chinglian* [Japanese], Tokyo, devoted its February issues in 1961, 1963, and 1967 largely to the 1947 affair. Because no foreign correspondents were on the scene and international attention was focused on European and mainland Chinese events, there was very little coverage in the world press at that time.

18. Interview with Ralph Blake, Washington, D.C., June 15, 1963.

19. Incident reported in *U.S. Relations With China, op. cit.,* p. 927.

20. Kerr, "Formosa: The March Massacres," *op. cit.,* p. 225. See also Kerr's *Formosa Betrayed, op. cit.,* chs. 12–14.

21. For the text of the 32 points in the Settlement Committee recommendation, see *U.S. Relations With China, op. cit.,* pp. 933–935. Additional demands are given in Lin's Chinese account, *op. cit.,* p. 14, mainly concerning replacement of mainland troops by native Formosans.

They may or may not be authentic, but reveal the more radical views of those outside the rebels' conservative leadership.

22. U.S. Relations With China, op. cit., p. 930, quoting the Hsin Sheng Pao, Taipei, March 9, 1947.

23. Kerr thought his diplomatic reports to the Nanking embassy had been leaked to the Nationalists, giving them the identity of dissidents even before March 1. During the massacre, the wife and infant children of one doomed Formosan sought asylum at the American Consulate but "had to be turned away" (Kerr, Formosa Betrayed, op. cit., p. 304 and pp. 322–323). Dr. Ira Hirschy, Chief Medical Officer for UNRRA-Taiwan, Edward E. Payne, UNNRA Reports Officer, and Allen Shackleton, a New Zealand UNRRA officer, supplied much of the data in the Kerr book.

24. Interview with Professor Shioya, April 5, 1963. (See Note 7.)

25. Kerr, "Formosa's Return to China," op. cit., p. 207.

26. Lin, February Revolution in Taiwan, op. cit., p. 29.

27. Kerr assumes a minimum of 5,000 Formosan and 100 mainlander deaths in March, probably 10,000 Formosans dead in connection with the affair, and "if we add to this the thousands who have been seized and done away with since March, 1947, on the pretext that they were involved in the affair, the number may reach the 20,000 figure often given by Formosan writers" (Formosa Betrayed, op. cit., p. 310).

28. Fifield, "Formosa in Transition," op. cit., pp. 216–217, and the same writer's "Formosa Acquires Strategic Value in China Crisis," Foreign Policy Bulletin, March 4, 1949, pp. 3–4.

29. Geraldine Fitch, Formosa Beachhead (Chicago: Henry Regnery, 1953), p. 74. Also see Mrs. Fitch's hostile review of Kerr's Formosa Betrayed in The Asian Student, March 19, 1966, p. 8.

30. Goddard, Formosa, A Study in Chinese History, op. cit., pp. 177–178. Goddard accepted fully the Nationalist China News Service press release of May 3, 1947, San Francisco, giving the official version of the March affair.

31. Fifield, "Formosa in Transition," op. cit., p. 215.

32. From the reply of a Formosan student in the United States to a series of written questions, dated October, 1964.

33. Interview with Frank Lim, Yokyo, June 23, 1961.

34. U.S. Relations With China, op. cit., p. 309.

35. Ibid., pp. 309–310. See George Kerr's article, "The Way Out: Formosa for the Formosans," The Reporter, February 6, 1951, pp. 5–8.

36. Interview in Washington, D.C., June 1961, with a diplomat who spent 1965–1967 on the Policy Planning Council of the State Department.

37. Kerr, Formosa Betrayed, op. cit., p. 309.

Chapter 3

1. Mark Mancall, "Introduction," *Formosa Today, op. cit.*, p. 24. Mancall attributes the older Taiwanese generation's disaffection to its Japanese heritage and memories of 1947.
2. The informant was quoting a young Formosan policeman in his town as an example of the many young people who felt themselves second-class citizens in their own island.
3. Letter from G. William Skinner, October 6, 1962.
4. See also comments by Albert Axelbank in "Chiang Kai-shek's Silent Enemies," *Harper's Magazine*, September 1963, p. 46. Axelbank, who was a correspondent in Taiwan for two years, says he "usually took a Japanese interpreter since most of the Formosans preferred to speak Japanese". Jonathan Mirsky in Mancall, *op. cit.*, p. 144 ("In the countryside Mandarin is met with scowls while the feeblest Japanese is greeted with open delight . . . people over forty prefer it to Formosan"). And Norma Diamond, "Traditional Values and Modernization in Taiwan," unpublished paper, read at the 17th annual meeting, Association for Asian Studies, April 2–4, 1965. Miss Diamond found fishing villages using Japan as their ideal to be imitated in food, clothing, and an "un-Chinese" open society.
5. The members of a model aborigine village south of Taitung seemed to speak only Japanese, and one week's observation in Taitung and Hualien revealed that east coast people used more Japanese words than Formosans on the western coast.
6. A government TV station began operating in 1962 and was followed the next year by a commercial station, both located in Taipei within range of 120,000 sets (*China Yearbook 1966–1967, op. cit.*, pp. 439–440). The Japanese Embassy in Taipei claimed that between 1962 and 1964, Formosa's annual import quota for Japanese films was about 60, compared with over 200 for Western nations. In October 1965 a mob of fans greeted a Japanese actress' arrival in Taipei "in sharp contrast to the handful of people who greeted the Chinese movie actors and actresses who arrived earlier from Hong Kong to receive awards in the Mandarin Film Festival" (*Japan Times*, October 29, 1965). The Associated Press reported that "shows by foreign performers, especially Japanese, are very popular in Taiwan" (*Japan Times*, April 4, 1967).
7. *China News* editorial, March 7, 1967.
8. Article in *Jiyu* (Freedom), Tokyo, August 1962, as reprinted in *Taiwan Chinglian*, Tokyo, August 1962, p. 36.
9. *China News*, May 22, 1967. Mayor Kao has been elected twice as a politically independent, native-born Formosan, but since Taipei was elevated to special status in 1967, he has served only at the pleasure of the central government.

10. *Ibid.*, May 31, 1967. See also the *China News* editorial of October 8, 1966, which asked, "Why don't our big corporations copy the Japanese lead?," referring to foreign language guides in department stores, railway stations, and hotel lobbies.

11. Ong Jok-tik, *Taiwan, op. cit.*, p. 133.

12. *China News*, September 18, 1965.

13. *Ibid.*, January 15, 1966.

14. Department of Statistics, Provincial Government of Taiwan, *Statistical Abstracts of Taiwan for the Past Fifty-One Years* (Taipei: Provincial Government, 1946), p. 1212. Pages 1211–1239 contain many tabular statistics on education under Japanese rule.

15. *China Yearbook 1966–1967, op. cit.*, pp. 386–387. There were 3 million enrolled in all schools during 1967, or about one-quarter of the entire population (*Free China Weekly*, June 9, 1968).

16. The free 9-year education system was inaugurated officially in September 1968 with 467 national, 429 provincial, and 38 Taipei city junior high schools accommodating a total of 520,000 students (*China News*, September 9, 1968).

17. *China News*, August 21, 1966; and Legislative Yuan testimony in its journal, *Li Fa Yuan Kung Pao*, March 8 and 18, 1966 (pp. 159 and 128, respectively).

18. Agency for International Development, *Economic and Social Trends (Taiwan)* (Washington, D.C.: AID, mimeo, 1964), p. 38. Almost all educational costs are borne by prefectural and municipal (50%), provincial (22%), and town and village governments (16%).

19. *China News*, February 8, 1967.

20. George L. Mackay, *From Far Formosa, op. cit.*, p. 117.

21. For the text of the Constitution, see the *China Yearbook 1966–1967, op. cit.*, Appendix, pp. 712–728. The document came into force December 25, 1947 but was amended in 1948, 1960, and 1966 to modify certain of its original provisions "during the period of Communist rebellion" (p. 729).

22. See Control Yuan member T'ao Po-ch'uan's report in the newspaper *Cheng Hsin Hsin Wen Pao*, Taipei, November 11, 1962, quoted in *The Young Formosan*, Tokyo, December, 1962, p. 15. See also the *China News*, November 17, 1965.

23. *Education and Development: The Role of Educational Planning in the Economic Development of the Republic of China* (Stanford Research Institute, October 1962, mimeo).

24. Bernard Gallin, "Rural Development in Taiwan: the Role of Government," *Rural Sociology*, 29, 3, September 1964, p. 320.

25. Peter Prugh, "The Lure of America," *Wall Street Journal*, November 21, 1966, p. 1. The wife of an American professor wrote friends in 1966: "The political dilemma of Taiwan today is undoubtedly one of the factors causing many young people to see little future for themselves here. Numerous Tunghai students, for example, view their education at this university, with its fine English teaching program and relatively high

proportion of foreign faculty, as a one-way ticket to another country, usually the U.S.A." See also results of a survey of graduate study preferences among 7,000 1965 college graduates, one-third of whom wished to study abroad (*Central Daily News*, October 23, 1966, p. 2).

26. For educational critiques by mainlander professors see Liang Shih-Ch'iu, "Some Opinions on Higher Education," *Wen Hsing*, Taipei, December 1963, p. 7; Ch'ien Ko-ch'uan, "Teachers in Taiwan," *Wen Hsing*, August 1958, p. 9; and Ch'ien Shih-liang (President of Taiwan National University), "How to Solve Some Problems of Higher Education in Taiwan," *New Age*, Taipei, February 15, 1961, pp. 2, 37.

27. A young American missionary professor and his wife who had taught in both Hong Kong and Taiwan reported that they "couldn't talk to Formosan students very long before they exploded into political complaints, but students may not take those ideas to you as a political scientist" (interview in Taichung, March 22, 1962). A group of U.S. Presbyterian youth leaders had similar experiences on its summer 1967 visit.

28. Interview in Taipei, December 21, 1957.

29. *China Yearbook 1966–1967*, *op. cit.*, p. 437. For editorial opinions of radio censorship, see Kondo Toshikyo, *Taiwan no Meiun* (Tokyo: Misuzu Shobo, 1961) by a Japanese author who was *Asahi Shimbun* correspondent in Taipei, 1952–1955. Both Kondo and his *Mainichi* colleague reported being followed and harassed.

30. Interview with Dr. Chiang Mon-lin, Taipei, December 20, 1957. At our last meeting on July 6, 1962, shortly before his death, he insisted Formosans could express their complaints freely: "Go around the island anywhere and ask whatever questions you wish. They have free elections and the central government doesn't interfere in local politics. Natives are in no danger if they criticize our government, but it's still too soon to expect American-style freedoms here."

31. *China Post*, May 1, 1965.

32. For an early Japanese colonial report, see *Report on the Control of the Aborigines in Formosa* (Takhoku: Government-General, 1911). For vivid descriptions of pre-1894 tribal customs, see Mackay, *op. cit.*, chs. 21–28. A Paiwan tribe in southern Formosa planned to spear imitation Chinese heads at a 1965 harvest festival "to commemorate the island's retrocession to China," but police banned the stunt because, they claimed (contrary to 19th century observers) headhunting had gone out of style after a Manchu official, Wu Feng, martyred himself in the early 1800's to shame the tribesmen out of the custom (*China News*, October 23, 1965).

33. When a tribal village near Taitung was afflicted by a rare disease, a group of Taipei doctors flown to the scene found 41 families "none of whom spoke Mandarin" (*China News*, January 30, 1966).

34. *China News*, October 8, 1965.

35. *China News*, May 19, 1967. After Taipei became a special city removed from provincial control in 1967, it could retain more tax income and possibly improve civic services as Mayor Kao had often promised.

36. *China News* editorial, January 12, 1966. See also the more pro-KMT *China Post:* "Taipei stands a good chance of becoming one of the dirtiest and unhealthiest cities in this part of the world" (May 18, 1965, editorial).

37. *China News,* November 17, 1966.

38. A student-conducted interview survey in three small villages within walking distance of the campus. Data from the first village, based on 162 of 305 householders visited in August and September of 1960, were available in 1962. There were dirt floors in 145 houses; 85% had either an outdoor privy or none at all; and 48% of the householders said sanitation was worse than before World War II. Few thought living conditions had improved under Nationalist rule. In 1962, graduates of the FSI Chinese Language School also reported farmers had told them, unsolicited, "life was better under Japan."

39. *China News,* May 24, 1967.

40. See *China News,* July 3, 1966.

41. Press conference held by the late Dr. Chiang on April 13, 1959, reprinted in *Wen Hsing,* Taipei, April 1963, pp. 13–15. The late Dr. Hu Shih also aroused conservative ire, but both Chiang and Hu were too prestigious to be silenced.

42. *China News,* July 9, 1966. Economics Minister K. T. Li, chairman of the CIECD, urged a rational population policy at the same seminar. Two months later, Dr. Sun Fo, son of the revered Sun Yat-sen and currently President of the Examination Yuan, in a message to the 12th anniversary of the Family Planning Association of China, defended "birth spacing" by saying the conditions under which his father opposed birth control had changed. "A UN estimate says Taiwan's population will be 21.3 million in 1980 and even the current 340,000 annual increase poses a very serious problem" (*China News,* October 8, 1966).

43. Statement by Tung Fang-wang quoted in *Wen Hsing,* Taipei, July 1959, p. 2.

44. *China News,* June 7, 1967. One of the women was Miss Lu Ching-hua, nicknamed "Mother of Foster Daughters."

45. For details of the early program see "Family Planning Health Program: Development of the Family Planning Extension Program," Annual Report, mimeo., Provincial Health Department, Taichung, Taiwan, 1964, and *Free China Weekly,* New York, May 26, 1964, pp. 1–2. Also the article by Ronald Freedman and John Takeshita, "Studies in Fertility and Family Limitation in Taiwan," Proceedings of the *University of Pittsburgh Symposium on Research Issues in Public Health and Population Change,* Pittsburgh, Pennsylvania, 1965. Three-fourths of 250,000 women polled in Taichung in 1964 favored birth control (*China News,* April 24, 1964).

46. A November 4, 1968 report in *The New York Times* quoted the Interior Ministry as planning to abolish all prostitution licenses by stages beginning in Taipei "at a date yet to be decided."

47. See articles by Mei Wen-li ("The Intellectuals on Formosa") and Lucy

H. Chen ("Literary Formosa") in Mark Mancall, ed., *Formosa Today*, *op. cit.*, pp. 121–141, and Mancall's own Introduction, pp. 28–35.

48. Sam Cohen, "Chinization' of Taiwan," *Honolulu Advertiser*, May 29, 1965. Cohen credits American aid for most Formosan progress.
49. D. J. Lee in *China News*, March 1, 1967.
50. Statistics on intermarriage are difficult to obtain, but most native and foreign observers agree with Mancall that "intermarriage is a much less common phenomenon than one would expect under the circumstances . . . On the whole, little social contact is found between Taiwanese and mainlanders, regardless of age or social level" (Mancall, *op. cit.*, p. 25). Occasionally a famous marriage is headlined, as that between the daughter of the Tatung Electric Company president and the son of a former KMT secretary-general.
51. Privately circulated letter written by an American woman after two years in Taiwan, dated November 1966.
52. Christmas letter, December 1966 (emphasis added).
53. Maurice Meisner in Mancall, *op. cit.*, p. 161.

Chapter 4

1. For commentaries on Sun's philosophy, see John K. Fairbank, *The United States and China* (New York: Viking Compass edition, 1962), ch. 9; Lyon Sharman, *Sun Yat-Sen* (New York: John Day, 1934); and Chen Cheng, *Land Reform in Taiwan* (Taipei: China Publishing Co., 1961), ch. 1.
2. For recent efforts of the Nationalist Government to give economic and technical aid to developing nations, see *China Yearbook 1966–1967*, *op. cit.*, chs. 20, 21, 23.
3. Chen Cheng, *op. cit.*, pp. 90–91.
4. Interview with Harry Schmidt in Taipei, May 1962. Professor Simon Kuznets of Harvard attributed Formosa's economic growth partly to the "large body of trained, efficient, and educated people who came from the mainland" (*China News*, June 23, 1967).
5. *China News*, May 10, 1967.
6. Press statement of Agency for International Development, Washington, D.C., mimeo., May 28, 1964. In an earlier AID Fact Sheet on "Aid to Free China" (Washington, D.C., undated), Taiwan was compared with Israel because both had received many educated refugees who were "capable technicians and administrators for future growth," and both relied on U.S. capital.
7. *Time*, May 12, 1967, pp. 92–94. William Glenn is even more enthusiastic in the *Far Eastern Economic Review*, June 22, 1967, p. 651.
8. See also the laudatory article by Robert P. Martin in *U.S. News and World Report*, January 1, 1962. ("Compared with many richer, more populous—but floundering—Asian countries, Formosa is a success story

any way you look at it . . . The Formosans no longer nurse the bitter hostility toward the mainlanders that was so marked in the first years after World War II.")

9. See Ed Meagher, "Taiwan Economy Model for Developing Nations," *Los Angeles Times*, August 10, 1965; and Thomas Blinkhorn, "Formosa's Bustling Economy Mushrooms," *Milwaukee Journal*, April 12, 1966. After admitting that "the 12 million local Taiwanese hold no political power," the *London Observer* News Service added, "But they own land and most of the businesses. They never had it so good." (*Milwaukee Journal*, June 17, 1968.)

10. *China News*, June 21, 1967.

11. Agency for International Development, U.S. Aid Mission to China, Program Office, *Taiwan: The U.S. Aid Program for FY 1964* (Taipei, 1964, mimeo.), Part IV, Economic and Social Trends, p. 12. This is an excellent source of both statistics and analyses. The reference is to data from the National Income Division, Directorate-General of Budgets, Accounts, and Statistics (DGBAS). The AID office used 1962 price data, actual free market rates of exchange for the New Taiwan dollar, and other deflators. It claimed that GNP was understated in amount but overstated in terms of growth rate by about 2%.

12. Data on 1965–1966 production, trade, and related items derived from *China Yearbook 1966–1967*, *op. cit.*, Part IV, The National Economy.

13. Neil H. Jacoby, *U.S. Aid to Taiwan* (New York: Frederick A. Praeger, 1966), p. 91, Chart VII-4 shows that the percentage of total industrial production contributed by the public sector declined from 65% in 1952 to 38% in 1963. The Jacoby volume is the best available source on the Formosan economy as well as U.S. aid, and is especially useful for the data in Appendices B–D, pp. 255–309.

14. *China News*, October 25, 1966. The legal minimum wage in 1967 was about US$11.50 per month, despite petitions from Chinese labor unions asking an increase to US$18.75.

15. Chen Cheng, *op. cit.*, pp. 7–10. Table 3, p. 308, shows that in 1940–1943 about 31% of all farm families were owner-farmers, a similar number were part-owners, and 38% were tenants.

16. *China Yearbook 1966–1967*, p. 284; also Chen Cheng, *op. cit.*, p. 76. By 1958, 40% of the island's 435,000 acres of public land had also been sold.

17. Dr. Ladejinsky had been active during the Allied Occupation land reform in Japan and visited Formosa twice in the years before land reform there. For his impressions, see the Chinese News Service press release, San Francisco, July 10, 1951, p. 3.

18. Riggs, *op. cit.*, p. 73, quotes native critics' charges that land reform "was largely undertaken to make the native landlords the scapegoats for the abuses perpetrated by the ruling mainland Chinese—it was easy for the Kuomintang to claim credit for a reform carried out at someone else's expense."

19. Arthur F. Raper, *Rural Taiwan—Problem and Promise* (Taipei: JCRR,

1953), p. 282. The survey of 48 villages in the 16 townships was sponsored by JCRR. Dr. Raper was a Project Evaluation Advisor to the U.S. Mutual Security Agency at that time.

20. *Japan Times*, December 3, 1966.

21. *Ibid.*

22. *China News*, October 4, 1964. Land consolidation plans are discussed in Chen, *op. cit.*, pp. 98–107.

23. Jacoby, *op. cit.*, p. 180–183.

24. Raper, *op. cit.*, p. 268. The follow-up survey in 1959, written by E. Stuart Kirby, was notably more restrained in reporting farmer complaints.

25. *China News*, February 18, 1967. Chen, *op. cit.*, p. 105, admits there was little Formosan or American support for the rice-fertilizer exchange system.

26. Riggs, *op. cit.*, p. 71.

27. *China News*, June 13, 1966. At Tunghai University in 1961 and 1962, I was told to pay my cookmaid US$15 a month because that was the standard wage and anything higher would create dissension among the other campus servants.

28. The Taipei retail commodity market prices (in US$) for July 11, 1962 included chicken, 70¢ lb.; beef, from 50¢ to 80¢ lb.; pork, from 40¢ to 65¢ lb.; rice, 9¢ lb.; eggs, 63¢ dozen; flour, 6¢ lb.; charcoal, 4¢ lb.; cabbage, 6¢ lb. (*China News*, July 11, 1962.) I had noted similar prices in native markets throughout the island during the previous year. Minister Yang Chi-tseng's comments are in *China News*, October 12, 1961.

29. *China News*, April 24, 1964, confirmed these figures. See also the Raper rural report, *op. cit.*, pp. 277–278.

30. Bernard Gallin, *Hsin Hsing* (Berkeley and Los Angeles, University of California Press, 1966), p. 55. Sweet potatoes are seldom served in any eating place, and the foreigner who likes them must buy them from street vendors or in the marketplace.

31. Bernard Gallin, "Rural Development in Taiwan: The Role of the Government," *Rural Sociology*, 29, 3, September 1964, p. 323.

32. *A Survey of Attitudes of the Local Population Toward U.S. Economic Aid to Taiwan* (Taipei: USIS Taiwan Office of Research and Evaluation, August 1960, in English and Chinese), p. 11. About 57 per cent of rural and urban respondents said their livelihood was only "so-so," while about 34 per cent said it was not good. Ten per cent more Taiwanese than mainlanders gave the latter reply to this and similar questions on present life compared with the years before 1945.

33. Interview in Kaohsiung harbor, January 1962.

34. *China News*, August 22, 1966.

35. E. Stuart Kirby, *Rural Progress in Taiwan* (Taipei: JCRR, 1960). The survey field work was directed by Martin M. C. Yang, of National Taiwan University, whose Department of Agricultural Economics staffed the study of 1,350 households.

36. Chen Cheng, *op. cit.*, pp. 87–89. Few outside objective observers or

native farmers would agree with the comparison of prewar Taiwan with the mainland, or that conditions have improved so much. Chen's charts all use 1948 as the base year for measuring the increase in the number of farmers holding public offices.

37. Kirby, *op. cit.*, p. 144.

38. For example, see Chen Sheng-huang, director of the provincial department of communication, in *China News*, April 25, 1966, on Japanese harbor reclamation.

39. Rats were estimated by the Taiwan Environmental Improvement Association to cause a daily grain loss of US$250,000 (*China News*, December 20, 1964). The late Chen Cheng, *op. cit.*, p. 106, says pests destroyed 13% of the total 1960 crop.

40. The USIS survey of 1960, *op. cit.*, pp. 59–63, tabulates the radio program preferences among 14 subjects ranging from music to world affairs. The categories of "music" and "cinema; entertainment" had the greatest following; politics was the third least popular topic. Civil servants, teachers, persons between 45 and 54 years of age, and the better educated of all ages, expressed the strongest interest in political news.

41. Raper, *Urban and Industrial Taiwan* (Taipei: Foreign Operations Administration and National Taiwan University, September 1954), p. 9. See also Raper's comments on pp. 131–134, and Jacoby's favorable opinions in his *U.S. Aid to Taiwan*, *op. cit.*, pp. 73–74: "While the motive was self-interest, Japan's policies were enlightened . . . the rise in agricultural productivity and output was impressive . . . Although figures are lacking, logic and much indirect evidence suggest that the real income, and the quality of living, of the Taiwanese people rose significantly during the Japanese period . . . Japan had laid the foundations of development for the industrious and talented Taiwanese people (to whom it gave) hard work, discipline, and social order . . . a receptivity to technological change, and an appetite for progress."

42. *China News*, January 5, 1962.

43. *Ibid.*, May 7, 1964.

44. *China Yearbook 1963–1964* (Taipei: China Publishing Co., 1964), p. 11.

45. *China Yearbook 1966–1967*, *op. cit.*, p. 295.

46. *Japan Times*, April 2, 1967.

47. Raper, *Urban and Industrial Taiwan*, *op. cit.*, pp. 114–118.

48. Jacoby, *op. cit.*, p. 236. Jacoby thought that some projects were approved for political reasons, despite objections from the screening committee, but that "AID wisely decided not to help finance an integrated steel plant, a nuclear reactor, and an international airline, which were desired by the Chinese government but clearly uneconomic for Taiwan." Many Formosans who were interviewed expressed gratitude for this type of American influence.

49. *China News*, February 21, 1965.

50. For press reports on the plans for a government steel plant, see *China News*, September 26, 1965.

51. *China News*, June 13, 1967. For an explanation of the free-trade zone see *Japan Times*, December 5, 1966. A pro-Nationalist account of Kaohsiung is given by A. A. Swyser, *Honolulu Star-Bulletin* editor, in "Taiwan Sister City is Bustling Trade Center," *China News*, August 29, 1966.

52. *China News*, June 14, 1967.

53. Raper, *Urban and Industrial Taiwan, op. cit.*, pp. 14–15 and pp. 351–353. Nine-tenths of the people knew of the American aid, but only 40 per cent of the city-dwellers (compared with 75 per cent of the farmers) thought it benefited them. See also USIS Taiwan, *A Survey of Attitudes of the Local Population toward U.S. Economic Aid to Taiwan, op. cit.*, pp. 17–42.

54. *China Post* and *China News*, November 16, 1961. The Yuan critics were Hoh Yu-lin and members of an economic affairs committee. "There is no denying the fact that government enterprises are functioning not so well as private firms . . . they have too many staff members in excess of their tables of organization," Hoh charged.

55. *China News*, November 19, 1965; February 23 and 25, 1967. Nissan Motors trucks were followed by Nissan "Bluebird" sedans, used mostly as taxis in Formosa. The *China News* and many of my informants were in favor of the regime's admitting more foreign automakers.

56. Interview in Taipei, July 13, 1962. Lin said, "The biggest need here is for managerial skills . . . and younger government leaders, such as [the United States] government has, even in the Kennedy Cabinet."

57. Raper, *Urban and Industrial Taiwan, op. cit.*, pp. 71–110, gives sketches of the 17 urban areas surveyed. Taipei had a population of 303,000 in 1937, 607,000 in 1953, and over 1 million in 1966; in the same 30-year period Kaohsiung rose from 100,000 to over 600,000; Taichung from 76,000 to 350,000; and Tainan from 120,000 to 400,000. Mainlander percentages ranged from over 25 in Taipei to around 20 per cent in other major cities, and under 10 per cent in towns.

58. *Ibid.*, p. 70, and elsewhere in the report. Raper's 1953 leader group objected most strongly to population increase, more small businesses operating in the streets, production of pork and fowl in previously forbidden areas of the cities, greater use of soft coal for cooking, war damage not yet repaired, and typhoon or earthquake damage to buildings and drainage systems. Ten years later, the average citizen made the same complaints, adding the continued failure of the Nationalists to match Japanese standards of nightsoil and garbage collection.

59. See *Ibid.*, chapter 9, for a graphic description of the Chunghua squatter section of Taipei, duplicated in other cities but less easily visible to foreigners. Raper makes a distinction between Taiwanese and mainlanders throughout his urban study, partly to point out that many mainlanders are low income people.

60. *China News*, May 9, 1966. Kao had served a previous term as Taipei mayor in the mid-1950's and, as a native-born political independent, was expected to ameliorate his city's problems.

61. *China Daily News* (Chinese), February 22, 1967, citing the *Cheng Hsin Hsin Wen Pao*. "Five hundred houses have been built by the city in the outskirts . . . but far short of the need. This simply indicates the authorities' lack of concern for the poor residents."

62. *China News*, May 17, 1966.

63. Jacoby, *op. cit.*, p. 234. On p. 93, *ibid.*, Jacoby said that unemployment in 1964 had increased to between 450,000 and 500,000, or 10 per cent of the labor force. ("Although the existence of unemployment was regrettable, it helped to hold down labor costs, and increased Taiwan's competitive strength in international markets.") The issue was debated by American economists and Nationalist officials at a 1967 Taipei conference (*China News*, June 23, 1967).

64. Interview in Naha, Okinawa, August 19, 1966 with a Ryukyu University professor who had just returned from a survey of Formosan labor conditions. Wages of industrial workers rose 71 per cent between 1958 and 1964, compared with commodity prices, which rose 48 per cent, but their productivity increased 175 per cent, according to the *Economic Daily News* of Taipei, which charged that the wage level was second lowest (after India) in all Asia (*China News*, June 1, 1967).

65. *China News*, May 7 and February 17, 1967.

66. Jacoby, *op. cit.*, p. 97.

67. *Ibid.*, p. 235.

68. *Ibid.*, pp. 145–146.

69. *China News*, February 12, 1967. See also mainlander Legislative Yuan member Yu Lin-yun's advocacy of direct taxation in the same newspaper, October 21, 1965. Richard Musgrave, a Harvard professor who was invited to Formosa as consultant to a Commission on Tax Reform in 1968, claimed "the tax burden is excessively regressive" (*China News*, July 31, 1968).

70. *China News*, May 4, 1962. The three papers quoted were the *Chen Hsin Hsin Wen Pao*, the *Independent Evening Post*, and the *Min Tsu Evening News*.

71. Jacoby, *op. cit.*, p. 148. See also *ibid.*, pp. 170–171, where Jacoby admitted that U.S. policy "tended to produce a lag in Taiwan's political development behind its economic and social development," but insisted that although aid strengthened the Nationalists politically, it helped to "energize the private sector and create new centers of economic power which would demand liberalized political rights, participation, and institutions." See also Allan Cole, "Political Roles of Taiwanese Entrepreneurs," *Asian Survey*, September 1967, pp. 645–654.

72. Farewell talk by Roy James, deputy director of ICA/China, in *China Post*, June 13, 1961. Wesley Haroldson made a similarly tough speech in June 1962 before his departure as AID director (interview with *Post* editor, Taipei, July 11, 1962).

73. Interviews with S. Y. Dao and Richard Hough, Taipei, July 13, 1962.

74. Jacoby, *op. cit.*, pp. 118–124. Jacoby's main point is that the U.S.

underwrote the major share of Nationalist defense costs, other than manpower.

75. Raper, *Urban and Industrial Taiwan, op. cit.*, p. 13. See Jacoby, *op. cit.*, p. 164, for the optimistic view that "Rising per capita income and the availability of a broader range and higher quality of consumer goods and public services helped to lessen unrest and enmity among dissident groups who lacked effective political power within the central government. Similarly, prosperity and greater economic opportunity tended to identify the 'out-groups' more with the current regime, to give them a vested interest in continued stability, and to counsel patience in the face of authoritarian controls."

76. AID, *Taiwan—The U.S. Aid Program for FY 1964, op cit.*, pp. 78–79 (emphasis added).

77. Interview with Oswald E. DeRuttia, Taipei, July 10, 1962.

78. Interview July 15, 1962.

Chapter 5

1. See Jacoby in *U.S. Aid to Taiwan, op. cit.*, p. 111: "In contrast to its rapid economic and social development, Taiwan experienced little basic change in its political structure during 1951–1965. Political development lagged, particularly in the central and provincial governments." Even the pro-Nationalist Australian W. G. Goddard spoke of excessive KMT influence in appointments and of the KMT's "outmoded ideas" on family influence, punishment of officials for minor causes, and the failure to hold national elections (*Formosa, A Study in Chinese History, op. cit.*, p. 209). For the degree of government control over mass media, see USIA, *Communication Fact Book: Taiwan* (Washington, D.C.: USIA, mimeo. 1962).

2. *China News*, May 25, 1967.

3. Jacoby, *op. cit.*, p. 113.

4. Comment at the annual meeting of the Association for Asian Studies, Palace Hotel, San Francisco, April 3, 1965.

5. Jacoby, *op. cit.*, p. 113. See *China News*, July 2 and October 23, 1967 for plans to hold partial elections on Formosa, raising the island's quota of central government representatives from 32 to 53.

6. Jacoby, *op. cit.*, p. 111. "The power base was narrow and maintained through internal unity and a refined and ordered dispensation of personal favors." Jacoby described the formal government structure and party system as "a conglomerate of the American presidential system, the British Cabinet system, and the Leninist principles of party organization . . ."

7. *Ibid.*, p. 112.

8. See account by Mark Plummer of the 1966 National Assembly voting,

"Taiwan: The Other China," *Current History*, September 1966, pp. 165–178; and "Chiang K'ai Shek and the National Assembly," in Sidney Brown, ed., *Studies on Asia 1967* (Lincoln: University of Nebraska Press, 1968). See also *China News*, July 2 and October 23, 1967 for plans to hold partial elections for national offices, raising Formosa's quota of seats.

9. *China Yearbook 1966–1967*, *op. cit.*, pp. 118–120.

10. *Ibid.*, p. 114. The provincial assembly had long urged such steps to elect new Formosan members of the three national bodies subject to popular election (*China News*, March 18, 1966).

11. *China Yearbook 1966–1967*, *op. cit.*, p. 161. See also Premier C. K. Yen's pledge to make Taiwan a "true democracy to defeat the Chinese Communists" (*China News*, October 25, 1965).

12. Jacoby, *op. cit.*, p. 112.

13. *China News*, March 15, 1966; *Central Daily News*, New York, April 8, 1966.

14. See the article by D. J. Lee, *China News*, June 21, 1967, claiming that the two small parties are very active and that either might "come to power sooner or later." None of their Formosan leaders with whom I talked had thought so.

15. Goddard, *op. cit.*, p. 185.

16. *Central Daily News*, April 8, 1966, p. 3.

17. Taipei was previously subject to provincial administration, and it is difficult to determine who originated the request for special city status or why the request was granted. See *China News*, March 25, 1966 and January 3, 1967.

18. Jacoby, *op. cit.*, p. 112.

19. See *China Yearbook 1966–1967*, *op. cit.*, p. 114, and the account of President Chiang's opposition to the Assembly's exercise of more powers in *China News*, December 25, 1965 and February 1, 1966, wherein he was quoted as declaring: "Everything should be subordinated to mainland recovery."

20. For evaluations of Chiang Ching-kuo, see *Japan Times*, September 28, 1966; *Milwaukee Journal*, October 25, 1964; two books in Chinese by Sun Chia-ch'i, *Why I Left the Nationalist Party in Taiwan* and *Chiang Ching-kuo Steals the State: An Inside Story* (Hong Kong: Li-Sheng Publication Centre, 1961), and Peter Arnett, "Return to China 'Dream' Says Chiang's Son-Heir," *San Francisco Sunday Examiner and Chronicle*, December 1, 1968.

21. Jacoby, *op. cit.*, p. 112.

22. Albert Axelbank, "Chiang Kai-shek's Silent Enemies," *Harper's*, September 1963, pp. 52–53.

23. *Ibid.*, p. 48.

24. Interview with Interior Minister Lien, Taipei, July 13, 1962.

25. Private report made by one of the participants in the discussion. See Axelbank, *op. cit.*, p. 53: "Some Formosans, who assume that the island's political complexion will remain unchanged for the next fifteen

or twenty years, foresee that the time will come when younger generation Formosans—and mainlanders who have become 'Formosanized'—
will live in harmony under a government run predominantly by Formosans."

26. *Ibid.*, p. 50.
27. Letter from Ng Yu-zin, executive of the Formosan Association (later
    the United Young Formosans for Independence), Tokyo, October 21,
    1964.
28. Tan Kheh-chiang, "Story about the Mayor of Taipei" (in Japanese),
    Taiwan Chinglian, Tokyo, March 1964, p. 21. Axelbank, *op. cit.*, p. 49,
    says the 1954 election involved voiding 10,000 of Kao's votes "because
    the ink on them had smudged" and bringing Nationalist soldiers to the
    city to vote, in violation of the residence requirement.
29. *Ibid.*, p. 21.
30. See Tan Kheh-chiang, "An Analysis of the Recent Election" (in
    Japanese), *Taiwan Chinglian*, May 1964, pp. 4–10, especially p. 10.
    Taiwanese held 310,000 of the city's 520,000 votes, but the KMT
    candidate, acting mayor Chou Pai-lien, commanded much native
    support.
31. Axelbank, *op. cit.*, p. 50.
32. Hosono Akio and others, *Taiwan no hyojo* [Conditions on Taiwan]
    (Tokyo: Kokon Shoin, 1963), p. 74. Pages 34–37 deal with Taiwanese-
    mainlander frictions observed by the authors; p. 73 contains statistics
    on the compositions of personnel in various levels of the Taiwan Pro-
    vincial Government, 1956, showing that the proportion of Chinese
    personnel ranged from 79 per cent at the top to 23 per cent in the
    lowest ranks.
33. Press reports on the 1968 election, *Milwaukee Journal*, April 23, 1968,
    and *Free China Weekly*, April 28, 1968. The two mayors were popular
    men in their community.
34. Axelbank, *op. cit.*, p. 49.
35. *Ibid.*, p. 48.
36. Both surveys are reported in English in a publication of the Chinese
    Institute of Public Opinion, Taipei, 1964. The original reports were
    titled, "A Survey of Attitudes of the Local Population toward U.S.
    Economic Aid to Taiwan" (August 1960) and "Radio Listenership in
    Taiwan: A Survey Report" (June 1961) both published by the Office
    of Research and Evaluation, USIS, Taiwan.
37. "A Survey of Attitudes . . . ," *op. cit.*, pp. 12–16. This survey used a
    1,000 sample properly balanced between mainlanders and Formosans
    but used quota sampling and an urban bias. The USIS introduction
    notes that "opinion research in Taiwan is still in its infancy. The CIPO
    . . . is neither adequately equipped nor experienced for precise attitude
    survey work . . . This was the first large-scale one ever attempted on
    the island" (p. 6).
38. See Mendel, "The Japanese Voter and Political Action," *Western Po-
    litical Quarterly*, XV, 3, May 1956, pp. 343–356.

39. Interview in Taichung, June 25, 1962.

40. Raper, *Rural Taiwan—Problem and Promise, op. cit.*, pp. 258, 270.

41. *Ibid.*, p. 192.

42. Kirby, *Rural Progress in Taiwan* (Taipei: Joint Commission on Rural Reconstruction, 1960), p. 110.

43. See Mendel, *The Japanese People and Foreign Policy, op. cit.*, pp. 240–243, citing the Conlon Report and other sources.

44. Raper, *Urban and Industrial Taiwan, op. cit.*, p. 351.

45. Interview in Milwaukee, July 26, 1965. Koo's Chinese passport expired after this trip, so he had to remain in Japan. The story of his organization is told in Chapter 7.

46. In addition to the account of Albert Axelbank, *op. cit.*, see articles by Mark Mancall, John Israel, and Maurice Meisner in Mancall, ed., *Formosa Today, op. cit.*; by Joyce Kallgren in the *Asian Survey*, January 1964, pp. 638–645 and January 1965, pp. 12–17; and Melvin Gurtov, *ibid.*, January 1967, pp. 40–45. An American student back from Formosa wrote in the *St. Louis Post-Dispatch*, May 12, 1967: "A staunch party-line representative of the KMT admits that if local newspapers were allowed to voice major criticisms of the government, the result would be the imminent danger of violent overthrow. Many observers feel that it is to prevent materialization of such a movement that the totalitarian practices which underlie the guise of democracy remain in effect on Taiwan."

47. Goddard, *op. cit.*, p. 213.

48. Jacoby, *op. cit.*, p. 244.

49. *China News*, November 10, 1961. See also *China News* editorials of December 28, 1964, January 8, 1966, and January 18, 1967 ("Overaged bureaucrats, misfits, and hacks are found at every level of government . . . Pay is so bad that few highly competent people can be persuaded to take government jobs . . . Moonlighting and petty cheating is widespread [and] large-scale peculations are not unusual").

50. *Ibid.*, October 29, 1964: "Literally, there is a watchdog at every turning of the government road. Yet we continue to have far too many corruption cases." (See also the *China News*, June 28, August 16, September 22, October 5, 1966, and January 28, 1967). The United Press estimated the total loss to taxpayers at NT$3 billion, or close to 4 per cent of one year's national income.

51. *China News*, July 1, 1963. (I myself was nearly expelled from Formosa in 1962 for criticizing the Army political staff college to one of its instructors.)

52. *China News*, December 12, 1965 and February 9 and April 2, 1966.

53. Quoted in *China Post*, January 29, 1962. The month before the regime rescinded the 72-hour visa-free privilege, Marvin Plake, director of the Pacific Area Travel Association, had told a Taipei audience that the provision was "convincing evidence to the world that the Republic of China is not a police state . . . and [it] has more political than economic significance" (*China Post*, May 20, 1965). The provision began

in November 1960 and expired June 30, 1965 over protests of travel agencies. The *China News*, noting the privilege had been withdrawn for security reasons remarked: "Yet Vietnam is scarcely less threatened than Taiwan [and] dares to permit entry of friendly nationals without a visa" (February 1, 1967).

54. Report from an American graduate student quoting his military interrogators. Others have experienced similar Chinese Nationalist resentment against "undue American influence."

55. Interview with Thomas Liao, Tokyo, February 1963.

56. Andrew Tully, *The C.I.A.* (New York: Morrow, 1961), contained a chapter titled "Foggy Bottom's Chiang," critical of U.S. support for guerrilla tactics.

57. John Israel in Mancall, *op. cit.*, p. 61.

58. *China Post*, October 19, 1963.

59. See *Tzu-yu-Chung-Kuo* (*Free China*), February 16, 1957, and an editorial stating that "the majority [of Formosans] generally feel that their rulers are foreigners" (July 16, 1960).

60. *Ibid.*, July 5, 1960, and Kondo, *op. cit.*, p. 20 refer to a speech by Chen Cheng in which he also warned such a new party not to oppose basic government policies.

61. Kondo, *op. cit.*, pp. 17–18. Sun Chia-ch'i, *Chiang Ching-kuo Steals the State, op. cit.*, pp. 91–98, tells how the KMT infiltrated minor parties and magazine staffs to plant evidence against dissenters. Sun specifically absolves Lei of knowing that the agent planted in his office was an ex-Communist: "It was just a convenient device to kill two birds with one stone . . . Lei was arrested because, as a non-native, his arrest would not antagonize the natives; he had been the main leader in organizing the new party; his magazine contained evidence available for official accusations of misconduct; and the magazine was so critical of Chiang, his son, and their government."

62. Kondo, *op. cit.*, p. 20. See also Hosono, *op. cit.*, p. 81, and Axelbank, *op. cit.*, p. 50. Axelbank said the party's leaders wanted to "bridge the gap which exists between Formosans and mainlanders," while the platform called for the lifting of martial law; freedom of speech, press, lawful political activity, and elections; no arbitrary arrests; and more opportunities for Formosans in the higher ranks of government."

63. Mancall, *op. cit.*, p. 39.

64. Axelbank, *op. cit.*, p. 51. A journalist and his wife working for the official Provincial Government newspaper, *Hsin Sheng Daily News*, were arrested for sedition as ex-Communists in 1966 (*China News*, June 23, 1966).

65. Mancall, *op. cit.*, p. 41. Two other politicians from other cities said they had experienced similar post-election discrimination, but that "Sung's case was more famous because it occurred in Taipei."

66. The director of the official Chinese News Service in New York, Lo I-cheng, "was equally surprised when the news came" (letter dated November 5, 1964).

67. The manifesto was translated and published by the United Formosans for Independence, Philadelphia, as *Declaration of Formosans* (May 1966, mimeo.) and is reproduced in the Appendix. For official Nationalist press releases on the case, see the *Daily News Report* of the Chinese News Service, New York, January 22, March 27, April 2, and November 3, 1965.

68. Letter from Ng Yu-zin, Tokyo, January 24, 1965. Roger Hilsman, then Assistant Secretary of State for Far East, reported that Nationalist Ambassador Tingfu Tsiang denied any power to influence the case (statement to students at Madison, Wisconsin, March 1965).

69. Hsieh Tsung-wen, formerly a magazine editor, and Wei Ting-chao, who had been on the research staff of *Academia Sinica*, repented "properly" (see the *China News*, July 24, 1966).

70. *Daily News Report* (New York: Chinese News Service, November 3, 1965), p. 2.

71. *China News*, July 20, 1966.

72. The *China Daily News*, September 17 and October 8, 1966.

73. See *ibid.*, December 9, 1964; *China Post*, April 18, 1965; and *China News*, December 28, 1965.

74. For the case of Hwang Chii-ming, see *New York Times*, March 4, May 14, July 4, and August 9, 1967; and ch. 7 below.

75. Anonymous, "A Report on Formosan Political Prisoners," *Formosan Readers Association Report*, 1 (November 1966), p. 11, reprinted in *The Progressive*, December 1967, as "Tyranny in Free Formosa." Friends of Thomas Liao said members of his immediate family had been tortured in prison to blackmail Liao into defecting in the hope they would be released.

Chapter 6

1. *Christian Science Monitor*, August 28, 1967.

2. *China News*, December 27, 1966.

3. Tung Chi-ping, "Red China," *Look Magazine*, December 1, 1964, pp. 21–27.

4. Peng et al, *Declaration of Formosans*, tr. by United Formosans for Independence, *op. cit.*, p. 5. See Appendix for complete text.

5. *China News*, April 20, 1964.

6. *Ibid.*, May 2, 1962.

7. *Central Daily News*, January 16, and February 1, 2 and 7, 1967; the latter two issues also reported that the NSC would contain thirteen high civil and military chiefs, with three standing committees headed by Chiang Ching-kuo and two Whampoa alumni. The planning that led to the NSC is reported in the *China News*, March 19 and May 19, 1966.

8. *New York Times*, August 9, 1967. "Nor do the Taiwanese accept as

uncomplainingly as the the mainlanders the heavy expenditures required by the large 'back-to-the-mainland' military establishment . . ." See also the statement of pro-Nationalist John C. Caldwell twelve years earlier: "American official policy is to build up the island of Formosa . . . As long as American policy is ambiguous and unrealistic, there will be friction (between the U.S. and Nationalist China)." (*Still the Rice Grows Green,* Chicago: Henry Regnery, 1955) p. 158.

9. Mendel, *The Japanese People* . . . , *op. cit.,* p. 241.

10. Comments heard in 1961 and 1962, confirmed by Professor Alfred Crofts, University of Denver, who witnessed the 1949 Nationalist army arrivals in Kaohsiung and Tainan.

11. An article by Chin Ta-fu in *Nippon Shuho* (Tokyo: March 20, 1953, pp. 5–7), "The Nationalist Counter-offensive against the Mainland Faces Difficulties," reported ground forces at 369,000, rear supply units at 60,000, the Navy at 40,000, and Air Forces 80,000. A 1965 research report on Taiwan by the Tokyo newspaper *Asahi* listed 400,000 Army, 62,000 Navy (including 27,000 Marines), and 82,000 Air Force (Tokyo: Asahi Shimbun, *Taiwan,* v. 2, May 1965, preface). The latter relied upon recent issues of the *Boei Nenkan* (Defense Yearbook) published by the Japanese Defense Agency, and on reports of the London Institute for Strategic Studies. Joyce Kallgren's chapter, "Nationalist China's Armed Forces," in Mark Mancall, ed., *Formosa Today* (New York: Frederick Praeger, 1964), pp. 91–100, cited the same sources plus the U.S. Congress, Senate Appropriations Committee, *Report on United States Military Operations and Mutual Security Programs Over-Seas* (86th Congress, Second Session, committee print, 1962).

12. Interview in Taipei, 1962.

13. Jeff Endrst, "Chiang's Military Punch," *Japan Times,* September 1, 1965, a résumé of the Nationalist strength and potential of that time. ROTC was made selective in 1967 with two years' service for those passing the exam and ordinary enlisted service for all other males (*Central Daily News,* Taipei, November 11, 1966).

14. *Boei Nenkan 1962, op. cit.,* pp. 431–433.

15. Asahi, *Taiwan, op. cit.,* gives the Japanese Defense Force strength in 1964 as 172,000 Army, 35,000 Navy, and 39,000 Air, but with about 1,700 planes—double the Nationalist air strength.

16. Endrst, *op. cit.;* but Kallgren, p. 93, quotes Japanese and British estimates of over 100,000 for the Chinese Air Force. In 1962 I saw some of the F-104's, to replace older F-86's, at the Taichung base, but the F5A models came later. Nationalist China seeks to attract Communist pilots by offering a bounty in gold for every MIG plane flown to Formosa.

17. President Eisenhower in January 1955 asked and secured a Congressional resolution going beyond the 1954 treaty with Nationalist China, by approving in advance American defense of "such related positions and territories . . . as he judges to be appropriate in assuring the defense of Formosa and the Pescadores." See Robert P. Newman, *Recog-*

nition of Communist China? (New York: Macmillan, 1961), pp. 93–94.

18. Endrst, *op. cit.*

19. Interview, July 15, 1962.

20. Reported by a friend of two eyewitnesses to the abortive coup. The island press claimed the rebels were demanding a quicker counterattack.

21. *China News,* July 29, 1966.

22. See *101 Questions About Taiwan* (Taipei: Free China Review Press, December 1960), pp. 64–65: "These political officers . . . are no 'commissars.' They are equivalent to the troop information and education officers, the special service officers, the counter-intelligence officers, and the chaplains of the U.S. Army all rolled into one. They help maintain the morale of the soldiers, teach them to read and write, give consultation on personal problems *and, in an unobtrusive manner, watch for possible sabotage and subversion.*" (Emphasis added.)

23. Letter from Ambassador Chen Ching-mai, Tokyo, October 1966, whom I had met when Chen was Nationalist envoy to Australia in 1963.

24. Axelbank, *op. cit.,* p. 52. Many veterans of the Nationalist military services, including a few mainland-born ROTC graduates, confirmed this rumor about ammunition control.

25. *Ibid.,* p. 52.

26. Jacoby, *op. cit.,* pp. 118–119.

27. *Ibid.,* p. 126.

28. *Declaration of Formosans, op. cit.,* p. 12. See Appendix for text.

29. Interview with a member of the Taiwan Provincial Assembly in southern Taiwan, 1963.

30. A. Doak Barnett, *Communist China and Asia* (New York: Random House Vintage Books, 1961), p. 103.

31. *101 Questions About Taiwan, op. cit.,* pp. 64–65.

32. Interview with Kaya Okinori, Tokyo, March 4, 1963.

33. Barnett, *op. cit.,* pp. 412–413.

34. *Ibid.,* p. 413.

35. *China News,* February 17, 1962.

36. *China News,* September 23, 1966.

37. *Ibid.,* November 1, 1966.

38. *Ibid.,* September 16, 1965.

39. Interview with State Department educational exchange officers, June 1963.

40. *Ibid.,* July 12, 1967.

41. *Ibid.,* February 23, 1967.

42. *Free China Weekly,* August 27, 1967.

43. *Japan Times,* January 14, 1967.

44. *China Post,* May 2, 1965; *China News,* November 4, 1965.

45. For the official Nationalist report of the incident, see *Free China Weekly,* August 15, 1965.

46. For interviews with mainland defectors, see *Free China Review,* February 1962, pp. 6–8 and *China News,* August 7, 9, and 15, 1967. A few

Nationalists defected at the 1964 Tokyo Olympic Games; but the most famous defector was former Vice President Li Tsung-jen, who flew from the United States to Peking in 1966 to denounce both his former Nationalist colleagues and his erstwhile American benefactors.

47. *101 Questions About Taiwan, op. cit.,* p. 114.

48. For a pro-Nationalist view of Quemoy's military status, see articles by TSgt. Robert Fisher, USAF, of the MAAG Public Information Office, in *China News,* Taipei, January 20 and March 2, 1966.

49. The Quemoy garrison was increased after the 1958 Communist shelling, and probably varies between 80,000 and 120,000 for all offshore islands.

50. Guards have orders to shoot anyone who does not give the correct password, so "very few of us wanted to venture out at night." The alternate-day Communist shellings took place normally before 11 p.m.

51. John Caldwell wrote ten years earlier that "The Chinese are realistic: men outnumber women on Kinmen by nearly ten to one, yet there has been no case of rape in two years. They have provided a huge house of prostitution in Hopu, equipped with dispensary, full-time doctor, reading room, ping-pong tables—and a nursery for the unfortunate mistakes that occur . . . There were 75 girls there, but few were busy. The price is cheap, thirty cents for an enlisted man, who draws his partner by lot, seventy-five cents for the officer, who can make a face-to-face choice . . ." (*Still the Rice Grows Green, op. cit.,* pp. 35–36).

52. Hanson Baldwin referred to Kinmen as "a whole island fortress" after his first visit in 1965. "The shelling is only a part of the propaganda struggle [and] the propaganda battle seems to have had little effect on either side" (*China News,* November 16, 1965, quoting an earlier *New York Times* dispatch from Kinmen).

53. Axelbank, *op. cit.,* p. 53.

54. *Declaration of Formosans, op. cit.,* complete text in Appendix.

55. Letter (October 1964) to an American graduate student at Stanford University.

56. *China News,* May 25, 1966.

57. Letter from an American student at the scene of the incident, January 25, 1966.

58. Letter dated May 1967.

Chapter 7

1. *China News,* August 18, 1967.

2. See *China News,* December 2, 1966, and related editorials in that newspaper, December 23, 1966 and January 18 and September 25, 1967 on ways of inducing scholars back home.

3. *Christian Science Monitor,* January 6, 1968.

4. The Japanese Government uses only "China" on its alien registration cards; welcomes one third as many Formosan students as the U.S. annually; and—with some exceptions, described in this chapter—tolerates

the continued presence of Formosans who have had their Nationalist passports revoked for political activity.

5. Interview in Tokyo, June 1961.
6. Joshua Liao died in Hong Kong about 1951. See Joshua Liao, *Formosa Speaks* (Hong Kong: Formosan League for Re-emancipation, 1950) and Fred Riggs, *Formosa Under Chinese Nationalist Rule* (New York: Macmillan, 1952), pp. 187–191.
7. For some of Liao's writings, see Thomas W. I. Liao, *Inside Formosa— Formosans vs. Chinese Since 1945* (Tokyo: Formosan Press, 1956, 2nd ed., 1960) and *Formosanism* (same publisher, 1957). Two newspapers of irregular publication, the provisional government's *Taiwan Minpo* (Tokyo: Taisei Bldg; Chuo-ku), and the affiliated Kansai group's *Taiwan Koheiho* (Kobe: Ko Kai-ichi, publisher) contain many of Liao's speeches and activities. In addition, another newspaper was published briefly in Tokyo in the early 1960's, *Taiwan Shimbun*. These three journals were in Japanese, but some had Chinese and English supplements. Evaluations of Liao and the provisional government can be found in Hosono and others, *Taiwan no hyojo*, pp. 82–91; Kondo, *Taiwan no meiun*, pp. 36–40; and Ong Jok-tik in Mancall, *Formosa Today*, pp. 163–170, a rather biased but valuable account.
8. Interview in Tokyo, January 31, 1963. See also *New York Times*, November 6, 1961.
9. Interview in Tokyo, February 1963 and August 1966.
10. Letter from George Kerr, October 25, 1965.
11. August 25, 1965, CBS radio program on "Problems of Group Cooperation."
12. Interview in the Tokyo Station Hotel, February 19, 1963.
13. For various reports on Liao's defection see the *Taiwan Minpo*, May 15, 1965 (his colleagues' view); *Taiwan Chinglian* (organ of the Formosan Association), May 25, 1965; and the Nationalist *Free China Weekly*, New York, May 12, 23, and 30, June 13, 1965. The official *Central Daily News* (Taipei) referred to Liao's defection on May 15, 18, 19, 29, 1965; the June 2, 1965 issue of the anti-Nationalist *China Daily News* (New York) editorially questioned the effect of Liao's return on the movement itself; the third-force *San Min Morning Paper* (Chicago) published similar editorials on June 18, 19, and 21, 1965.
14. Letters from a relative of Thomas Liao and another well-informed Formosan in the United States, September 24, 1967 and May 29, 1965, respectively. The latter claimed that more than 100 political prisoners had been released from jail after Liao's return; the former explained in detail the persecution of Liao's family and his efforts on their behalf after returning. *The New York Times*, May 17, 1965, reported that it was Chiang Ching-kuo who had arranged Liao's return.
15. *China Post*, Taipei, May 16, 1965.
16. *Ibid.*, May 16, 1965.
17. See *China Post*, May 21, 1965, and *China News*, April 30, 1965, for the announced defection of Cheng Wan-fu. Dr. Wu Chen-nan, Liao's vice-

president in Tokyo, also defected in 1966 (*Japan Times*, October 29, 1966). None of these men had played an active role in Japan. Scholars in Hong Kong, where I made exhaustive inquiries in 1961 and 1964, knew none of Liao's alleged associates in Macao and Hong Kong.

18. *The New York Times Book Review*, March 27, 1966. Trumbull stood by his opinions in an interview in Tokyo, August 1966.

19. *Japan Times*, October 29, 1966; see also *China Post*, May 21, 1965 and April 13, 1966.

20. A Formosan who attended two American universities before joining Liao's group in 1960 warned me "never to contact the Young Formosan Association" because he regarded one of its leaders who had been his colleague in military service in Taiwan as unreliable. After Liao's defection, the same man admitted his error during a meeting in Tokyo, August 1966. Kaku Ko-yu, described below, warned me in early 1964 not to see any Formosans in Japan "except those loyal to Dr. Liao."

21. *Taiwan Minpo*, organ of the provisional government, Tokyo, May 15, 1965 (issue #150), and July 1, 1965. The latter issue also gives the biographies of the new provisional government leaders who succeeded the defectors.

22. *Taiwan Minpo*, July 1, 1965, p. 4, and *Taiwan Chinglian*, May 25, 1965.

23. Letter from Tokyo dated June 3, 1965. See also a letter by Ng Yu-zin of the *Formosan Association*, June 11, 1965.

24. Such a boomerang effect was predicted by Professor John Lin, New York State University, New Paltz, N.Y., in a letter of July 29, 1965.

25. Interview in Tokyo, February 20, 1963. See also Ryo's article in the magazine *Dokuritsu Taiwan* [Independent Formosa], Tokyo, August 1967, pp. 27–29, and the excellent book by Kan Bun-kai, *Taiwan no Dokuritsu* [The Independence of Formosa] (Tokyo: Yuki Shobo, 1962).

26. Interview in Yokohama, August 23, 1964.

27. Interview in Tokyo, December 17, 1962, with an informant connected with the magazine *Taiwan*, published annually from 1961 by the *Taiwan Mondai Kenkyu Kyokai* (Formosan Problems Research Association).

28. Interviews with Nagoya area Formosans, November 21, 1962, and March 20, 1963.

29. The verdict of the Osaka District Court was handed down on September 4, 1962, and the Supreme Court appeal filed March 12, 1964. Kaku wrote May 29, 1965 on the eve of his imprisonment asking me to appeal to Justice Minister Ishii Mitsujiro, who had spent his youth in Formosa. Ishii replied in September that the best way to help Kaku was to "send money to Mrs. Kaku." He was held under grade 4, the strictest of Japanese prison grades, unable to send or receive mail or food from the outside, to possess books, or to write while in prison. "I had only 3 days in Sugamo with good treatment, then was sent in

manacles to Utsunomiya Prison where I was given no rice, fruit, vegetables, milk, meat, or fish. The daily budget for my food was 4¢, according to the guards, and no insecticide against bugs—it was worse than a
Formosan prison," claimed Kaku on August 27, 1966.

30. For an account of one of Kaku's street demonstrations in Tokyo, see
Japan Times, July 2, 1967.

31. Interview in Tokyo, July 29, 1966. See Shi Mei's book, *Taiwan—
Yonhyakunen-shi* [400 Year History of Formosa] (Tokyo: Otoba Shobo,
1962).

32. Interview at Kyu Ei-kan's home in Tokyo, August 25, 1966.

33. The magazine *Dokuritsu Taiwan* [Independent Formosa] is published
by Shi Mei, 1–23–4 Nishi Ikebukuro, Toshima-ku, Tokyo.

34. Ong Jok-tik, "The Formosan Independence Movement," in Mancall,
op. cit., p. 169. In 1968, Ong's group (now called United Young
Formosans for Independence) published monthly journals in Japanese
(*Taiwan*, formerly *Taiwan Chinglian*) and also in Chinese.

35. Interview in Tokyo, January 30, 1963.

36. Interviews at Ong's home in Tokyo, February 1963, and at the Palace
Hotel,Tokyo, August 28, 1964.

37. Interview in Tokyo, February 18, 1963.

38. Interview in Tokyo, August 21, 1964; and a letter, August 27, 1965.

39. The visa denial was reported in the *Japan Times*, August 5, 1966. An
editorial in the Chicago *San Min Morning Star* of August 15, 1966
insisted that denial of the visa on grounds of my work for overseas
Formosan journals proved there were Formosan independence movements abroad even after Thomas Liao's defection: "The visa denial is a
stupid act." See also my "Open Letter to Ambassador Goldberg,"
Independent Formosa (Tokyo: U.Y.F.I.), VI, 2, April 1967, pp. 11–12.

40. Discussion in Milwaukee, Wis., July 26, 1965.

41. See "Formosans' Protest to U.S. Secretary of State Dean Rusk," *Independent Formosa*, August 1966, pp. 1–2, and *Japan Times*, July 6,
1966. As the Formosans were not permitted near the Kyoto conference
hall, they staged a hunger strike nearby from July 5–7, in which the
United Young Formosans joined members of the provisional government groups (see *Japan Times*, November 25, 1967, and *Free China
Weekly*, December 10, 1967, p. 4).

42. Recent refugee publications in Tokyo are *Taiwan Dokuritsuho* [Report
on Formosan Independence] (Tokyo: Taiwan Dokuritsu Doshisha)
which began in 1963, and the *Taiwan Seinenho* [Formosan Youth
News], published by the United Young Formosans in 1966.

43. See *Independent Formosa*, October 1967, for complete details of the
arrest, and petitions, and protests to the Japanese government. *Japan
Times*, March 4, 1967, reported the suicide of Lu Chuan-sin, 31, to
avoid deportation to Taiwan, and a letter from an overseas Chinese held
at the Yokohama deportation center (*Japan Times*, August 21, 1966).
Other Formosans held at Omura, Kyushu, according to a letter from
an inmate, July 9, 1966, were moved to Yokohama in 1969.

44. See the April 1968 issue of the UYFI magazine *Taiwan,* and *Japan Times,* March 28, 1968 for details of the Liu case. In a similar incident, friends of a 29-year-old Formosan graduate student, who had been at the University of Hawaii before continuing his research in Japan, claimed the Tokyo immigration office had bundled him aboard a China Air Lines plane February 9, 1968. They learned of a Nationalist five-year sentence against him the following June (*Yomiuri Shimbun,* June 20, 1968).

45. *Japan Times,* November 25 and 28, 1967.

46. Interview in Okayama, November 30, 1962.

47. Interviews in Okayama, August 9, 1962 and August 1966.

48. See my letters in the *Christian Science Monitor,* December 29, 1967 and February 5, 1968, and the rebuttal by Nationalist Chinese information officer I-cheng Loh of New York, January 20, 1968.

49. Unpublished letter from Professor Ronald Chen, Kansas State College of Pittsburg, February 10, 1968 to *Christian Science Monitor,* giving names of two Tokyo University students and one National Taiwan University graduate arrested in 1967.

50. Conversations of September 1 and 2, 1965.

51. See pro-independence ads in the Kansas State University student newspaper, *Collegian,* March 1 and November 29, 1966, and articles in the same paper January 14, 17, 18, and 19; and February 7, 1966 and March 29 and May 2, 1967. The last-cited was a letter from Richard Wang, alumnus of KSU who told of difficulties obtaining extension of his passport in 1963 and 1966.

52. Letter, June 5, 1966, applauding my objection to a review of George Kerr's *Formosa Betrayed* in the *Asian Student,* a publication of the Asia Foundation in San Francisco (see the *Asian Student* issues of April 9 and 23, 1966).

53. Letter, July 26, 1967.

54. Letter, March 5, 1967.

55. Letter, 1966. "I was the only Formosan in the X Ministry, and gradually became disgusted with the mainlander officials . . ." At last report, he was employed safely in Formosa "awaiting an opportune time to do something to reach our aim: the independence of Formosa, which cannot be achieved without risks and sacrifices."

56. Letter, January 16, 1968.

57. *The New York Times,* March 4, 1967. See also *Independent Formosa,* VI, 3 (June 1967), pp. 4–5.

58. Telegram, March 17, 1967.

59. See *The New York Times,* May 14 and August 9, 1967; and Melvin Gurtov, "Recent Developments in Formosa," *China Quarterly,* July–September 1967, pp. 59–95, especially p. 88.

60. Letter from Timothy Bradbury of NSA, May 8, 1967.

61. *China News,* July 21, 1967.

62. Letter, May 3, 1965.

63. Letter, February 8, 1966.

64. Letter, May 29, 1965.
65. Conversations in Chicago and Milwaukee, September and November, 1967.
66. Letter, April 9, 1965.
67. Letter, October 31, 1964.

Chapter 8

1. Peter P. C. Cheng, "The Formosa Tangle: A Formosan's View," *Asian Survey,* November 1967, p. 806.
2. See, especially, John K. Fairbank, *The United States and China,* revised edition (New York: The Viking Press, 1962); Edgar Snow, *China, Russia, and the U.S.A.* (New York: Marzani and Munsell, 1962); Robert Blum and A. Doak Barnett, *The United States and China in World Affairs* (New York: McGraw-Hill, 1966); and A. T. Steele, *The American People and China* (New York: McGraw-Hill, 1966).
3. David Schoenbrun, "The Empty Chair at the UN," *Diplomat Magazine,* XVII, 196, (September 1966), p. 121.
4. U.S. Department of State, *United States Relations with China, with Special Reference to the Period 1944–1949* (Washington, D.C.: Department of State Publication 3573, Far Eastern Series 30, 1949). Kerr's report of 1947 is on pp. 923–938. For other versions of this period, see Tang Tsou, *America's Failure in China 1941–1950* (Chicago: University of Chicago Press, 1963), chs. 9–11; and Herbert Feis, *Japan Subdued* (Princeton: Princeton University Press, 1961).
5. *Department of State Bulletin,* January 15, 1950, p. 79.
6. *Ibid.,* July 3, 1950, p. 50.
7. Kerr, *Formosa Betrayed, op. cit.,* pp. 404–405.
8. *Department of State Bulletin,* September 19, 1951, p. 462.
9. *Ibid.,* (XXXI), 1954, p. 899.
10. *Congressional Record,* February 9, 1955, p. 138. For arguments favoring the Nationalists' legal right to Formosa see Frank Morello, *The International Legal Status of Formosa* (The Hague: Martinus Nijhoff, 1966), pp. 93–98.
11. U.S. Senate Committee on Foreign Relations, *Report on Mutual Security Treaty with the Republic of China.* Executive Report No. 2, 84th Congress, 1st Session 1955, p. 14.
12. See D. F. Fleming, "Our Brink-of-War Diplomacy," *Western Political Quarterly,* IX, September 1956, pp. 535–552 and Robert P. Newman, *Recognition of Communist China?* (New York: Macmillan paperback, 1961), ch. 5.
13. For the Dulles and Herter statements, and Chiang Kai-shek's bitter reaction, see *The New York Times,* September 29, October 1, and October 2, 1958.
14. William J. Lederer, *A Nation of Sheep* (New York: W. W. Norton,

1961), ch. 3, "What We Aren't Told About Formosa." Lederer cites an article by Tang Tsou as a good background to the offshore island issue: "The Quemoy Imbroglio: Chiang Kai-shek and the United States," *Western Political Quarterly*, December 1959, pp. 1075–1091.

15. Arthur M. Schlesinger, Jr., *A Thousand Days* (Boston: Houghton-Mifflin, 1965) p. 483–484.

16. Harry S Truman, *Memoirs, v. 2, Years of Trial and Hope* (New York: Doubleday, 1956), p. 403.

17. Kenneth Young, "American Dealings with Peking," *Foreign Affairs*, (45,1) October 1966, pp. 81–82. Harold Hinton reports the 1962 crisis in more detail in his *Communist China in World Politics* (Boston: Houghton-Mifflin, 1966), especially pp. 270–272.

18. Reuters dispatch, *Christian Science Monitor*, July 11, 1967.

19. *China News*, August 6, 1967. This editorial typifies Nationalist press suspicions of American reliability throughout the 1961–1968 period.

20. Rowland Evans and Robert Novak, *Lyndon B. Johnson: The Exercise of Power* (New York: New American Library, 1966), p. 171.

21. Letter, May 23, 1966.

22. *Department of State Bulletin*, September 8, 1958, p. 389.

23. *Ibid.*, March 14, 1960, p. 410.

24. Letter from Mr. Popple, April 23, 1963.

25. Interviews in Taichung, April 1962, and with a press officer in the Tokyo Embassy later that year.

26. Interview in Taichung, April 1962.

27. Statement of Marshall Green, later Assistant Secretary of State (Far East) at the University of Wisconsin-Milwaukee, March 21, 1964, as reported in *Foreign Policy Problems—1964, Proceedings of the Eighth Annual Institute on United States Foreign Policy* (Milwaukee: UWM Institute for World Affairs Education, 1964) p. 64.

28. Harriman's reply to a Formosan student's question at Madison, May 13, 1965.

29. George W. Ball, *The Discipline of Power* (Boston: Little, Brown, 1968), pp. 178–179.

30. Interview with Mr. Kennan at the Woodrow Wilson School of Public and International Affairs, Princeton, January 16, 1964.

31. *China Daily News*, New York, January 20, 1965, quoting Tao Pai-chuan's article in the Taipei *Lien Ho Pao*, January 4. Kennan's article, "Japanese Security and American Policy," appeared in *Foreign Affairs*, October 1964, pp. 14–28.

32. *Foreign Affairs*, April 1960, pp. 478–479.

33. Statement by Reischauer in *Asia, the Pacific, and the United States*, a Hearing before the Committee on Foreign Relations, U.S. Senate, January 31, 1967 (Washington: U.S. Government Printing Office, 1967) p. 26.

34. Edwin O. Reischauer, *Wanted—An Asian Policy* (New York: Alfred A. Knopf) p. 242.

35. *China News*, February 3, 1967. See also Reischauer's *Beyond Vietnam*

(New York: Alfred A. Knopf, 1967), pp. 174–177, for reiteration of his support for self-determination, qualified as "two Chinas" rather than Formosan native control.

36. Allen S. Whiting and Robert A. Scalapino, "The United States and Taiwan," in Willard Thorp, ed., *The United States and the Far East* (Englewood Cliffs, N.J.: Prentice-Hall-Spectrum 1962), pp. 171–172.

37. See, for example, the exchange between Senators Knowland and Fulbright in the *Congressional Record*, 83rd Congress, 2nd Session, August 17, 1954, pp. 14793–14796.

38. *China News*, April 11, 1967. Another ex-member of Congress considered very friendly to the Nationalists, Clare Boothe Luce, told a San Francisco audience that Washington should recognize Peking if the latter accepted Taiwan's independence (Daniel Tretiak, "Sino-American Impasse," *Far Eastern Economic Review*, January 7, 1965, p. 16).

39. Letter, June 19, 1964.

40. Letter, November 3, 1966.

41. Allen J. Ellender, A *Report of United States Foreign Policy and Operations* (Washington, D.C.: Senate Document 73, 87th Congress, 2nd Session, March 1, 1962), pp. 125–130.

42. *Congressional Record*, September 4, 1964, pp. 15486–15490.

43. *Ibid.*, July 9, 1963, p. 11606.

44. *Asahi*, Tokyo, March 28, 1966.

45. *China News*, May 10, 1966.

46. Senate speech of May 26, 1958 as reprinted in *The Voice of Korea* (Washington, D.C.: Korean Affairs Institute), June 27, 1958. For Mansfield's 1968 view, see "China: Retrospect and Prospect," in the *War/Peace Report*, May 1968, pp. 7–11.

47. Letter, January 24, 1967. Senator George McGovern wrote similar opinions ("I agree with you about the importance of self-determination for the people of Formosa") in a letter of July 6, 1966 (see McGovern's Senate Speech on China policy in the *Congressional Record*, May 3, 1966).

48. Letter, January 15, 1964.

49. See *China News*, January 28, 1967. Justice Douglas confirmed this view in a letter, February 10, 1967 ("The quote . . . is an accurate one. I have no manuscript. It was a speech I made from notes.").

50. *Cheng Fu-sheng and Lin Fu-mei v. William F. Rogers*, Civil Action 2580-59, United States District Court for the District of Columbia, October 6, 1959. See also Ely Maurer, "Legal Problems Regarding Formosa and the Offshore Islands," Department of State Bulletin, December 22, 1958, pp. 1005–1011. Judge Holtzoff took the last sentence quoted here directly from p. 1009 of this article by the then Assistant Legal Officer for Far Eastern Affairs, delivered originally on November 20, 1958 to the Washington chapter of the Federal Bar Association. Mr. Maurer confirmed his view to my assistant in August 1965.

51. Letter, February 24, 1969.

52. A. T. Steele, *The American People and China* (New York: McGraw-Hill for the Council on Foreign Relations, 1966), Appendix, p. 257.

The national survey was conducted by the University of Michigan Survey Research Center in May and June 1964. Survey data are available from the Council in a pamphlet, *The American Public's View of U.S. Policy Toward China* (1964).

53. *Ibid.*, p. 272.
54. *Ibid.*, pp. 47–48.
55. Gallup poll data from the American Institute of Public Opinion, Princeton, New Jersey, as filed in the Roper Public Opinion Research Center, Williamstown, Mass. The September 1958 Poll was #605 in the AIPO series, which also includes periodic questions on U.N. representation, trust in Nationalist China as a reliable ally, and related topics. Sentiment against the seating of Peking in the U.N. ranged from 6 to 1 in the mid-1950's to less than 3 to 1 in 1968.
56. Steele, *op. cit.*, pp. 49, 52.
57. *Ibid.*, p. 50.
58. For the Wrights' testimony on their firm's relations with Nationalist China, see U.S. Senate, Committee on Foreign Relations, *Activities of Non-diplomatic Representatives of Foreign Principals in the United States, Part 10* (Washington: July 10, 1963), pp. 1481–1482. Hamilton Wright, Jr.'s letter was dated November 15, 1963. In conversation with me, he claimed his firm cancelled the contract because the Nationalists wanted the firm to promote U.S. support for a counterattack, "which was a propaganda job we could not approve."
59. Conversations in Kaohsiung, March and April 1962, and in Tokyo, August 1966.
60. Letter, April 6, 1967.
61. Letters sent from Taipei, August 15, and Hong Kong, August 19, 1966.
62. *New York Times*, December 22, 1964, from an editorial titled "Taiwan Success Story." See also *Washington Post*, April 4, 1968: "Taiwan is not ours to lump into one China or cement into two Chinas. It is, ultimately, the birthright of the people who live there."
63. *Capitol Times*, Madison, November 13, 1965.
64. Letter, April 21, 1965.
65. David Schoenbrun, "The Empty Chair at the U.N.," *op. cit.*, p. 120.
66. Letter, May 27, 1966.
67. William J. Lederer, *A Nation of Sheep*, *op. cit.*, ch. 3.
68. Letter, March 9, 1967, when Lederer was a research associate at Harvard University. See also Albert Axelbank, "Chiang Kai-shek's Secret Enemies," *Harper's*, September 1963, pp. 45–52, and his articles, "The Shackled Press in Formosa," International Press Institute *Report*, September 1963, and "News Management in Asia," *Bulletin* of the Overseas Press Club of America, June 8, 1963. Ironically, the Nationalist regime included three of Axelbank's 1961 UPI stories in its information pamphlet, *After Seeing Free China* (Taipei: Government Information Office, 1962).
69. *Saturday Evening Post*, November 14, 1964, editorial, "Needed: A China policy that makes sense," p. 86.
70. *Wall Street Journal*, editorial, "After Mao," November 14, 1967.

71. The *Christian Science Monitor* editorialized on "Formosa in Calmer Waters," discounting native opposition, December 7, 1967. See my rebuttal letter (December 29, 1967) and one by an anonymous Cambridge student (January 3, 1968).

72. For the text of the statement, see *The New York Times*, March 21, 1966 p. 12. Most signatories belonged to the Association for Asian Studies, but that organization disavowed any connection.

73. Letter, July 16, 1964, and various conversations.

74. Letter, December 14, 1963.

75. Letter, January 12, 1964.

76. Letter, September 27, 1967.

77. Letter, October 14, 1966. This man avoided discussing politics with Formosans because he wished to remain on the island for a long time, and to stay on good terms with the Nationalist officials whose cooperation facilitated his research.

78. John K. Fairbank, "Taiwan: Myth, Dream, and Nightmare," *The New Republic*, February 5, 1966, pp. 11–13. See also Fairbank's testimony in *U.S. Policy with Respect to Mainland China*, U.S. Senate Committee on Foreign Relations, 89th Congress, 2nd Session, 1966, p. 177: "I have been concerned for a long time about the future of Taiwan because it seems to me it deserves to be an independent country in its own right. It has its own resources and native life now. It is, in fact, a country bigger than about two-thirds of the U.N. members . . . When one mentions the idea of an independent Taiwan, one is known as a capitalist spy in Peking, and a Communist traitor in Taipei."

79. Robert A. Scalapino, *New Perspectives on Northeast Asia* (San Francisco: Northern California ADA, 1961), p. 31. See also Scalapino's strong letter of protest against the imprisonment of Lei Chen in *The New York Times*, September 27, 1960: "Where is Free China? Not on the mainland certainly, but not in Taiwan either . . . We shall either develop a China policy that includes the principle that all citizens of Taiwan shall have a voice in determining their future and participating in their government, or we shall ultimately face the hostility of the Taiwanese people themselves. Once again history will charge us with shielding a decadent dictatorship."

80. *China News*, December 10, 1966.

81. Barnett, *Communist China and Asia* (New York: Random House, 1960), p. 422. See also U.S. Senate, *U.S. Policy with Respect to China*, *op. cit.*, pp. 14 and 57.

82. *Japan Times* (Tokyo), January 3, 1967.

83. U.S. Senate, *U.S. Policy with Respect to China*, *op. cit.*, pp. 456, 466–467. Judd said "the pressures toward democracy are irresistible on Taiwan . . . but no country goes too far in holding wholly free elections during war . . . Considering circumstances, I admire the extent to which they have gone toward democracy of our sort." Taylor agreed, stressing the "truly remarkable economic revolution in Taiwan."

84. *Ibid.*, pp. 496–505. Rowe disputed a letter by Vera Micheles Dean, pub-

lished in *The New York Times,* March 18, 1966, in which she hoped that "the ghosts of Senator McCarthy and the Committee of One Million would be exorcised." See also *The Reporter* articles on "The China Lobby," April 12 and 29, 1952.

85. Harold S. Quigley, *China's Politics in Perspective* (Minneapolis: University of Minnesota Press, 1962) p. 172. Harold M. Vinacke, another prewar specialist on Asian politics, took a more pro-Nationalist position in his *United States Policy Toward China* (Occasional Paper No. 1, Center for the Study of U.S. Foreign Policy, University of Cincinnati, 1961), p. 52: "It would be clearly within the limits set by our treaty obligations to the National Government for Washington to seek to bring about acceptance of status for Taiwan separate from China. The advantage of such a change of United States policy is not clear unless proposed by the National Government itself or urged by others. Consequently, on balance, it must be concluded that there should be no immediate change in policy *vis-à-vis* Taiwan and support of the National Government."

86. Harold Hinton, *Communist China in World Politics, op. cit.,* p. 496. Also: "In general, it is clear that the United States is in no position to dislodge entrenched governments, however disagreeable . . . there is no alternative but to wait for the passage of time, aided to be sure by discreet pressures when appropriate, to mellow the KMT and its relations with the Formosans, who will probably tend to absorb them over the long run. More drastic action might have even worse results, such as forcing the KMT into the arms of the Communists" (from a letter from Dr. Hinton, February 26, 1966).

87. O. Edmund Clubb, "Sino-American Relations and the Future of Formosa," *Political Science Quarterly,* March 1965, pp. 17, 21.

88. Letter, July 20, 1965.

89. Conversation with Professor James W. Morley, June 9, 1963. Professor Martin Wilbur of Columbia University objected to American scholars writing critical articles after having enjoyed Nationalist hospitality (comment at the Association for Asian Studies meeting, San Francisco, April 1965).

90. Letter, January 4, 1967.

91. Andrew T. Roy, *On Asia's Rim* (New York: Friendship Press, 1962), pp. 94, 98, 113, 119. Roy expanded his comments in conversation with me at Chung Chi College, now part of the Chinese University, Hong Kong, where he served as dean, May 1963.

Chapter 9

1. Interview at the Japanese Foreign Ministry, December 1957.

2. See especially: Shao Chuan Leng, *Japan and Communist China* (Kyoto: Doshisha University Press, 1958); Shigeharu Matsumoto, "Japan and

China" in A. M. Halpern, ed., *Policies Toward China: Views from Six Continents* (New York: McGraw-Hill, 1965); A. Doak Barnett, *Communist China and Asia* (New York: Harper and Brothers, 1960) ch. 10; and Harold Hinton, *Communist China in World Politics* (Boston: Houghton-Mifflin, 1966), ch. 14.

3. *China News*, December 3, 1967.
4. *Ibid.*, October 25, 1967.
5. *Japan Times*, September 9, 1967.
6. *Mainichi*, Tokyo, December 7, 1956.
7. Interview at the Japanese Foreign Ministry, November 19, 1962.
8. *Yomiuri Shimbun*, Tokyo, April 4, 1958, and *Mainichi Shimbun*, January 6, 1959. A Japanese rightist tore down the Chinese Communist flag at the Nagasaki trade fair, but legally this was a minor offense because Japan had no diplomatic relations with Peking. During 1959, Japan relaxed the fingerprinting requirement for alien registration cards, mainly because of the Peking objections. For developments prior to 1958, see James W. Morley, *Soviet and Chinese Communist Policies toward Japan* (New York: Institute of Pacific Relations, 1958); for related issues, Martin Wilbur, "Japan and the Rise of Communist China," in Hugh Borton, ed., *Japan Between East and West* (New York: Harper's, 1957).
9. *Seikai Orai*, Tokyo, November 1963; *Summary of Selected Japanese Magazines* (Tokyo: U.S. Embassy), January 13, 1964.
10. *Japan Times*, September 30, 1963; *Asahi Evening News*, October 12, 1963.
11 *Asahi Evening News*, October 10, 1963.
12. *Japan Times*, November 2, 1963 and January 11–14, 1964.
13. Letter, October 12, 1964. This graduate student wrote to agree with opinions expressed in my article, "Japan's Taiwan Tangle," *Asian Survey*, October 1964, pp. 1073–1084. Formosan and foreign observers whom I interviewed in Taiwan during September 1964 confirmed this report. They said the front door of the Japanese Embassy was patched, and that officials and shopkeepers nearby believed the vandals had been Nationalist-inspired.
14. *Japan Times*, August 3 and October 29, 1965, and March 8, 1968. Sato reaffirmed the Yoshida letter in a 1968 campaign speech (*Free China Weekly*, July 7, 1968).
15. *China Yearbook 1965–1966*, *op. cit.*, pp. 228–229.
16. *China News* editorial, May 20, 1967.
17. Melvin Gurtov, "Taiwan in 1966: Political Rigidity, Economic Growth," *Asian Survey*, January 1967, p. 42.
18. *China Post*, May 1, 1965; *China News*, June 28, 1963, and May 30, 1967.
19. Interview, Taipei, July 9, 1962.
20. *China News*, January 9, 1966.
21. Interview at the Japanese Foreign Ministry, September 8, 1964.
22. Interviews in Tokyo, July 9, 1961; February 1962; and February 1963.

23. Interview, February 25, 1963, in Tokyo.
24. Interview in Tokyo, July 27, 1966.
25. Interview in Tokyo, August 1, 1966.
26. Interview in Tokyo, August 1, 1966.
27. Interview in Hong Kong, November 2, 1962.
28. Interview in Hong Kong, November 2, 1962.
29. Interview in Canberra, September 18, 1962.
30. Interview in Washington, D.C., September 10, 1965.
31. Interview with Admiral Hasegawa, Tokyo, February 14, 1963.
32. Interview with Admiral Takahashi, Tokyo, January 14, 1963.
33. Interview with Marshal Hata, Tokyo, November 20, 1957.
34. See Kazuo Kuroda in the *Japan Times*, July 15, 1967. Kuroda expressed the same view earlier to the writer.
35. Okinori Kaya, *The Communist China Policy of the Government and the Liberal-Democratic Party* (Tokyo: Japan National Foreign Affairs Association, n.d.), pp. 14–20. Kaya is president of this Association.
36. Interview in Tokyo March 4, 1963. Kaya later criticized the LDP "doves (whose) policy of appeasement toward Communist China is meaningless and rather dangerous" (*Japan Times*, June 1, 1968).
37. *Japan Times*, Tokyo, May 20, 1967.
38. Interview in Tokyo, March 12, 1963.
39. Interview in Tokyo, March 5, 1963.
40. Interview in Tokyo, August 28, 1964.
41. Interview in Tokyo, July 27, 1962.
42. Interview in Tokyo, July 22, 1966.
43. See Miki's statement on China policy, *Japan Times*, July 12, 1967.
44. Interview, August 24, 1961.
45. Interview, August 21, 1964.
46. Interview, Hotel New Japan, July 26, 1962.
47. Interview at Ishii's home in Tokyo, July 25, 1962.
48. Interview, September 8, 1961.
49. Interview with Osaka assemblyman Kaginaka, November 26, 1962 in Osaka City Hall.
50. Interview with Matsumura in Tokyo, July 27, 1961. See also Matsumura's views in the *Toyo Keizai* (*Selected Summaries of Japanese Magazines* (SSJM), June 27, 1966) and the *Tokyo Shimbun* (*Daily Summary of Japanese Press*, December 2, 1964), the latter following the exchange of newsmen.
51. Interview in Tokyo, July 27, 1966.
52. Quoted in the *Seikai Orai*, Tokyo, as translated in the *SSJM*, January 13, 1964, pp. 1–8.
53. *Ibid.*, p. 14.
54. Interview with Nishio, September 5, 1961.
55. Quoted in *Doko*, as translated in the *SSJM*, October 17, 1966. Some Eki of the DSP had told me on February 18, 1963 that "Our party doesn't take a clear stand on Taiwan's future, but it should be some kind of UN settlement, then a plebiscite ten years later . . . There is

much support for a separate Taiwan because the natives there don't like
Chiang government and our policy succeeded in Taiwan better than in
Korea . . ."

56. From an article in the party organ, *Komei Shimbun*, May 21, 1968,
quoting Ninomiya Bunzo.

57. Interview with Matsumoto in Tokyo, August 2, 1961.

58. Speech by Hozumi at the Kudan Kaidan, Tokyo, February 28, 1962.

59. Interview with Wada at the JSP party headquarters, Tokyo, August 16,
1961.

60. Interview with Katsumata, July 1966, *China News*, Taipei, February 11,
1966.

61. Interview with Kanzaki at the Osaka City Hall, November 29, 1962.

62. Interview with Shiga, August 24, 1964. Shiga lost his Diet seat in 1966
due to JCP opposition.

63. *Japan Times*, July 11, 1967.

64. Mendel, *The Japanese People* . . . , *op. cit.*, pp. 238–239. A December 1965 study approved the UN seating of Peking by 34—11 per cent,
compared with a 40—13 per cent vote in a 1958 USIA survey. See the
writer's articles, "Japan Reviews her American Alliance," *Public Opinion Quarterly*, Spring 1966, pp. 1–18, and "Japanese Views of Sato's
Foreign Policy: The Credibility Gap," *Asian Survey*, July 1967, pp.
444–456.

65. *Asian Survey*, *ibid.*, pp. 452–455, and my article, "Security Without
Arms" in *Far Eastern Economic Review* (Hong Kong), January 16,
1969, pp. 102–103.

66. My 1957 Japanese national and regional samples were asked if they
favored the use of force to protect Japanese fishermen then being seized
by South Korean gunboats (often converted from captured Japanese
fishing vessels). Only 10 per cent approved. See *The Japanese People*
. . . , *op. cit.*, pp. 184–186.

67. *Ibid.*, pp. 230–232.

68. Interview with Kondo Toshikyo, author of the excellent book *Taiwan no
Meiun* [The Fate of Formosa] (Tokyo: Misuzu Books, 1961), in Tokyo,
1963.

69. Interviews in Tokyo, August 12, 1966. The Asahi Research Room study
is titled, *Taiwan, Its international status, politics, and economics* (To-
kyo: Asahi Shimbun Chosa Kenkyushitsu, 2 vols., 1965, confidential).
Other Japanese studies include *Taiwan no Hyojo* [The Face of Formosa]
by Hosono Akio and five other members of the Southeast Asia Study
Group (Tokyo: Kokon Shoin, 1963); Omura Tatsuzo, *Futatsu no
Chukoku* [The Two Chinas], (Tokyo: Kobundo, 1961); and Kiuchi
Nobutane, *Gendai no Taiwan* [Contemporary Formosa], (Tokyo: Sekai
Keizai Chosokai, 1961).

70. Interview in Tokyo, February 28, 1963.

71. Interview in Tokyo, January 18, 1963.

72. Interview with Hasegawa Saiji of *Jiji Press*, February 26, 1963.

73. Hosono and others, *op. cit.*, pp. 35–37.

74. Interview in Tokyo, February 7, 1963.
75. Reported in an interview at American Embassy, Tokyo, February 12, 1962. Later that year a group of more conservative Kyoto University scholars assured me that "Taiwanese are indeed different from Chinese and it is easy for us to spot the difference . . . Taiwan has the base for a viable economy, unlike South Korea . . . and we should all study it more" (interviews, December 9, 1962).
76. "Principles of Red Chinese Foreign Policy Conduct," *Jiyu* (Freedom), February 1965, pp. 44–45, written with Okabe Tatsumi. See also their article in *Sekai*, March 1965.
77. Interview in Fukuoka, April 4, 1963.
78. Ohira Zengo, "Two Chinas is No Myth," *Jiyu*, May 1961, pp. 2–9, as translated in the *Journal of Japanese Social and Political Ideas*, April 1966, pp. 69–72. (Ohira signed the 1967 petition against the deportation of two Formosan students; see details in the *Independent Formosa*, October 1967, pp. 22–23.)
79. Interview in Tokyo, August 28, 1964.
80. Interview with Okazaki Kaheita, August 26, 1964.
81. Interview with Sakaguchi Shuzei, Kumamoto, April 3, 1963.
82. Interview in Hong Kong, November 5, 1962.
83. Letter, November 8, 1966.
84. *Free China Weekly*, February 4, 1968. Wei spoke to a closed session of the Control Yuan.
85. *China News*, September 17, 1967.
86. *Ibid.*, November 18, 1967 (an editorial titled "Japan is Close Enough"). See also an editorial in the *China Post*, August 2, 1967. The dean of the Soochow University Law School near Taipei, often a spokesman for the KMT regime, told me on May 8, 1962 that "Japan would not be satisfied with Okinawa as she wasn't satisfied with it before, but would also want Taiwan, Manchuria, and other areas. We cannot trust her."
87. American authorities in Okinawa have sent hundreds of Okinawans to Formosa for periods up to six months on technical training assignments, and even to study "freedom of the press." See *Konnichi no Ryukyu* [Ryukyus Today], published monthly by the U.S. Civil Administration of the Ryukyu Islands, 1 February 1965 and the two succeeding issues, for the article "Formosa as we saw it," written by three Okinawan travellers to Formosa. The same magazine published a three-part report by Ryukyu Chief Executive Ota Seisaku, prewar governor of the Pescadores islands ("My Trip to Taiwan," October–December 1963).
88. Interview in Naha, April 16, 1963.
89. Interview in Naha, April 14, 1963.
90. Interview in Naha office of *Okinawa Times*, August 17, 1966.
91. Interview in Naha, August 18, 1966.

Chapter 10

1. Letter from Washington, October 14, 1965.
2. See *China News*, January 1, 1968, for President Chiang's dismissal of the Communist nuclear threat to Formosa.
3. Chen Han-seng, "Taiwan—China's Largest Island," *China Reconstructs* (Peking), January 1955, pp. 18–21.
4. *New York Times*, January 19, 1956.
5. *New York Times*, September 26, 1956.
6. For examples, see *Oppose U.S. Occupation of Taiwan and the "Two Chinas" Plot—A Selection of Important Documents* (Peking: Foreign Language Press, 1958) and occasional issues that year of the weekly *Peking Review*.
7. Letter from the China Publications Centre, Peking, September 9, 1964.
8. Letter from Chiang Chun of the China Publications Centre (*Guozi Shudian*) October 27, 1964. See also a statement of Chou En-lai reported by Felix Greene: "The United States seeks to set up what they call an 'independent state' of Taiwan, or a 'Sino-Formosan nation,' or to conduct what they call a 'plebiscite' in Taiwan, or even to place Taiwan 'under trusteeship,' and so on. All this is aimed at dismembering Chinese territory, violating China's sovereign rights and legalizing the seizure of Taiwan by the United States. All the Chinese people, including those on Taiwan, are firmly opposed to these schemes; even those members of the Chiang Kai-shek clique who have the slightest concern for the national interest don't approve of them" (quoted in H. Arthur Steiner, "Communist China in the World Community," *International Conciliation*, May 1961), p. 442.
9. Edgar Snow, *The Other Side of the River* (New York: Random House, 1962), pp. 760, 765–766. Chou's interview appears in the appendix which, along with chapters 80–86, was reprinted in a paperback edition titled, *China, Russia, and the U.S.A.* (New York: Marzani and Munsell, 1962).
10. Interview with Mori Shonai, Osaka, November 26, 1962.
11. Interview with Nishimura Chiuro of the *Yomiuri*, Tokyo, August 5, 1966.
12. Letter from Dr. H. C. Ling, December 28, 1966. In our interview in his Hong Kong offices the previous August, Dr. Ling had denied the possibility of an independent future for Formosa.
13. Peter P. C. Cheng, "The Formosan Tangle: A Formosan's View," *Asian Survey*, November 1967, p. 797. All attempts to meet such pro-Peking Formosans in Japan were rebuffed, and I heard of none inside the island.
14. Kondo, *Taiwan no meiun* [The Fate of Taiwan], p. 164.
15. See Thomas W. Robinson, "A National Interest Analysis of Sino-Soviet Relations," *International Studies Quarterly*, June 1967, pp. 135–175.

Robinson considers "control of Taiwan" a major Chinese interest not shared by Russia: "Witness Soviet refusal to back the Chinese in the Taiwan Straits in 1958" (p. 170).

16. *Christian Science Monitor,* May 26, 1966. The same theme was repeated in many issues of *Peking Review* and domestic Chinese publications throughout the 1963–1969 period. See especially *Peking Review,* March 7 and 14, 1969.

17. Interview at Princeton, January 1964.

18. Quoted in *Tokyo Shimbun,* December 12, 1967, as translated in *Daily Summary of Japanese Press* (Tokyo: American Embassy, Political Section, Translation Services Branch), December 16–18, 1967, pp. 13–15.

19. See Premier Fidel Castro's attack on Mao in *The New York Times,* March 15, 1966: "Someday the Chinese will rid themselves of their rulers."

20. *Hsinhua* news release, July 1956, 062837, VI, p. 350.

21. *London Observer,* August 12, 1962. See also *The New York Times,* August 12, 1962 and February 8, 1957, and Snow, *op. cit.,* pp. 765–766.

22. *The New York Times,* August 13, 1962, and *Free China* (Taipei), July 16, 1956, pp. 3–4, detail the Nationalist denials.

23. *Japan Times,* July 21, 1965, reported that Li was greeted at the Peking airport by Premier Chou En-lai and three vice-premiers.

24. *China News,* September 27, 1965. Li said "The U.S. has publicly announced at home and abroad that it has no territorial ambition, then why does it deem it necessary to intervene in the internal affairs of China and send its Seventh Fleet to occupy China's territory of Taiwan?" (Li died in early 1969.)

25. Letter from "D. J. Spencer," July 12, 1966.

26. Warren Unna, "New View of Peking," *Washington Post,* December 1, 1964. See also a similar view by a Japanese writer, Mori Kyojo, in *Taiwan Chinglian,* November 1966, p. 14.

27. Interviews in the Department of Defense, Washington, September 1964 and June 1966.

28. Dennis Bloodworth, *The Chinese Looking Glass* (New York: Farrar, Straus, and Giroux, 1967), pp. 358–360.

29. Interview in Tokyo, August 1, 1966. For American statements favoring peaceful amalgamation see Harold Hinton, *Communist China in World Affairs* (Boston: Houghton-Mifflin, 1966), p. 496, and *A New China Policy: Some Quaker Proposals* (New Haven: Yale University Press, 1965), p. 57.

30. "Peking asserted that these ambitions [to reoccupy Taiwan] had motivated Premier Eisaku Sato and Foreign Minister Etsusaburo Shiina in giving support to the concept of self-determination for the eight million Formosans" (*Milwaukee Journal,* December 13, 1964, part 1, p. 3).

31. Frank Morello, *International Legal Status of Formosa* (The Hague: Martinus Nijhoff, 1966), pp. 28 and 94.

32. Letter from I-chung Loh, director of the Chinese News Service, New York, February 28, 1964.

33. *China News,* December 19, 1967.
34. *Ibid.,* December 24, 1967.
35. Interview in Tokyo, August 28, 1964.
36. Chiao-min Hsieh, *China—Ageless Land and Countless People* (Princeton: D. Van Nostrand, 1967), p. 104.
37. Interview in Milwaukee, Wis., July 26, 1965.
38. For background on Ching-kuo see the *Japan Times,* September 28, 1966; the *Asia Magazine,* August 21, 1966, and James Cattey, "Chiang's Son and Formosa's Future," *Milwaukee Journal,* October 25, 1964. Cattey, *op. cit.,* See also a report in the *Central Daily News,* Taipei, January 31, 1967, of the appointment of Ching-kuo's son, Shao-wen, as director of the Anti-Communist Youth Corps. Formosan students who had known Shao-wen as a youth called him Chiang III because he always reminded people he was the Gimo's grandson. He was said to have engaged in gang fights, and to have been "expelled from a school in California for numerous speeding offenses" (letter from a Formosan student, February 1967).
39. Lung-chu Chen and Harold Lasswell, *Formosa, China, and the United Nations* (New York: St. Martin's Press, 1967), pp. 152–153.
40. Joshua Liao, *Formosa Speaks* (Hong Kong: Formosan League for Re-emancipation, 1950), iv. The late Joshua Liao was the elder brother of Dr. Thomas Liao. This 59-page pamphlet was the Formosan nationalists' first major appeal in English directed to the U.N.
41. For a fuller treatment of how every U.N. member voted on these resolutions see Chen and Lasswell, *op. cit.,* Appendix, pp. 403–412.
42. *China News,* November 18, 1967. See also Kao Yung-an, "Justice Prevails at the U.N.," *Free China Review,* January 1967, pp. 9–18.
43. Urban Whitaker, "The United Nations and the Future of Formosa," *Ilha Formosa,* January 1963, pp. 5–8. Dr. Whitaker's unpublished interviews with a large number of U.N. missions in the 1962–1963 session showed wide off-the-record support for a "one China, one Formosa" formula, but the votes on the study committee proposal indicated a continuing lack of open support.
44. Chen and Lasswell, *op. cit.,* p. 240.
45. Richard Harris, "Britain and China," in A. M. Halpern, ed., *Policies toward China: Views from Six Continents* (New York: McGraw-Hill, 1965), pp. 28–29. Harris was the Far Eastern correspondent for *The Times* of London. The Labour M.P. quoted therein, John Mendelson, expressed similar views in a 1967 conversation.
46. *Japan Times,* October 26, 1965.
47. Letter from Victor J. Lloyd, December 1, 1966.
48. *Economist* (London), April 2, 1966, as quoted in the *Chosa Geppo* (Monthly survey) (Tokyo: Cabinet Research Office), May 1966, pp. 78–79.
49. *The Times* (London), October 30, 1967.
50. John W. Holmes, in "Canada and China," in A. M. Halpern, *op. cit.,*

p. 106, 111. Holmes was director general of the Canadian Institute of International Affairs.

51. *Ibid.*, p. 110.
52. *Far Eastern Economic Review* (Hong Kong), October 15, 1967, p. 132.
53. Coral Bell, "Australia and China," in A. M. Halpern, *op. cit.*, p. 186. See also Henry Albinski, *Australian Policies and Attitudes toward China* (Princeton: Princeton University Press, 1966).
54. *Sydney Morning Herald*, September 11, 1958. Three-fourths of Australian Liberal party voters but only 59 per cent of Laborites favored defense of Formosa in 1955. Another poll showed that 60 per cent of Australians and 64 per cent of New Zealanders would be willing to visit mainland China if invited (from a Roy Morgan Australian Gallup Survey in December 1957–January 1958).
55. Conversation with Sir William Cawthorn, October 3, 1962.
56. Letter from Peter Sinclair, University of Kentucky Medical School, February 13, 1968.
57. See Edgar Faure, *The Serpent and the Tortoise* (New York: St. Martin's Press, 1958) and François Fejto, "France and China," in A. M. Halpern, *op. cit.*, pp. 42–76. Fejto is a specialist on Communist Affairs for Agence France-Presse.
58. Heinrich Bechtoldt, "The Federal Republic of Germany and China," in A. M. Halpern, *op. cit.*, p. 80. See also Chancellor Ludwig Erhard's comment in the Italian journal, *Le Ore*, February 13, 1964. Bechtoldt is editor of the West German magazine *Aussen-politik* and a professor at the University of Tübingen.
59. Conversation atop Victoria Peak, Hong Kong, August 1966. Other German businessmen in Hong Kong made similar comments in 1962 and 1964.
60. See *Japan Times*, October 10, 1965, reporting about 2,500 overseas trainees inside Formosa and almost as many Chinese personnel abroad. For other details, see *Japan Times* January 30 and October 10, 1966, *Free China Weekly*, October 22, 1967, and *Central Daily News* (Taipei), February 13, 1966.
61. Reported in the *China News*, January 26, 1967, and William Clifford, "Free China's Dirt Farm Diplomacy," *The Lion*, October 1967, pp. 30–32.
62. Letter from a Formosan graduate student, May 3, 1965.
63. See Colin Legum, "Africa and China," in A. M. Halpern, *op. cit.*, pp. 389–436. Legum, Commonwealth correspondent of the *Observer* (London) notes that "when Africans speak about 'the Chinese,' they usually mean the People's Republic of China. They tend to regard Taiwan as the exile base of Marshal Chiang Kai-shek, who lost the mainland to the revolution and will never regain it. Those who recognized Taiwan did so either because of grievances against the Peking regime . . . or, in most cases, out of deference to the wishes of France or the United States" (p. 393). For a pro-Nationalist interpretation, see

David N. Rowe, "Cooperation between the Republic of China and African Countries," *International Bulletin of the African Institute* (Pretoria), August 1963.

64. Malcolm Kerr, "The Middle East and China," in Halpern, *op. cit.*, pp. 437–456.

65. Arnold Brackman, "The Malay World and China," in Halpern, *op. cit.*, pp. 262–302. Brackman reports that "the Provisional Taiwan Government in Tokyo sent a mission to Indonesia to draw a distinction between Taiwanese and Chinese on Taiwan and to deny that Taiwanese were implicated in the PRRI-Permesta revolt (a native uprising openly supported by the Nationalists). The mission's arrival incensed Peking, which scented an 'intrigue at creating two Chinas.' Djakarta expelled the mission and reaffirmed its 'one-China policy'" (p. 278).

66. Robert Elegant, "The Red Dragon: Are There Ways To Tame It?" *The National Observer*, January 18, 1965, p. 13.

67. For reports on referenda in Gilbraltar and Puerto Rico, see *Milwaukee Journal*, July 22 and 24, 1967 (Nationalist China joined Spain in opposing any Gilbraltar referendum).

68. See W. G. Goddard, *Formosa: A Study in Chinese History* (East Lansing: Michigan State University Press, 1966) p. 213.

69. Letter, October 5, 1963.

70. Letter from Robert Newman, July 11, 1963. Newman's book, *Recognition of Communist China?* (New York: Macmillan, 1961) has been cited above.

INDEX